Tower Air Fryer
Cookbook For Beginners

600
Frying, baking, grilling and roasting with your Tower Air Fryer is easy for Beginners to Have Fun Cooking and Eating.

Ellie Davis

Copyright © 2022 by Ellie Davis All rights reserved.

The content contained within this book may not be reproduced, duplicated, or transmitted without direct written permission from the author or the publisher. Under no circumstances will any blame or legal responsibility be held against the publisher, or author, for any damages, reparation, or monetary loss due to the information contained within this book, either directly or indirectly.

Legal Notice: This book is copyright protected. It is only for personal use. You cannot amend, distribute, sell, use, quote or paraphrase any part, or the content within this book, without the consent of the author or publisher.

Disclaimer Notice: Please note the information contained within this document is for educational and entertainment purposes only. All effort has been executed to present accurate, up to date, reliable, complete information. No warranties of any kind are declared or implied. Readers acknowledge that the author is not engaged in the rendering of legal, financial, medical, or professional advice. The content within this book has been derived from various sources. Please consult a licensed professional before attempting any techniques outlined in this book. By reading this document, the reader agrees that under no circumstances is the author responsible for any losses, direct or indirect, that are incurred as a result of the use of the information contained within this document, including, but not limited to, errors, omissions, or inaccuracies.

Table of Contents

Table of Contents 3
Introduction 9
    What a Tower Air Fryer is 9
    10 Useful Tower Air Fryer Tricks and Tips 9
    Some Common Questions about the Tower Air Fryers 10

Measurement Conversions 11
    BASIC KITCHEN CONVERSIONS & EQUIVALENTS 11

Appetizers And Snacks 12

Avocado Fries With Quick Salsa Fresca 12	Honey-mustard Chicken Wings 21
Honey Tater Tots With Bacon 12	Beet Chips 21
Rich Clam Spread 12	Avocado Fries, Vegan 21
Cinnamon Sweet Potato Fries 12	Fried String Beans With Greek Sauce 21
Grilled Ham & Muenster Cheese On Raisin Bread 13	Fried Gyoza 22
Fried Peaches 13	Paprika Onion Blossom 22
String Bean Fries 13	Granola Three Ways 22
Nicoise Deviled Eggs 13	Bagel Chips 23
Sweet Potato Chips 13	Balsamic Grape Dip 23
Buffalo French Fries 14	Fiery Bacon-wrapped Dates 23
Garlic Wings 14	Cheesy Spinach Dip(2) 23
No-guilty Spring Rolls 14	Classic Potato Chips 23
Sweet And Salty Snack Mix 14	Beer-battered Onion Rings 23
Curried Pickle Chips 14	Artichoke Samosas 24
Cheddar Stuffed Jalapeños 15	Popcorn Chicken Bites 24
Shrimp Egg Rolls 15	Cinnamon Apple Crisps 24
Roasted Jalapeño Salsa Verde 15	Avocado Egg Rolls 24
Veggie Cheese Bites 15	Bacon Candy 25
Crispy Chicken Bites With Gorgonzola Sauce 15	Cheesy Green Dip 25
Five Spice Fries 16	Sausage & Cauliflower Balls 25
Stuffed Baby Bella Caps 16	Buttery Spiced Pecans 25
Spiced Parsnip Chips 16	Cauliflower-crust Pizza 25
Canadian-inspired Waffle Poutine 16	Onion Ring Nachos 26
Cheesy Green Pitas 16	Black-olive Jalapeño Poppers 26
Smoked Whitefish Spread 17	Buffalo Cauliflower 26
Corn Dog Muffins 17	Herbed Cheese Brittle 26
Poutine 17	Avocado Toast With Lemony Shrimp 27
Pizza Bagel Bites 17	Corn Dog Bites 27
Cheesy Green Wonton Triangles 18	Parmesan Pizza Nuggets 27
Vegetable Spring Rolls 18	Plantain Chips 27
Taquito Quesadillas 18	Breaded Mozzarella Sticks 28
Smoked Salmon Puffs 18	Bacon & Blue Cheese Tartlets 28
Orange-glazed Carrots 19	Sausage And Cheese Rolls 28
Garlic-herb Pita Chips 19	Crab Rangoon Dip With Wonton Chips 28
Fried Brie With Cherry Tomatoes 19	Chicken Nachos 29
Blooming Onion 19	Fried Cheese Ravioli With Marinara Sauce 29
Crunchy Pickle Chips 20	Artichoke-spinach Dip 29
Warm Spinach Dip With Pita Chips 20	Crispy Spiced Chickpeas 29
Vegetarian Fritters With Green Dip 20	Garlic Breadsticks 29
Mozzarella Sticks 21	Seafood Egg Rolls 30

Bread And Breakfast 31

Nutty Whole Wheat Muffins 31	French Toast And Turkey Sausage Roll-ups 32
Banana-strawberry Cakecups 31	Crispy Bacon 32
Parmesan Garlic Naan 31	Maple-peach And Apple Oatmeal 32
Cherry Beignets 31	Green Onion Pancakes 32

Tower Air Fryer Cookbook

Vegetarian Quinoa Cups	32
Egg Muffins	33
Morning Loaded Potato Skins	33
Sweet Potato & Mushroom Hash	33
Light Frittata	33
Orange Cran-bran Muffins	33
Wild Blueberry Lemon Chia Bread	33
Easy Vanilla Muffins	34
Banana Bread	34
Cinnamon Sugar Donut Holes	34
Carrot Muffins	35
English Scones	35
Spinach-bacon Rollups	35
Eggless Mung Bean Tart	35
Avocado Toasts With Poached Eggs	35
Crispy Samosa Rolls	35
Mascarpone Iced Cinnamon Rolls	36
Morning Apple Biscuits	36
Morning Burrito	36
Pumpkin Empanadas	36
Cream Cheese Deviled Eggs	36
Hashbrown Potatoes Lyonnaise	37
Mushroom & Cavolo Nero Egg Muffins	37
English Muffin Sandwiches	37
Chorizo Sausage & Cheese Balls	37
Southwest Cornbread	37
Soft Pretzels	37
Cinnamon Pumpkin Donuts	38
Cheddar-ham-corn Muffins	38
Shakshuka Cups	38
Pizza Dough	39
Colorful French Toast Sticks	39
Veggie & Feta Scramble Bowls	39
Southern Sweet Cornbread	39
Coffee Cake	39
Cheddar & Sausage Tater Tots	40
Blueberry Muffins	40
Breakfast Pot Pies	40
Cheddar Cheese Biscuits	40
Huevos Rancheros	41
Wake-up Veggie & Ham Bake	41
Classic Cinnamon Rolls	41
Easy Corn Dog Cupcakes	41
Breakfast Chimichangas	41
Garlic Bread Knots	42
Oat Muffins With Blueberries	42
Bacon Puff Pastry Pinwheels	42
Breakfast Sausage Bites	42
Hole In One	42
Morning Chicken Frittata Cups	43
Cajun Breakfast Potatoes	43
Whole-grain Cornbread	43
Seasoned Herbed Sourdough Croutons	43
Carrot Orange Muffins	43
Honey Donuts	44
Strawberry Streusel Muffins	44
Cinnamon-coconut Doughnuts	44
Pigs In A Blanket	44
Western Frittata	45
Ham & Cheese Sandwiches	45
Hush Puffins	45
Not-so-english Muffins	45
Aromatic Mushroom Omelet	45
Smooth Walnut-banana Loaf	46
Favorite Blueberry Muffins	46
Banana-blackberry Muffins	46
Fried Pb&j	46
Honey Oatmeal	46
Viking Toast	47
Quiche Cups	47
Almond-pumpkin Porridge	47
Brown Sugar Grapefruit	47

Vegetarians Recipes 48

Pesto Pepperoni Pizza Bread	48
Creamy Broccoli & Mushroom Casserole	48
Tropical Salsa	48
Cheddar Bean Taquitos	48
Crunchy Rice Paper Samosas	48
Green Bean Sautée	49
Rigatoni With Roasted Onions, Fennel, Spinach And Lemon Pepper Ricotta	49
Italian-style Fried Cauliflower	49
Spaghetti Squash And Kale Fritters With Pomodoro Sauce	49
Roasted Vegetable Thai Green Curry	50
Easy Zucchini Lasagna Roll-ups	50
Mushroom And Fried Onion Quesadilla	50
Zucchini Tamale Pie	51
Veggie-stuffed Bell Peppers	51
Chicano Rice Bowls	51
Mushroom Bolognese Casserole	51
Stuffed Portobellos	51
Green Bean & Baby Potato Mix	52
Garlicky Roasted Mushrooms	52
Grilled Cheese Sandwich	52
Chive Potato Pierogi	52
Spicy Vegetable And Tofu Shake Fry	52
Rainbow Quinoa Patties	53
Gorgeous Jalapeño Poppers	53
Ricotta Veggie Potpie	53
Spiced Vegetable Galette	53
General Tso's Cauliflower	54
Rice & Bean Burritos	54
Pizza Portobello Mushrooms	54
Zucchini & Bell Pepper Stir-fry	55
Tofu & Spinach Lasagna	55
Colorful Vegetable Medley	55
Italian Stuffed Bell Peppers	55
Tacos	55
Roasted Vegetable Pita Pizza	56
Garlicky Brussel Sprouts With Saffron Aioli	56
Veggie Samosas	56
Hearty Salad	56
Home-style Cinnamon Rolls	56
Vegetarian Paella	57
Spinach And Cheese Calzone	57
Tex-mex Potatoes With Avocado Dressing	57
Powerful Jackfruit Fritters	57
Honey Pear Chips	57

Vegan Buddha Bowls(2)	58
Spicy Bean Patties	58
Lentil Burritos With Cilantro Chutney	58
Farfalle With White Sauce	58
Effortless Mac `n´ Cheese	59
Sweet Corn Bread	59
Berbere Eggplant Dip	59
Caprese-style Sandwiches	59
Vegetable Couscous	59
Easy Cheese & Spinach Lasagna	60
Smoked Paprika Sweet Potato Fries	60
Curried Potato, Cauliflower And Pea Turnovers	60
Roasted Vegetable, Brown Rice And Black Bean Burrito	61
Chili Tofu & Quinoa Bowls	61
Bengali Samosa With Mango Chutney	61
Sicilian-style Vegetarian Pizza	61
Crispy Apple Fries With Caramel Sauce	62
Cheddar Stuffed Portobellos With Salsa	62
Zucchini Tacos	62
Fennel Tofu Bites	62
Breaded Avocado Tacos	62
Egg Rolls	62
Falafel	63
Vegetarian Shepherd´s Pie	63
Mushroom, Zucchini And Black Bean Burgers	63
Cheesy Enchilada Stuffed Baked Potatoes	64

Poultry Recipes 65

Chicken Souvlaki Gyros	65
Teriyaki Chicken Legs	65
Christmas Chicken & Roasted Grape Salad	65
Chicken Cordon Bleu	65
Country Chicken Hoagies	66
Basic Chicken Breasts(2)	66
Spicy Honey Mustard Chicken	66
Chicken & Rice Sautée	66
Guajillo Chile Chicken Meatballs	66
Katsu Chicken Thighs	66
Intense Buffalo Chicken Wings	67
Japanese-style Turkey Meatballs	67
Spinach & Turkey Meatballs	67
Boss Chicken Cobb Salad	67
Garlic Chicken	68
Glazed Chicken Thighs	68
Sunday Chicken Skewers	68
Peanut Butter-barbeque Chicken	68
Korean-style Chicken Bulgogi	68
Sweet-and-sour Chicken	69
Chicken Hand Pies	69
Punjabi-inspired Chicken	69
Easy Turkey Meatballs	69
Italian Roasted Chicken Thighs	69
Gluten-free Nutty Chicken Fingers	70
Farmer´s Fried Chicken	70
Chicken Burgers With Blue Cheese Sauce	70
Buttered Turkey Breasts	70
Parmesan Chicken Meatloaf	71
Jerk Chicken Drumsticks	71
Chicken Chimichangas	71
Simple Buttermilk Fried Chicken	71
Rich Turkey Burgers	72
Chicken Pasta Pie	72
Gingery Turkey Meatballs	72
Gruyère Asparagus & Chicken Quiche	72
Poblano Bake	73
Greek Chicken Wings	73
Cheesy Chicken-avocado Paninis	73
Southern-style Chicken Legs	73
Mexican Turkey Meatloaves	73
Cajun Chicken Livers	74
Pulled Turkey Quesadillas	74
Honey Lemon Thyme Glazed Cornish Hen	74
Chicken Adobo	74
Fantasy Sweet Chili Chicken Strips	74
Chicken Tenders With Basil-strawberry Glaze	75
Southern-fried Chicken Livers	75
Japanese-inspired Glazed Chicken	75
Chicken Wellington	75
Chicken Cutlets With Broccoli Rabe And Roasted Peppers	76
Mexican-inspired Chicken Breasts	76
Greek Gyros With Chicken & Rice	76
Chicken Nuggets	76
Harissa Chicken Wings	77
Asian Meatball Tacos	77
Herb-marinated Chicken	77
Kale & Rice Chicken Rolls	77
Chicken Parmigiana	77
Mustardy Chicken Bites	78
Restaurant-style Chicken Thighs	78
Chicken & Fruit Biryani	78
Cal-mex Turkey Patties	78
Chipotle Chicken Drumsticks	78
Mom's Chicken Wings	78
Family Chicken Fingers	79
Crispy Cordon Bleu	79
Chicken Wings Al Ajillo	79
Chicken Breast Burgers	79
Sage & Paprika Turkey Cutlets	79

Fish And Seafood Recipes 80

Coconut-shrimp Po' Boys	80
Hot Calamari Rings	80
Almond-crusted Fish	80
Garlicky Sea Bass With Root Veggies	80
Breaded Parmesan Perch	81
Fish Tacos With Jalapeño-lime Sauce	81
King Prawns Al Ajillo	81
Filled Mushrooms With Crab & Cheese	81
Stuffed Shrimp	81
Saucy Shrimp	82
Shrimp Patties	82
Mom´s Tuna Melt Toastie	82
Californian Tilapia	83
Five Spice Red Snapper With Green Onions And Orange Salsa	83
Fish Sticks With Tartar Sauce	83

Tower Air Fryer Cookbook

Family Fish Nuggets With Tartar Sauce	83
Cajun-seasoned Shrimp	83
Easy Asian-style Tuna	84
Sardinas Fritas	84
Shrimp Al Pesto	84
Crab Cakes On A Budget	84
Catalan Sardines With Romesco Sauce	84
Shrimp Teriyaki	84
Coconut Shrimp	85
Lime Flaming Halibut	85
Sweet Potato–wrapped Shrimp	85
Mojo Sea Bass	85
Shrimp-jalapeño Poppers In Prosciutto	86
The Best Shrimp Risotto	86
Stuffed Shrimp Wrapped In Bacon	86
Buttered Swordfish Steaks	86
Lemon-roasted Salmon Fillets	86
Sea Scallops	87
Dilly Red Snapper	87
Seared Scallops In Beurre Blanc	87
Holliday Lobster Salad	87
Buttery Lobster Tails	87
Shrimp "scampi"	88
Chinese Fish Noodle Bowls	88
Peppery Tilapia Roulade	88
Shrimp & Grits	88
Fried Shrimp	89
Bbq Fried Oysters	89
Holiday Shrimp Scampi	89
Crunchy Clam Strips	89
Tilapia Al Pesto	89
Mojito Fish Tacos	90
Cajun Flounder Fillets	90
Crabmeat-stuffed Flounder	90
Catfish Nuggets	90
Crunchy And Buttery Cod With Ritz® Cracker Crust	91
Tuscan Salmon	91
Mahi-mahi "burrito" Fillets	91
Horseradish-crusted Salmon Fillets	91
Garlic And Dill Salmon	91
Southeast Asian-style Tuna Steaks	92
Cheese & Crab Stuffed Mushrooms	92
Easy-peasy Shrimp	92
Fish Tortillas With Coleslaw	92
Summer Sea Scallops	92
Rich Salmon Burgers With Broccoli Slaw	92
The Best Oysters Rockefeller	93
Quick Tuna Tacos	93
Cilantro Sea Bass	93
Crab Cakes	93
Crunchy Flounder Gratin	93
Herb-crusted Sole	94
Restaurant-style Breaded Shrimp	94
Black Cod With Grapes, Fennel, Pecans And Kale	94
Dijon Shrimp Cakes	94

Beef, pork & Lamb Recipes 95

Beef Short Ribs	95
Stress-free Beef Patties	95
Honey Pork Links	95
Beef Fajitas	95
Country-style Pork Ribs(2)	95
Sweet Potato–crusted Pork Rib Chops	96
Beef & Barley Stuffed Bell Peppers	96
Barbecue-style London Broil	96
Sage Pork With Potatoes	96
Rack Of Lamb With Pistachio Crust	96
Crispy Steak Subs	97
Italian Sausage & Peppers	97
Sweet And Sour Pork	97
Chipotle Pork Meatballs	98
City "chicken"	98
Crispy Smoked Pork Chops	98
Fried Spam	98
Pork Chops	99
Italian Meatballs	99
Ground Beef Calzones	99
Spicy Hoisin Bbq Pork Chops	99
Meatloaf With Tangy Tomato Glaze	99
Balsamic Beef & Veggie Skewers	100
Extra Crispy Country-style Pork Riblets	100
Indonesian Pork Satay	100
Pork Cutlets With Almond-lemon Crust	100
Golden Pork Quesadillas	101
Broccoli & Mushroom Beef	101
Tarragon Pork Tenderloin	101
Crispy Pork Medallions With Radicchio And Endive Salad	101
Lamb Chops In Currant Sauce	102
Pesto-rubbed Veal Chops	102
Bacon, Blue Cheese And Pear Stuffed Pork Chops	102
Smokehouse-style Beef Ribs	102
Berbere Beef Steaks	103
Authentic Sausage Kartoffel Salad	103
Tandoori Lamb Samosas	103
Chinese-style Lamb Chops	103
French-style Pork Medallions	103
Pizza Tortilla Rolls	104
Garlic-buttered Rib Eye Steak	104
Vietnamese Beef Lettuce Wraps	104
Tamari-seasoned Pork Strips	105
Wasabi Pork Medallions	105
Grilled Pork & Bell Pepper Salad	105
Argentinian Steak Asado Salad	105
Homemade Pork Gyoza	105
Wiener Schnitzel	106
Pork Chops With Cereal Crust	106
Orange Glazed Pork Tenderloin	106
Sausage-cheese Calzone	106
Italian Sausage Rolls	107
Peachy Pork Chops	107
Bbq Back Ribs	107
Lazy Mexican Meat Pizza	107
Zesty London Broil	107
Glazed Meatloaf	107
Carne Asada	108
Jerk Meatballs	108
Lamb Koftas Meatballs	108
Barbecue Country-style Pork Ribs	108

Chile Con Carne Galette 109	Meat Loaves 111
Mongolian Beef 109	Flank Steak With Roasted Peppers And Chimichurri 111
Tonkatsu 109	Paprika Fried Beef 112
Lemon-garlic Strip Steak 110	Lamb Meatballs With Quick Tomato Sauce 112
Cal-mex Chimichangas 110	Stuffed Cabbage Rolls 112
Basil Cheese & Ham Stromboli 110	Perfect Strip Steaks 112
Thyme Steak Finger Strips 110	Friday Night Cheeseburgers 113
Pepperoni Bagel Pizzas 110	Barbecue-style Beef Cube Steak 113
Leftover Roast Beef Risotto 110	Chicken Fried Steak 113
Balsamic Marinated Rib Eye Steak With Balsamic Fried Cipollini Onions 111	

Vegetable Side Dishes Recipes 114

Sriracha Green Beans 114	Broccoli Au Gratin 121
Horseradish Potato Mash 114	Dilly Sesame Roasted Asparagus 121
Pecorino Dill Muffins 114	Asparagus 121
Layered Mixed Vegetables 114	Mexican-style Frittata 121
Perfect Asparagus 114	Stuffed Onions 122
Fried Cauliflowerwith Parmesan Lemon Dressing 115	Easy Parmesan Asparagus 122
Vegetable Roast 115	Honey-mustard Asparagus Puffs 122
Perfect Broccolini 115	Parmesan Asparagus 122
Summer Watermelon And Cucumber Salad 115	Sticky Broccoli Florets 122
Honey-roasted Parsnips 115	Smoky Roasted Veggie Chips 123
Corn On The Cob 115	Simple Green Bake 123
Grits Casserole 116	Sesame Carrots And Sugar Snap Peas 123
Butternut Medallions With Honey Butter And Sage 116	Roasted Broccoli And Red Bean Salad 123
Honey-mustard Roasted Cabbage 116	Asparagus Wrapped In Pancetta 123
Speedy Baked Caprese With Avocado 116	Chicken Eggrolls 124
Crunchy Green Beans 116	Lemony Fried Fennel Slices 124
Best-ever Brussels Sprouts 117	Citrusy Brussels Sprouts 124
Simple Roasted Sweet Potatoes 117	Jerk Rubbed Corn On The Cob 124
Roasted Heirloom Carrots With Orange And Thyme 117	Tasty Brussels Sprouts With Guanciale 124
Five-spice Roasted Sweet Potatoes 117	Crispy Brussels Sprouts 124
Green Peas With Mint 117	Rosemary Potato Salad 125
Garlic-parmesan Popcorn 117	Sage Hasselback Potatoes 125
Rosemary New Potatoes 117	Garlicky Brussels Sprouts 125
Chili-oiled Brussels Sprouts 118	Carrots & Parsnips With Tahini Sauce 125
Hot Okra Wedges 118	Provence French Fries 125
Smashed Fried Baby Potatoes 118	Cheese & Bacon Pasta Bake 125
Gorgonzola Stuffed Mushrooms 118	Onion Rings 126
Roasted Brussels Sprouts 118	Roasted Eggplant Halves With Herbed Ricotta 126
Mom´s Potatoes Au Gratin 118	Buttery Radish Wedges 126
Cheesy Texas Toast 119	Mushrooms, Sautéed 126
Balsamic Beet Chips 119	Grilled Lime Scallions 126
Sage & Thyme Potatoes 119	Fingerling Potatoes 127
Onions 119	Basic Corn On The Cob 127
Crispy, Cheesy Leeks 119	Buttery Stuffed Tomatoes 127
Salmon Salad With Steamboat Dressing 120	Farmers' Market Veggie Medley 127
Yellow Squash 120	Crispy Cauliflower Puffs 127
Zucchini Fries 120	Balsamic Stuffed Mushrooms 128
Acorn Squash Halves With Maple Butter Glaze 120	Moroccan-spiced Carrots 128
Sweet Roasted Pumpkin Rounds 121	Rosemary Roasted Potatoes With Lemon 128
Blistered Shishito Peppers 121	Smoked Avocado Wedges 128

Desserts And Sweets 129

Cherry Cheesecake Rolls 129	Carrot-oat Cake Muffins 130
S'mores Pockets 129	Strawberry Donuts 130
Home-style Pumpkin Pie Pudding 129	Coconut Rice Cake 130
Lemon Iced Donut Balls 129	Fried Cannoli Wontons 130
Mixed Berry Pie 129	Cheesecake Wontons 131
Nutty Banana Bread 130	Mini Carrot Cakes 131

Black And Blue Clafoutis	131
Fudgy Brownie Cake	131
Cherry Hand Pies	132
Pumpkin Brownies	132
Honey-roasted Mixed Nuts	132
Chocolate Macaroons	132
Giant Buttery Oatmeal Cookie	133
Famous Chocolate Lava Cake	133
Vanilla-strawberry Muffins	133
Party S´mores	134
Chocolate Bars	134
Molten Chocolate Almond Cakes	134
Carrot Cake With Cream Cheese Icing	134
Apple-carrot Cupcakes	135
Nutty Cookies	135
Fried Snickers Bars	135
Cinnamon Pear Cheesecake	135
Baked Apple Crisp	135
Cinnamon Canned Biscuit Donuts	136
Air-fried Beignets	136
Baked Stuffed Pears	136
Apple & Blueberry Crumble	136
Giant Buttery Chocolate Chip Cookie	136
Holiday Peppermint Cake	137
Fluffy Orange Cake	137
Custard	137
Rich Blueberry Biscuit Shortcakes	137
British Bread Pudding	138
Apple Dumplings	138
One-bowl Chocolate Buttermilk Cake	138
Fall Pumpkin Cake	138
Annie's Chocolate Chunk Hazelnut Cookies	139
Apple Crisp	139
Caramel Blondies With Macadamia Nuts	139
Cinnamon Sugar Banana Rolls	140
White Chocolate Cranberry Blondies	140
Honeyed Tortilla Fritters	140
Berry Streusel Cake	140
Peanut Butter S'mores	141
Oatmeal Blackberry Crisp	141
Strawberry Donut Bites	141
Cheese Blintzes	141
Cheese & Honey Stuffed Figs	141
Maple Cinnamon Cheesecake	142
Spiced Fruit Skewers	142
Coconut Cream Roll-ups	142
Mango-chocolate Custard	142
Grilled Pineapple Dessert	142
Fruit Turnovers	142
Coconut Crusted Bananas With Pineapple Sauce	143
Brownies After Dark	143
Puff Pastry Apples	143
Baked Caramelized Peaches	144
Roasted Pears	144
Banana-almond Delights	144
Lemon Pound Cake Bites	144
Chocolate Rum Brownies	144
Ricotta Stuffed Apples	144

RECIPE INDEX 145

Introduction

You can fit so much into this Tower Air Fryer, making it a useful helper in the kitchen. With most models, all food goes into one basket, but with this model, it's possible to have multiple layers of food cooking at the same time. As with other 'health' fryers, the shelves are basket-like, so any fat or juices will fall to the bottom tray – bear this in mind when stacking ingredients. Or, you can always use roasting tins, as you would in a conventional oven. We heated pies and a filo pastry dish in enamel tins on top of the trays, and that worked really well.

If you have a fussy family with differing dinner demands, we could see this helping a lot, because of the ability to cook multiple dishes at once. You could, for example, cook a pizza on top, then wedges and goujons on the remaining shelves to keep everyone happy. When oven space is at a premium – on Christmas Day, for example – this would be a really useful extra appliance, as it could sort out stuffing, pigs in blankets and extra roasties with ease. With the rotisserie function, this air fryer is better still. There's a timer that can be set up to an hour, so we seasoned a chicken, basted it with olive oil, and left it to spin its way to juicy, crisp perfection. A turkey crown would also work well, as would any other roast. Pork with crackling was a real success, too.

What a Tower Air Fryer is

An Air Fryer is a kitchen appliance that utilizes super-heated air to cook food in a special chamber using the convection mechanism. Technically speaking, a mechanical fan blows heat around the space so the hot air circulates around your food at high speed, cooking evenly from all sides, producing crispy browning results. This is called the Maillard effect. According to Wikipedia "The Maillard reaction is a chemical reaction between amino acids and reducing sugars that gives browned food its distinctive flavor. Seared steaks, pan-fried dumplings, cookies and other kinds of biscuits, bread, toasted marshmallows, and many other foods undergo this reaction.

This simple but intelligent machine radiates heat from heating elements and uses rapid air technology to fry roast, and bake your food with less oil. The Air Fryer can also warm your food. You don't have slave over a hot stove since the Air Fryer features an automatic temperature control. Thanks to its convection settings, it produces crispier and more flavorful food than conventional cooking methods.

If you are thinking of cutting down on fat consumption, here is a great solution. Studies have shown that air fried veggies contain up to 80% less fat in comparison to veggies that are deep fried. Just to give you an idea of the calorie content – deep-fried onion rings contain about 411 Calories vs air fried that contain about 176 Calories. Deep-fried Chicken Nuggets = 305 calories vs air fried = 180 Calories.

In order to understand how to use an Air Fryer, it would be good to find out more about the anatomy of this magical device. There is the inside i.e. electric-coil heating elements. A specially designed fan distributes the hot air evenly throughout the cooking basket. Then, the Air Fryer has a removable cooking basket with a mesh bottom that is coated with a non-stick material. It is placed in a frying basket drawer, cooking your food in the sealed environment. Air Fryers come with accessories, such as baking dishes, pans, trays, grill pans, skewer racks, and so forth; it will vary from model to model. However, make sure to use pans and racks that are designed to fit into the Air Fryer.

How the Tower Air Fryer Works

The technology of the Tower Air Fryer is very simple. Fried foods get their crunchy texture because hot oil heats foods quickly and evenly on their surface. Oil is an excellent heat conductor, which helps with fast and simultaneous cooking across all of the ingredients. For decades cooks have used convection ovens to try to mimic the effects of frying or cooking the whole surface of food. But the air never circulates quickly enough to achieve that delicious surface crisp we all love in fried foods.

With this mechanism the air is circulated on high degrees, up to 200° C, to "air fry" any food such as fish, chicken or chips etc. This technology has changed the whole idea of cooking by reducing the fat up to 80% compared to old-fashioned deep fat frying.

The Tower air fryer cooking releases the heat through a heating element which cooks the food in a healthier and more appropriate way. There's also an exhaust fan right above the cooking chamber which provides the food required airflow. This way food is cooked with constant heated air. This leads to the same heating temperature reaching every single part of the food that is being cooked. So, this is only grill and the exhaust fan that is helping the Tower air fryer to boost air at a constantly high speed in order to cook healthy food with less fat.

The internal pressure increases the temperature that will then be controlled by the exhaust system. Exhaust fan also releases filtered extra air to cook the food in a much healthier way.

Tower air fryer has no odor at all and it is absolutely harmless making it user and environment friendly.

10 Useful Tower Air Fryer Tricks and Tips

Here is an easy-to-follow list to get you fully acquainted with your new purchase and creating some amazing meals in the shortest time.

1. Always make sure you place the fryer on a nice level surface with a good gap behind it when using it. This is because it has vents at the back to release steam so make sure it is pulled safely away from any wall power sockets. And definitely do not put it on top of your stove!

2. Don't put too much food in the basket as it needs air to circulate all surfaces in order to cook it evenly and get it nice and crispy. A single layer of food is best so cook in batches, if necessary.

3. Never spray the food with oil or sprinkle with seasoning once it is in the air fryer. Always do this before placing the food in the basket.

4. It is always best to preheat your air fryer to get optimum results. Just 2-3 minutes is fine and I recommend using the timer and then resetting it with the cooking time once you have put the food inside.

5. Please note that batter doesn't do well in an air fryer as the fan splatters it everywhere, creating smoke and making a mess that can be pretty tough to clean. Breaded foods are far safer and better but need to be prepared properly. So, make sure you coat the food first with flour, then egg and then the breadcrumbs, pressing them firmly with your hand into the surface of the food. Finally, spray the surface with oil to ensure the crumbs don't blow off and to give your food that wonderfully crispy fried coating.

6. Turn the food over halfway through cooking just like you would if regular frying or roasting to ensure even browning and crisping.

7. Check the food regularly when first using your air fryer to check if it's done. This is until you get used to it because you don't want to burn or dry out your food.

8. Make sure you place the basket on a heat proof mat or rack when you remove it as it will be extremely hot and damage your countertop.

9. Use oven mitts and tongs or other suitable utensils to remove any items to avoid seriously burning yourself.

10. After use, don't scrub the racks or basket with metal scourers as you will damage the coating. They can be left in soak in hot soapy water for about 30 mins and then will clean easily with a regular sponge or cloth.

So now it's time for you to dive right into our delectable and diverse super-size collection of fabulous air-fryer recipes and get cooking without the guilt and minus the extra pounds!

Some Common Questions about the Tower Air Fryers

1. **Can you cook battered food in an Tower Air Fryers?**

Crispy food needs enough oil to bind batters and coatings, but not too much or you'll end up with soggy results. If the food has a crumbly or floury outside texture, try spraying it with a little bit more oil.

If you're making air fried food from scratch, spray your homemade items with a light coating of oil (too much and the food won't get crispy) and arrange foods so the hot air circulates around each piece as much as possible.

2. **Can you use olive oil while Tower Air Fryers?**

Using cooking oils that can stand up to high temperatures is key while air frying, so avocado, grapeseed, and peanut oil are great for achieving crispy goodness. For best results, brush on lightly or spray an even coat of cooking spray made from these oils. Extra virgin olive oil is not an air fry-friendly oil due to its low smoke point, but extra light olive oil can be used for air frying because of its high smoke point. Other types of olive oil and some vegetable oils smoke at lower temperatures, meaning they will cause food to dry up quickly and prevent them from getting crispy.

3. **Can you use aluminum foil in an Tower Air Fryers?**

Air fry works best on dark pans because they get and stay hot very quickly. Shiny foil reflects heat off the bakeware, which may change your results. When cooking with the Air fry Tray, we suggest putting a baking sheet on a rack a couple of positions below your tray. You can line that sheet with foil or parchment (or both) to catch any drips or crumbs, but you should never put aluminum foil, liners, or bakeware on the oven bottom. Items in this location can cause issues with air circulation and direct heat in any oven. Always keep the bottom of the oven clear so the air can circulate properly.

4. **How do I keep my Tower Air Fryers clean?**

Before using the air fry feature, place a cookie or baking sheet a rack or two under the Air Fry Tray to catch crumbs or drips. This will keep the bottom of the oven clean and free of fallen bits that can burn or cause odors later. Remember, do not place pans directly on the oven bottom to keep heat circulating correctly.

The Air Fry Tray is dishwasher safe, but for optimal cleaning, we recommend washing it by hand. It's designed to hold foods that already have some oil on them, which should keep food from sticking.

5. **How do I limit the amount of smoke when using the Tower Air Fryers?**

Air fry uses really hot air to cook food fast and make it crunchy. Although air fry uses hot air to cook, remember that you are still frying your food so that it gets crispy! When some high-fat or greasy foods (like fresh wings) meet that hot air inside an oven, some smoke is normal. If air fry is making a lot of smoke, try these tips. When using the Air Fry Tray, put a baking sheet on a rack or two below the Air Fry Tray. This keeps drips and crumbs from landing on the oven bottom, where they can burn and create smoke. For additional protection, place some foil-lined parchment paper on the baking sheet. Parchment paper traps oil and keeps it from smoking. Use cooking oils that can stand up to high temperatures like avocado, grapeseed, and peanut oils. Cooking sprays made from these oils are available at the grocery store.

Measurement Conversions

BASIC KITCHEN CONVERSIONS & EQUIVALENTS

DRY MEASUREMENTS CONVERSION CHART
3 TEASPOONS = 1 TABLESPOON = 1/16 CUP
6 TEASPOONS = 2 TABLESPOONS = 1/8 CUP
12 TEASPOONS = 4 TABLESPOONS = 1/4 CUP
24 TEASPOONS = 8 TABLESPOONS = 1/2 CUP
36 TEASPOONS = 12 TABLESPOONS = 3/4 CUP
48 TEASPOONS = 16 TABLESPOONS = 1 CUP

METRIC TO US COOKING CONVER SIONS
OVEN TEMPERATURES
120 °C = 250 °F
160 °C = 320 °F
180° C = 360 °F
205 °C = 400 °F
220 °C = 425 °F

LIQUID MEASUREMENTS CONVERSION CHART
8 FLUID OUNCES = 1 CUP = 1/2 PINT = 1/4 QUART
16 FLUID OUNCES = 2 CUPS = 1 PINT = 1/2 QUART
32 FLUID OUNCES = 4 CUPS = 2 PINTS = 1 QUART = 1/4 GALLON
128 FLUID OUNCES = 16 CUPS = 8 PINTS = 4 QUARTS = 1 GALLON

BAKING IN GRAMS
1 CUP FLOUR = 140 GRAMS
1 CUP SUGAR = 150 GRAMS
1 CUP POWDERED SUGAR = 160 GRAMS
1 CUP HEAVY CREAM = 235 GRAMS

VOLUME
1 MILLILITER = 1/5 TEASPOON
5 ML = 1 TEASPOON
15 ML = 1 TABLESPOON
240 ML = 1 CUP OR 8 FLUID OUNCES
1 LITER = 34 FL. OUNCES

WEIGHT
1 GRAM = .035 OUNCES
100 GRAMS = 3.5 OUNCES
500 GRAMS = 1.1 POUNDS
1 KILOGRAM = 35 OUNCES

US TO METRIC COOKING CONVERSIONS
1/5 TSP = 1 ML
1 TSP = 5 ML
1 TBSP = 15 ML
1 FL OUNCE = 30 ML
1 CUP = 237 ML
1 PINT (2 CUPS) = 473 ML
1 QUART (4 CUPS) = .95 LITER
1 GALLON (16 CUPS) = 3.8 LITERS
1 OZ = 28 GRAMS
1 POUND = 454 GRAMS

BUTTER
1 CUP BUTTER = 2 STICKS = 8 OUNCES = 230 GRAMS = 8 TABLESPOONS

WHAT DOES 1 CUP EQUAL
1 CUP = 8 FLUID OUNCES
1 CUP = 16 TABLESPOONS
1 CUP = 48 TEASPOONS
1 CUP = 1/2 PINT
1 CUP = 1/4 QUART
1 CUP = 1/16 GALLON
1 CUP = 240 ML

BAKING PAN CONVERSIONS
1 CUP ALL-PURPOSE FLOUR = 4.5 OZ
1 CUP ROLLED OATS = 3 OZ 1 LARGE EGG = 1.7 OZ
1 CUP BUTTER = 8 OZ 1 CUP MILK = 8 OZ
1 CUP HEAVY CREAM = 8.4 OZ
1 CUP GRANULATED SUGAR = 7.1 OZ
1 CUP PACKED BROWN SUGAR = 7.75 OZ
1 CUP VEGETABLE OIL = 7.7 OZ
1 CUP UNSIFTED POWDERED SUGAR = 4.4 OZ

BAKING PAN CONVERSIONS
9-INCH ROUND CAKE PAN = 12 CUPS
10-INCH TUBE PAN =16 CUPS
11-INCH BUNDT PAN = 12 CUPS
9-INCH SPRINGFORM PAN = 10 CUPS
9 X 5 INCH LOAF PAN = 8 CUPS
9-INCH SQUARE PAN = 8 CUPS

Tower Air Fryer Cookbook

Appetizers And Snacks

Avocado Fries With Quick Salsa Fresca

Servings: 4
Cooking Time: 6 Minutes
Ingredients:
- ½ cup flour*
- 2 teaspoons salt
- 2 eggs, lightly beaten
- 1 cup panko breadcrumbs*
- ⅛ teaspoon cayenne pepper
- ¼ teaspoon smoked paprika (optional)
- 2 large avocados, just ripe
- vegetable oil, in a spray bottle
- Quick Salsa Fresca
- 1 cup cherry tomatoes
- 1 tablespoon-sized chunk of shallot or red onion
- 2 teaspoons fresh lime juice
- 1 teaspoon chopped fresh cilantro or parsley
- salt and freshly ground black pepper

Directions:
1. Set up a dredging station with three shallow dishes. Place the flour and salt in the first shallow dish. Place the eggs into the second dish. Combine the breadcrumbs, cayenne pepper and paprika (if using) in the third dish.
2. Preheat the air fryer to 400°F/205°C.
3. Cut the avocado in half around the pit and separate the two sides. Slice the avocados into long strips while still in their skin. Run a spoon around the slices, separating them from the avocado skin. Try to keep the slices whole, but don't worry if they break – you can still coat and air-fry the pieces.
4. Coat the avocado slices by dredging them first in the flour, then the egg and then the breadcrumbs, pressing the crumbs on gently with your hands. Set the coated avocado fries on a tray and spray them on all sides with vegetable oil.
5. Air-fry the avocado fries, one layer at a time, at 400°F/205°C for 6 minutes, turning them over halfway through the cooking time and spraying lightly again if necessary. When the fries are nicely browned on all sides, season with salt and remove.
6. While the avocado fries are air-frying, make the salsa fresca by combining everything in a food processor. Pulse several times until the salsa is a chunky purée. Serve the fries warm with the salsa on the side for dipping.

Honey Tater Tots With Bacon

Servings: 4
Cooking Time: 25 Minutes
Ingredients:
- 24 frozen tater tots
- 6 bacon slices
- 1 tbsp honey
- 1 cup grated cheddar

Directions:
1. Preheat air fryer to 400°F/205°C. Air Fry the tater tots for 10 minutes, shaking the basket once halfway through cooking. Cut the bacon into pieces. When the tater tots are done, remove them from the fryer to a baking pan. Top them with bacon and drizzle with honey. Air Fry for 5 minutes to crisp up the bacon. Top the tater tots with cheese and cook for 2 minutes to melt the cheese. Serve.

Rich Clam Spread

Servings: 6
Cooking Time: 40 Minutes
Ingredients:
- 2 cans chopped clams in clam juice
- 1/3 cup panko bread crumbs
- 1 garlic clove, minced
- 1 tbsp olive oil
- 1 tbsp lemon juice
- ¼ tsp hot sauce
- 1 tsp Worcestershire sauce
- ½ tsp shallot powder
- ¼ tsp dried dill
- Salt and pepper to taste
- ½ tsp sweet paprika
- 4 tsp grated Parmesan cheese
- 2 celery stalks, chopped

Directions:
1. Completely drain one can of clams. Add them to a bowl along with the entire can of clams, breadcrumbs, garlic, olive oil, lemon juice, Worcestershire sauce, hot sauce, shallot powder, dill, pepper, salt, paprika, and 2 tbsp Parmesan. Combine well and set aside for 10 minutes. After that time, put the mixture in a greased baking dish.
2. Preheat air fryer to 325°F/160°C. Put the dish in the air fryer and Bake for 10 minutes. Sprinkle the remaining paprika and Parmesan, and continue to cook until golden brown on top, 8-10 minutes. Serve hot along with celery sticks.

Cinnamon Sweet Potato Fries

Servings: 5
Cooking Time: 30 Minutes
Ingredients:
- 3 sweet potatoes
- 2 tsp butter, melted
- 1 tsp cinnamon
- Salt and pepper to taste

Directions:
1. Preheat air fryer to 400°F/205°C. Peel the potatoes and slice them thinly crosswise. Transfer the slices to a large bowl. Toss with butter, cinnamon, salt, and pepper until fully coated. Place half of the slices into the air fryer. Stacking is ok. Air Fry for 10 minutes. Shake the basket, and cook for another 10-12 minutes until crispy. Serve hot.

Grilled Ham & Muenster Cheese On Raisin Bread

Servings: 1
Cooking Time: 10 Minutes
Ingredients:
- 2 slices raisin bread
- 2 tablespoons butter, softened
- 2 teaspoons honey mustard
- 3 slices thinly sliced honey ham (about 3 ounces)
- 4 slices Muenster cheese (about 3 ounces)
- 2 toothpicks

Directions:
1. Preheat the air fryer to 370°F/185°C.
2. Spread the softened butter on one side of both slices of raisin bread and place the bread, buttered side down on the counter. Spread the honey mustard on the other side of each slice of bread. Layer 2 slices of cheese, the ham and the remaining 2 slices of cheese on one slice of bread and top with the other slice of bread. Remember to leave the buttered side of the bread on the outside.
3. Transfer the sandwich to the air fryer basket and secure the sandwich with toothpicks.
4. Air-fry at 370°F/185°C for 5 minutes. Flip the sandwich over, remove the toothpicks and air-fry for another 5 minutes. Cut the sandwich in half and enjoy!!

Fried Peaches

Servings: 4
Cooking Time: 8 Minutes
Ingredients:
- 2 egg whites
- 1 tablespoon water
- ¼ cup sliced almonds
- 2 tablespoons brown sugar
- ½ teaspoon almond extract
- 1 cup crisp rice cereal
- 2 medium, very firm peaches, peeled and pitted
- ¼ cup cornstarch
- oil for misting or cooking spray

Directions:
1. Preheat air fryer to 390°F/200°C.
2. Beat together egg whites and water in a shallow dish.
3. In a food processor, combine the almonds, brown sugar, and almond extract. Process until ingredients combine well and the nuts are finely chopped.
4. Add cereal and pulse just until cereal crushes. Pour crumb mixture into a shallow dish or onto a plate.
5. Cut each peach into eighths and place in a plastic bag or container with lid. Add cornstarch, seal, and shake to coat.
6. Remove peach slices from bag or container, tapping them hard to shake off the excess cornstarch. Dip in egg wash and roll in crumbs. Spray with oil.
7. Place in air fryer basket and cook for 5minutes. Shake basket, separate any that have stuck together, and spritz a little oil on any spots that aren't browning.
8. Cook for 3 minutes longer, until golden brown and crispy.

String Bean Fries

Servings: 4
Cooking Time: 6 Minutes
Ingredients:
- ½ pound fresh string beans
- 2 eggs
- 4 teaspoons water
- ½ cup white flour
- ½ cup breadcrumbs
- ¼ teaspoon salt
- ¼ teaspoon ground black pepper
- ¼ teaspoon dry mustard (optional)
- oil for misting or cooking spray

Directions:
1. Preheat air fryer to 360°F/180°C.
2. Trim stem ends from string beans, wash, and pat dry.
3. In a shallow dish, beat eggs and water together until well blended.
4. Place flour in a second shallow dish.
5. In a third shallow dish, stir together the breadcrumbs, salt, pepper, and dry mustard if using.
6. Dip each string bean in egg mixture, flour, egg mixture again, then breadcrumbs.
7. When you finish coating all the string beans, open air fryer and place them in basket.
8. Cook for 3minutes.
9. Stop and mist string beans with oil or cooking spray.
10. Cook for 3 moreminutes or until string beans are crispy and nicely browned.

Nicoise Deviled Eggs

Servings:4
Cooking Time: 20 Minutes
Ingredients:
- 4 eggs
- 2 tbsp mayonnaise
- 10 chopped Nicoise olives
- 2 tbsp goat cheese crumbles
- Salt and pepper to taste
- 2 tbsp chopped parsley

Directions:
1. Preheat air fryer to 260ºF/180°C. Place the eggs in silicone muffin cups to avoid bumping around and cracking during the cooking process. Add silicone cups to the frying basket and Air Fry for 15 minutes. Remove and run the eggs under cold water. When cool, remove the shells and halve them lengthwise.
2. Spoon yolks into a separate medium bowl and arrange white halves on a large plate. Mash the yolks with a fork. Stir in the remaining ingredients. Spoon mixture into white halves and scatter with mint to serve.

Sweet Potato Chips

Servings: 4
Cooking Time: 10 Minutes
Ingredients:
- 2 medium sweet potatoes, washed
- 2 cups filtered water
- 1 tablespoon avocado oil
- 2 teaspoons brown sugar
- ½ teaspoon salt

Directions:
1. Using a mandolin, slice the potatoes into ⅛-inch pieces.
2. Add the water to a large bowl. Place the potatoes in the bowl, and soak for at least 30 minutes.
3. Preheat the air fryer to 350°F/175°C.
4. Drain the water and pat the chips dry with a paper towel or kitchen cloth. Toss the chips with the avocado oil, brown sugar, and salt. Liberally spray the air fryer basket with olive oil mist.

5. Set the chips inside the air fryer, separating them so they're not on top of each other. Cook for 5 minutes, shake the basket, and cook another 5 minutes, or until browned.
6. Remove and let cool a few minutes prior to serving. Repeat until all the chips are cooked.

Buffalo French Fries

Servings: 6
Cooking Time: 35 Minutes
Ingredients:
- 3 large russet potatoes
- 2 tbsp buffalo sauce
- 2 tbsp extra-virgin olive oil
- Salt and pepper to taste

Directions:
1. Preheat air fryer to 380°F/195°C. Peel and cut potatoes lengthwise into French fries. Place them in a bowl, then coat with olive oil, salt and pepper. Air Fry them for 10 minutes. Shake the basket, then cook for five minutes. Serve drizzled with Buffalo sauce immediately.

Garlic Wings

Servings: 4
Cooking Time: 15 Minutes
Ingredients:
- 2 pounds chicken wings
- oil for misting
- cooking spray
- Marinade
- 1 cup buttermilk
- 2 cloves garlic, mashed flat
- 1 teaspoon Worcestershire sauce
- 1 bay leaf
- Coating
- 1½ cups grated Parmesan cheese
- ¾ cup breadcrumbs
- 1½ tablespoons garlic powder
- ½ teaspoon salt

Directions:
1. Mix all marinade ingredients together.
2. Remove wing tips (the third joint) and discard or freeze for stock. Cut the remaining wings at the joint and toss them into the marinade, stirring to coat well. Refrigerate for at least an hour but no more than 8 hours.
3. When ready to cook, combine all coating ingredients in a shallow dish.
4. Remove wings from marinade, shaking off excess, and roll in coating mixture. Press coating into wings so that it sticks well. Spray wings with oil.
5. Spray air fryer basket with cooking spray. Place wings in basket in single layer, close but not touching.
6. Cook at 360°F/180°C for 15minutes or until chicken is done and juices run clear.
7. Repeat previous step to cook remaining wings.

No-guilty Spring Rolls

Servings: 6
Cooking Time: 20 Minutes
Ingredients:
- 2 cups shiitake mushrooms, thinly sliced
- 4 cups green cabbage, shredded
- 4 tsp sesame oil
- 6 garlic cloves, minced
- 1 tbsp grated ginger
- 1 cup grated carrots
- Salt to taste
- 16 rice paper wraps
- ½ tsp ground cumin
- ½ tsp ground coriander

Directions:
1. Warm the sesame oil in a pan over medium heat. Add garlic, ginger, mushrooms, cabbage, carrots, cumin, coriander, and salt and stir-fry for 3-4 minutes or until the cabbage is wilted. Remove from heat. Get a piece of rice paper, wet with water, and lay it on a flat, non-absorbent surface. Place ¼ cup of the filling in the middle, then fold the bottom over the filling and fold the sides in. Roll up to make a mini burrito. Repeat until you have the number of spring rolls you want.
2. Preheat air fryer to 390°F/200°C. Place the spring rolls in the greased frying basket. Spray the tops with cooking oil and Air Fry for 8-10 minutes until golden. Serve immediately.

Sweet And Salty Snack Mix

Servings: 10
Cooking Time: 12 Minutes
Ingredients:
- ½ cup honey
- 3 tablespoons butter, melted
- 1 teaspoon salt
- 2 cups sesame sticks
- 1 cup pepitas (pumpkin seeds)
- 2 cups granola
- 1 cup cashews
- 2 cups crispy corn puff cereal (Kix® or Corn Pops®)
- 2 cups mini pretzel crisps
- 1 cup dried cherries

Directions:
1. Combine the honey, butter and salt in a small bowl or measuring cup and stir until combined.
2. Combine the sesame sticks, pepitas, granola, cashews, corn puff cereal and pretzel crisps in a large bowl. Pour the honey mixture over the top and toss to combine.
3. Preheat air fryer to 370°F/185°C.
4. Air-fry the snack mix in two batches. Place half the mixture in the air fryer basket and air-fry for 12 minutes, or until the snack mix is lightly toasted. Toss the basket several times throughout the process so that the mix cooks evenly and doesn't get too dark on top.
5. Transfer the snack mix to a cookie sheet and let it cool completely. Mix in the dried cherries and store the mix in an airtight container for up to a week or two.

Curried Pickle Chips

Servings: 4
Cooking Time: 25 Minutes
Ingredients:
- 2 dill pickles, sliced
- 1 cup breadcrumbs
- 2 eggs, beaten
- A pinch of white pepper
- 1 tsp curry powder
- ½ tsp mustard powder

Directions:
1. Preheat air fryer to 350°F/175°C. Combine the breadcrumbs, curry, mustard powder, and white pepper in a mixing bowl. Coat the pickle slices with the crumb mixture; then dip into the eggs, then dip again into the dry ingredients. Arrange the coated pickle pieces on the greased frying basket in an even layer. Air Fry for 15 minutes, shaking the basket several times during cooking until crispy, golden brown and perfect. Serve warm.

Cheddar Stuffed Jalapeños

Servings: 5
Cooking Time: 15 Minutes
Ingredients:
- 10 jalapeño peppers
- 6 oz ricotta cheese
- ¼ cup grated cheddar
- 2 tbsp bread crumbs

Directions:
1. Preheat air fryer to 340°F/170°C. Cut jalapeños in half lengthwise. Clean out the seeds and membrane. Set aside. Microwave ricotta cheese in a small bowl for 15 seconds to soften. Stir in cheddar cheese to combine. Stuff each jalapeño half with the cheese mixture. Top the poppers with bread crumbs. Place in air fryer and lightly spray with cooking oil. Bake for 5-6 minutes. Serve warm.

Shrimp Egg Rolls

Servings: 8
Cooking Time: 10 Minutes
Ingredients:
- 1 tablespoon vegetable oil
- ½ head green or savoy cabbage, finely shredded
- 1 cup shredded carrots
- 1 cup canned bean sprouts, drained
- 1 tablespoon soy sauce
- ½ teaspoon sugar
- 1 teaspoon sesame oil
- ¼ cup hoisin sauce
- freshly ground black pepper
- 1 pound cooked shrimp, diced
- ¼ cup scallions
- 8 egg roll wrappers
- vegetable oil
- duck sauce

Directions:
1. Preheat a large sauté pan over medium-high heat. Add the oil and cook the cabbage, carrots and bean sprouts until they start to wilt – about 3 minutes. Add the soy sauce, sugar, sesame oil, hoisin sauce and black pepper. Sauté for a few more minutes. Stir in the shrimp and scallions and cook until the vegetables are just tender. Transfer the mixture to a colander in a bowl to cool. Press or squeeze out any excess water from the filling so that you don't end up with soggy egg rolls.
2. To make the egg rolls, place the egg roll wrappers on a flat surface with one of the points facing towards you so they look like diamonds. Dividing the filling evenly between the eight wrappers, spoon the mixture onto the center of the egg roll wrappers. Spread the filling across the center of the wrappers from the left corner to the right corner, but leave 2 inches from each corner empty. Brush the empty sides of the wrapper with a little water. Fold the bottom corner of the wrapper tightly up over the filling, trying to avoid making any air pockets. Fold the left corner in toward the center and then the right corner toward the center. It should now look like an envelope. Tightly roll the egg roll from the bottom to the top open corner. Press to seal the egg roll together, brushing with a little extra water if need be. Repeat this technique with all 8 egg rolls.
3. Preheat the air fryer to 370°F/185°C.
4. Spray or brush all sides of the egg rolls with vegetable oil. Air-fry four egg rolls at a time for 10 minutes, turning them over halfway through the cooking time.
5. Serve hot with duck sauce or your favorite dipping sauce.

Roasted Jalapeño Salsa Verde

Servings: 4
Cooking Time: 20 Minutes
Ingredients:
- ¾ lb fresh tomatillos, husked
- 1 jalapeño, stem removed
- 4 green onions, sliced
- 3 garlic cloves, peeled
- ½ tsp salt
- 1 tsp lime juice
- ¼ tsp apple cider vinegar
- ¼ cup cilantro leaves

Directions:
1. Preheat air fryer to 400°F/205°C. Add tomatillos and jalapeño to the frying basket and Bake for 5 minutes. Put in green onions and garlic and Bake for 5 more minutes. Transfer it into a food processor along with salt, lime juice, vinegar and cilantro and blend until the sauce is finely chopped. Pour it into a small sealable container and refrigerate it until ready to use up to five days.

Veggie Cheese Bites

Servings: 4
Cooking Time: 8 Minutes
Ingredients:
- 2 cups riced vegetables (see the Note below)
- ½ cup shredded zucchini
- ½ teaspoon garlic powder
- ¼ teaspoon black pepper
- ¼ teaspoon salt
- 1 large egg
- ¾ cup shredded cheddar cheese
- ⅓ cup whole-wheat flour

Directions:
1. Preheat the air fryer to 350°F/175°C.
2. In a large bowl, mix together the riced vegetables, zucchini, garlic powder, pepper, and salt. Mix in the egg. Stir in the shredded cheese and whole-wheat flour until a thick, doughlike consistency forms. If you need to, add 1 teaspoon of flour at a time so you can mold the batter into balls.
3. Using a 1-inch scoop, portion the batter out into about 12 balls.
4. Liberally spray the air fryer basket with olive oil spray. Then place the veggie bites inside. Leave enough room between each bite so the air can flow around them.
5. Cook for 8 minutes, or until the outside is slightly browned. Depending on the size of your air fryer, you may need to cook these in batches.
6. Remove and let cool slightly before serving.

Crispy Chicken Bites With Gorgonzola Sauce

Servings: 4
Cooking Time: 30 Minutes
Ingredients:
- ¼ cup crumbled Gorgonzola cheese
- ¼ cup creamy blue cheese salad dressing
- 1 lb chicken tenders, cut into thirds crosswise
- ½ cup sour cream
- 1 celery stalk, chopped
- 3 tbsp buffalo chicken sauce

- 1 cup panko bread crumbs
- 2 tbsp olive oil

Directions:
1. Preheat air fryer to 350°F/175°C. Blend together sour cream, salad dressing, Gorgonzola cheese, and celery in a bowl. Set aside. Combine chicken pieces and Buffalo wing sauce in another bowl until the chicken is coated.
2. In a shallow bowl or pie plate, mix the bread crumbs and olive oil. Dip the chicken into the bread crumb mixture, patting the crumbs to keep them in place. Arrange the chicken in the greased frying basket and Air Fry for 8-9 minutes, shaking once halfway through cooking until the chicken is golden. Serve with the blue cheese sauce.

Five Spice Fries

Servings: 2
Cooking Time: 30 Minutes
Ingredients:
- 1 Yukon Gold potato, cut into fries
- 1 tbsp coconut oil
- 1 tsp coconut sugar
- 1 tsp garlic powder
- ½ tsp Chinese five-spice
- Salt to taste
- ¼ tsp turmeric
- ¼ tsp paprika

Directions:
1. Preheat air fryer to 390°F/200°C. Toss the potato pieces with coconut oil, sugar, garlic, Chinese five-spice, salt, turmeric, and paprika in a bowl and stir well. Place in the greased frying basket and Air Fry for 18-25 minutes, tossing twice until softened and golden. Serve warm.

Stuffed Baby Bella Caps

Servings: 16
Cooking Time: 12 Minutes
Ingredients:
- 16 fresh, small Baby Bella mushrooms
- 2 green onions
- 4 ounces mozzarella cheese
- ½ cup diced ham
- 2 tablespoons breadcrumbs
- ½ teaspoon garlic powder
- ¼ teaspoon ground oregano
- ¼ teaspoon ground black pepper
- 1 to 2 teaspoons olive oil

Directions:
1. Remove stems and wash mushroom caps.
2. Cut green onions and cheese in small pieces and place in food processor.
3. Add ham, breadcrumbs, garlic powder, oregano, and pepper and mince ingredients.
4. With food processor running, dribble in just enough olive oil to make a thick paste.
5. Divide stuffing among mushroom caps and pack down lightly.
6. Place stuffed mushrooms in air fryer basket in single layer and cook at 390°F/200°C for 12minutes or until tops are golden brown and mushrooms are tender.
7. Repeat step 6 to cook remaining mushrooms.

Spiced Parsnip Chips

Servings:2
Cooking Time: 35 Minutes
Ingredients:
- ½ tsp smoked paprika
- ¼ tsp chili powder
- ¼ tsp garlic powder
- ⅛ tsp onion powder
- ⅛ tsp cayenne pepper
- ⅛ tsp granulated sugar
- 1 tsp salt
- 1 parsnip, cut into chips
- 2 tsp olive oil

Directions:
1. Preheat air fryer to 400ºF/205°C. Mix all spices in a bowl and reserve. In another bowl, combine parsnip chips, olive oil, and salt. Place parsnip chips in the lightly greased frying basket and Air Fry for 12 minutes, shaking once. Transfer the chips to a bowl, toss in seasoning mix, and let sit for 15 minutes before serving.

Canadian-inspired Waffle Poutine

Servings: 4
Cooking Time: 30 Minutes
Ingredients:
- 1 cup frozen waffle cut fries
- 2 tsp olive oil
- 1 red bell pepper, chopped
- 2 green onions, sliced
- 1 cup grated mozzarella
- ½ cup beef gravy

Directions:
1. Preheat air fryer to 380°F/195°C. Toss the waffle fries with olive oil, then place in the frying basket. Air Fry for about 10-12 minutes, shake the basket once until crisp and lightly golden. Take the fries out of the basket and place in a baking pan. Top with peppers, green onions, and mozzarella cheese. Cook until the vegetables are tender, about 3 minutes. Remove the pan from the fryer and drizzle beef gravy over all of the fries and vegetables. Heat the gravy through for about 2 minutes, then serve.

Cheesy Green Pitas

Servings: 4
Cooking Time: 15 Minutes
Ingredients:
- ½ cup canned artichoke hearts, sliced
- 2 whole-wheat pitas
- 2 tbsp olive oil, divided
- 2 garlic cloves, minced
- ¼ tsp salt
- ¼ cup green olives
- ¼ cup grated Pecorino
- ¼ cup crumbled feta
- 2 tbsp chopped chervil

Directions:
1. Preheat air fryer to 380°F/195°C. Lightly brush each pita with some olive oil, then top with garlic and salt. Divide the artichoke hearts, green olives, and cheeses evenly between the two pitas, and put both into the air fryer. Bake for 10 minutes. Remove the pitas and cut them into 4 pieces each before serving. Top with chervil. Enjoy!
2. Roast the shrimp for 4 minutes, then open the air fryer and place the ramekin with oil and garlic in the basket beside the shrimp packet. Cook for 2 more minutes. Place the shrimp on a serving plate or platter with the ramekin of garlic olive oil on the side for dipping.

Smoked Whitefish Spread

Servings: 1
Cooking Time: 10 Minutes
Ingredients:
- ¾ pound Boneless skinless white-flesh fish fillets, such as hake or trout
- 3 tablespoons Liquid smoke
- 3 tablespoons Regular, low-fat, or fat-free mayonnaise (gluten-free, if a concern)
- 2 teaspoons Jarred prepared white horseradish (optional)
- ¼ teaspoon Onion powder
- ¼ teaspoon Celery seeds
- ¼ teaspoon Table salt
- ¼ teaspoon Ground black pepper

Directions:
1. Put the fish fillets in a zip-closed bag, add the liquid smoke, and seal closed. Rub the liquid smoke all over the fish , then refrigerate the sealed bag for 2 hours.
2. Preheat the air fryer to 400°F/205°C.
3. Set a 12-inch piece of aluminum foil on your work surface. Remove the fish fillets from the bag and set them in the center of this piece of foil (the fillets can overlap). Fold the long sides of the foil together and crimp them closed. Make a tight seam so no steam can escape. Fold up the ends and crimp to seal well.
4. Set the packet in the basket and air-fry undisturbed for 10 minutes.
5. Use kitchen tongs to transfer the foil packet to a wire rack. Cool for a minute or so. Open the packet, transfer the fish to a plate, and refrigerate for 30 minutes.
6. Put the cold fish in a food processor. Add the mayonnaise, horseradish (if using), onion powder, celery seeds, salt, and pepper. Cover and pulse to a slightly coarse spread, certainly not fully smooth.
7. For a more traditional texture, put the fish fillets in a bowl, add the other ingredients, and stir with a wooden spoon, mashing the fish with everything else to make a coarse paste.
8. Scrape the spread into a bowl and serve at once, or cover with plastic wrap and store in the fridge for up to 4 days.

Corn Dog Muffins

Servings: 8
Cooking Time: 10 Minutes
Ingredients:
- 1¼ cups sliced kosher hotdogs (3 or 4, depending on size)
- ½ cup flour
- ½ cup yellow cornmeal
- 2 teaspoons baking powder
- ½ cup skim milk
- 1 egg
- 2 tablespoons canola oil
- 8 foil muffin cups, paper liners removed
- cooking spray
- mustard or your favorite dipping sauce

Directions:
1. Slice each hot dog in half lengthwise, then cut in ¼-inch half-moon slices. Set aside.
2. Preheat air fryer to 390°F/200°C.
3. In a large bowl, stir together flour, cornmeal, and baking powder.
4. In a small bowl, beat together the milk, egg, and oil until just blended.
5. Pour egg mixture into dry ingredients and stir with a spoon to mix well.
6. Stir in sliced hot dogs.
7. Spray the foil cups lightly with cooking spray.
8. Divide mixture evenly into muffin cups.
9. Place 4 muffin cups in the air fryer basket and cook for 5 minutes.
10. Reduce temperature to 360°F/180°C and cook 5 minutes or until toothpick inserted in center of muffin comes out clean.
11. Repeat steps 9 and 10 to bake remaining corn dog muffins.
12. Serve with mustard or other sauces for dipping.

Poutine

Servings: 2
Cooking Time: 25 Minutes
Ingredients:
- 2 russet potatoes, scrubbed and cut into ½-inch sticks
- 2 teaspoons vegetable oil
- 2 tablespoons butter
- ¼ onion, minced (about ¼ cup)
- 1 clove garlic, smashed
- ¼ teaspoon dried thyme
- 3 tablespoons flour
- 1 teaspoon tomato paste
- 1½ cups strong beef stock
- salt and lots of freshly ground black pepper
- a few dashes of Worcestershire sauce
- ⅔ cup chopped string cheese or cheese curds

Directions:
1. Bring a large saucepan of salted water to a boil on the stovetop while you peel and cut the potatoes. Blanch the potatoes in the boiling salted water for 4 minutes while you Preheat the air fryer to 400°F/205°C. Strain the potatoes and rinse them with cold water. Dry them well with a clean kitchen towel.
2. Toss the dried potato sticks gently with the oil and place them in the air fryer basket. Air-fry for 25 minutes, shaking the basket a few times while the fries cook to help them brown evenly.
3. While the fries are cooking, make the gravy. Melt the butter in a small saucepan over medium heat. Add the onion, garlic and thyme and cook for five minutes, until soft and just starting to brown. Stir in the flour and cook for another two minutes, stirring regularly. Finally, add the tomato paste and continue to cook for another minute or two. Whisk in the beef stock and bring the mixture to a boil to thicken. Season to taste with salt, lots of freshly ground black pepper and a few dashes of Worcestershire sauce. Keep the gravy warm.
4. As soon as the fries are done, season them with salt and transfer to a plate or basket. Top the fries with the cheese curds or string cheese, and pour the warm gravy over the top.

Pizza Bagel Bites

Servings: 2
Cooking Time: 5 Minutes
Ingredients:
- 2 Mini bagel(s), split into two rings
- ¼ cup Purchased pizza sauce

Tower Air Fryer Cookbook

- ½ cup Finely grated or shredded cheese, such as Parmesan cheese, semi-firm mozzarella, fontina, or (preferably) a cheese blend

Directions:
1. Preheat the air fryer to 375°F/190°C.
2. Spread the cut side of each bagel half with 1 tablespoon pizza sauce; top each half with 2 tablespoons shredded cheese.
3. When the machine is at temperature, put the bagels cheese side up in the basket in one layer. Air-fry undisturbed for 4 minutes, or until the cheese has melted and is gooey. You may need to air-fry the pizza bagel bites for 1 minute extra if the temperature is at 360°F/180°C.
4. Use a nonstick-safe spatula to transfer the topped bagel halves to a wire rack. Cool for at least 5 minutes before serving.

Cheesy Green Wonton Triangles

Servings: 20 Wontons
Cooking Time: 55 Minutes

Ingredients:
- 6 oz marinated artichoke hearts
- 6 oz cream cheese
- ¼ cup sour cream
- ¼ cup grated Parmesan
- ¼ cup grated cheddar
- 5 oz chopped kale
- 2 garlic cloves, chopped
- Salt and pepper to taste
- 20 wonton wrappers

Directions:
1. Microwave cream cheese in a bowl for 20 seconds. Combine with sour cream, Parmesan, cheddar, kale, artichoke hearts, garlic, salt, and pepper. Lay out the wrappers on a cutting board. Scoop 1 ½ tsp of cream cheese mixture on top of the wrapper. Fold up diagonally to form a triangle. Bring together the two bottom corners. Squeeze out any air and press together to seal the edges.
2. Preheat air fryer to 375°F/190°C. Place a batch of wonton in the greased frying basket and Bake for 10 minutes. Flip them and cook for 5-8 minutes until crisp and golden. Serve.

Vegetable Spring Rolls

Servings: 6
Cooking Time: 8 Minutes

Ingredients:
- ¾ cup (a little more than 2½ ounces) Fresh bean sprouts
- 6 tablespoons Shredded carrots
- 6 tablespoons Slivered, drained, sliced canned bamboo shoots
- 1½ tablespoons Regular or low-sodium soy sauce or gluten-free tamari sauce
- 1½ teaspoons Granulated white sugar
- 1½ teaspoons Toasted sesame oil
- 6 Spring roll wrappers (gluten-free, if a concern)
- 1 Large egg, well beaten
- Vegetable oil spray

Directions:
1. Gently stir the bean sprouts, carrots, bamboo shoots, soy or tamari sauce, sugar, and oil in a large bowl until the vegetables are evenly coated. Set aside at room temperature for 10 to 15 minutes.
2. Preheat the air fryer to 400°F/205°C.
3. Set a spring roll wrapper on a clean, dry work surface. Pick up about ¼ cup of the vegetable mixture and gently squeeze it in your clean hand to release most of the liquid. Set this bundle of vegetables along one edge of the wrapper.
4. Fold two opposing sides (at right angles to the filling) up and over the filling, concealing part of it and making a folded-over border down two sides of the wrapper. Brush the top half of the wrapper (including the folded parts) with beaten egg so it will seal when you roll it closed.
5. Starting with the side nearest the filling, roll the wrapper closed, working to make a tight fit, eliminating as much air as possible from inside the wrapper. Set it aside seam side down and continue making more filled rolls using the same techniques.
6. Lightly coat all the sealed rolls with vegetable oil spray on all sides. Set them seam side down in the basket and air-fry undisturbed for 8 minutes, or until golden brown and very crisp.
7. Use a nonstick-safe spatula and a flatware fork for balance to transfer the rolls to a wire rack. Cool for at least 5 minutes or up to 15 minutes before serving.

Taquito Quesadillas

Servings: 4
Cooking Time: 35 Minutes

Ingredients:
- 8 tbsp Mexican blend shredded cheese
- 8 soft corn tortillas
- 2 tsp olive oil
- ¼ cup chopped cilantro

Directions:
1. Preheat air fryer at 350°F/175°C. Spread cheese and coriander over 4 tortillas; top each with the remaining tortillas and brush the tops lightly with oil. Place quesadillas in the frying basket and Air Fry for 6 minutes. Serve warm.

Smoked Salmon Puffs

Servings: 2
Cooking Time: 8 Minutes

Ingredients:
- Two quarters of one thawed sheet (that is, a half of the sheet; wrap and refreeze the remainder) A 17.25-ounce box frozen puff pastry
- 4 ½-ounce smoked salmon slices
- 2 tablespoons Softened regular or low-fat cream cheese (not fat-free)
- Up to 2 teaspoons Drained and rinsed capers, minced
- Up to 2 teaspoons Minced red onion
- 1 Large egg white
- 1 tablespoon Water

Directions:
1. Preheat the air fryer to 400°F/205°C.
2. For a small air fryer, roll the piece of puff pastry into a 6 x 6-inch square on a clean, dry work surface.
3. For a medium or larger air fryer, roll each piece of puff pastry into a 6 x 6-inch square.
4. Set 2 salmon slices on the diagonal, corner to corner, on each rolled-out sheet. Smear the salmon with cream cheese, then sprinkle with capers and red onion. Fold the sheet closed by picking up one corner that does not have an edge of salmon near it and folding the dough across the salmon to its opposite corner. Seal the edges closed by pressing the tines of a flatware fork into them.

5. Whisk the egg white and water in a small bowl until uniform. Brush this mixture over the top(s) of the packet(s).
6. Set the packet(s) in the basket (if you're working with more than one, they cannot touch). Air-fry undisturbed for 8 minutes, or until golden brown and flaky.
7. Use a nonstick-safe spatula to transfer the packet(s) to a wire rack. Cool for 5 minutes before serving.

Orange-glazed Carrots

Servings: 3
Cooking Time: 25 Minutes
Ingredients:
- 3 carrots, cut into spears
- 1 tbsp orange juice
- 2 tsp balsamic vinegar
- 1 tsp avocado oil
- 1 tsp clear honey
- ½ tsp dried rosemary
- ¼ tsp salt
- ¼ tsp lemon zest

Directions:
1. Preheat air fryer to 390°F/200°C. Put the carrots in a baking pan. Add the orange juice, balsamic vinegar, oil, honey, rosemary, salt, and zest. Stir well. Roast for 15-18 minutes, shaking them once or twice until the carrots are bright orange, glazed, and tender. Serve while hot.

Garlic-herb Pita Chips

Servings: 4
Cooking Time: 6 Minutes
Ingredients:
- ¼ teaspoon dried basil
- ¼ teaspoon marjoram
- ¼ teaspoon ground oregano
- ¼ teaspoon garlic powder
- ¼ teaspoon ground thyme
- ¼ teaspoon salt
- 2 whole 6-inch pitas, whole grain or white
- oil for misting or cooking spray

Directions:
1. Mix all seasonings together.
2. Cut each pita half into 4 wedges. Break apart wedges at the fold.
3. Mist one side of pita wedges with oil. Sprinkle with half of seasoning mix.
4. Turn pita wedges over, mist the other side with oil, and sprinkle with remaining seasonings.
5. Place pita wedges in air fryer basket and cook at 330°F/165°C for 2minutes.
6. Shake basket and cook for 2minutes longer. Shake again, and if needed cook for 2 moreminutes, until crisp. Watch carefully because at this point they will cook very quickly.

Fried Brie With Cherry Tomatoes

Servings: 8
Cooking Time: 15 Minutes
Ingredients:
- 1 baguette*
- 2 pints red and yellow cherry tomatoes
- 1 tablespoon olive oil
- salt and freshly ground black pepper
- 1 teaspoon balsamic vinegar
- 1 tablespoon chopped fresh parsley
- 1 (8-ounce) wheel of Brie cheese
- olive oil
- ½ teaspoon Italian seasoning (optional)
- 1 tablespoon chopped fresh basil

Directions:
1. Preheat the air fryer to 350°F/175°C.
2. Start by making the crostini. Slice the baguette diagonally into ½-inch slices and brush the slices with olive oil on both sides. Air-fry the baguette slices at 350°F in batches for 6 minutes or until lightly browned on all sides. Set the bread aside on your serving platter.
3. Toss the cherry tomatoes in a bowl with the olive oil, salt and pepper. Air-fry the cherry tomatoes for 3 to 5 minutes, shaking the basket a few times during the cooking process. The tomatoes should be soft and some of them will burst open. Toss the warm tomatoes with the balsamic vinegar and fresh parsley and set aside.
4. Cut a circle of parchment paper the same size as your wheel of Brie cheese. Brush both sides of the Brie wheel with olive oil and sprinkle with Italian seasoning, if using. Place the circle of parchment paper on one side of the Brie and transfer the Brie to the air fryer basket, parchment side down. Air-fry at 350°F/175°C for 8 to 10 minutes, or until the Brie is slightly puffed and soft to the touch.
5. Watch carefully and remove the Brie before the rind cracks and the cheese starts to leak out. Transfer the wheel to your serving platter and top with the roasted tomatoes. Sprinkle with basil and serve with the toasted bread slices.

Blooming Onion

Servings: 4
Cooking Time: 25 Minutes
Ingredients:
- 1 large Vidalia onion, peeled
- 2 eggs
- ½ cup milk
- 1 cup flour
- 1 teaspoon salt
- ½ teaspoon freshly ground black pepper
- ¼ teaspoon ground cayenne pepper
- ½ teaspoon paprika
- ½ teaspoon garlic powder
- Dipping Sauce:
- ½ cup mayonnaise
- ½ cup ketchup
- 1 teaspoon Worcestershire sauce
- ½ teaspoon ground cayenne pepper
- ½ teaspoon paprika
- ½ teaspoon onion powder

Directions:
1. Cut off the top inch of the onion, leaving the root end of the onion intact. Place the now flat, stem end of the onion down on a cutting board with the root end facing up. Make 16 slices around the onion, starting with your knife tip ½-inch away from the root so that you never slice through the root. Begin by making slices at 12, 3, 6 and 9 o'clock around the onion. Then make three slices down the onion in between each of the original four slices. Turn the onion over, gently separate the onion petals, and remove the loose pieces of onion in the center.
2. Combine the eggs and milk in a bowl. In a second bowl, combine the flour, salt, black pepper, cayenne pepper, paprika, and garlic powder.
3. Preheat the air fryer to 350°F/175°C.

4. Place the onion cut side up into a third empty bowl. Sprinkle the flour mixture all over the onion to cover it and get in between the onion petals. Turn the onion over to carefully shake off the excess flour and then transfer the onion to the empty flour bowl, again cut side up.

5. Pour the egg mixture all over the onion to cover all the flour. Let it soak for a minute in the mixture. Carefully remove the onion, tipping it upside down to drain off any excess egg, and transfer it to the empty egg bowl, again cut side up.

6. Finally, sprinkle the flour mixture over the onion a second time, making sure the onion is well coated and all the petals have the seasoned flour mixture on them. Carefully turn the onion over, shake off any excess flour and transfer it to a plate or baking sheet. Spray the onion generously with vegetable oil.

7. Transfer the onion, cut side up to the air fryer basket and air-fry for 25 minutes. The onion petals will open more fully as it cooks, so spray with more vegetable oil at least twice during the cooking time.

8. While the onion is cooking, make the dipping sauce by combining all the dip ingredients and mixing well. Serve the Blooming Onion as soon as it comes out of the air fryer with dipping sauce on the side.

Crunchy Pickle Chips

Servings: 4
Cooking Time: 20 Minutes
Ingredients:
- 1 lb dill pickles, sliced
- 2 eggs
- 1/3 cup flour
- 1/3 cup bread crumbs
- 1 tsp Italian seasoning

Directions:
1. Preheat air fryer to 400°F/205°C. Set out three small bowls. In the first bowl, add flour. In the second bowl, beat eggs. In the third bowl, mix bread crumbs with Italian seasoning. Dip the pickle slices in the flour. Shake, then dredge in egg. Roll in bread crumbs and shake excess. Place the pickles in the greased frying basket and Air Fry for 6 minutes. Flip them halfway through cooking and fry for another 3 minutes until crispy. Serve warm.

Warm Spinach Dip With Pita Chips

Servings: 6
Cooking Time: 40 Minutes
Ingredients:
- Pita Chips:
- 4 pita breads
- 1 tablespoon olive oil
- ½ teaspoon paprika
- salt and freshly ground black pepper
- Spinach Dip:
- 8 ounces cream cheese, softened at room , Temperature: 1 cup ricotta cheese
- 1 cup grated Fontina cheese
- ½ teaspoon Italian seasoning
- ½ teaspoon garlic powder
- ¾ teaspoon salt
- freshly ground black pepper
- 16 ounces frozen chopped spinach, thawed and squeezed dry
- ¼ cup grated Parmesan cheese
- ½ tomato, finely diced
- ¼ teaspoon dried oregano

Directions:
1. Preheat the air fryer to 390°F/200°C.
2. Split the pita breads open so you have 2 circles. Cut each circle into 8 wedges. Place all the wedges into a large bowl and toss with the olive oil. Season with the paprika, salt and pepper and toss to coat evenly. Air-fry the pita triangles in two batches for 5 minutes each, shaking the basket once or twice while they cook so they brown and crisp evenly.
3. Combine the cream cheese, ricotta cheese, Fontina cheese, Italian seasoning, garlic powder, salt and pepper in a large bowl. Fold in the spinach and mix well.
4. Transfer the spinach-cheese mixture to a 7-inch ceramic baking dish or cake pan. Sprinkle the Parmesan cheese on top and wrap the dish with aluminum foil. Transfer the dish to the basket of the air fryer, lowering the dish into the basket using a sling made of aluminum foil (fold a piece of aluminum foil into a strip about 2-inches wide by 24-inches long). Fold the ends of the aluminum foil over the top of the dish before returning the basket to the air fryer. Air-fry for 30 minutes at 390°F. With 4 minutes left on the air fryer timer, remove the foil and let the cheese brown on top.
5. Sprinkle the diced tomato and oregano on the warm dip and serve immediately with the pita chips.

Vegetarian Fritters With Green Dip

Servings: 6
Cooking Time: 40 Minutes
Ingredients:
- ½ cup grated carrots
- ½ cup grated zucchini
- ¼ cup minced yellow onion
- 1 garlic clove, minced
- 1 large egg
- ¼ cup flour
- ¼ cup bread crumbs
- Salt and pepper to taste
- ½ tsp ground cumin
- ½ avocado, peeled and pitted
- ½ cup plain Greek yogurt
- 1 tsp lime juice
- 1 tbsp white vinegar
- ¼ cup chopped cilantro

Directions:
1. Preheat air fryer to 375°F/190°C. Combine carrots, zucchini, onion, garlic, egg, flour, bread crumbs, salt, pepper, and cumin in a large bowl. Scoop out 12 equal portions of the vegetables and form them into patties. Arrange the patties on the greased basket. Air Fry for 5 minutes, then flip the patties. Air Fry for another 5 minutes. Check if the fritters are golden and cooked through. If more time is needed, cook for another 3-5 minutes.
2. While the fritters are cooking, prepare the avocado sauce. Mash the avocado in a small bowl to the desired texture. Stir in yogurt, white vinegar, chopped cilantro, lime juice, and salt. When the fritter is done, transfer to a serving plate along with the avocado sauce for dipping. Serve warm and enjoy.

Mozzarella Sticks

Servings: 4
Cooking Time: 5 Minutes
Ingredients:
- 1 egg
- 1 tablespoon water
- 8 eggroll wraps
- 8 mozzarella string cheese "sticks"
- sauce for dipping

Directions:
1. Beat together egg and water in a small bowl.
2. Lay out egg roll wraps and moisten edges with egg wash.
3. Place one piece of string cheese on each wrap near one end.
4. Fold in sides of egg roll wrap over ends of cheese, and then roll up.
5. Brush outside of wrap with egg wash and press gently to seal well.
6. Place in air fryer basket in single layer and cook 390°F/200°C for 5 minutes. Cook an additional 1 or 2minutes, if necessary, until they are golden brown and crispy.
7. Serve with your favorite dipping sauce.

Honey-mustard Chicken Wings

Servings: 2
Cooking Time: 14 Minutes
Ingredients:
- 2 pounds chicken wings
- salt and freshly ground black pepper
- 2 tablespoons butter
- ¼ cup honey
- ¼ cup spicy brown mustard
- pinch ground cayenne pepper
- 2 teaspoons Worcestershire sauce

Directions:
1. Prepare the chicken wings by cutting off the wing tips and discarding (or freezing for chicken stock). Divide the drumettes from the wingettes by cutting through the joint. Place the chicken wing pieces in a large bowl.
2. Preheat the air fryer to 400°F/205°C.
3. Season the wings with salt and freshly ground black pepper and air-fry the wings in two batches for 10 minutes per batch, shaking the basket half way through the cooking process.
4. While the wings are air-frying, combine the remaining ingredients in a small saucepan over low heat.
5. When both batches are done, toss all the wings with the honey-mustard sauce and toss them all back into the basket for another 4 minutes to heat through and finish cooking. Give the basket a good shake part way through the cooking process to redistribute the wings. Remove the wings from the air fryer and serve.

Beet Chips

Servings: 4
Cooking Time: 20 Minutes
Ingredients:
- 2 large red beets, washed and skinned
- 1 tablespoon avocado oil
- ¼ teaspoon salt

Directions:
1. Preheat the air fryer to 330°F/165°C.
2. Using a mandolin or sharp knife, slice the beets in ⅛-inch slices. Place them in a bowl of water and let them soak for 30 minutes. Drain the water and pat the beets dry with a paper towel or kitchen cloth.
3. In a medium bowl, toss the beets with avocado oil and sprinkle them with salt.
4. Lightly spray the air fryer basket with olive oil mist and place the beet chips into the basket. To allow for even cooking, don't overlap the beets; cook in batches if necessary.
5. Cook the beet chips 15 to 20 minutes, shaking the basket every 5 minutes, until the outer edges of the beets begin to flip up like a chip. Remove from the basket and serve warm. Repeat with the remaining chips until they're all cooked.

Avocado Fries, Vegan

Servings: 4
Cooking Time: 10 Minutes
Ingredients:
- ¼ cup almond or coconut milk
- 1 tablespoon lime juice
- ⅛ teaspoon hot sauce
- 2 tablespoons flour
- ¾ cup panko breadcrumbs
- ¼ cup cornmeal
- ¼ teaspoon salt
- 1 large avocado
- oil for misting or cooking spray

Directions:
1. In a small bowl, whisk together the almond or coconut milk, lime juice, and hot sauce.
2. Place flour on a sheet of wax paper.
3. Mix panko, cornmeal, and salt and place on another sheet of wax paper.
4. Split avocado in half and remove pit. Peel or use a spoon to lift avocado halves out of the skin.
5. Cut avocado lengthwise into ½-inch slices. Dip each in flour, then milk mixture, then roll in panko mixture.
6. Mist with oil or cooking spray and cook at 390°F/200°C for 10minutes, until crust is brown and crispy.

Fried String Beans With Greek Sauce

Servings: 4
Cooking Time: 10 Minutes
Ingredients:
- 1 egg
- 1 tbsp flour
- ¼ tsp paprika
- ½ tsp garlic powder
- Salt to taste
- ¼ cup bread crumbs
- ¼ lemon zest
- ½ lb whole string beans
- ½ cup Greek yogurt
- 1 tbsp lemon juice
- ⅛ tsp cayenne pepper

Directions:
1. Preheat air fryer to 380°F195°C. Whisk the egg and 2 tbsp of water in a bowl until frothy. Sift the flour, paprika, garlic powder, and salt in another bowl, then stir in the bread crumbs. Dip each string bean into the egg mixture, then roll into the bread crumb mixture. Put the string beans in a single layer in the greased frying basket. Air Fry them for 5 minutes until the breading is golden brown. Stir the yogurt, lemon juice and zest, salt, and cayenne in a small bowl. Serve the bean fries with lemon-yogurt sauce.

Fried Gyoza

Servings: 18
Cooking Time: 6 Minutes
Ingredients:
- 5 ounces Lean ground pork
- 2½ tablespoons Very thinly sliced scallion
- 1 tablespoon plus 2 teaspoons Minced peeled fresh ginger
- 1¼ teaspoons Toasted sesame oil
- ⅛ teaspoon Table salt
- ⅛ teaspoon Ground black pepper
- 18 Round gyoza or square wonton wrappers (thawed, if necessary)
- Vegetable oil spray

Directions:
1. Preheat the air fryer to 350°F/175°C.
2. Mix the ground pork, scallion, ginger, sesame oil, salt, and pepper in a bowl until well combined.
3. Set a bowl of water on a clean, dry surface or next to a clean, dry cutting board. Set one gyoza or wonton wrapper on that surface. Dip your clean finger in the water and run it around the perimeter of the gyoza wrapper or the edge of the wonton wrapper. Put about 1 ½ teaspoons of the meat mixture in the center of the wrapper.
4. For the gyoza wrapper, fold the wrapper in half to close, pressing the edge to seal, then wet the outside of the edge of both sides of the seam and pleat it into little ridges to seal.
5. For the wonton wrapper, fold it in half lengthwise to make a rectangle, then seal the sides together, flattening the packet a bit as you do.
6. Set the filled wrapper aside and continue making more in the same way. When done, generously coat them on all sides with vegetable oil spray.
7. Place the gyoza in the basket in one layer and air-fry undisturbed for 6 minutes, or until browned and crisp at the edges.
8. Use kitchen tongs or a nonstick-safe spatula to gently transfer the gyoza to a wire rack. Cool for only 2 or 3 minutes before serving hot.

Paprika Onion Blossom

Servings: 4
Cooking Time: 35 Minutes + Cooling Time
Ingredients:
- 1 large onion
- 1 ½ cups flour
- 1 tsp garlic powder
- 1 tsp paprika
- ½ tsp bell pepper powder
- Salt and pepper to taste
- 2 eggs
- 1 cup milk

Directions:
1. Remove the tip of the onion but leave the root base intact. Peel the onion to the root and remove skin. Place the onion cut-side down on a cutting board. Starting ½-inch down from the root, cut down to the bottom. Repeat until the onion is divided into quarters. Starting ½-inch down from the root, repeat the cuts in between the first cuts. Repeat this process in between the cuts until you have 16 cuts in the onion. Flip the onion onto the root and carefully spread the inner layers. Set aside.
2. In a bowl, add flour, garlic, paprika, bell pepper, salt, and pepper, then stir. In another large bowl, whisk eggs and milk. Place the onion in the flour bowl and cover with flour mixture. Transfer the onion into the egg mixture and coat completely with either a spoon or basting brush. Return the onion to the flour bowl and cover completely. Take a sheet of foil and wrap the onion with the foil. Freeze for 45 minutes.
3. Preheat air fryer to 400°F/205°C. Remove the onion from the foil and place in the greased frying basket. Air Fry for 10 minutes. Lightly spray the onion with cooking oil, then cook for another 10-15 minutes. Serve immediately.

Granola Three Ways

Servings: 4
Cooking Time: 10 Minutes
Ingredients:
- Nantucket Granola
- ¼ cup maple syrup
- ¼ cup dark brown sugar
- 1 tablespoon butter
- 1 teaspoon vanilla extract
- 1 cup rolled oats
- ½ cup dried cranberries
- ½ cup walnuts, chopped
- ¼ cup pumpkin seeds
- ¼ cup shredded coconut
- Blueberry Delight
- ¼ cup honey
- ¼ cup light brown sugar
- 1 tablespoon butter
- 1 teaspoon lemon extract
- 1 cup rolled oats
- ½ cup sliced almonds
- ½ cup dried blueberries
- ¼ cup pumpkin seeds
- ¼ cup sunflower seeds
- Cherry Black Forest Mix
- ¼ cup honey
- ¼ cup light brown sugar
- 1 tablespoon butter
- 1 teaspoon almond extract
- 1 cup rolled oats
- ½ cup sliced almonds
- ½ cup dried cherries
- ¼ cup shredded coconut
- ¼ cup dark chocolate chips
- oil for misting or cooking spray

Directions:
1. Combine the syrup or honey, brown sugar, and butter in a small saucepan or microwave-safe bowl. Heat and stir just until butter melts and sugar dissolves. Stir in the extract.
2. Place all other dry ingredients in a large bowl. (For the Cherry Black Forest Mix, don't add the chocolate chips yet.)
3. Pour melted butter mixture over dry ingredients and stir until oat mixture is well coated.
4. Lightly spray a baking pan with oil or cooking spray.
5. Pour granola into pan and cook at 390°F/200°C for 5minutes. Stir. Continue cooking for 5minutes, stirring every minute or two, until golden brown. Watch closely. Once the mixture begins to brown, it will cook quickly.
6. Remove granola from pan and spread on wax paper. It will become crispier as it cools.
7. For the Cherry Black Forest Mix, stir in chocolate chips after granola has cooled completely.
8. Store in an airtight container.

Bagel Chips

Servings: 2
Cooking Time: 4 Minutes
Ingredients:
- Sweet
- 1 large plain bagel
- 2 teaspoons sugar
- 1 teaspoon ground cinnamon
- butter-flavored cooking spray
- Savory
- 1 large plain bagel
- 1 teaspoon Italian seasoning
- ½ teaspoon garlic powder
- oil for misting or cooking spray

Directions:
1. Preheat air fryer to 390°F/200°C.
2. Cut bagel into ¼-inch slices or thinner.
3. Mix the seasonings together.
4. Spread out the slices, mist with oil or cooking spray, and sprinkle with half of the seasonings.
5. Turn over and repeat to coat the other side with oil or cooking spray and seasonings.
6. Place in air fryer basket and cook for 2minutes. Shake basket or stir a little and continue cooking for 2 minutes or until toasty brown and crispy.

Balsamic Grape Dip

Servings: 6
Cooking Time: 25 Minutes
Ingredients:
- 2 cups seedless red grapes
- 1 tbsp balsamic vinegar
- 1 tbsp honey
- 1 cup Greek yogurt
- 2 tbsp milk
- 2 tbsp minced fresh basil

Directions:
1. Preheat air fryer to 380°F/195°C. Add the grapes and balsamic vinegar to the frying basket, then pour honey over and toss to coat. Roast for 8-12 minutes, shriveling the grapes, and take them out of the air fryer. Mix the milk and yogurt together, then gently stir in the grapes and basil. Serve and enjoy!

Fiery Bacon-wrapped Dates

Servings: 16
Cooking Time: 6 Minutes
Ingredients:
- 8 Thin-cut bacon strips, halved widthwise (gluten-free, if a concern)
- 16 Medium or large Medjool dates, pitted
- 3 tablespoons (about ¾ ounce) Shredded semi-firm mozzarella
- 32 Pickled jalapeño rings

Directions:
1. Preheat the air fryer to 400°F/205°C.
2. Lay a bacon strip half on a clean, dry work surface. Split one date lengthwise without cutting through it, so that it opens like a pocket. Set it on one end of the bacon strip and open it a bit. Place 1 teaspoon of the shredded cheese and 2 pickled jalapeño rings in the date, then gently squeeze it together without fully closing it (just to hold the stuffing inside). Roll up the date in the bacon strip and set it bacon seam side down on a cutting board. Repeat this process with the remaining bacon strip halves, dates, cheese, and jalapeño rings.
3. Place the bacon-wrapped dates bacon seam side down in the basket. Air-fry undisturbed for 6 minutes, or until crisp and brown.
4. Use kitchen tongs to gently transfer the wrapped dates to a wire rack or serving platter. Cool for a few minutes before serving.

Cheesy Spinach Dip[2]

Servings: 8
Cooking Time: 30 Minutes
Ingredients:
- 1 can refrigerated biscuit dough
- 4 oz cream cheese, softened
- ¼ cup mayonnaise
- 1 cup spinach
- 2 oz cooked bacon, crumbled
- 2 scallions, chopped
- 2 cups grated Fontina cheese
- 1 cup grated cheddar
- ½ tsp garlic powder

Directions:
1. Preheat the air fryer to 350°F/175°C. Divide the dough into 8 biscuits and press each one into and up the sides of the silicone muffin cup, then set aside. Combine the cream cheese and mayonnaise and beat until smooth. Stir in the spinach, bacon, scallions, 1 cup of cheddar cheese and garlic powder. Then divide the mixture between the muffin cups. Put them in the basket and top each with 1 tbsp of Fontina cheese. Bake for 8-13 minutes or until the dough is golden and the filling is hot and bubbling. Remove from the air fryer and cool on a wire rack. Serve.

Classic Potato Chips

Servings: 4
Cooking Time: 8 Minutes
Ingredients:
- 2 medium russet potatoes, washed
- 2 cups filtered water
- 1 tablespoon avocado oil
- ½ teaspoon salt

Directions:
1. Using a mandolin, slice the potatoes into ⅛-inch-thick pieces.
2. Pour the water into a large bowl. Place the potatoes in the bowl and soak for at least 30 minutes.
3. Preheat the air fryer to 350°F/175°C.
4. Drain the water and pat the potatoes dry with a paper towel or kitchen cloth. Toss with avocado oil and salt. Liberally spray the air fryer basket with olive oil mist.
5. Set the potatoes inside the air fryer basket, separating them so they're not on top of each other. Cook for 5 minutes, shake the basket, and cook another 5 minutes, or until browned.
6. Remove and let cool a few minutes prior to serving. Repeat until all the chips are cooked.

Beer-battered Onion Rings

Servings: 4
Cooking Time: 25 Minutes
Ingredients:
- 2 sliced onions, rings separated
- 1 cup flour

- Salt and pepper to taste
- 1 tsp garlic powder
- 1 cup beer

Directions:
1. Preheat air fryer to 350°F/175°C. In a mixing bowl, combine the flour, garlic powder, beer, salt, and black pepper. Dip the onion rings into the bowl and lay the coated rings in the frying basket. Air Fry for 15 minutes, shaking the basket several times during cooking to jostle the onion rings and ensure a good even fry. Once ready, the onions should be crispy and golden brown. Serve hot.

Artichoke Samosas

Servings: 6
Cooking Time: 25 Minutes
Ingredients:
- ½ cup minced artichoke hearts
- ¼ cup ricotta cheese
- 1 egg white
- 3 tbsp grated mozzarella
- ½ tsp dried thyme
- 6 phyllo dough sheets
- 2 tbsp melted butter
- 1 cup mango chutney

Directions:
1. Preheat air fryer to 400°F/205°C. Mix together ricotta cheese, egg white, artichoke hearts, mozzarella cheese, and thyme in a small bowl until well blended. When you bring out the phyllo dough, cover it with a damp kitchen towel so that it doesn't dry out while you are working with it. Take one sheet of phyllo and place it on the work surface.
2. Cut it into thirds lengthwise. At the base of each strip, place about 1 ½ tsp of filling. Fold the bottom right-hand tip of the strip over to the left-hand side to make a triangle. Continue flipping and folding triangles along the strip. Brush the triangle with butter to seal the edges. Place triangles in the greased frying basket and Bake until golden and crisp, 4 minutes. Serve with mango chutney.

Popcorn Chicken Bites

Servings: 2
Cooking Time: 8 Minutes
Ingredients:
- 1 pound chicken breasts, cutlets or tenders
- 1 cup buttermilk
- 3 to 6 dashes hot sauce (optional)
- 8 cups cornflakes (or 2 cups cornflake crumbs)
- ½ teaspoon salt
- 1 tablespoon butter, melted
- 2 tablespoons chopped fresh parsley

Directions:
1. Cut the chicken into bite-sized pieces (about 1-inch) and place them in a bowl with the buttermilk and hot sauce (if using). Cover and let the chicken marinate in the buttermilk for 1 to 3 hours in the refrigerator.
2. Preheat the air fryer to 380°F/195°C.
3. Crush the cornflakes into fine crumbs by either crushing them with your hands in a bowl, rolling them with a rolling pin in a plastic bag or processing them in a food processor. Place the crumbs in a bowl, add the salt, melted butter and parsley and mix well. Working in batches, remove the chicken from the buttermilk marinade, letting any excess drip off and transfer the chicken to the cornflakes. Toss the chicken pieces in the cornflake mixture to coat evenly, pressing the crumbs onto the chicken.
4. Air-fry the chicken in two batches for 8 minutes per batch, shaking the basket halfway through the cooking process. Re-heat the first batch with the second batch for a couple of minutes if desired.
5. Serve the popcorn chicken bites warm with BBQ sauce or honey mustard for dipping.

Cinnamon Apple Crisps

Servings: 1
Cooking Time: 22 Minutes
Ingredients:
- 1 large apple
- ½ teaspoon ground cinnamon
- 2 teaspoons avocado oil or coconut oil

Directions:
1. Preheat the air fryer to 300°F/150°C.
2. Using a mandolin or knife, slice the apples to ¼-inch thickness. Pat the apples dry with a paper towel or kitchen cloth. Sprinkle the apple slices with ground cinnamon. Spray or drizzle the oil over the top of the apple slices and toss to coat.
3. Place the apple slices in the air fryer basket. To allow for even cooking, don't overlap the slices; cook in batches if necessary.
4. Cook for 20 minutes, shaking the basket every 5 minutes. After 20 minutes, increase the air fryer temperature to 330°F/155°C and cook another 2 minutes, shaking the basket every 30 seconds. Remove the apples from the basket before they get too dark.
5. Spread the chips out onto paper towels to cool completely, at least 5 minutes. Repeat with the remaining apple slices until they're all cooked.

Avocado Egg Rolls

Servings: 8
Cooking Time: 8 Minutes
Ingredients:
- 8 full-size egg roll wrappers
- 1 medium avocado, sliced into 8 pieces
- 1 cup cooked black beans, divided
- ½ cup mild salsa, divided
- ½ cup shredded Mexican cheese, divided
- ⅓ cup filtered water, divided
- ½ cup sour cream
- 1 teaspoon chipotle hot sauce

Directions:
1. Preheat the air fryer to 400°F/205°C.
2. Place the egg roll wrapper on a flat surface and place 1 strip of avocado down in the center.
3. Top the avocado with 2 tablespoons of black beans, 1 tablespoon of salsa, and 1 tablespoon of shredded cheese.
4. Place two of your fingers into the water, and then moisten the four outside edges of the egg roll wrapper with water (so the outer edges will secure shut).
5. Fold the bottom corner up, covering the filling. Then secure the sides over the top, remembering to lightly moisten them so they stick. Tightly roll the egg roll up and moisten the final flap of the wrapper and firmly press it into the egg roll to secure it shut.
6. Repeat Steps 2–5 until all 8 egg rolls are complete.
7. When ready to cook, spray the air fryer basket with olive oil spray and place the egg rolls into the basket.

Depending on the size and type of air fryer you have, you may need to do this in two sets.
8. Cook for 4 minutes, flip, and then cook the remaining 4 minutes.
9. Repeat until all the egg rolls are cooked. Meanwhile, mix the sour cream with the hot sauce to serve as a dipping sauce.
10. Serve warm.

Bacon Candy
Servings: 6
Cooking Time: 6 Minutes
Ingredients:
- 1½ tablespoons Honey
- 1 teaspoon White wine vinegar
- 3 Extra thick–cut bacon strips, halved widthwise (gluten-free, if a concern)
- ½ teaspoon Ground black pepper

Directions:
1. Preheat the air fryer to 350°F/175°C.
2. Whisk the honey and vinegar in a small bowl until incorporated.
3. When the machine is at temperature, remove the basket. Lay the bacon strip halves in the basket in one layer. Brush the tops with the honey mixture; sprinkle each bacon strip evenly with black pepper.
4. Return the basket to the machine and air-fry undisturbed for 6 minutes, or until the bacon is crunchy. Or a little less time if you prefer bacon that's still pliable, an extra minute if you want the bacon super crunchy. Take care that the honey coating doesn't burn. Remove the basket from the machine and set aside for 5 minutes. Use kitchen tongs to transfer the bacon strips to a serving plate.

Cheesy Green Dip
Servings: 6
Cooking Time: 30 Minutes
Ingredients:
- ½ cup canned artichoke hearts, chopped
- ½ cup cream cheese, softened
- 2 tbsp grated Romano cheese
- ¼ cup grated mozzarella
- ½ cup spinach, chopped
- ½ cup milk
- Salt and pepper to taste

Directions:
1. Preheat air fryer to 350°F/175°C. Whisk the milk, cream cheese, Romano cheese, spinach, artichoke hearts, salt, and pepper in a mixing bowl. Pour the mixture into a greased baking pan, and sprinkle the grated mozzarella cheese over the top. Bake in the air fryer for 20 minutes. Serve.

Sausage & Cauliflower Balls
Servings: 4
Cooking Time: 30 Minutes
Ingredients:
- 2 chicken sausage links, casings removed
- 1 cup shredded Monterey jack cheese
- 4 ½ cups riced cauliflower
- ½ tsp salt
- 1 ¼ cups pizza sauce
- 2 eggs
- ½ cup breadcrumbs
- 3 tsp grated Parmesan cheese

Directions:
1. In a large skillet over high heat, cook the sausages while breaking them up into smaller pieces with a spoon. Cook through completely for 4 minutes. Add cauliflower, salt, and ¼ cup of pizza sauce. Lower heat to medium and stir-fry for 7 minutes or until the cauliflower is tender. Remove from heat and stir in Monterey cheese. Allow to cool slightly, 4 minutes or until it is easy to handle.
2. Lightly coat a ¼-cup measuring cup with cooking spray. Pack and level the cup with the cauliflower mixture. Remove from the cup and roll it into a ball in your palm. Set aside and repeat until you have 12 balls. In a bowl, beat eggs and 1 tbsp of water until combined. In another bowl, combine breadcrumbs and Parmesan. Dip one cauliflower ball into the egg mixture, then in the crumbs. Press the crumbs so that they stick to the ball. Put onto a workspace and spray with cooking oil. Repeat for all balls.
3. Preheat air fryer to 400°F/205°C. Place the balls on the bottom of the frying basket in a single layer. Air Fry for about 8-10 minutes, flipping once until the crumbs are golden and the balls are hot throughout. Warm up the remaining pizza sauce as a dip.

Buttery Spiced Pecans
Servings: 6
Cooking Time: 4 Minutes
Ingredients:
- 2 cups (½ pound) Pecan halves
- 2 tablespoons Butter, melted
- 1 teaspoon Mild paprika
- ½ teaspoon Ground cumin
- Up to ½ teaspoon Cayenne
- ½ teaspoon Table salt

Directions:
1. Preheat the air fryer to 400°F/205°C.
2. Toss the pecans, butter, paprika, cumin, cayenne, and salt in a bowl until the nuts are evenly coated.
3. When the machine is at temperature, pour the nuts into the basket, spreading them into as close to one layer as you can. Air-fry for 4 minutes, tossing after every minute, and perhaps even more frequently for the last minute if the pecans are really browning, until the pecans are warm, dark brown in spots, and very aromatic.
4. Pour the contents of the basket onto a lipped baking sheet and spread the nuts into one layer. Cool for at least 5 minutes before serving. The nuts can be stored at room temperature in a sealed container for up to 1 week.

Cauliflower-crust Pizza
Servings: 3
Cooking Time: 14 Minutes
Ingredients:
- 1 pound 2 ounces Riced cauliflower
- 1 plus 1 large egg yolk Large egg(s)
- 3 tablespoons (a little more than ½ ounce) Finely grated Parmesan cheese
- 1½ tablespoons Potato starch
- ¾ teaspoon Dried oregano
- ¾ teaspoon Table salt
- Vegetable oil spray
- 3 tablespoons Purchased pizza sauce
- 6 tablespoons (about 1½ ounces) Shredded semi-firm mozzarella

Directions:

1. Pour the riced cauliflower into a medium microwave-safe bowl. Microwave on high for 4 minutes. Stir well, then cool for 15 minutes.
2. Preheat the air fryer to 400°F/205°C.
3. Pour the riced cauliflower into a clean kitchen towel or a large piece of cheesecloth. Gather the towel or cheesecloth together. Working over the sink, squeeze the moisture out of the cauliflower, getting out as much of the liquid as you can.
4. Pour the squeezed cauliflower back into that same medium bowl and stir in the egg, egg yolk (if using), cheese, potato starch, oregano, and salt to form a loose, uniform "dough."
5. Cut a piece of aluminum foil or parchment paper into a 6-inch circle for a small pizza, a 7-inch circle for a medium one, or an 8-inch circle for a large one. Coat the circle with vegetable oil spray, then place it in the air-fryer basket. Using a small offset spatula or the back of a flatware tablespoon, spread and smooth the cauliflower mixture onto the circle right to the edges. Air-fry undisturbed for 10 minutes.
6. Remove the basket from the air fryer. Reduce the machine's temperature to 350°F.
7. Using a large nonstick-safe spatula, flip over the cauliflower circle along with its foil or parchment paper right in the basket. Peel off and discard the foil or parchment paper. Spread the pizza sauce evenly over the crust and sprinkle with the cheese.
8. Air-fry undisturbed for 4 minutes, or until the cheese has melted and begun to bubble. Remove the basket from the machine and cool for 5 minutes. Use the same spatula to transfer the pizza to a wire rack to cool for 5 minutes more before cutting the pie into wedges to serve.

Onion Ring Nachos

Servings: 3
Cooking Time: 8 Minutes
Ingredients:
- ¾ pound Frozen breaded (not battered) onion rings (do not thaw)
- 1½ cups (about 6 ounces) Shredded Cheddar, Monterey Jack, or Swiss cheese, or a purchased Tex-Mex blend
- Up to 12 Pickled jalapeño rings

Directions:
1. Preheat the air fryer to 400°F/205°C.
2. When the machine is at temperature, spread the onion rings in the basket in a fairly even layer. Air-fry undisturbed for 6 minutes, or until crisp. Remove the basket from the machine.
3. Cut a circle of parchment paper to line a 6-inch round cake pan for a small air fryer, a 7-inch round cake pan for a medium air fryer, or an 8-inch round cake pan for a large machine.
4. Pour the onion rings into a fairly even layer in the cake pan, then sprinkle the cheese evenly over them. Dot with the jalapeño rings.
5. Set the pan in the basket and air-fry undisturbed for 2 minutes, until the cheese has melted and is bubbling.
6. Remove the pan from the basket. Cool for 5 minutes before serving.

Black-olive Jalapeño Poppers

Servings: 5
Cooking Time: 20 Minutes
Ingredients:
- 5 jalapeño peppers, cut lengthwise, seeded
- ¼ cup cream cheese, softened
- ¼ cup grated cheddar
- 1 tbsp chopped black olives
- 1 tbsp chopped green olives
- 1 tsp dried oregano
- 1 tbsp mayonnaise
- 1 tbsp Parmesan cheese
- 1 tbsp dried parsley

Directions:
1. Preheat air fryer at 350ºF/175°C. Mix all ingredients, except jalapeños, in a bowl. Add prepared mixture into each jalapeño half. Lay stuffed peppers in the frying basket and Bake for 8 minutes. Transfer them to a serving plate. Serve right away and sprinkle with dried parsley.

Buffalo Cauliflower

Servings: 6
Cooking Time: 12 Minutes
Ingredients:
- 1 large head of cauliflower, washed and cut into medium-size florets
- ½ cup all-purpose flour
- ¼ cup melted butter
- 3 tablespoons hot sauce
- ½ teaspoon garlic powder
- ½ cup blue cheese dip or ranch dressing (optional)

Directions:
1. Preheat the air fryer to 350°F/175°C.
2. Make sure the cauliflower florets are dry, and then coat them in flour.
3. Liberally spray the air fryer basket with an olive oil mist. Place the cauliflower into the basket, making sure not to stack them on top of each other. Depending on the size of your air fryer, you may need to do this in two batches.
4. Cook for 6 minutes, then shake the basket, and cook another 6 minutes.
5. While cooking, mix the melted butter, hot sauce, and garlic powder in a large bowl.
6. Carefully remove the cauliflower from the air fryer. Toss the cauliflower into the butter mixture to coat. Repeat Steps 2–4 for any leftover cauliflower. Serve warm with the dip of your choice.

Herbed Cheese Brittle

Servings: 4
Cooking Time: 5 Minutes
Ingredients:
- ½ cup shredded Parmesan cheese
- ½ cup shredded white cheddar cheese
- 1 tablespoon fresh chopped rosemary
- 1 teaspoon garlic powder
- 1 large egg white

Directions:
1. Preheat the air fryer to 400°F/205°C.
2. In a large bowl, mix the cheeses, rosemary, and garlic powder. Mix in the egg white. Then pour the batter into a 7-inch pan (or an air-fryer-compatible pan). Place the pan in the air fryer basket and cook for 4 to 5 minutes, or until the cheese is melted and slightly browned.
3. Remove the pan from the air fryer, and let it cool for 2 minutes. Invert the pan before the cheese brittle completely cools but is semi-hardened to allow it to easily slide out of the pan.
4. Let the pan cool another 5 minutes. Break into pieces and serve.

Avocado Toast With Lemony Shrimp

Servings: 4
Cooking Time: 6 Minutes
Ingredients:
- 6 ounces Raw medium shrimp (30 to 35 per pound), peeled and deveined
- 1½ teaspoons Finely grated lemon zest
- 2 teaspoons Lemon juice
- 1½ teaspoons Minced garlic
- 1½ teaspoons Ground black pepper
- 4 Rye or whole-wheat bread slices (gluten-free, if a concern)
- 2 Ripe Hass avocado(s), halved, pitted, peeled and roughly chopped
- For garnishing Coarse sea salt or kosher salt

Directions:
1. Preheat the air fryer to 400°F/205°C.
2. Toss the shrimp, lemon zest, lemon juice, garlic, and pepper in a bowl until the shrimp are evenly coated.
3. When the machine is at temperature, use kitchen tongs to place the shrimp in a single layer in the basket. Air-fry undisturbed for 4 minutes, or until the shrimp are pink and barely firm. Use kitchen tongs to transfer the shrimp to a cutting board.
4. Working in batches, set as many slices of bread as will fit in the basket in one layer. Air-fry undisturbed for 2 minutes, just until warmed through and crisp. The bread will not brown much.
5. Arrange the bread slices on a clean, dry work surface. Divide the avocado bits among them and gently smash the avocado into a coarse paste with the tines of a flatware fork. Top the toasts with the shrimp and sprinkle with salt as a garnish.

Corn Dog Bites

Servings: 3
Cooking Time: 12 Minutes
Ingredients:
- 3 cups Purchased cornbread stuffing mix
- ⅓ cup All-purpose flour
- 2 Large egg(s), well beaten
- 3 Hot dogs, cut into 2-inch pieces (vegetarian hot dogs, if preferred)
- Vegetable oil spray

Directions:
1. Preheat the air fryer to 375°F/190°C .
2. Put the cornbread stuffing mix in a food processor. Cover and pulse to grind into a mixture like fine bread crumbs.
3. Set up and fill three shallow soup plates or small pie plates on your counter: one for the flour, one for the egg(s), and one for the stuffing mix crumbs.
4. Dip a hot dog piece in the flour to coat it completely, then gently shake off any excess. Dip the hot dog piece into the egg(s) and gently roll it around to coat all surfaces, then pick it up and allow any excess egg to slip back into the rest. Set the hot dog piece in the stuffing mix crumbs and roll it gently to coat it evenly and well on all sides, even the ends. Set it aside on a cutting board and continue dipping and coating the remaining hot dog pieces.
5. Give the coated hot dog pieces a generous coating of vegetable oil spray on all sides, then set them in the basket in one layer with some space between them. Air-fry undisturbed for 10 minutes, or until golden brown and crunchy. (You'll need to add 2 minutes in the air fryer if the temperature is at 360°F/180°C.)
6. Use a nonstick-safe spatula, and perhaps a flatware fork for balance, to transfer the corn dog bites to a wire rack. Cool for 5 minutes before serving.

Parmesan Pizza Nuggets

Servings: 8
Cooking Time: 6 Minutes
Ingredients:
- ¾ cup warm filtered water
- 1 package fast-rising yeast
- ½ teaspoon salt
- 2 cups all-purpose flour
- ¼ cup finely grated Parmesan cheese
- 1 teaspoon Italian seasoning
- 2 tablespoon extra-virgin olive oil
- 1 teaspoon kosher salt

Directions:
1. Preheat the air fryer to 370°F/185°C.
2. In a large microwave-safe bowl, add the water. Heat for 40 seconds in the microwave. Remove and mix in the yeast and salt. Let sit 5 minutes.
3. Meanwhile, in a medium bowl, mix the flour with the Parmesan cheese and Italian seasoning. Set aside.
4. Using a stand mixer with a dough hook attachment, add the yeast liquid and then mix in the flour mixture ⅓ cup at a time until all the flour mixture is added and a dough is formed.
5. Remove the bowl from the stand, and then let the dough rise for 1 hour in a warm space, covered with a kitchen towel.
6. After the dough has doubled in size, remove it from the bowl and punch it down a few times on a lightly floured flat surface.
7. Divide the dough into 4 balls, and then roll each ball out into a long, skinny, sticklike shape.
8. Using a sharp knife, cut each dough stick into 6 pieces. Repeat for the remaining dough balls until you have about 24 nuggets formed.
9. Lightly brush the top of each bite with the egg whites and cover with a pinch of sea salt.
10. Spray the air fryer basket with olive oil spray and place the pizza nuggets on top. Cook for 6 minutes, or until lightly browned. Remove and keep warm.
11. Repeat until all the nuggets are cooked.
12. Serve warm.

Plantain Chips

Servings: 2
Cooking Time: 14 Minutes
Ingredients:
- 1 large green plantain
- 2½ cups filtered water, divided
- 2 teaspoons sea salt, divided

Directions:
1. Slice the plantain into 1-inch pieces. Place the plantains into a large bowl, cover with 2 cups water and 1 teaspoon salt. Soak the plantains for 30 minutes; then remove and pat dry.
2. Preheat the air fryer to 390°F/200°C.
3. Place the plantain pieces into the air fryer basket, leaving space between the plantain rounds. Cook the

plantains for 5 minutes, and carefully remove them from the air fryer basket.
4. Add the remaining water to a small bowl.
5. Using a small drinking glass, dip the bottom of the glass into the water and mash the warm plantains until they're ¼-inch thick. Return the plantains to the air fryer basket, sprinkle with the remaining sea salt, and spray lightly with cooking spray.
6. Cook for another 6 to 8 minutes, or until lightly golden brown edges appear.

Breaded Mozzarella Sticks

Servings: 6
Cooking Time: 25 Minutes
Ingredients:
- 2 tbsp flour
- 1 egg
- 1 tbsp milk
- ½ cup bread crumbs
- ¼ tsp salt
- ¼ tsp Italian seasoning
- 10 mozzarella sticks
- 2 tsp olive oil
- ½ cup warm marinara sauce

Directions:
1. Place the flour in a bowl. In another bowl, beat the egg and milk. In a third bowl, combine the crumbs, salt, and Italian seasoning. Cut the mozzarella sticks into thirds. Roll each piece in flour, then dredge in egg mixture, and finally roll in breadcrumb mixture. Shake off the excess between each step. Place them in the freezer for 10 minutes.
2. Preheat air fryer to 400ºF/205°C. Place mozzarella sticks in the frying basket and Air Fry for 5 minutes, shake twice and brush with olive oil. Serve the mozzarella sticks immediately with marinara sauce.

Bacon & Blue Cheese Tartlets

Servings: 6
Cooking Time: 30 Minutes
Ingredients:
- 6 bacon slices
- 16 phyllo tartlet shells
- ½ cup diced blue cheese
- 3 tbsp apple jelly

Directions:
1. Preheat the air fryer to 400°F/205°C. Put the bacon in a single layer in the frying basket and Air Fry for 14 minutes, turning once halfway through. Remove and drain on paper towels, then crumble when cool. Wipe the fryer clean. Fill the tartlet shells with bacon and the blue cheese cubes and add a dab of apple jelly on top of the filling. Lower the temperature to 350°F, then put the shells in the frying basket. Air Fry until the cheese melts and the shells brown, about 5-6 minutes. Remove and serve.

Sausage And Cheese Rolls

Servings: 3
Cooking Time: 18 Minutes
Ingredients:
- 3 3- to 3½-ounce sweet or hot Italian sausage links
- 2 1-ounce string cheese stick(s), unwrapped and cut in half lengthwise
- Three quarters from one thawed sheet (cut the sheet into four quarters; wrap and refreeze one of them) A 17.25-ounce box frozen puff pastry

Directions:
1. Preheat the air fryer to 400°F/205°C.
2. When the machine is at temperature, set the sausage links in the basket and air-fry undisturbed for 12 minutes, or until cooked through.
3. Use kitchen tongs to transfer the links to a wire rack. Cool for 15 minutes. (If necessary, pour out any rendered fat that has collected below the basket in the machine.)
4. Cut the sausage links in half lengthwise. Sandwich half a string cheese stick between two sausage halves, trimming the ends so the cheese doesn't stick out beyond the meat.
5. Roll each piece of puff pastry into a 6 x 6-inch square on a clean, dry work surface. Set the sausage-cheese sandwich at one edge and roll it up in the dough. The ends will be open like a pig-in-a-blanket. Repeat with the remaining puff pastry, sausage, and cheese.
6. Set the rolls seam side down in the basket. Air-fry undisturbed for 6 minutes, or until puffed and golden brown.
7. Use a nonstick-safe spatula, and perhaps a flatware fork for balance, to transfer the rolls to a wire rack. Cool for at least 5 minutes before serving.

Crab Rangoon Dip With Wonton Chips

Servings: 6
Cooking Time: 18 Minutes
Ingredients:
- Wonton Chips:
- 1 (12-ounce) package wonton wrappers
- vegetable oil
- sea salt
- Crab Rangoon Dip:
- 8 ounces cream cheese, softened
- ¾ cup sour cream
- 1 teaspoon Worcestershire sauce
- 1½ teaspoons soy sauce
- 1 teaspoon sesame oil
- ⅛ teaspoon ground cayenne pepper
- ¼ teaspoon salt
- freshly ground black pepper
- 8 ounces cooked crabmeat
- 1 cup grated white Cheddar cheese
- ⅓ cup chopped scallions
- paprika (for garnish)

Directions:
1. Cut the wonton wrappers in half diagonally to form triangles. Working in batches, lay the wonton triangles on a flat surface and brush or spray both sides with vegetable oil.
2. Preheat the air fryer to 370°F/185°C.
3. Place about 10 to 12 wonton triangles in the air fryer basket, letting them overlap slightly. Air-fry for just 2 minutes, shaking the basket halfway through the cooking time. Transfer the wonton chips to a large bowl and season immediately with sea salt. (You'll hear the chips start to spin around in the air fryer when they are almost done.) Repeat with the rest of wontons (keeping those fishing hands at bay!).
4. To make the dip, combine the cream cheese, sour cream, Worcestershire sauce, soy sauce, sesame oil, cayenne pepper,

salt, and freshly ground black pepper in a bowl. Mix well and then fold in the crabmeat, Cheddar cheese, and scallions.
5. Transfer the dip to a 7-inch ceramic baking pan or shallow casserole dish. Sprinkle paprika on top and cover the dish with aluminum foil. Lower the dish into the air fryer basket using a sling made of aluminum foil (fold a piece of aluminum foil into a strip about 2-inches wide by 24-inches long). Air-fry for 11 minutes. Remove the aluminum foil and air-fry for another 5 minutes to finish cooking and brown the top. Serve hot with the wonton chips.

Chicken Nachos

Servings: 6
Cooking Time: 25 Minutes
Ingredients:
- 2 oz baked corn tortilla chips
- 1 cup leftover roast chicken, shredded
- ½ cup canned black beans
- 1 red bell pepper, chopped
- ½ grated carrot
- 1 jalapeño pepper, minced
- 1/3 cup grated Swiss cheese
- 1 tomato, chopped

Directions:
1. Preheat air fryer to 360°F/180°C. Lay the tortilla chips in a single layer in a baking pan. Add the chicken, black beans, red bell pepper, carrot, jalapeño, and cheese on top. Bake in the air fryer for 9-12 minutes. Make sure the cheese melts and is slightly browned. Serve garnished with tomatoes.

Fried Cheese Ravioli With Marinara Sauce

Servings: 4
Cooking Time: 7 Minutes
Ingredients:
- 1 pound cheese ravioli, fresh or frozen
- 2 eggs, lightly beaten
- 1 cup plain breadcrumbs
- ½ teaspoon paprika
- ½ teaspoon dried oregano
- ½ teaspoon salt
- grated Parmesan cheese
- chopped fresh parsley
- 1 to 2 cups marinara sauce (jarred or homemade)

Directions:
1. Bring a stockpot of salted water to a boil. Boil the ravioli according to the package directions and then drain. Let the cooked ravioli cool to a temperature where you can comfortably handle them.
2. While the pasta is cooking, set up a dredging station with two shallow dishes. Place the eggs into one dish. Combine the breadcrumbs, paprika, dried oregano and salt in the other dish.
3. Preheat the air fryer to 380°F/195°C.
4. Working with one at a time, dip the cooked ravioli into the egg, coating all sides. Then press the ravioli into the breadcrumbs, making sure that all sides are covered. Transfer the ravioli to the air fryer basket, cooking in batches, one layer at a time. Air-fry at 380°F/195°C for 7 minutes.
5. While the ravioli is air-frying, bring the marinara sauce to a simmer on the stovetop. Transfer to a small bowl.
6. Sprinkle a little Parmesan cheese and chopped parsley on top of the fried ravioli and serve warm with the marinara sauce on the side for dipping.

Artichoke-spinach Dip

Servings: 4
Cooking Time: 25 Minutes
Ingredients:
- 4 oz canned artichoke hearts, chopped
- ½ cup Greek yogurt
- ¼ cup cream cheese
- ½ cup spinach, chopped
- ½ red bell pepper, chopped
- 1 garlic clove, minced
- ½ tsp dried oregano
- 3 tsp grated Parmesan cheese

Directions:
1. Preheat air fryer to 340°F/170°C. Mix the yogurt and cream cheese. Add the artichoke, spinach, red bell pepper, garlic, and oregano, then put the mix in a pan and scatter Parmesan cheese on top. Put the pan in the frying basket and Bake for 9-14 minutes. The dip should be bubble and brown. Serve hot.

Crispy Spiced Chickpeas

Servings: 2
Cooking Time: 20 Minutes
Ingredients:
- 1 (15-ounce) can chickpeas, drained (or 1½ cups cooked chickpeas)
- ½ teaspoon salt
- ½ teaspoon chili powder
- ¼ teaspoon ground cinnamon
- ⅛ teaspoon smoked paprika
- pinch ground cayenne pepper
- 1 tablespoon olive oil

Directions:
1. Preheat the air fryer to 400°F/205°C.
2. Dry the chickpeas as well as you can with a clean kitchen towel, rubbing off any loose skins as necessary. Combine the spices in a small bowl. Toss the chickpeas with the olive oil and then add the spices and toss again.
3. Air-fry for 15 minutes, shaking the basket a couple of times while they cook.
4. Check the chickpeas to see if they are crispy enough and if necessary, air-fry for another 5 minutes to crisp them further. Serve warm, or cool to room temperature and store in an airtight container for up to two weeks.

Garlic Breadsticks

Servings: 12
Cooking Time: 7 Minutes
Ingredients:
- 1½ tablespoons Olive oil
- 1½ teaspoons Minced garlic
- ¼ teaspoon Table salt
- ¼ teaspoon Ground black pepper
- 6 ounces Purchased pizza dough (vegan dough, if that's a concern)

Directions:
1. Preheat the air fryer to 400°F/205°C. Mix the oil, garlic, salt, and pepper in a small bowl.
2. Divide the pizza dough into 4 balls for a small air fryer, 6 for a medium machine, or 8 for a large, each ball about the

size of a walnut in its shell. (Each should weigh 1 ounce, if you want to drag out a scale and get obsessive.) Roll each ball into a 5-inch-long stick under your clean palms on a clean, dry work surface. Brush the sticks with the oil mixture.

3. When the machine is at temperature, place the prepared dough sticks in the basket, leaving a 1-inch space between them. Air-fry undisturbed for 7 minutes, or until puffed, golden, and set to the touch.

4. Use kitchen tongs to gently transfer the breadsticks to a wire rack and repeat step 3 with the remaining dough sticks.

Seafood Egg Rolls

Servings: 6
Cooking Time: 35 Minutes
Ingredients:
- 2 tbsp olive oil
- 1 shallot, chopped
- 2 garlic cloves, minced
- ½ cup shredded carrots
- 1 lb cooked shrimp, chopped
- 1 cup corn kernels
- 1/3 cup chopped cashews
- 1 tbsp soy sauce
- 2 tsp fish sauce
- 12 egg roll wrappers

Directions:
1. Preheat the air fryer to 400°F/205°C. Combine the olive oil, shallot, garlic, and carrots in a 6-inch. Put the pan in the frying basket and Air Fry for 3-5 minutes, stirring once. Remove the pan and put the veggies in a bowl. Add shrimp, corn, cashews, soy sauce, and fish sauce to the veggies and combine. Lay the egg roll wrappers on the clean work surface and brush the edges with water. Divide the filling equally and fill them, then brush the edges with water again. Roll up, folding in the side, enclosing the filling inside. Place 4 egg rolls in the basket and spray with cooking oil. Air Fry for 10-12 minutes, rotating once halfway through cooking until golden and crispy. Repeat with remaining rolls. Serve hot.

Tower Air Fryer Cookbook

Bread And Breakfast

Nutty Whole Wheat Muffins
Servings: 8
Cooking Time: 11 Minutes
Ingredients:
- ½ cup whole-wheat flour, plus 2 tablespoons
- ¼ cup oat bran
- 2 tablespoons flaxseed meal
- ¼ cup brown sugar
- ½ teaspoon baking soda
- ½ teaspoon baking powder
- ¼ teaspoon salt
- ½ teaspoon cinnamon
- ½ cup buttermilk
- 2 tablespoons melted butter
- 1 egg
- ½ teaspoon pure vanilla extract
- ½ cup grated carrots
- ¼ cup chopped pecans
- ¼ cup chopped walnuts
- 1 tablespoon pumpkin seeds
- 1 tablespoon sunflower seeds
- 16 foil muffin cups, paper liners removed
- cooking spray

Directions:
1. Preheat air fryer to 330°F/165°C.
2. In a large bowl, stir together the flour, bran, flaxseed meal, sugar, baking soda, baking powder, salt, and cinnamon.
3. In a medium bowl, beat together the buttermilk, butter, egg, and vanilla. Pour into flour mixture and stir just until dry ingredients moisten. Do not beat.
4. Gently stir in carrots, nuts, and seeds.
5. Double up the foil cups so you have 8 total and spray with cooking spray.
6. Place 4 foil cups in air fryer basket and divide half the batter among them.
7. Cook at 330°F/165°C for 11minutes or until toothpick inserted in center comes out clean.
8. Repeat step 7 to cook remaining 4 muffins.

Banana-strawberry Cakecups
Servings: 6
Cooking Time: 25 Minutes
Ingredients:
- ½ cup mashed bananas
- ¼ cup maple syrup
- ½ cup Greek yogurt
- 1 tsp vanilla extract
- 1 egg
- 1 ½ cups flour
- 1 tbsp cornstarch
- ½ tsp baking soda
- ½ tsp baking powder
- ½ tsp salt
- ½ cup strawberries, sliced

Directions:
1. Preheat air fryer to 360°F/180°C. Place the mashed bananas, maple syrup, yogurt, vanilla, and egg in a large bowl and mix until smooth. Sift in 1 ½ cups of the flour, baking soda, baking powder, and salt, then stir to combine.
2. In a small bowl, toss the strawberries with the cornstarch. Fold the mixture into the muffin batter. Divide the mixture evenly between greased muffin cups and place into the air frying basket. Bake for 12-15 minutes until golden brown on top and a toothpick inserted into the middle of one of the muffins comes out clean. Leave to cool for 5 minutes. Serve and enjoy!

Parmesan Garlic Naan
Servings: 6
Cooking Time: 4 Minutes
Ingredients:
- 1 cup bread flour
- 1 teaspoon baking powder
- ⅛ teaspoon salt
- 1 teaspoon garlic powder
- 2 tablespoon shredded parmesan cheese
- 1 cup plain 2% fat Greek yogurt
- 1 tablespoon extra-virgin olive oil

Directions:
1. Preheat the air fryer to 400°F/205°C.
2. In a medium bowl, mix the flour, baking powder, salt, garlic powder, and cheese. Mix the yogurt into the flour, using your hands to combine if necessary.
3. On a flat surface covered with flour, divide the dough into 6 equal balls and roll each out into a 4-inch-diameter circle.
4. Lightly brush both sides of each naan with olive oil and place one naan at a time into the basket. Cook for 3 to 4 minutes (or until the bread begins to rise and brown on the outside). Remove and repeat for the remaining breads.
5. Serve warm.

Cherry Beignets
Servings: 4
Cooking Time: 25 Minutes
Ingredients:
- 2 tsp baking soda
- 1 ½ cups flour
- ¼ tsp salt
- 3 tbsp brown sugar
- 4 tsp chopped dried cherries
- ½ cup buttermilk
- 1 egg
- 3 tbsp melted lard

Directions:
1. Preheat air fryer to 330°F/165°C. Combine baking soda, flour, salt, and brown sugar in a bowl. Then stir in dried cherries. In a small bowl, beat together buttermilk and egg until smooth. Pour in with the dry ingredients and stir until just moistened.
2. On a floured work surface, pat the dough into a square. Divide it by cutting into 16 pieces. Lightly brush with melted lard. Arrange the squares in the frying basket, without overlapping. Air Fry until puffy and golden brown, 5-8 minutes. Serve.

French Toast And Turkey Sausage Roll-ups

Servings: 3
Cooking Time: 24 Minutes
Ingredients:
- 6 links turkey sausage
- 6 slices of white bread, crusts removed*
- 2 eggs
- ½ cup milk
- ½ teaspoon ground cinnamon
- ½ teaspoon vanilla extract
- 1 tablespoon butter, melted
- powdered sugar (optional)
- maple syrup

Directions:
1. Preheat the air fryer to 380°F/195°C and pour a little water into the bottom of the air fryer drawer. (This will help prevent the grease that drips into the bottom drawer from burning and smoking.)
2. Air-fry the sausage links at 380°F for 8 to 10 minutes, turning them a couple of times during the cooking process. (If you have pre-cooked sausage links, omit this step.)
3. Roll each sausage link in a piece of bread, pressing the finished seam tightly to seal shut.
4. Preheat the air fryer to 370°F/185°C.
5. Combine the eggs, milk, cinnamon, and vanilla in a shallow dish. Dip the sausage rolls in the egg mixture and let them soak in the egg for 30 seconds. Spray or brush the bottom of the air fryer basket with oil and transfer the sausage rolls to the basket, seam side down.
6. Air-fry the rolls at 370°F/185°C for 9 minutes. Brush melted butter over the bread, flip the rolls over and air-fry for an additional 5 minutes. Remove the French toast roll-ups from the basket and dust with powdered sugar, if using. Serve with maple syrup and enjoy.

Crispy Bacon

Servings: 6
Cooking Time: 20 Minutes
Ingredients:
- 12 ounces bacon

Directions:
1. Preheat the air fryer to 350°F/175°C for 3 minutes.
2. Lay out the bacon in a single layer, slightly overlapping the strips of bacon.
3. Air fry for 10 minutes or until desired crispness.
4. Repeat until all the bacon has been cooked.

Maple-peach And Apple Oatmeal

Servings: 4
Cooking Time: 15 Minutes
Ingredients:
- 2 cups old-fashioned rolled oats
- ½ tsp baking powder
- 1 ½ tsp ground cinnamon
- ¼ tsp ground flaxseeds
- ⅛ tsp salt
- 1 ¼ cups vanilla almond milk
- ¼ cup maple syrup
- 1 tsp vanilla extract
- 1 peeled peach, diced
- 1 peeled apple, diced

Directions:
1. Preheat air fryer to 350°F/175°C. Mix oats, baking powder, cinnamon, flaxseed, and salt in a large bowl. Next, stir in almond milk, maple syrup, vanilla, and ¾ of the diced peaches, and ¾ of the diced apple. Grease 6 ramekins. Divide the batter evenly between the ramekins and transfer the ramekins to the frying basket. Bake in the air fryer for 8-10 minutes until the top is golden and set. Garnish with the rest of the peaches and apples. Serve.

Green Onion Pancakes

Servings: 4
Cooking Time: 8 Minutes
Ingredients:
- 2 cup all-purpose flour
- ½ teaspoon salt
- ¾ cup hot water
- 1 tablespoon vegetable oil
- 1 tablespoon butter, melted
- 2 cups finely chopped green onions
- 1 tablespoon black sesame seeds, for garnish

Directions:
1. In a large bowl, whisk together the flour and salt. Make a well in the center and pour in the hot water. Quickly stir the flour mixture together until a dough forms. Knead the dough for 5 minutes; then cover with a warm, wet towel and set aside for 30 minutes to rest.
2. In a small bowl, mix together the vegetable oil and melted butter.
3. On a floured surface, place the dough and cut it into 8 pieces. Working with 1 piece of dough at a time, use a rolling pin to roll out the dough until it's ¼ inch thick; then brush the surface with the oil and butter mixture and sprinkle with green onions. Next, fold the dough in half and then in half again. Roll out the dough again until it's ¼ inch thick and brush with the oil and butter mixture and green onions. Fold the dough in half and then in half again and roll out one last time until it's ¼ inch thick. Repeat this technique with all 8 pieces.
4. Meanwhile, preheat the air fryer to 400°F/205°C.
5. Place 1 or 2 pancakes into the air fryer basket (or as many as will fit in your fryer), and cook for 2 minutes or until crispy and golden brown. Repeat until all the pancakes are cooked. Top with black sesame seeds for garnish, if desired.

Vegetarian Quinoa Cups

Servings: 6
Cooking Time: 25 Minutes
Ingredients:
- 1 carrot, chopped
- 1 zucchini, chopped
- 4 asparagus, chopped
- ¾ cup quinoa flour
- 2 tbsp lemon juice
- ¼ cup nutritional yeast
- ¼ tsp garlic powder
- Salt and pepper to taste

Directions:
1. Preheat air fryer to 340°F/170°C. Combine the vegetables, quinoa flour, water, lemon juice, nutritional yeast, garlic powder, salt, and pepper in a medium bowl, and mix well. Divide the mixture between 6 cupcake molds. Place the filled molds into the air fryer and Bake for 20 minutes, or until the tops are lightly browned and a toothpick inserted into the center comes out clean. Serve cooled.

Egg Muffins

Servings: 4
Cooking Time: 11 Minutes
Ingredients:
- 4 eggs
- salt and pepper
- olive oil
- 4 English muffins, split
- 1 cup shredded Colby Jack cheese
- 4 slices ham or Canadian bacon

Directions:
1. Preheat air fryer to 390°F/200°C.
2. Beat together eggs and add salt and pepper to taste. Spray air fryer baking pan lightly with oil and add eggs. Cook for 2minutes, stir, and continue cooking for 4minutes, stirring every minute, until eggs are scrambled to your preference. Remove pan from air fryer.
3. Place bottom halves of English muffins in air fryer basket. Take half of the shredded cheese and divide it among the muffins. Top each with a slice of ham and one-quarter of the eggs. Sprinkle remaining cheese on top of the eggs. Use a fork to press the cheese into the egg a little so it doesn't slip off before it melts.
4. Cook at 360°F/180°C for 1 minute. Add English muffin tops and cook for 4minutes to heat through and toast the muffins.

Morning Loaded Potato Skins

Servings: 4
Cooking Time: 55 Minutes
Ingredients:
- 2 large potatoes
- 1 fried bacon slice, chopped
- Salt and pepper to taste
- 1 tbsp chopped dill
- 1 ½ tbsp butter
- 2 tbsp milk
- 4 eggs
- 1 scallion, sliced
- ¼ cup grated fontina cheese
- 2 tbsp chopped parsley

Directions:
1. Preheat air fryer to 400°F/205°C. Wash each potato and poke with fork 3 or 4 times. Place in the frying basket and bake for 40-45 minutes. Remove the potatoes and let cool until they can be handled. Cut each potato in half lengthwise. Scoop out potato flesh but leave enough to maintain the structure of the potato. Transfer the potato flesh to a medium bowl and stir in salt, pepper, dill, bacon, butter, and milk until mashed with some chunky pieces.
2. Fill the potato skin halves with the potato mixture and press the center of the filling with a spoon about ½-inch deep. Crack an egg in the center of each potato, then top with scallions and cheese. Return the potatoes to the air fryer and bake for 3 to 5 minutes until the egg is cooked to preferred doneness and cheese is melted. Serve immediately sprinkled with parsley.

Sweet Potato & Mushroom Hash

Servings: 6
Cooking Time: 35 Minutes
Ingredients:
- 2 peeled sweet potatoes, cubed
- 4 oz baby Bella mushrooms, diced
- ½ red bell pepper, diced
- ½ red onion, diced
- 2 tbsp olive oil
- 1 garlic clove, minced
- Salt and pepper to taste
- ½ tbsp chopped marjoram

Directions:
1. Preheat air fryer to 380°F/195°C. Place all ingredients in a large bowl and toss until the vegetables are well coated. Pour the vegetables into the frying basket. Bake for 8-10 minutes, then shake the vegetables. Cook for 8-10 more minutes. Serve and enjoy!

Light Frittata

Servings: 4
Cooking Time: 25 Minutes
Ingredients:
- ½ red bell pepper, chopped
- 1 shallot, chopped
- 1 baby carrot, chopped
- 1 tbsp olive oil
- 8 egg whites
- 1/3 cup milk
- 2 tsp grated Parmesan cheese

Directions:
1. Preheat air fryer to 350°F/175°C. Toss the red bell pepper, shallot, carrot, and olive oil in a baking pan. Put in the fryer and Bake for 4-6 minutes until the veggies are soft. Shake the basket once during cooking. Whisk the egg whites in a bowl until fluffy and stir in milk. Pour the mixture over the veggies. Toss some Parmesan cheese on top and put the pan back into the fryer. Bake for 4-6 minutes or until the frittata puffs. Serve and enjoy!

Orange Cran-bran Muffins

Servings: 4
Cooking Time: 30 Minutes
Ingredients:
- 1 ½ cups bran cereal flakes
- 1 cup flour
- 3 tbsp granulated sugar
- 1 tbsp orange zest
- 1 tsp baking powder
- 1 cup milk
- 3 tbsp peanut oil
- 1 egg
- ½ cup dried cranberries

Directions:
1. Preheat air fryer to 320°F/160°C. Combine the cereal, flour, granulated sugar, orange zest, and baking powder in a bowl, and in another bowl, beat the milk, oil, and egg. Add the egg mix to the dry ingredients and stir, then add the cranberries and stir again. Make 8 foil muffin cups by doubling 16 cups. Set 4 cups in the frying basket and spoon the batter in the cups until they're ¾ full. Bake for 15 minutes or until the tops bounce when touched. Set the muffins on a wire rack for 10 minutes, then serve.

Wild Blueberry Lemon Chia Bread

Servings: 6
Cooking Time: 27 Minutes
Ingredients:
- ¼ cup extra-virgin olive oil
- 1/3 cup plus 1 tablespoon cane sugar
- 1 large egg
- 3 tablespoons fresh lemon juice

- 1 tablespoon lemon zest
- ⅔ cup milk
- 1 cup all-purpose flour
- ¾ teaspoon baking powder
- ⅛ teaspoon salt
- 2 tablespoons chia seeds
- 1 cup frozen wild blueberries
- ⅓ cup powdered sugar
- 2 teaspoons milk

Directions:
1. Preheat the air fryer to 310°F/155°C.
2. In a medium bowl, mix the olive oil with the sugar. Whisk in the egg, lemon juice, lemon zest, and milk; set aside.
3. In a small bowl, combine the all-purpose flour, baking powder, and salt.
4. Slowly mix the dry ingredients into the wet ingredients. Stir in the chia seeds and wild blueberries.
5. Liberally spray a 7-inch springform pan with olive-oil spray. Pour the batter into the pan and place the pan in the air fryer. Bake for 25 to 27 minutes, or until a toothpick inserted in the center comes out clean.
6. Remove and let cool on a wire rack for 10 minutes prior to removing from the pan.
7. Meanwhile, in a small bowl, mix the powdered sugar with the milk to create the glaze.
8. Slice and serve with a drizzle of the powdered sugar glaze.

Easy Vanilla Muffins

Servings: 6
Cooking Time: 35 Minutes + Cooling Time
Ingredients:
- 1 1/3 cups flour
- 5 tbsp butter, melted
- ¼ cup brown sugar
- 2 tbsp raisins
- ½ tsp ground cinnamon
- 1/3 cup granulated sugar
- ¼ cup milk
- 1 large egg
- 1 tsp vanilla extract
- 1 tsp baking powder
- Pinch of salt

Directions:
1. Preheat the air fryer to 330°F/165°C. Combine 1/3 cup of flour, 2 ½ tbsp of butter, brown sugar, and cinnamon in a bowl and mix until crumbly. Set aside. In another bowl, combine the remaining butter, granulated sugar, milk, egg, and vanilla and stir well. Add the remaining flour, baking powder, raisins, and salt and stir until combined.
2. Spray 6 silicone muffin cups with baking spray and spoon half the batter into them. Add a tsp of the cinnamon mixture, then add the rest of the batter and sprinkle with the remaining cinnamon mixture, pressing into the batter. Put the muffin cups in the frying basket and Bake for 14-18 minutes or until a toothpick inserted into the center comes out clean. Cool for 10 minutes, then remove the muffins from the cups. Serve and enjoy!

Banana Bread

Servings: 6
Cooking Time: 20 Minutes
Ingredients:
- cooking spray
- 1 cup white wheat flour
- ½ teaspoon baking powder
- ¼ teaspoon salt
- ¼ teaspoon baking soda
- 1 egg
- ½ cup mashed ripe banana
- ¼ cup plain yogurt
- ¼ cup pure maple syrup
- 2 tablespoons coconut oil
- ½ teaspoon pure vanilla extract

Directions:
1. Preheat air fryer to 330°F/165°C.
2. Lightly spray 6 x 6-inch baking dish with cooking spray.
3. In a medium bowl, mix together the flour, baking powder, salt, and soda.
4. In a separate bowl, beat the egg and add the mashed banana, yogurt, syrup, oil, and vanilla. Mix until well combined.
5. Pour liquid mixture into dry ingredients and stir gently to blend. Do not beat. Batter may be slightly lumpy.
6. Pour batter into baking dish and cook at 330°F/165°C for 20 minutes or until toothpick inserted in center of loaf comes out clean.

Cinnamon Sugar Donut Holes

Servings: 12
Cooking Time: 6 Minutes
Ingredients:
- 1 cup all-purpose flour
- 6 tablespoons cane sugar, divided
- 1 teaspoon baking powder
- 3 teaspoons ground cinnamon, divided
- ¼ teaspoon salt
- 1 large egg
- 1 teaspoon vanilla extract
- 2 tablespoons melted butter

Directions:
1. Preheat the air fryer to 370°F/185°C.
2. In a small bowl, combine the flour, 2 tablespoons of the sugar, the baking powder, 1 teaspoon of the cinnamon, and the salt. Mix well.
3. In a larger bowl, whisk together the egg, vanilla extract, and butter.
4. Slowly add the dry ingredients into the wet until all the ingredients are uniformly combined. Set the bowl inside the refrigerator for at least 30 minutes.
5. Before you're ready to cook, in a small bowl, mix together the remaining 4 tablespoons of sugar and 2 teaspoons of cinnamon.
6. Liberally spray the air fryer basket with olive oil mist so the donut holes don't stick to the bottom. Note: You do not want to use parchment paper in this recipe; it may burn if your air fryer is hotter than others.
7. Remove the dough from the refrigerator and divide it into 12 equal donut holes. You can use a 1-ounce serving scoop if you have one.
8. Roll each donut hole in the sugar and cinnamon mixture; then place in the air fryer basket. Repeat until all the donut holes are covered in the sugar and cinnamon mixture.
9. When the basket is full, cook for 6 minutes. Remove the donut holes from the basket using oven-safe tongs and let cool 5 minutes. Repeat until all 12 are cooked.

Carrot Muffins

Servings: 4
Cooking Time: 35 Minutes + Cooling Time
Ingredients:
- 1 ½ cups flour
- ½ tsp baking soda
- ½ tsp baking powder
- 1/3 cup brown sugar
- ½ tsp ground cinnamon
- 2 eggs
- 2/3 cup almond milk
- 3 tbsp sunflower oil
- ½ cup shredded carrots
- 1/3 cup golden raisins

Directions:
1. Preheat air fryer to 320°F/160°C. Mix the flour, baking powder, baking soda, brown sugar, and cinnamon in a bowl. In a smaller bowl, whisk the eggs, almond milk, and oil. Combine the mixtures, stir, but leave some lumps in the batter. Add the carrots and raisins and stir. Make 8 foil muffin cups by doubling 16 cups. Set 4 cups in the air fryer and put the batter in the cups until they're ¾ full. Bake in the fryer for 13-17 minutes; the muffin tops should bounce when touched. Repeat until all muffins are done. Let the muffins cool on a rack, then serve.

English Scones

Servings: 8
Cooking Time: 8 Minutes
Ingredients:
- 2 cups all-purpose flour
- 1 tablespoon baking powder
- ½ teaspoon salt
- 2 tablespoons sugar
- ¼ cup unsalted butter
- ⅔ cup plus 1 tablespoon whole milk, divided

Directions:
1. Preheat the air fryer to 380°F/195°C.
2. In a large bowl, whisk together the flour, baking powder, salt, and sugar. Using a pastry blender or your fingers, cut in the butter until pea-size crumbles appear. Make a well in the center and pour in ⅔ cup of the milk. Quickly mix the batter until a ball forms. Knead the dough 3 times.
3. Place the dough onto a floured surface and, using your hands or a rolling pin, flatten the dough until it's ¾ inch thick. Using a biscuit cutter or drinking glass, cut out 10 circles, reforming the dough and flattening as needed to use up the batter.
4. Brush the tops lightly with the remaining 1 tablespoon of milk.
5. Place the scones into the air fryer basket. Cook for 8 minutes or until golden brown and cooked in the center.

Spinach-bacon Rollups

Servings: 4
Cooking Time: 9 Minutes
Ingredients:
- 4 flour tortillas (6- or 7-inch size)
- 4 slices Swiss cheese
- 1 cup baby spinach leaves
- 4 slices turkey bacon

Directions:
1. Preheat air fryer to 390°F/200°C.
2. On each tortilla, place one slice of cheese and ¼ cup of spinach.
3. Roll up tortillas and wrap each with a strip of bacon. Secure each end with a toothpick.
4. Place rollups in air fryer basket, leaving a little space in between them.
5. Cook for 4 minutes. Turn and rearrange rollups (for more even cooking) and cook for 5 minutes longer, until bacon is crisp.

Eggless Mung Bean Tart

Servings: 2
Cooking Time: 20 Minutes
Ingredients:
- 2 tsp soy sauce
- 1 tsp lime juice
- 1 large garlic clove, minced or pressed
- ½ tsp red chili flakes
- ½ cup mung beans, soaked
- Salt and pepper to taste
- ½ minced shallot
- 1 green onion, chopped

Directions:
1. Preheat the air fryer to 390°F/200°C. Add the soy sauce, lime juice, garlic, and chili flakes to a bowl and stir. Set aside. Place the drained beans in a blender along with ½ cup of water, salt, and pepper. Blend until smooth. Stir in shallot and green onion, but do not blend.
2. Pour the batter into a greased baking pan. Bake for 15 minutes in the air fryer until golden. A knife inserted in the center should come out clean. Once cooked, cut the "quiche" into quarters. Drizzle with sauce and serve.

Avocado Toasts With Poached Eggs

Servings: 4
Cooking Time: 15 Minutes
Ingredients:
- 4 eggs
- Salt and pepper to taste
- 4 bread pieces, toasted
- 1 pitted avocado, sliced
- ½ tsp chili powder
- ½ tsp dried rosemary

Directions:
1. Preheat air fryer to 320°F/160°C. Crack 1 egg into each greased ramekin and season with salt and black pepper. Place the ramekins into the air frying basket. Bake for 6-8 minutes.
2. Scoop the flesh of the avocado into a small bowl. Season with salt, black pepper, chili powderp and rosemary. Using a fork, smash the avocado lightly. Spread the smashed avocado evenly over toasted bread slices. Remove the eggs from the air fryer and gently spoon one onto each slice of avocado toast. Serve and enjoy!

Crispy Samosa Rolls

Servings: 4
Cooking Time: 30 Minutes
Ingredients:
- 2/3 cup canned peas
- 4 scallions, finely sliced
- 2 cups grated potatoes
- 2 tbsp lemon juice

- 1 tsp ground ginger
- 1 tsp curry powder
- 1 tsp Garam masala
- ¼ cup chickpea flour
- 1 tbsp tahini
- 8 rice paper wrappers

Directions:
1. Preheat air fryer to 350°F/175°C. Mix the peas, scallions, potatoes, lemon juice, ginger, curry powder, Garam masala, and chickpea flour in a bowl. In another bowl, whisk tahini and 1/3 cup of water until combined. Set aside on a plate.
2. Submerge the rice wrappers, one by one, into the tahini mixture until they begin to soften and set aside on a plate.
3. Fill each wrap with 1/3 cup of the veggie mixture and wrap them into a roll. Bake for 15 minutes until golden brown and crispy, turning once. Serve right away.

Mascarpone Iced Cinnamon Rolls

Servings: 6
Cooking Time: 40 Minutes
Ingredients:
- ¼ cup mascarpone cheese, softened
- 9 oz puff pastry sheet
- 3 tbsp light brown sugar
- 2 tsp ground cinnamon
- 2 tsp butter, melted
- ¼ tsp vanilla extract
- ¼ tsp salt
- 2 tbsp milk
- 1 tbsp lemon zest
- ¼ cup confectioners' sugar

Directions:
1. Preheat air fryer to 320°F/160°C. Mix the brown sugar and cinnamon in a small bowl. Unroll the pastry sheet on its paper and brush it with melted butter. Then sprinkle with cinnamon sugar. Roll up the dough tightly, then cut into rolls about 1-inch wide. Put into a greased baking pan with the spiral side showing. Put the pan into the air fryer and Bake until golden brown, 18-20 minutes. Set aside to cool for 5-10 minutes.
2. Meanwhile, add the mascarpone cheese, vanilla, and salt in a small bowl, whisking until smooth and creamy. Add the confectioners' sugar and continue whisking until fully blended. Pour and mix in 1 tsp of milk at a time until the glaze is pourable but still with some thickness. Spread the glaze over the warm cinnamon rolls and scatter with lemon zest. Serve and enjoy!

Morning Apple Biscuits

Servings: 6
Cooking Time: 15 Minutes
Ingredients:
- 1 apple, grated
- 1 cup oat flour
- 2 tbsp honey
- ¼ cup peanut butter
- 1/3 cup raisins
- ½ tsp ground cinnamon

Directions:
1. Preheat air fryer to 350°F/175°C. Combine the apple, flour, honey, peanut butter, raisins, and cinnamon in a bowl until combined. Make balls out of the mixture. Place them onto parchment paper and flatten them. Bake for 9 minutes until slightly brown. Serve warm.

Morning Burrito

Servings: 4
Cooking Time: 15 Minutes
Ingredients:
- 2 oz cheddar cheese, torn into pieces
- 2 hard-boiled eggs, chopped
- 1 avocado, chopped
- 1 red bell pepper, chopped
- 3 tbsp salsa
- 4 flour tortillas

Directions:
1. Whisk the eggs, avocado, red bell pepper, salsa, and cheese. Pout the tortillas on a clean surface and divide the egg mix between them. Fold the edges and roll up; poke a toothpick through so they hold. Preheat air fryer to 390°F/200°C. Place the burritos in the frying basket and Air Fry for 3-5 minutes until crispy and golden. Serve hot.

Pumpkin Empanadas

Servings: 4
Cooking Time: 30 Minutes
Ingredients:
- 1 can pumpkin purée
- ¼ cup white sugar
- 2 tsp cinnamon
- 1 tbsp brown sugar
- ½ tbsp cornstarch
- ¼ tsp vanilla extract
- 2 tbsp butter
- 4 empanada dough shells

Directions:
1. Place the puree in a pot and top with white and brown sugar, cinnamon, cornstarch, vanilla extract, 1 tbsp of water and butter and stir thoroughly. Bring to a boil over medium heat. Simmer for 4-5 minutes. Allow to cool.
2. Preheat air fryer to 360°F/180°C. Lay empanada shells flat on a clean counter. Spoon the pumpkin mixture into each of the shells. Fold the empanada shells over to cover completely. Seal the edges with water and press down with a fork to secure. Place the empanadas on the greased frying basket and Bake for 15 minutes, flipping once halfway through until golden. Serve hot.

Cream Cheese Deviled Eggs

Servings: 4
Cooking Time: 20 Minutes
Ingredients:
- 2 cooked bacon slices, crumbled
- 4 whole eggs
- 2 tbsp mayonnaise
- 1 tsp yellow mustard
- ½ tsp dill pickle juice
- 1 tsp diced sweet pickles
- Salt and pepper to taste
- 2 tbsp cream cheese
- Parsley for sprinkling

Directions:
1. Preheat air fryer at 250°F/120°C. Place egg in the frying basket and Air Fry for 15 minutes. Then place them immediately into a bowl with ice and 1 cup of water to stop the cooking process. Let chill for 5 minutes, then carefully

peel them. Cut egg in half lengthwise and spoon yolks into a bowl. Arrange the egg white halves on a plate.
2. Mash egg yolks with a fork. Stir in mayonnaise, mustard, pickle juice, diced pickles, salt, pepper and cream cheese. Pour 1 tbsp of the mixture into egg white halves, scatter with crumbled bacon and parsley and serve.

Hashbrown Potatoes Lyonnaise
Servings: 4
Cooking Time: 33 Minutes
Ingredients:
- 1 Vidalia (or other sweet) onion, sliced
- 1 teaspoon butter, melted
- 1 teaspoon brown sugar
- 2 large russet potatoes (about 1 pound), sliced ½-inch thick
- 1 tablespoon vegetable oil
- salt and freshly ground black pepper

Directions:
1. Preheat the air fryer to 370°F/185°C.
2. Toss the sliced onions, melted butter and brown sugar together in the air fryer basket. Air-fry for 8 minutes, shaking the basket occasionally to help the onions cook evenly.
3. While the onions are cooking, bring a 3-quart saucepan of salted water to a boil on the stovetop. Par-cook the potatoes in boiling water for 3 minutes. Drain the potatoes and pat them dry with a clean kitchen towel.
4. Add the potatoes to the onions in the air fryer basket and drizzle with vegetable oil. Toss to coat the potatoes with the oil and season with salt and freshly ground black pepper.
5. Increase the air fryer temperature to 400°F/205°C and air-fry for 22 minutes tossing the vegetables a few times during the cooking time to help the potatoes brown evenly. Season to taste again with salt and freshly ground black pepper and serve warm.

Mushroom & Cavolo Nero Egg Muffins
Servings: 6
Cooking Time: 20 Minutes
Ingredients:
- 8 oz baby Bella mushrooms, sliced
- 6 eggs, beaten
- 1 garlic clove, minced
- Salt and pepper to taste
- ½ tsp chili powder
- 1 cup cavolo nero
- 2 scallions, diced

Directions:
1. Preheat air fryer to 320°F/160°C. Place the eggs, garlic, salt, pepper, and chili powder in a bowl and beat until well combined. Fold in the mushrooms, cavolo nero, and scallions. Divide the mixture between greased muffin cups. Place into the air fryer and Bake for 12-15 minutes, or until the eggs are set. Cool for 5 minutes. Enjoy!

English Muffin Sandwiches
Servings: 4
Cooking Time: 15 Minutes
Ingredients:
- 4 English muffins
- 8 pepperoni slices
- 4 cheddar cheese slices
- 1 tomato, sliced

Directions:
1. Preheat air fryer to 370°F/185°C. Split open the English muffins along the crease. On the bottom half of the muffin, layer 2 slices of pepperoni and one slice of the cheese and tomato. Place the top half of the English muffin to finish the sandwich. Lightly spray with cooking oil. Place the muffin sandwiches in the air fryer. Bake for 8 minutes, flipping once. Let cool slightly before serving.

Chorizo Sausage & Cheese Balls
Servings: 4
Cooking Time: 25 Minutes
Ingredients:
- 1 egg white
- 1 lb chorizo ground sausage
- ¼ tsp smoked paprika
- 2 tbsp canned green chiles
- ¼ cup bread crumbs
- ¼ cup grated cheddar

Directions:
1. Preheat air fryer to 400°F/205°C. Mix all ingredients in a large bowl. Form into 16 balls. Put the sausage balls in the frying basket and Air Fry for 6 minutes. When done, shake the basket and cook for an additional 6 minutes. Transfer to a serving plate and serve.

Southwest Cornbread
Servings: 6
Cooking Time: 18 Minutes
Ingredients:
- cooking spray
- ½ cup yellow cornmeal
- ½ cup flour
- 2 teaspoons baking powder
- ½ teaspoon salt
- ½ cup frozen corn kernels, thawed and drained
- ¼ cup finely chopped onion
- 1 or 2 small jalapeño peppers, seeded and chopped
- 1 egg
- ½ cup milk
- 2 tablespoons melted butter
- 2 ounces sharp Cheddar cheese, grated

Directions:
1. Preheat air fryer to 360°F/180°C.
2. Spray air fryer baking pan with nonstick cooking spray.
3. In a medium bowl, stir together the cornmeal, flour, baking powder, and salt.
4. Stir in the corn, onion, and peppers.
5. In a small bowl, beat together the egg, milk, and butter. Stir into dry ingredients until well combined.
6. Spoon half the batter into prepared baking pan, spreading to edges. Top with grated cheese. Spoon remaining batter on top of cheese and gently spread to edges of pan so it completely covers the cheese.
7. Cook at 360°F/180°C for 18 minutes, until cornbread is done and top is crispy brown.

Soft Pretzels
Servings: 12
Cooking Time: 6 Minutes
Ingredients:
- 2 teaspoons yeast
- 1 cup water, warm
- 1 teaspoon sugar
- 1 teaspoon salt

- 2½ cups all-purpose flour
- 2 tablespoons butter, melted
- 1 cup boiling water
- 1 tablespoon baking soda
- coarse sea salt
- melted butter

Directions:
1. Combine the yeast and water in a small bowl. Combine the sugar, salt and flour in the bowl of a stand mixer. With the mixer running and using the dough hook, drizzle in the yeast mixture and melted butter and knead dough until smooth and elastic – about 10 minutes. Shape into a ball and let the dough rise for 1 hour.
2. Punch the dough down to release any air and decide what size pretzels you want to make.
3. a. To make large pretzels, divide the dough into 12 portions.
4. b. To make medium sized pretzels, divide the dough into 24 portions.
5. c. To make mini pretzel knots, divide the dough into 48 portions.
6. Roll each portion into a skinny rope using both hands on the counter and rolling from the center to the ends of the rope. Spin the rope into a pretzel shape (or tie the rope into a knot) and place the tied pretzels on a parchment lined baking sheet.
7. Preheat the air fryer to 350°F/175°C.
8. Combine the boiling water and baking soda in a shallow bowl and whisk to dissolve (this mixture will bubble, but it will settle down). Let the water cool so that you can put your hands in it. Working in batches, dip the pretzels (top side down) into the baking soda-water mixture and let them soak for 30 seconds to a minute. (This step is what gives pretzels their texture and helps them to brown faster.) Then, remove the pretzels carefully and return them (top side up) to the baking sheet. Sprinkle the coarse salt on the top.
9. Air-fry in batches for 3 minutes per side. When the pretzels are finished, brush them generously with the melted butter and enjoy them warm with some spicy mustard.

Cinnamon Pumpkin Donuts

Servings: 6
Cooking Time: 30 Minutes
Ingredients:
- 1/3 cup canned pumpkin purée
- 1 cup flour
- 3 tbsp brown sugar
- ½ tsp ground cinnamon
- 1/8 tsp ground nutmeg
- 1 tsp baking powder
- 3 tbsp milk
- 2 tbsp butter, melted
- 1 large egg
- 3 tbsp powdered sugar

Directions:
1. Combine the flour, brown sugar, cinnamon, nutmeg, and baking powder in a bowl. Whisk the pumpkin, milk, butter, and egg white in another bowl. Pour the pumpkin mixture over the dry ingredients and stir. Add more milk or flour if necessary to make a soft dough. Cover your hands in flour, make 12 pieces from the dough, and form them into balls. Measure the frying basket, then cut foil or parchment paper about an inch smaller than the measurement. Poke holes in it and put it in the basket.
2. Preheat air fryer to 360°F/180°C. Set the donut holes in the basket and Air Fry for 5-7 minutes. Allow the donuts to chill for 5 minutes, then roll in powdered sugar. Serve.

Cheddar-ham-corn Muffins

Servings: 8
Cooking Time: 8 Minutes
Ingredients:
- ¾ cup yellow cornmeal
- ¼ cup flour
- 1½ teaspoons baking powder
- ¼ teaspoon salt
- 1 egg, beaten
- 2 tablespoons canola oil
- ½ cup milk
- ½ cup shredded sharp Cheddar cheese
- ½ cup diced ham
- 8 foil muffin cups, liners removed and sprayed with cooking spray

Directions:
1. Preheat air fryer to 390°F/200°C.
2. In a medium bowl, stir together the cornmeal, flour, baking powder, and salt.
3. Add egg, oil, and milk to dry ingredients and mix well.
4. Stir in shredded cheese and diced ham.
5. Divide batter among the muffin cups.
6. Place 4 filled muffin cups in air fryer basket and bake for 5 minutes.
7. Reduce temperature to 330°F/165°C and bake for 1 to 2 minutes or until toothpick inserted in center of muffin comes out clean.
8. Repeat steps 6 and 7 to cook remaining muffins.

Shakshuka Cups

Servings: 4
Cooking Time: 25 Minutes
Ingredients:
- 2 tbsp tomato paste
- ½ cup chicken broth
- 4 tomatoes, diced
- 2 garlic cloves, minced
- ½ tsp dried oregano
- ½ tsp dried coriander
- ½ tsp dried basil
- ¼ tsp red pepper flakes
- ¼ tsp paprika
- 4 eggs
- Salt and pepper to taste
- 2 scallions, diced
- ½ cup grated cheddar cheese
- ½ cup Parmesan cheese
- 4 bread slices, toasted

Directions:
1. Preheat air fryer to 350°F/175°C. Combine the tomato paste, chicken broth, tomatoes, garlic, oregano, coriander, basil, red pepper flakes, and paprika. Pour the mixture evenly into greased ramekins. Bake in the air fryer for 5 minutes. Carefully remove the ramekins and crack one egg in each ramekin, then season with salt and pepper. Top with scallions, grated cheese, and Parmesan cheese. Return the ramekins to the frying basket and bake for 3-5 minutes until the eggs are set, and the cheese is melted. Serve with toasted bread immediately.

Pizza Dough

Servings: 3
Cooking Time: 10 Minutes
Ingredients:
- 4 cups bread flour, pizza ("00") flour or all-purpose flour
- 1 teaspoon active dry yeast
- 2 teaspoons sugar
- 2 teaspoons salt
- 1½ cups water
- 1 tablespoon olive oil

Directions:
1. Combine the flour, yeast, sugar and salt in the bowl of a stand mixer. Add the olive oil to the flour mixture and start to mix using the dough hook attachment. As you're mixing, add 1¼ cups of the water, mixing until the dough comes together. Continue to knead the dough with the dough hook for another 10 minutes, adding enough water to the dough to get it to the right consistency.
2. Transfer the dough to a floured counter and divide it into 3 equal portions. Roll each portion into a ball. Lightly coat each dough ball with oil and transfer to the refrigerator, covered with plastic wrap. You can place them all on a baking sheet, or place each dough ball into its own oiled zipper sealable plastic bag or container. (You can freeze the dough balls at this stage, removing as much air as possible from the oiled bag.) Keep in the refrigerator for at least one day, or as long as five days.
3. When you're ready to use the dough, remove your dough from the refrigerator at least 1 hour prior to baking and let it sit on the counter, covered gently with plastic wrap.

Colorful French Toast Sticks

Servings: 4
Cooking Time: 20 Minutes
Ingredients:
- 1 egg
- 1/3 cup whole milk
- Salt to taste
- ½ tsp ground cinnamon
- ½ tsp ground chia seeds
- 1 cup crushed pebbles
- 4 sandwich bread slices, each cut into 4 sticks
- ¼ cup honey

Directions:
1. Preheat air fryer at 375ºF/190°C. Whisk the egg, milk, salt, cinnamon and chia seeds in a bowl. In another bowl, add crushed cereal. Dip breadsticks in the egg mixture, then dredge them in the cereal crumbs. Place breadsticks in the greased frying basket and Air Fry for 5 minutes, flipping once. Serve with honey as a dip.

Veggie & Feta Scramble Bowls

Servings: 2
Cooking Time: 25 Minutes
Ingredients:
- 1 russet potato, cubed
- 1 bell pepper, cut into strips
- ½ feta, cubed
- 1 tbsp nutritional yeast
- ½ tsp garlic powder
- ½ tsp onion powder
- ¼ tsp ground turmeric
- 1 tbsp apple cider vinegar

Directions:
1. Preheat air fryer to 400°F/205°C. Put in potato cubes and bell pepper strips and Air Fry for 10 minutes. Combine the feta, nutritional yeast, garlic, onion, turmeric, and apple vinegar in a small pan. Fit a trivet in the fryer, lay the pan on top, and Air Fry for 5 more minutes until potatoes are tender and feta cheese cooked. Share potatoes and bell peppers into 2 bowls and top with feta scramble. Serve.

Southern Sweet Cornbread

Servings: 6
Cooking Time: 17 Minutes
Ingredients:
- cooking spray
- ½ cup white cornmeal
- ½ cup flour
- 2 teaspoons baking powder
- ½ teaspoon salt
- 4 teaspoons sugar
- 1 egg
- 2 tablespoons oil
- ½ cup milk

Directions:
1. Preheat air fryer to 360°F/180°C.
2. Spray air fryer baking pan with nonstick cooking spray.
3. In a medium bowl, stir together the cornmeal, flour, baking powder, salt, and sugar.
4. In a small bowl, beat together the egg, oil, and milk. Stir into dry ingredients until well combined.
5. Pour batter into prepared baking pan.
6. Cook at 360°F for 17 minutes or until toothpick inserted in center comes out clean or with crumbs clinging.

Coffee Cake

Servings: 8
Cooking Time: 35 Minutes
Ingredients:
- 4 tablespoons butter, melted and divided
- ⅓ cup cane sugar
- ¼ cup brown sugar
- 1 large egg
- 1 cup plus 6 teaspoons milk, divided
- 1 teaspoon vanilla extract
- 2 cups all-purpose flour
- 1½ teaspoons baking powder
- ¼ teaspoon salt
- 2 teaspoons ground cinnamon
- ⅓ cup chopped pecans
- ⅓ cup powdered sugar

Directions:
1. Preheat the air fryer to 325°F/160°C.
2. Using a hand mixer or stand mixer, in a medium bowl, cream together the butter, cane sugar, brown sugar, the egg, 1 cup of the milk, and the vanilla. Set aside.
3. In a small bowl, mix together the flour, baking powder, salt, and cinnamon. Slowly combine the dry ingredients into the wet. Fold in the pecans.
4. Liberally spray a 7-inch springform pan with cooking spray. Pour the batter into the pan and place in the air fryer basket.
5. Bake for 30 to 35 minutes. While the cake is baking, in a small bowl, add the powdered sugar and whisk together with the remaining 6 teaspoons of milk. Set aside.
6. When the cake is done baking, remove the pan from the basket and let cool on a wire rack. After 10 minutes, remove and invert the cake from pan. Drizzle with the powdered sugar glaze and serve.

Cheddar & Sausage Tater Tots
Servings: 4
Cooking Time: 25 Minutes
Ingredients:
- 12 oz ground chicken sausage
- 4 eggs
- 1 cup sour cream
- 1 tsp Worcestershire sauce
- 1 tsp shallot powder
- Salt and pepper to taste
- 1 lb frozen tater tots
- ¾ cup grated cheddar

Directions:
1. Whisk eggs, sour cream, Worcestershire sauce and shallot in a bowl. Add salt and pepper to taste. Coat a skillet with cooking spray. Over medium heat, brown the ground sausage for 3-4 minutes. Break larger pieces with a spoon or spatula. Set aside.
2. Preheat air fryer to 330°F/165°C. Prepare a baking pan with a light spray of cooking oil. Layer the bottom of the pan with tater tots, then place in the air fryer. Bake for 6 minutes, then shake the pan. Cover tater tots with cooked sausage and egg mixture. Continue cooking for 6 minutes. Top with cheese, then cook for another 2-3 minutes or until cheese is melted. Serve warm.

Blueberry Muffins
Servings: 8
Cooking Time: 14 Minutes
Ingredients:
- 1⅓ cups flour
- ½ cup sugar
- 2 teaspoons baking powder
- ¼ teaspoon salt
- ⅓ cup canola oil
- 1 egg
- ½ cup milk
- ⅔ cup blueberries, fresh or frozen and thawed
- 8 foil muffin cups including paper liners

Directions:
1. Preheat air fryer to 330°F/165°C.
2. In a medium bowl, stir together flour, sugar, baking powder, and salt.
3. In a separate bowl, combine oil, egg, and milk and mix well.
4. Add egg mixture to dry ingredients and stir just until moistened.
5. Gently stir in blueberries.
6. Spoon batter evenly into muffin cups.
7. Place 4 muffin cups in air fryer basket and bake at 330°F/165°C for 14 minutes or until tops spring back when touched lightly.
8. Repeat previous step to cook remaining muffins.

Breakfast Pot Pies
Servings: 4
Cooking Time: 20 Minutes
Ingredients:
- 1 refrigerated pie crust
- ½ pound pork breakfast sausage
- ¼ cup diced onion
- 1 garlic clove, minced
- ½ teaspoon ground black pepper
- ¼ teaspoon salt
- 1 cup chopped bell peppers
- 1 cup roasted potatoes
- 2 cups milk
- 2 to 3 tablespoons all-purpose flour

Directions:
1. Flatten the store-bought pie crust out on an even surface. Cut 4 equal circles that are slightly larger than the circumference of ramekins (by about ¼ inch). Set aside.
2. In a medium pot, sauté the breakfast sausage with the onion, garlic, black pepper, and salt. When browned, add in the bell peppers and potatoes and cook an additional 3 to 4 minutes to soften the bell peppers. Remove from the heat and portion equally into the ramekins.
3. To the same pot (without washing it), add the milk. Heat over medium-high heat until boiling. Slowly reduce to a simmer and stir in the flour, 1 tablespoon at a time, until the gravy thickens and coats the back of a wooden spoon (about 5 minutes).
4. Remove from the heat and equally portion ½ cup of gravy into each ramekin on top of the sausage and potato mixture.
5. Place the circle pie crusts on top of the ramekins, lightly pressing them down on the perimeter of each ramekin with the prongs of a fork. Gently poke the prongs into the center top of the pie crust a few times to create holes for the steam to escape as the pie cooks.
6. Bake in the air fryer for 6 minutes (or until the tops are golden brown).
7. Remove and let cool 5 minutes before serving.

Cheddar Cheese Biscuits
Servings: 8
Cooking Time: 22 Minutes
Ingredients:
- 2⅓ cups self-rising flour
- 2 tablespoons sugar
- ½ cup butter (1 stick), frozen for 15 minutes
- ½ cup grated Cheddar cheese, plus more to melt on top
- 1⅓ cups buttermilk
- 1 cup all-purpose flour, for shaping
- 1 tablespoon butter, melted

Directions:
1. Line a buttered 7-inch metal cake pan with parchment paper or a silicone liner.
2. Combine the flour and sugar in a large mixing bowl. Grate the butter into the flour. Add the grated cheese and stir to coat the cheese and butter with flour. Then add the buttermilk and stir just until you can no longer see streaks of flour. The dough should be quite wet.
3. Spread the all-purpose (not self-rising) flour out on a small cookie sheet. With a spoon, scoop 8 evenly sized balls of dough into the flour, making sure they don't touch each other. With floured hands, coat each dough ball with flour and toss them gently from hand to hand to shake off any excess flour. Place each floured dough ball into the prepared pan, right up next to the other. This will help the biscuits rise up, rather than spreading out.
4. Preheat the air fryer to 380°F/195°C.
5. Transfer the cake pan to the basket of the air fryer, lowering it into the basket using a sling made of aluminum foil (fold a piece of aluminum foil into a strip about 2-inches wide by 24-inches long). Let the ends of the aluminum foil sling hang across the cake pan before returning the basket to the air fryer.
6. Air-fry for 20 minutes. Check the biscuits a couple of times to make sure they are not getting too brown on top. If

they are, re-arrange the aluminum foil strips to cover any brown parts. After 20 minutes, check the biscuits by inserting a toothpick into the center of the biscuits. It should come out clean. If it needs a little more time, continue to air-fry for a couple of extra minutes. Brush the tops of the biscuits with some melted butter and sprinkle a little more grated cheese on top if desired. Pop the basket back into the air fryer for another 2 minutes. Remove the cake pan from the air fryer using the aluminum sling. Let the biscuits cool for just a minute or two and then turn them out onto a plate and pull apart. Serve immediately.

Huevos Rancheros

Servings: 4
Cooking Time: 45 Minutes + Cooling Time
Ingredients:
- 1 tbsp olive oil
- 20 cherry tomatoes, halved
- 2 chopped plum tomatoes
- ¼ cup tomato sauce
- 2 scallions, sliced
- 2 garlic cloves, minced
- 1 tsp honey
- ½ tsp salt
- ⅛ tsp cayenne pepper
- ¼ tsp grated nutmeg
- ¼ tsp paprika
- 4 eggs

Directions:
1. Preheat the air fryer to 370°F/185°C. Combine the olive oil, cherry tomatoes, plum tomatoes, tomato sauce, scallions, garlic, nutmeg, honey, salt, paprika and cayenne in a 7-inch springform pan that has been wrapped in foil to prevent leaks. Put the pan in the frying basket and
2. Bake the mix for 15-20 minutes, stirring twice until the tomatoes are soft. Mash some of the tomatoes in the pan with a fork, then stir them into the sauce. Also, break the eggs into the sauce, then return the pan to the fryer and Bake for 2 minutes. Remove the pan from the fryer and stir the eggs into the sauce, whisking them through the sauce. Don't mix in completely. Cook for 4-8 minutes more or until the eggs are set. Let cool, then serve.

Wake-up Veggie & Ham Bake

Servings: 4
Cooking Time: 25 Minutes
Ingredients:
- 25 Brussels sprouts, halved
- 2 mini sweet peppers, diced
- 1 yellow onion, diced
- 3 deli ham slices, diced
- 2 tbsp orange juice
- ¼ tsp salt
- 1 tsp orange zest

Directions:
1. Preheat air fryer to 350°F/175°C. Mix the sprouts, sweet peppers, onion, deli ham, orange juice, and salt in a bowl. Transfer to the frying basket and Air Fry for 12 minutes, tossing once. Scatter with orange zest and serve.

Classic Cinnamon Rolls

Servings: 4
Cooking Time: 6 Minutes
Ingredients:
- 1½ cups all-purpose flour
- 1 tablespoon granulated sugar
- 2 teaspoons baking powder
- ½ teaspoon salt
- 4 tablespoons butter, divided
- ½ cup buttermilk
- 2 tablespoons brown sugar
- 1 teaspoon cinnamon
- 1 cup powdered sugar
- 2 tablespoons milk

Directions:
1. Preheat the air fryer to 360°F/180°C.
2. In a large bowl, stir together the flour, sugar, baking powder, and salt. Cut in 3 tablespoons of the butter with a pastry blender or two knives until coarse crumbs remain. Stir in the buttermilk until a dough forms.
3. Place the dough onto a floured surface and roll out into a square shape about ½ inch thick.
4. Melt the remaining 1 tablespoon of butter in the microwave for 20 seconds. Using a pastry brush or your fingers, spread the melted butter onto the dough.
5. In a small bowl, mix together the brown sugar and cinnamon. Sprinkle the mixture across the surface of the dough. Roll the dough up, forming a long log. Using a pastry cutter or sharp knife, cut 10 cinnamon rolls.
6. Carefully place the cinnamon rolls into the air fryer basket. Then bake at 360°F/180°C for 6 minutes or until golden brown.
7. Meanwhile, in a small bowl, whisk together the powdered sugar and milk.
8. Plate the cinnamon rolls and drizzle the glaze over the surface before serving.

Easy Corn Dog Cupcakes

Servings: 6
Cooking Time: 30 Minutes
Ingredients:
- 1 cup cornbread Mix
- 2 tsp granulated sugar
- Salt to taste
- 3/4 cup cream cheese
- 3 tbsp butter, melted
- 1 egg
- ¼ cup minced onions
- 1 tsp dried parsley
- 2 beef hot dogs, sliced and cut into half-moons

Directions:
1. Preheat air fryer at 350ºF/175°C. Combine cornbread, sugar, and salt in a bowl. In another bowl, whisk cream cheese, parsley, butter, and egg. Pour wet ingredients to dry ingredients and toss to combine. Fold in onion and hot dog pieces. Transfer it into 8 greased silicone cupcake liners. Place it in the frying basket and Bake for 8-10 minutes. Serve right away.

Breakfast Chimichangas

Servings: 4
Cooking Time: 8 Minutes
Ingredients:
- Four 8-inch flour tortillas
- ½ cup canned refried beans
- 1 cup scrambled eggs
- ½ cup grated cheddar or Monterey jack cheese
- 1 tablespoon vegetable oil
- 1 cup salsa

Directions:

1. Lay the flour tortillas out flat on a cutting board. In the center of each tortilla, spread 2 tablespoons refried beans. Next, add ¼ cup eggs and 2 tablespoons cheese to each tortilla.
2. To fold the tortillas, begin on the left side and fold to the center. Then fold the right side into the center. Next fold the bottom and top down and roll over to completely seal the chimichanga. Using a pastry brush or oil mister, brush the tops of the tortilla packages with oil.
3. Preheat the air fryer to 400°F/205°C for 4 minutes. Place the chimichangas into the air fryer basket, seam side down, and air fry for 4 minutes. Using tongs, turn over the chimichangas and cook for an additional 2 to 3 minutes or until light golden brown.

Garlic Bread Knots
Servings: 8
Cooking Time: 5 Minutes
Ingredients:
- ¼ cup melted butter
- 2 teaspoons garlic powder
- 1 teaspoon dried parsley
- 1 (11-ounce) tube of refrigerated French bread dough

Directions:
1. Mix the melted butter, garlic powder and dried parsley in a small bowl and set it aside.
2. To make smaller knots, cut the long tube of bread dough into 16 slices. If you want to make bigger knots, slice the dough into 8 slices. Shape each slice into a long rope about 6 inches long by rolling it on a flat surface with the palm of your hands. Tie each rope into a knot and place them on a plate.
3. Preheat the air fryer to 350°F/175°C.
4. Transfer half of the bread knots into the air fryer basket, leaving space in between each knot. Brush each knot with the butter mixture using a pastry brush.
5. Air-fry for 5 minutes. Remove the baked knots and brush a little more of the garlic butter mixture on each. Repeat with the remaining bread knots and serve warm.

Oat Muffins With Blueberries
Servings: 6
Cooking Time: 25 Minutes
Ingredients:
- ¾ cup old-fashioned rolled oats
- 1 ½ cups flour
- ½ cup evaporated cane sugar
- 1 tbsp baking powder
- 1 tsp ground cinnamon
- ¼ tsp ground chia seeds
- ¼ tsp ground sesame seeds
- ½ tsp salt
- 1 cup vanilla almond milk
- 4 tbsp butter, softened
- 2 eggs
- 1 tsp vanilla extract
- 1 cup blueberries
- 2 tbsp powdered sugar

Directions:
1. Preheat air fryer to 350°F/175°C. Combine flour oats, sugar, baking powder, chia seeds, sesame seeds, cinnamon, and salt in a bowl. Mix the almond milk, butter, eggs, and vanilla in another bowl until smooth. Pour in dry ingredients and stir to combine. Fold in blueberries. Fill 12 silicone muffin cups about halfway and place them in the frying basket. Bake for 12-15 minutes until just browned, and a toothpick in the center comes out clean. Cool for 5 minutes. Serve topped with powdered sugar.

Bacon Puff Pastry Pinwheels
Servings: 8
Cooking Time: 10 Minutes
Ingredients:
- 1 sheet of puff pastry
- 2 tablespoons maple syrup
- ¼ cup brown sugar
- 8 slices bacon (not thick cut)
- coarsely cracked black pepper
- vegetable oil

Directions:
1. On a lightly floured surface, roll the puff pastry out into a square that measures roughly 10 inches wide by however long your bacon strips are (usually about 11 inches). Cut the pastry into eight even strips.
2. Brush the strips of pastry with the maple syrup and sprinkle the brown sugar on top, leaving 1 inch of dough exposed at the far end of each strip. Place a slice of bacon on each strip of puff pastry, letting 1/8-inch of the length of bacon hang over the edge of the pastry. Season generously with coarsely ground black pepper.
3. With the exposed end of the pastry strips away from you, roll the bacon and pastry strips up into pinwheels. Dab a little water on the exposed end of the pastry and pinch it to the pinwheel to seal the pastry shut.
4. Preheat the air fryer to 360°F/180°C.
5. Brush or spray the air fryer basket with a little vegetable oil. Place the pinwheels into the basket and air-fry at 360°F for 8 minutes. Turn the pinwheels over and air-fry for another 2 minutes to brown the bottom. Serve warm.

Breakfast Sausage Bites
Servings: 4
Cooking Time: 30 Minutes
Ingredients:
- 1 lb ground pork sausages
- ¼ cup diced onions
- 1 tsp rubbed sage
- ¼ tsp ground nutmeg
- ½ tsp fennel
- ¼ tsp garlic powder
- 2 tbsp parsley, chopped
- Salt and pepper to taste

Directions:
1. Preheat air fryer at 350°F/175°C. Combine all ingredients, except the parsley, in a bowl. Form mixture into balls. Place them in the greased frying basket and Air Fry for 10 minutes, flipping once. Sprinkle with parsley and serve immediately.

Hole In One
Servings: 1
Cooking Time: 7 Minutes
Ingredients:
- 1 slice bread
- 1 teaspoon soft butter
- 1 egg
- salt and pepper
- 1 tablespoon shredded Cheddar cheese
- 2 teaspoons diced ham

Directions:

1. Place a 6 x 6-inch baking dish inside air fryer basket and preheat fryer to 330°F/165°C.
2. Using a 2½-inch-diameter biscuit cutter, cut a hole in center of bread slice.
3. Spread softened butter on both sides of bread.
4. Lay bread slice in baking dish and crack egg into the hole. Sprinkle egg with salt and pepper to taste.
5. Cook for 5 minutes.
6. Turn toast over and top it with shredded cheese and diced ham.
7. Cook for 2 more minutes or until yolk is done to your liking.

Morning Chicken Frittata Cups

Servings: 6
Cooking Time: 30 Minutes
Ingredients:
- ¼ cup shredded cooked chicken breasts
- 3 eggs
- 2 tbsp heavy cream
- 4 tsp Tabasco sauce
- ¼ cup grated Asiago cheese
- 2 tbsp chives, chopped

Directions:
1. Preheat air fryer to 350°F/175°C. Beat all ingredients in a bowl. Divide the egg mixture between greased 6 muffin cups and place them in the frying basket. Bake for 8-10 minutes until set. Let cool slightly before serving. Enjoy!

Cajun Breakfast Potatoes

Servings: 4
Cooking Time: 20 Minutes
Ingredients:
- 1 pound roasting potatoes (like russet), scrubbed clean
- 1 tablespoon vegetable oil
- 2 teaspoons paprika
- ½ teaspoon garlic powder
- ¼ teaspoon onion powder
- ¼ teaspoon ground cumin
- 1 teaspoon thyme
- 1 teaspoon sea salt
- ½ teaspoon black pepper

Directions:
1. Cut the potatoes into 1-inch cubes.
2. In a large bowl, toss the cut potatoes with vegetable oil.
3. Sprinkle paprika, garlic powder, onion powder, cumin, thyme, salt, and pepper onto the potatoes, and toss to coat well.
4. Preheat the air fryer to 400°F/205°C for 4 minutes.
5. Add the potatoes to the air fryer basket and bake for 10 minutes. Stir or toss the potatoes and continue baking for an additional 5 minutes. Stir or toss again and continue baking for an additional 5 minutes or until the desired crispness is achieved.

Whole-grain Cornbread

Servings: 6
Cooking Time: 25 Minutes
Ingredients:
- 1 cup stoneground cornmeal
- ½ cup brown rice flour
- 1 teaspoon sugar
- 2 teaspoons baking powder
- ¼ teaspoon salt
- 1 cup milk
- 2 tablespoons oil
- 2 eggs
- cooking spray

Directions:
1. Preheat the air fryer to 360°F/180°C.
2. In a medium mixing bowl, mix cornmeal, brown rice flour, sugar, baking powder, and salt together.
3. Add the remaining ingredients and beat with a spoon until batter is smooth.
4. Spray air fryer baking pan with nonstick cooking spray and add the cornbread batter.
5. Bake at 360°F/180°C for 25 minutes, until center is done.

Seasoned Herbed Sourdough Croutons

Servings: 4
Cooking Time: 7 Minutes
Ingredients:
- 4 cups cubed sourdough bread, 1-inch cubes (about 8 ounces)
- 1 tablespoon olive oil
- 1 teaspoon fresh thyme leaves
- ¼ – ½ teaspoon salt
- freshly ground black pepper

Directions:
1. Combine all ingredients in a bowl and taste to make sure it is seasoned to your liking.
2. Preheat the air fryer to 400°F/205°C.
3. Toss the bread cubes into the air fryer and air-fry for 7 minutes, shaking the basket once or twice while they cook.
4. Serve warm or store in an airtight container.

Carrot Orange Muffins

Servings: 12
Cooking Time: 12 Minutes
Ingredients:
- 1½ cups all-purpose flour
- ½ cup granulated sugar
- ½ teaspoon ground cinnamon
- 2 teaspoons baking powder
- ¼ teaspoon baking soda
- ½ teaspoon salt
- 2 large eggs
- ¼ cup vegetable oil
- ⅓ cup orange marmalade
- 2 cups grated carrots

Directions:
1. Preheat the air fryer to 320°F/160°C.
2. In a large bowl, whisk together the flour, sugar, cinnamon, baking powder, baking soda, and salt; set aside.
3. In a separate bowl, whisk together the eggs, vegetable oil, orange marmalade, and grated carrots.
4. Make a well in the dry ingredients; then pour the wet ingredients into the well of the dry ingredients. Using a rubber spatula, mix the ingredients for 1 minute or until slightly lumpy.
5. Using silicone muffin liners, fill 6 muffin liners two-thirds full.
6. Carefully place the muffin liners in the air fryer basket and bake for 12 minutes (or until the tops are browned and a toothpick inserted in the center comes out clean). Carefully remove the muffins from the basket and repeat with remaining batter.
7. Serve warm.

Honey Donuts

Servings: 6
Cooking Time: 25 Minutes + Chilling Time
Ingredients:
- 1 refrigerated puff pastry sheet
- 2 tsp flour
- 2 ½ cups powdered sugar
- 3 tbsp honey
- 2 tbsp milk
- 2 tbsp butter, melted
- ½ tsp vanilla extract
- ½ tsp ground cinnamon
- Pinch of salt

Directions:
1. Preheat the air fryer to 325°F/160°C. Dust a clean work surface with flour and lay the puff pastry on it, then cut crosswise into five 3-inch wide strips. Cut each strip into thirds for 15 squares. Lay round parchment paper in the bottom of the basket, then add the pastry squares in a single layer.
2. Make sure none are touching. Bake for 13-18 minutes or until brown, then leave on a rack to cool. Repeat for all dough. Combine the sugar, honey, milk, butter, vanilla, cinnamon, and salt in a small bowl and mix with a wire whisk until combined. Dip the top half of each donut in the glaze, turn the donut glaze side up, and return to the wire rack. Let cool until the glaze sets, then serve.

Strawberry Streusel Muffins

Servings: 12
Cooking Time: 14 Minutes
Ingredients:
- 1¾ cups all-purpose flour
- ½ cup granulated sugar
- 2 teaspoons baking powder
- ¼ teaspoon baking soda
- ½ teaspoon salt
- ½ cup plain yogurt
- ½ cup milk
- ¼ cup vegetable oil
- 2 large eggs
- 1 teaspoon vanilla extract
- ½ cup freeze-dried strawberries
- 2 tablespoons brown sugar
- ¼ cup oats
- 2 tablespoons butter

Directions:
1. Preheat the air fryer to 330°F/165°C.
2. In a large bowl, whisk together the flour, sugar, baking powder, baking soda, and salt; set aside.
3. In a separate bowl, whisk together the yogurt, milk, vegetable oil, eggs, and vanilla extract.
4. Make a well in the dry ingredients; then pour the wet ingredients into the well of the dry ingredients. Using a rubber spatula, mix the ingredients for 1 minute or until slightly lumpy. Fold in the strawberries.
5. In a small bowl, use your fingers to mix together the brown sugar, oats, and butter until coarse crumbles appear. Divide the mixture in half.
6. Using silicone muffin liners, fill 6 muffin liners two-thirds full.
7. Crumble half of the streusel topping onto the first batch of muffins.
8. Carefully place the muffin liners in the air fryer basket and bake for 14 minutes (or until the tops are browned and a toothpick inserted in the center comes out clean). Carefully remove the muffins from the basket and repeat with the remaining batter and topping.
9. Serve warm.

Cinnamon-coconut Doughnuts

Servings: 6
Cooking Time: 35 Minutes
Ingredients:
- 1 egg, beaten
- ¼ cup milk
- 2 tbsp safflower oil
- 1 ½ tsp vanilla
- ½ tsp lemon zest
- 1 ½ cups all-purpose flour
- ¾ cup coconut sugar
- 2 ½ tsp cinnamon
- ½ tsp ground nutmeg
- ¼ tsp salt
- ¾ tsp baking powder

Directions:
1. Preheat air fryer to 350°F/175°C. Add the egg, milk, oil, vanilla, and lemon zest. Stir well and set this wet mixture aside. In a different bowl, combine the flour, ½ cup coconut sugar, ½ teaspoon cinnamon, nutmeg, salt, and baking powder. Stir well. Add this mixture to the wet mix and blend. Pull off bits of the dough and roll into balls.
2. Place in the greased frying basket, leaving room between as they get bigger. Spray the tops with oil and Air Fry for 8-10 minutes, flipping once. During the last 2 minutes of frying, place 4 tbsp of coconut sugar and 2 tsp of cinnamon in a bowl and stir to combine. After frying, coat each donut by spraying with oil and toss in the cinnamon-sugar mix. Serve and enjoy!

Pigs In A Blanket

Servings: 10
Cooking Time: 8 Minutes
Ingredients:
- 1 cup all-purpose flour, plus more for rolling
- 1 teaspoon baking powder
- ¼ cup salted butter, cut into small pieces
- ½ cup buttermilk
- 10 fully cooked breakfast sausage links

Directions:
1. In a large mixing bowl, whisk together the flour and baking powder. Using your fingers or a pastry blender, cut in the butter until you have small pea-size crumbles.
2. Using a rubber spatula, make a well in the center of the flour mixture. Pour the buttermilk into the well, and fold the mixture together until you form a dough ball.
3. Place the sticky dough onto a floured surface and, using a floured rolling pin, roll out until ½-inch thick. Using a round biscuit cutter, cut out 10 rounds, reshaping the dough and rolling out, as needed.
4. Place 1 fully cooked breakfast sausage link on the left edge of each biscuit and roll up, leaving the ends slightly exposed.
5. Using a pastry brush, brush the biscuits with the whisked eggs, and spray them with cooking spray.
6. Place the pigs in a blanket into the air fryer basket with at least 1 inch between each biscuit. Set the air fryer to 340°F/170°C and cook for 8 minutes.

Western Frittata

Servings: 1
Cooking Time: 19 Minutes
Ingredients:
- ½ red or green bell pepper, cut into ½-inch chunks
- 1 teaspoon olive oil
- 3 eggs, beaten
- ¼ cup grated Cheddar cheese
- ¼ cup diced cooked ham
- salt and freshly ground black pepper, to taste
- 1 teaspoon butter
- 1 teaspoon chopped fresh parsley

Directions:
1. Preheat the air fryer to 400°F/205°C.
2. Toss the peppers with the olive oil and air-fry for 6 minutes, shaking the basket once or twice during the cooking process to redistribute the ingredients.
3. While the vegetables are cooking, beat the eggs well in a bowl, stir in the Cheddar cheese and ham, and season with salt and freshly ground black pepper. Add the air-fried peppers to this bowl when they have finished cooking.
4. Place a 6- or 7-inch non-stick metal cake pan into the air fryer basket with the butter using an aluminum sling to lower the pan into the basket. (Fold a piece of aluminum foil into a strip about 2-inches wide by 24-inches long.) Air-fry for 1 minute at 380°F/195°C to melt the butter. Remove the cake pan and rotate the pan to distribute the butter and grease the pan. Pour the egg mixture into the cake pan and return the pan to the air fryer, using the aluminum sling.
5. Air-fry at 380°F/195°C for 12 minutes, or until the frittata has puffed up and is lightly browned. Let the frittata sit in the air fryer for 5 minutes to cool to an edible temperature and set up. Remove the cake pan from the air fryer, sprinkle with parsley and serve immediately.

Ham & Cheese Sandwiches

Servings: 2
Cooking Time: 15 Minutes
Ingredients:
- 1 tsp butter
- 4 bread slices
- 4 deli ham slices
- 4 Cheddar cheese slices
- 4 thick tomato slices
- 1 tsp dried oregano

Directions:
1. Preheat air fryer to 370°F/185°C. Smear ½ tsp of butter on only one side of each slice of bread and sprinkle with oregano. On one of the slices, layer 2 slices of ham, 2 slices of cheese, and 2 slices of tomato on the unbuttered side. Place the unbuttered side of another piece of bread onto the toppings. Place the sandwiches butter side down into the air fryer. Bake for 8 minutes, flipping once until crispy. Let cool slightly, cut in half and serve.

Hush Puffins

Servings: 20
Cooking Time: 8 Minutes
Ingredients:
- 1 cup buttermilk
- ¼ cup butter, melted
- 2 eggs
- 1½ cups all-purpose flour
- 1½ cups cornmeal
- ⅓ cup sugar
- 1 teaspoon baking soda
- 1 teaspoon salt
- 4 scallions, minced
- vegetable oil

Directions:
1. Combine the buttermilk, butter and eggs in a large mixing bowl. In a second bowl combine the flour, cornmeal, sugar, baking soda and salt. Add the dry ingredients to the wet ingredients, stirring just to combine. Stir in the minced scallions and refrigerate the batter for 30 minutes.
2. Shape the batter into 2-inch balls. Brush or spray the balls with oil.
3. Preheat the air fryer to 360°F/180°C.
4. Air-fry the hush puffins in two batches at 360°F/180°C for 8 minutes, turning them over after 6 minutes of the cooking process.
5. Serve warm with butter.

Not-so-english Muffins

Servings: 4
Cooking Time: 10 Minutes
Ingredients:
- 2 strips turkey bacon, cut in half crosswise
- 2 whole-grain English muffins, split
- 1 cup fresh baby spinach, long stems removed
- ¼ ripe pear, peeled and thinly sliced
- 4 slices Provolone cheese

Directions:
1. Place bacon strips in air fryer basket and cook for 2minutes. Check and separate strips if necessary so they cook evenly. Cook for 4 more minutes, until crispy. Remove and drain on paper towels.
2. Place split muffin halves in air fryer basket and cook at 390°F/200°C for 2minutes, just until lightly browned.
3. Open air fryer and top each muffin with a quarter of the baby spinach, several pear slices, a strip of bacon, and a slice of cheese.
4. Cook at 360°F for 2minutes, until cheese completely melts.

Aromatic Mushroom Omelet

Servings: 4
Cooking Time: 30 Minutes
Ingredients:
- 6 eggs
- 2 tbsp milk
- ½ yellow onion, diced
- ½ cup diced mushrooms
- 2 tbsp chopped parsley
- 1 tsp dried oregano
- 1 tbsp chopped chives
- ½ tbsp chopped dill
- ½ cup grated Gruyère cheese

Directions:
1. Preheat air fryer to 350°F/175°C. Beat eggs in a medium bowl, then add the rest of the ingredients, except for the parsley. Stir until completely combined. Pour the mixture into a greased pan and bake in the air fryer for 18-20 minutes until the eggs are set. Top with parsley and serve.

Smooth Walnut-banana Loaf

Servings: 4
Cooking Time: 40 Minutes
Ingredients:
- 1/3 cup peanut butter, melted
- 2 tbsp butter, melted and cooled
- ¾ cup flour
- ½ tsp salt
- ¼ tsp baking soda
- 2 ripe bananas
- 2 eggs
- 1 tsp lemon juice
- ½ cup evaporated cane sugar
- ½ cup ground walnuts
- 1 tbsp blackstrap molasses
- 1 tsp vanilla extract

Directions:
1. Preheat air fryer to 310°F/155°C. Mix flour, salt, and baking soda in a small bowl. Mash together bananas and eggs in a large bowl, then stir in sugar, peanut butter, lemon juice, butter, walnuts, molasses, and vanilla. When it is well incorporated, stir in the flour mixture until just combined. Transfer the batter to a parchment-lined baking dish and make sure it is even. Bake in the air fryer for 30 to 35 minutes until a toothpick in the middle comes out clean, and the top is golden. Serve and enjoy.

Favorite Blueberry Muffins

Servings: 8
Cooking Time: 25 Minutes
Ingredients:
- 1 cup all-purpose flour
- ½ tsp baking soda
- 1/3 cup granulated sugar
- ¼ tsp salt
- 1 tbsp lemon juice
- 1 tsp lemon zest
- ¼ cup milk
- ½ tsp vanilla extract
- 1 egg
- 1 tbsp vegetable oil
- ¼ cup halved blueberries
- 1 tbsp powdered sugar

Directions:
1. Preheat air fryer at 375°F/190°C. Combine dry ingredients in a bowl. Mix ¼ cup of fresh milk with 1 tsp of lemon juice and leave for 10 minutes. Put it in another bowl with the wet ingredients. Pour wet ingredients into dry ingredients and gently toss to combine. Fold in blueberries. Spoon mixture into 8 greased silicone cupcake liners and Bake them in the fryer for 6-8 minutes. Let cool onto a cooling rack. Serve right away sprinkled with powdered sugar.

Banana-blackberry Muffins

Servings: 6
Cooking Time: 20 Minutes
Ingredients:
- 1 ripe banana, mashed
- ½ cup milk
- 1 tsp apple cider vinegar
- 1 tsp vanilla extract
- 2 tbsp ground flaxseed
- 2 tbsp coconut sugar
- ¾ cup flour
- 1 tsp baking powder
- ½ tsp baking soda
- ¾ cup blackberries

Directions:
1. Preheat air fryer to 350°F/175°C. Place the banana in a bowl. Stir in milk, apple vinegar, vanilla extract, flaxseed, and coconut sugar until combined. In another bowl, combine flour, baking powder, and baking soda. Pour it into the banana mixture and toss to combine. Divide the batter between 6 muffin molds and top each with blackberries, pressing slightly. Bake for 16 minutes until golden brown and a toothpick comes out clean. Serve cooled.

Fried Pb&j

Servings: 4
Cooking Time: 8 Minutes
Ingredients:
- ½ cup cornflakes, crushed
- ¼ cup shredded coconut
- 8 slices oat nut bread or any whole-grain, oversize bread
- 6 tablespoons peanut butter
- 2 medium bananas, cut into ½-inch-thick slices
- 6 tablespoons pineapple preserves
- 1 egg, beaten
- oil for misting or cooking spray

Directions:
1. Preheat air fryer to 360°F/180°C.
2. In a shallow dish, mix together the cornflake crumbs and coconut.
3. For each sandwich, spread one bread slice with 1½ tablespoons of peanut butter. Top with banana slices. Spread another bread slice with 1½ tablespoons of preserves. Combine to make a sandwich.
4. Using a pastry brush, brush top of sandwich lightly with beaten egg. Sprinkle with about 1½ tablespoons of crumb coating, pressing it in to make it stick. Spray with oil.
5. Turn sandwich over and repeat to coat and spray the other side.
6. Cooking 2 at a time, place sandwiches in air fryer basket and cook for 6 to 7minutes or until coating is golden brown and crispy. If sandwich doesn't brown enough, spray with a little more oil and cook at 390°F/200°C for another minute.
7. Cut cooked sandwiches in half and serve warm.

Honey Oatmeal

Servings: 6
Cooking Time: 35 Minutes
Ingredients:
- 2 cups rolled oats
- 2 cups oat milk
- ¼ cup honey
- ½ cup Greek yogurt
- 1 tsp vanilla extract
- ½ tsp ground cinnamon
- ¼ tsp salt
- 1 ½ cups diced mango

Directions:
1. Preheat air fryer to 380°F/195°C. Stir together the oats, milk, honey, yogurt, vanilla, cinnamon, and salt in a large bowl until well combined. Fold in ¾ cup of the mango and then pour the mixture into a greased cake pan. Sprinkle the remaining manog across the top of the oatmeal mixture. Bake in the air fryer for 30 minutes. Leave to set and cool for 5 minutes. Serve and enjoy!

Viking Toast

Servings: 2
Cooking Time: 20 Minutes
Ingredients:
- 2 tbsp minced green chili pepper
- 1 avocado, pressed
- 1 clove garlic, minced
- ¼ tsp lemon juice
- Salt and pepper to taste
- 2 bread slices
- 2 plum tomatoes, sliced
- 4 oz smoked salmon
- ¼ diced peeled red onion

Directions:
1. Preheat air fryer at 350°F/175°C. Combine the avocado, garlic, lemon juice, and salt in a bowl until you reach your desired consistency. Spread avocado mixture on the bread slices.
2. Top with tomato slices and sprinkle with black pepper. Place bread slices in the frying basket and Bake for 5 minutes. Transfer to a plate. Top each bread slice with salmon, green chili pepper, and red onion. Serve.

Quiche Cups

Servings: 10
Cooking Time: 16 Minutes
Ingredients:
- ¼ pound all-natural ground pork sausage
- 3 eggs
- ¾ cup milk
- 20 foil muffin cups
- cooking spray
- 4 ounces sharp Cheddar cheese, grated

Directions:
1. Divide sausage into 3 portions and shape each into a thin patty.
2. Place patties in air fryer basket and cook 390°F/200°C for 6minutes.
3. While sausage is cooking, prepare the egg mixture. A large measuring cup or bowl with a pouring lip works best. Combine the eggs and milk and whisk until well blended. Set aside.
4. When sausage has cooked fully, remove patties from basket, drain well, and use a fork to crumble the meat into small pieces.
5. Double the foil cups into 10 sets. Remove paper liners from the top muffin cups and spray the foil cups lightly with cooking spray.
6. Divide crumbled sausage among the 10 muffin cup sets.
7. Top each with grated cheese, divided evenly among the cups.
8. Place 5 cups in air fryer basket.
9. Pour egg mixture into each cup, filling until each cup is at least ⅔ full.
10. Cook for 8 minutes and test for doneness. A knife inserted into the center shouldn't have any raw egg on it when removed.
11. If needed, cook 2 more minutes, until egg completely sets.
12. Repeat steps 8 through 11 for the remaining quiches.

Almond-pumpkin Porridge

Servings: 4
Cooking Time: 10 Minutes
Ingredients:
- 1 cup pumpkin seeds
- 2/3 cup chopped pecans
- 1/3 cup quick-cooking oats
- ¼ cup pumpkin purée
- ¼ cup diced pitted dates
- 1 tsp chia seeds
- 1 tsp sesame seeds
- 1 tsp dried berries
- 2 tbsp butter
- 2 tsp pumpkin pie spice
- ¼ cup honey
- 1 tbsp dark brown sugar
- ¼ cup almond flour
- Salt to taste

Directions:
1. Preheat air fryer at 350°F/175°C. Combine the pumpkin seeds, pecans, oats, pumpkin purée, dates, chia seeds, sesame seeds, dried berries, butter, pumpkin pie spice, honey, sugar, almond flour, and salt in a bowl. Press mixture into a greased cake pan. Place cake pan in the frying basket and Bake for 5 minutes, stirring once. Let cool completely for 10 minutes before crumbling.

Brown Sugar Grapefruit

Servings: 2
Cooking Time: 4 Minutes
Ingredients:
- 1 grapefruit
- 2 to 4 teaspoons brown sugar

Directions:
1. Preheat the air fryer to 400°F/205°C.
2. While the air fryer is Preheating, cut the grapefruit in half horizontally (in other words not through the stem or blossom end of the grapefruit). Slice the bottom of the grapefruit to help it sit flat on the counter if necessary. Using a sharp paring knife (serrated is great), cut around the grapefruit between the flesh of the fruit and the peel. Then, cut each segment away from the membrane so that it is sitting freely in the fruit.
3. Sprinkle 1 to 2 teaspoons of brown sugar on each half of the prepared grapefruit. Set up a rack in the air fryer basket (use an air fryer rack or make your own rack with some crumpled up aluminum foil). You don't have to use a rack, but doing so will get the grapefruit closer to the element so that the brown sugar can caramelize a little better. Transfer the grapefruit half to the rack in the air fryer basket. Depending on how big your grapefruit are and what size air fryer you have, you may need to do each half separately to make sure they sit flat.
4. Air-fry at 400°F/205°C for 4 minutes.
5. Remove and let it cool for just a minute before enjoying.

Vegetarians Recipes

Pesto Pepperoni Pizza Bread

Servings: 4
Cooking Time: 25 Minutes
Ingredients:
- 2 eggs, beaten
- 2 tbsp flour
- 2 tbsp cassava flour
- 1/3 cup whipping cream
- ¼ cup chopped pepperoni
- 1/3 cup grated mozzarella
- 2 tsp Italian seasoning
- ½ tsp baking powder
- ⅛ tsp salt
- 3 tsp grated Parmesan cheese
- ½ cup pesto

Directions:
1. Preheat air fryer to 300ºF/150°C. Combine all ingredients, except for the Parmesan and pesto sauce, in a bowl until mixed. Pour the batter into a pizza pan. Place it in the frying basket and Bake for 20 minutes. After, sprinkle Parmesan on top and cook for 1 minute. Let chill for 5 minutes before slicing. Serve with warmed pesto sauce.

Creamy Broccoli & Mushroom Casserole

Servings: 4
Cooking Time: 30 Minutes
Ingredients:
- 4 cups broccoli florets, chopped
- 1 cup crushed cheddar cheese crisps
- ¼ cup diced onion
- ¼ tsp dried thyme
- ¼ tsp dried marjoram
- ¼ tsp dried oregano
- ½ cup diced mushrooms
- 1 egg
- 2 tbsp sour cream
- ¼ cup mayonnaise
- Salt and pepper to taste

Directions:
1. Preheat air fryer to 350ºF/175°C. Combine all ingredients, except for the cheese crisps, in a bowl. Spoon mixture into a round cake pan. Place cake pan in the frying basket and Bake for 14 minutes. Let sit for 10 minutes. Distribute crushed cheddar cheese crisps over the top and serve.

Tropical Salsa

Servings: 4
Cooking Time: 15 Minutes
Ingredients:
- 1 cup pineapple cubes
- ½ apple, cubed
- Salt to taste
- ¼ tsp olive oil
- 2 tomatoes, diced
- 1 avocado, diced
- 3-4 strawberries, diced
- ¼ cup diced red onion
- 1 tbsp chopped cilantro
- 1 tbsp chopped parsley
- 2 cloves garlic, minced
- ½ tsp granulated sugar
- ½ lime, juiced

Directions:
1. Preheat air fryer at 400ºF/205°C. Combine pineapple cubes, apples, olive oil, and salt in a bowl. Place pineapple in the greased frying basket, and Air Fry for 8 minutes, shaking once. Transfer it to a bowl. Toss in tomatoes, avocado, strawberries, onion, cilantro, parsley, garlic, sugar, lime juice, and salt. Let chill in the fridge before using.

Cheddar Bean Taquitos

Servings: 4
Cooking Time: 25 Minutes
Ingredients:
- 1 cup refried beans
- 2 cups cheddar shreds
- ½ jalapeño pepper, minced
- ¼ chopped white onion
- 1 tsp oregano
- 15 soft corn tortillas

Directions:
1. Preheat air fryer at 350ºF/175°C. Spread refried beans, jalapeño pepper, white onion, oregano and cheddar shreds down the center of each corn tortilla. Roll each tortilla tightly. Place tacos, seam side down, in the frying basket, and Air Fry for 4 minutes. Serve immediately.

Crunchy Rice Paper Samosas

Servings: 2
Cooking Time: 20 Minutes
Ingredients:
- 1 boiled potato, mashed
- ¼ cup green peas
- 1 tsp garam masala powder
- ½ tsp ginger garlic paste
- ½ tsp cayenne pepper
- ½ tsp turmeric powder
- Salt and pepper to taste
- 3 rice paper wrappers

Directions:
1. Preheat air fryer to 350°F/175°C. Place the mashed potatoes in a bowl. Add the peas, garam masala powder, ginger garlic paste, cayenne pepper, turmeric powder, salt, and pepper and stir until ingredients are evenly blended.
2. Lay the rice paper wrappers out on a lightly floured surface. Divide the potato mixture between the wrappers and fold the top edges over to seal. Transfer the samosas to the greased frying basket and Air Fry for 12 minutes, flipping once until the samosas are crispy and flaky. Remove and leave to cool for 5 minutes. Serve and enjoy!

Green Bean Sautée

Servings: 4
Cooking Time: 25 Minutes
Ingredients:
- 1 ½ lb green beans, trimmed
- 1 tbsp olive oil
- ½ tsp garlic powder
- Salt and pepper to taste
- 4 garlic cloves, thinly sliced
- 1 tbsp fresh basil, chopped

Directions:
1. Preheat the air fryer to 375°F/190°C. Toss the beans with the olive oil, garlic powder, salt, and pepper in a bowl, then add to the frying basket. Air Fry for 6 minutes, shaking the basket halfway through the cooking time. Add garlic to the air fryer and cook for 3-6 minutes or until the green beans are tender and the garlic slices start to brown. Sprinkle with basil and serve warm.

Rigatoni With Roasted Onions, Fennel, Spinach And Lemon Pepper Ricotta

Servings: 2
Cooking Time: 13 Minutes
Ingredients:
- 1 red onion, rough chopped into large chunks
- 2 teaspoons olive oil, divided
- 1 bulb fennel, sliced ¼-inch thick
- ¾ cup ricotta cheese
- 1½ teaspoons finely chopped lemon zest, plus more for garnish
- 1 teaspoon lemon juice
- salt and freshly ground black pepper
- 8 ounces (½ pound) dried rigatoni pasta
- 3 cups baby spinach leaves

Directions:
1. Bring a large stockpot of salted water to a boil on the stovetop and Preheat the air fryer to 400°F.
2. While the water is coming to a boil, toss the chopped onion in 1 teaspoon of olive oil and transfer to the air fryer basket. Air-fry at 400°F/205°C for 5 minutes. Toss the sliced fennel with 1 teaspoon of olive oil and add this to the air fryer basket with the onions. Continue to air-fry at 400°F for 8 minutes, shaking the basket a few times during the cooking process.
3. Combine the ricotta cheese, lemon zest and juice, ¼ teaspoon of salt and freshly ground black pepper in a bowl and stir until smooth.
4. Add the dried rigatoni to the boiling water and cook according to the package directions. When the pasta is cooked al dente, reserve one cup of the pasta water and drain the pasta into a colander.
5. Place the spinach in a serving bowl and immediately transfer the hot pasta to the bowl, wilting the spinach. Add the roasted onions and fennel and toss together. Add a little pasta water to the dish if it needs moistening. Then, dollop the lemon pepper ricotta cheese on top and nestle it into the hot pasta. Garnish with more lemon zest if desired.

Italian-style Fried Cauliflower

Servings: 4
Cooking Time: 35 Minutes
Ingredients:
- 2 eggs
- 1/3 cup all-purpose flour
- ½ tsp Italian seasoning
- ½ cup bread crumbs
- 1 tsp garlic powder
- 3 tsp grated Parmesan cheese
- Salt and pepper to taste
- 1 head cauliflower, cut into florets
- ½ tsp ground coriander

Directions:
1. Preheat air fryer to 370°F/185°C. Set out 3 small bowls. In the first, mix the flour with Italian seasoning. In the second, beat the eggs. In the third bowl, combine the crumbs, garlic, Parmesan, ground coriander, salt, and pepper.
2. Dip the cauliflower in the flour, then dredge in egg, and finally in the bread crumb mixture. Place a batch of cauliflower in the greased frying basket and spray with cooking oil. Bake for 10-12 minutes, shaking once until golden. Serve warm and enjoy!

Spaghetti Squash And Kale Fritters With Pomodoro Sauce

Servings: 3
Cooking Time: 45 Minutes
Ingredients:
- 1½-pound spaghetti squash (about half a large or a whole small squash)
- olive oil
- ½ onion, diced
- ½ red bell pepper, diced
- 2 cloves garlic, minced
- 4 cups coarsely chopped kale
- salt and freshly ground black pepper
- 1 egg
- 1/3 cup breadcrumbs, divided*
- 1/3 cup grated Parmesan cheese
- ½ teaspoon dried rubbed sage
- pinch nutmeg
- Pomodoro Sauce:
- 2 tablespoons olive oil
- ½ onion, chopped
- 1 to 2 cloves garlic, minced
- 1 (28-ounce) can peeled tomatoes
- ¼ cup red wine
- 1 teaspoon Italian seasoning
- 2 tablespoons chopped fresh basil, plus more for garnish
- salt and freshly ground black pepper
- ½ teaspoon sugar (optional)

Directions:
1. Preheat the air fryer to 370°F/185°C.
2. Cut the spaghetti squash in half lengthwise and remove the seeds. Rub the inside of the squash with olive oil and season with salt and pepper. Place the squash, cut side up, into the air fryer basket and air-fry for 30 minutes, flipping the squash over halfway through the cooking process.
3. While the squash is cooking, Preheat a large sauté pan over medium heat on the stovetop. Add a little olive oil and sauté the onions for 3 minutes, until they start to soften. Add the red pepper and garlic and continue to sauté for an additional 4 minutes. Add the kale and season with salt and pepper. Cook for 2 more minutes, or until the kale is soft. Transfer the mixture to a large bowl and let it cool.
4. While the squash continues to cook, make the Pomodoro sauce. Preheat the large sauté pan again over

medium heat on the stovetop. Add the olive oil and sauté the onion and garlic for 2 to 3 minutes, until the onion begins to soften. Crush the canned tomatoes with your hands and add them to the pan along with the red wine and Italian seasoning and simmer for 20 minutes. Add the basil and season to taste with salt, pepper and sugar (if using).

5. When the spaghetti squash has finished cooking, use a fork to scrape the inside flesh of the squash onto a sheet pan. Spread the squash out and let it cool.
6. Once cool, add the spaghetti squash to the kale mixture, along with the egg, breadcrumbs, Parmesan cheese, sage, nutmeg, salt and freshly ground black pepper. Stir to combine well and then divide the mixture into 6 thick portions. You can shape the portions into patties, but I prefer to keep them a little random and unique in shape. Spray or brush the fritters with olive oil.
7. Preheat the air fryer to 370°F/185°C.
8. Brush the air fryer basket with a little olive oil and transfer the fritters to the basket. Air-fry the squash and kale fritters at 370°F/185°C for 15 minutes, flipping them over halfway through the cooking process.
9. Serve the fritters warm with the Pomodoro sauce spooned over the top or pooled on your plate. Garnish with the fresh basil leaves.

Roasted Vegetable Thai Green Curry

Servings: 4
Cooking Time: 16 Minutes
Ingredients:
- 1 (13-ounce) can coconut milk
- 3 tablespoons green curry paste
- 1 tablespoon soy sauce*
- 1 tablespoon rice wine vinegar
- 1 teaspoon sugar
- 1 teaspoon minced fresh ginger
- ½ onion, chopped
- 3 carrots, sliced
- 1 red bell pepper, chopped
- olive oil
- 10 stalks of asparagus, cut into 2-inch pieces
- 3 cups broccoli florets
- basmati rice for serving
- fresh cilantro
- crushed red pepper flakes (optional)

Directions:
1. Combine the coconut milk, green curry paste, soy sauce, rice wine vinegar, sugar and ginger in a medium saucepan and bring to a boil on the stovetop. Reduce the heat and simmer for 20 minutes while you cook the vegetables. Set aside.
2. Preheat the air fryer to 400°F/205°C.
3. Toss the onion, carrots, and red pepper together with a little olive oil and transfer the vegetables to the air fryer basket. Air-fry at 400°F/205°C for 10 minutes, shaking the basket a few times during the cooking process. Add the asparagus and broccoli florets and air-fry for an additional 6 minutes, again shaking the basket for even cooking.
4. When the vegetables are cooked to your liking, toss them with the green curry sauce and serve in bowls over basmati rice. Garnish with fresh chopped cilantro and crushed red pepper flakes.

Easy Zucchini Lasagna Roll-ups

Servings: 2
Cooking Time: 40 Minutes
Ingredients:
- 2 medium zucchini
- 2 tbsp lemon juice
- 1 ½ cups ricotta cheese
- 1 tbsp allspice
- 2 cups marinara sauce
- 1/3 cup mozzarella cheese

Directions:
1. Preheat air fryer to 400°F/205°C. Cut the ends of each zucchini, then slice into 1/4-inch thick pieces and drizzle with lemon juice. Roast for 5 minutes until slightly tender. Let cool slightly. Combine ricotta cheese and allspice in a bowl; set aside. Spread 2 tbsp of marinara sauce on the bottom of a baking pan. Spoon 1-2 tbsp of the ricotta mixture onto each slice, roll up each slice and place them spiral-side up in the pan. Scatter with the remaining ricotta mixture and drizzle with marinara sauce. Top with mozzarella cheese and Bake at 360°F/180°C for 20 minutes until the cheese is bubbly and golden brown. Serve warm.

Mushroom And Fried Onion Quesadilla

Servings: 2
Cooking Time: 33 Minutes
Ingredients:
- 1 onion, sliced
- 2 tablespoons butter, melted
- 10 ounces button mushrooms, sliced
- 2 tablespoons Worcestershire sauce
- salt and freshly ground black pepper
- 4 (8-inch) flour tortillas
- 2 cups grated Fontina cheese
- vegetable or olive oil

Directions:
1. Preheat the air fryer to 400°F/205°C.
2. Toss the onion slices with the melted butter and transfer them to the air fryer basket. Air-fry at 400°F for 15 minutes, shaking the basket several times during the cooking process. Add the mushrooms and Worcestershire sauce to the onions and stir to combine. Air-fry at 400°F for an additional 10 minutes. Season with salt and freshly ground black pepper.
3. Lay two of the tortillas on a cutting board. Top each tortilla with ½ cup of the grated cheese, half of the onion and mushroom mixture and then finally another ½ cup of the cheese. Place the remaining tortillas on top of the cheese and press down firmly.
4. Brush the air fryer basket with a little oil. Place a quesadilla in the basket and brush the top with a little oil. Secure the top tortilla to the bottom with three toothpicks and air-fry at 400°F/205°C for 5 minutes. Flip the quesadilla over by inverting it onto a plate and sliding it back into the basket. Remove the toothpicks and brush the other side with oil. Air-fry for an additional 3 minutes.
5. Invert the quesadilla onto a cutting board and cut it into 4 or 6 triangles. Serve immediately.

Zucchini Tamale Pie

Servings: 4
Cooking Time: 45 Minutes
Ingredients:
- 1 cup canned diced tomatoes with juice
- 1 zucchini, diced
- 3 tbsp safflower oil
- 1 cup cooked pinto beans
- 3 garlic cloves, minced
- 1 tbsp corn masa flour
- 1 tsp dried oregano
- ½ tsp ground cumin
- 1 tsp onion powder
- Salt to taste
- ½ tsp red chili flakes
- ½ cup ground cornmeal
- 1 tsp nutritional yeast
- 2 tbsp chopped cilantro
- ½ tsp lime zest

Directions:
1. Warm 2 tbsp of the oil in a skillet over medium heat and sauté the zucchini for 3 minutes or until they begin to brown. Add the beans, tomatoes, garlic, flour, oregano, cumin, onion powder, salt, and chili flakes. Cook over medium heat, stirring often, about 5 minutes until the mix is thick and no liquid remains. Remove from heat. Spray a baking pan with oil and pour the mix inside. Smooth out the top and set aside.
2. In a pot over high heat, add the cornmeal, 1 ½ cups of water, and salt. Whisk constantly as the mix begins to boil. Once it boils, reduce the heat to low. Add the yeast and oil and continue to cook, stirring often, for 10 minutes or until the mix is thick and hard to stir. Remove. Preheat air fryer to 325°F/160°C. Add the cilantro and lime zest into the cornmeal mix and thoroughly combine. Using a rubber spatula, spread it evenly over the filling in the baking pan to form a crust topping. Put in the frying basket and Bake for 20 minutes or until the top is golden. Let it cool for 5 to 10 minutes, then cut and serve.

Veggie-stuffed Bell Peppers

Servings: 4
Cooking Time: 40 Minutes
Ingredients:
- ½ cup canned fire-roasted diced tomatoes, including juice
- 2 red bell peppers
- 4 tsp olive oil
- ½ yellow onion, diced
- 1 zucchini, diced
- ¾ cup chopped mushrooms
- ¼ cup tomato sauce
- 2 tsp Italian seasoning
- ¼ tsp smoked paprika
- Salt and pepper to taste

Directions:
1. Cut bell peppers in half from top to bottom and discard the seeds. Brush inside and tops of the bell peppers with some olive oil. Set aside. Warm the remaining olive oil in a skillet over medium heat. Stir-fry the onion, zucchini, and mushrooms for 5 minutes until the onions are tender. Combine tomatoes and their juice, tomato sauce, Italian seasoning, paprika, salt, and pepper in a bowl.
2. Preheat air fryer to 350°F/175°C. Divide both mixtures between bell pepper halves. Place bell pepper halves in the frying basket and Air Fry for 8 minutes. Serve immediately.

Chicano Rice Bowls

Servings: 4
Cooking Time: 10 Minutes
Ingredients:
- 1 cup sour cream
- 2 tbsp milk
- 1 tsp ground cumin
- 1 tsp chili powder
- 1/8 tsp cayenne pepper
- 1 tbsp tomato paste
- 1 white onion, chopped
- 1 clove garlic, minced
- ½ tsp ground turmeric
- ½ tsp salt
- 1 cup canned black beans
- 1 cup canned corn kernels
- 1 tsp olive oil
- 4 cups cooked brown rice
- 3 tomatoes, diced
- 1 avocado, diced

Directions:
1. Whisk the sour cream, milk, cumin, ground turmeric, chili powder, cayenne pepper, and salt in a bowl. Let chill covered in the fridge until ready to use.
2. Preheat air fryer at 350°F/175°C. Combine beans, white onion, tomato paste, garlic, corn, and olive oil in a bowl. Transfer it into the frying basket and Air Fry for 5 minutes. Divide cooked rice into 4 serving bowls. Top each with bean mixture, tomatoes, and avocado and drizzle with sour cream mixture over. Serve immediately.

Mushroom Bolognese Casserole

Servings: 4
Cooking Time: 20 Minutes
Ingredients:
- 1 cup canned diced tomatoes
- 2 garlic cloves, minced
- 1 tsp onion powder
- ¾ tsp dried basil
- ¾ tsp dried oregano
- 1 cup chopped mushrooms
- 16 oz cooked spaghetti

Directions:
1. Preheat air fryer to 400°F/205°C. Whisk the tomatoes and their juices, garlic, onion powder, basil, oregano, and mushrooms in a baking pan. Cover with aluminum foil and Bake for 6 minutes. Slide out the pan and add the cooked spaghetti; stir to coat. Cover with aluminum foil and Bake for 3 minutes until and bubbly. Serve and enjoy!

Stuffed Portobellos

Servings: 4
Cooking Time: 45 Minutes
Ingredients:
- 1 cup cherry tomatoes
- 2 ¼ tsp olive oil
- 3 tbsp grated mozzarella
- 1 cup chopped baby spinach
- 1 garlic clove, minced

- ¼ tsp dried oregano
- ¼ tsp dried thyme
- Salt and pepper to taste
- ¼ cup bread crumbs
- 4 portobello mushrooms, stemmed and gills removed
- 1 tbsp chopped parsley

Directions:
1. Preheat air fryer to 360°F/180°C. Combine tomatoes, ¼ teaspoon olive oil, and salt in a small bowl. Arrange in a single layer in the parchment-lined frying basket and Air Fry for 10 minutes. Stir and flatten the tomatoes with the back of a spoon, then Air Fry for another 6-8 minutes. Transfer the tomatoes to a medium bowl and combine with spinach, garlic, oregano, thyme, pepper, bread crumbs, and the rest of the olive oil.
2. Place the mushrooms on a work surface with the gills facing up. Spoon tomato mixture and mozzarella cheese equally into the mushroom caps and transfer the mushrooms to the frying basket. Air Fry for 8-10 minutes until the mushrooms have softened and the tops are golden. Garnish with chopped parsley and serve.

Green Bean & Baby Potato Mix

Servings: 4
Cooking Time: 25 Minutes

Ingredients:
- 1 lb baby potatoes, halved
- 4 garlic cloves, minced
- 2 tbsp olive oil
- Salt and pepper to taste
- ½ tsp hot paprika
- ½ tbsp taco seasoning
- 1 tbsp chopped parsley
- ½ lb green beans, trimmed

Directions:
1. Preheat air fryer to 375°F/190°C. Toss potatoes, garlic, olive oil, salt, pepper, hot paprika, and taco seasoning in a large bowl. Arrange the potatoes in a single layer in the air fryer basket. Air Fry for 10 minutes, then stir in green beans. Air Fry for another 10 minutes. Serve hot sprinkled with parsley.

Garlicky Roasted Mushrooms

Servings: 4
Cooking Time: 30 Minutes

Ingredients:
- 16 garlic cloves, peeled
- 2 tsp olive oil
- 16 button mushrooms
- 2 tbsp fresh chives, snipped
- Salt and pepper to taste
- 1 tbsp white wine

Directions:
1. Preheat air fryer to 350°F/175°C. Coat the garlic with some olive oil in a baking pan, then Roast in the air fryer for 12 minutes. When done, take the pan out and stir in the mushrooms, salt, and pepper. Then add the remaining olive oil and white wine. Put the pan back into the fryer and Bake for 10-15 minutes until the mushrooms and garlic soften. Sprinkle with chives and serve warm.

Grilled Cheese Sandwich

Servings: 1
Cooking Time: 15 Minutes

Ingredients:
- 2 sprouted bread slices
- 1 tsp sunflower oil
- 2 Halloumi cheese slices
- 1 tsp mellow white miso
- 1 garlic clove, minced
- 2 tbsp kimchi
- 1 cup Iceberg lettuce, torn

Directions:
1. Preheat air fryer to 390°F/200°C. Brush the outside of the bread with sunflower oil. Put the sliced cheese, buttered sides facing out inside and close the sandwich. Put the sandwich in the frying basket and Air Fry for 12 minutes, flipping once until golden and crispy on the outside.
2. On a plate, open the sandwich and spread the miso and garlic clove over the inside of one slice. Top with kimchi and lettuce, close the sandwich, cut in half, and serve.

Chive Potato Pierogi

Servings: 4
Cooking Time: 55 Minutes

Ingredients:
- 2 boiled potatoes, mashed
- Salt and pepper to taste
- 1 tsp cumin powder
- 2 tbsp sour cream
- ¼ cup grated Parmesan
- 2 tbsp chopped chives
- 1 tbsp chopped parsley
- 1 ¼ cups flour
- ¼ tsp garlic powder
- ¾ cup Greek yogurt
- 1 egg

Directions:
1. Combine the mashed potatoes along with sour cream, cumin, parsley, chives, pepper, and salt and stir until slightly chunky. Mix the flour, salt, and garlic powder in a large bowl. Stir in yogurt until it comes together as a sticky dough. Knead in the bowl for about 2-3 minutes to make it smooth. Whisk the egg and 1 teaspoon of water in a small bowl. Roll out the dough on a lightly floured work surface to ¼-inch thickness. Cut out 12 circles with a cookie cutter.
2. Preheat air fryer to 350°F/175°C. Divide the potato mixture and Parmesan cheese between the dough circles. Brush the edges of them with the egg wash and fold the dough over the filling into half-moon shapes. Crimp the edges with a fork to seal. Arrange the on the greased frying basket and Air Fry for 8-10 minutes, turning the pierogies once, until the outside is golden. Serve warm.

Spicy Vegetable And Tofu Shake Fry

Servings: 4
Cooking Time: 17 Minutes

Ingredients:
- 4 teaspoons canola oil, divided
- 2 tablespoons rice wine vinegar
- 1 tablespoon sriracha chili sauce
- ¼ cup soy sauce*
- ½ teaspoon toasted sesame oil
- 1 teaspoon minced garlic
- 1 tablespoon minced fresh ginger
- 8 ounces extra firm tofu

- ½ cup vegetable stock or water
- 1 tablespoon honey
- 1 tablespoon cornstarch
- ½ red onion, chopped
- 1 red or yellow bell pepper, chopped
- 1 cup green beans, cut into 2-inch lengths
- 4 ounces mushrooms, sliced
- 2 scallions, sliced
- 2 tablespoons fresh cilantro leaves
- 2 teaspoons toasted sesame seeds

Directions:
1. Combine 1 tablespoon of the oil, vinegar, sriracha sauce, soy sauce, sesame oil, garlic and ginger in a small bowl. Cut the tofu into bite-sized cubes and toss the tofu in with the marinade while you prepare the other vegetables. When you are ready to start cooking, remove the tofu from the marinade and set it aside. Add the water, honey and cornstarch to the marinade and bring to a simmer on the stovetop, just until the sauce thickens. Set the sauce aside.
2. Preheat the air fryer to 400°F/205°C.
3. Toss the onion, pepper, green beans and mushrooms in a bowl with a little canola oil and season with salt. Air-fry at 400°F/205°C for 11 minutes, shaking the basket and tossing the vegetables every few minutes. When the vegetables are cooked to your preferred doneness, remove them from the air fryer and set aside.
4. Add the tofu to the air fryer basket and air-fry at 400°F/205°C for 6 minutes, shaking the basket a few times during the cooking process. Add the vegetables back to the basket and air-fry for another minute. Transfer the vegetables and tofu to a large bowl, add the scallions and cilantro leaves and toss with the sauce. Serve over rice with sesame seeds sprinkled on top.

Rainbow Quinoa Patties
Servings: 4
Cooking Time: 20 Minutes
Ingredients:
- 1 cup canned tri-bean blend, drained and rinsed
- 2 tbsp olive oil
- ½ tsp ground cumin
- ½ tsp garlic salt
- 1 tbsp paprika
- 1/3 cup uncooked quinoa
- 2 tbsp chopped onion
- ¼ cup shredded carrot
- 2 tbsp chopped cilantro
- 1 tsp chili powder
- ½ tsp salt
- 2 tbsp mascarpone cheese

Directions:
1. Place 1/3 cup of water, 1 tbsp of olive oil, cumin, and salt in a saucepan over medium heat and bring it to a boil. Remove from the heat and stir in quinoa. Let rest covered for 5 minutes.
2. Preheat air fryer at 350°F/175°C. Using the back of a fork, mash beans until smooth. Toss in cooked quinoa and the remaining ingredients. Form mixture into 4 patties. Place patties in the greased frying basket and Air Fry for 6 minutes, turning once, and brush with the remaining olive oil. Serve immediately.

Gorgeous Jalapeño Poppers
Servings: 6
Cooking Time: 25 Minutes
Ingredients:
- 6 center-cut bacon slices, halved
- 6 jalapeños, halved lengthwise
- 4 oz cream cheese
- ¼ cup grated Gruyere cheese
- 2 tbsp chives, chopped

Directions:
1. Scoop out seeds and membranes of the jalapeño halves, discard. Combine cream cheese, Gruyere cheese, and chives in a bowl. Fill the jalapeño halves with the cream cheese filling using a small spoon. Wrap each pepper with a slice of bacon and secure with a toothpick.
2. Preheat air fryer to 325°F/160°C. Put the stuffed peppers in a single layer on the greased frying basket and Bake until the peppers are tender, cheese is melted, and the bacon is brown, 11-13minutes. Serve warm and enjoy!

Ricotta Veggie Potpie
Servings: 4
Cooking Time: 30 Minutes
Ingredients:
- 1 ¼ cup flour
- ¾ cup ricotta cheese
- 1 tbsp olive oil
- 1 potato, peeled and diced
- ¼ cup diced mushrooms
- ¼ cup diced carrots
- ¼ cup diced celery
- ¼ cup diced yellow onion
- 1 garlic clove, minced
- 1 tbsp unsalted butter
- 1 cup milk
- ½ tsp ground black pepper
- 1 tsp dried thyme
- 2 tbsp dill, chopped

Directions:
1. Preheat air fryer to 350°F/175°C. Combine 1 cup flour and ricotta cheese in a medium bowl and stir until the dough comes together. Heat oil over medium heat in a small skillet. Stir in potato, mushroom, carrots, dill, thyme, celery, onion, and garlic. Cook for 4-5 minutes, often stirring, until the onions are soft and translucent.
2. Add butter and melt, then stir in the rest of the flour. Slowly pour in the milk and keep stirring. Simmer for 5 minutes until the sauce has thickened, then stir in pepper and thyme. Spoon the vegetable mixture into four 6-ounce ramekins. Cut the dough into 4 equal sections and work it into rounds that fit over the size of the ramekins. Top the ramekins with the dough, then place the ramekins in the frying basket. Bake for 10 minutes until the crust is golden. Serve hot and enjoy.

Spiced Vegetable Galette
Servings: 4
Cooking Time: 30 Minutes
Ingredients:
- ¼ cup cooked eggplant, chopped
- ¼ cup cooked zucchini, chopped
- 1 refrigerated pie crust
- 2 eggs
- ¼ cup milk
- Salt and pepper to taste

- 1 red chili, finely sliced
- ¼ cup tomato, chopped
- ½ cup shredded mozzarella cheese

Directions:
1. Preheat air fryer to 360°F/180°C. In a baking dish, add the crust and press firmly. Trim off any excess edges. Poke a few holes. Beat the eggs in a bowl. Stir in the milk, half of the cheese, eggplant, zucchini, tomato, red chili, salt, and pepper. Mix well. Transfer the mixture to the baking dish and place in the air fryer. Bake for 15 minutes or until firm and almost crusty. Slide the basket out and top with the remaining cheese. Cook further for 5 minutes, or until golden brown. Let cool slightly and serve.

General Tso's Cauliflower

Servings: 4
Cooking Time: 15 Minutes
Ingredients:
- 1 head cauliflower cut into florets
- ¾ cup all-purpose flour, divided*
- 3 eggs, lightly beaten
- 1 cup panko breadcrumbs*
- canola or peanut oil, in a spray bottle
- 2 tablespoons oyster sauce
- ¼ cup soy sauce
- 2 teaspoons chili paste
- 2 tablespoons rice wine vinegar
- 2 tablespoons sugar
- ¼ cup water
- white or brown rice for serving
- steamed broccoli

Directions:
1. Set up dredging station using three bowls. Place the cauliflower in a large bowl and sprinkle ¼ cup of the flour over the top. Place the eggs in a second bowl and combine the panko breadcrumbs and remaining ½ cup flour in a third bowl. Toss the cauliflower in the flour to coat all the florets thoroughly. Dip the cauliflower florets in the eggs and finally toss them in the breadcrumbs to coat on all sides. Place the coated cauliflower florets on a baking sheet and spray generously with canola or peanut oil.
2. Preheat the air fryer to 400°F/205°C.
3. Air-fry the cauliflower at 400°F/205°C for 15 minutes, flipping the florets over for the last 3 minutes of the cooking process and spraying again with oil.
4. While the cauliflower is air-frying, make the General Tso Sauce. Combine the oyster sauce, soy sauce, chili paste, rice wine vinegar, sugar and water in a saucepan and bring the mixture to a boil on the stove top. Lower the heat and let it simmer for 10 minutes, stirring occasionally.
5. When the timer is up on the air fryer, transfer the cauliflower to a large bowl, pour the sauce over it all and toss to coat. Serve with white or brown rice and some steamed broccoli.

Rice & Bean Burritos

Servings: 4
Cooking Time: 20 Minutes
Ingredients:
- 1 bell pepper, sliced
- ½ red onion, thinly sliced
- 2 garlic cloves, peeled
- 1 tbsp olive oil
- 1 cup cooked brown rice
- 1 can pinto beans
- ½ tsp salt
- ¼ tsp chili powder
- ¼ tsp ground cumin
- ¼ tsp smoked paprika
- 1 tbsp lime juice
- 4 tortillas
- 2 tsp grated Parmesan cheese
- 1 avocado, diced
- 4 tbsp salsa
- 2 tbsp chopped cilantro

Directions:
1. Preheat air fryer to 400°F/205°C. Combine bell pepper, onion, garlic, and olive oil. Place in the frying basket and Roast for 5 minutes. Shake and roast for another 5 minutes.
2. Remove the garlic from the basket and mince finely. Add to a large bowl along with brown rice, pinto beans, salt, chili powder, cumin, paprika, and lime juice. Divide the roasted vegetable mixture between the tortillas. Top with rice mixture, Parmesan, avocado, cilantro, and salsa. Fold in the sides, then roll the tortillas over the filling. Serve.

Pizza Portobello Mushrooms

Servings: 2
Cooking Time: 18 Minutes
Ingredients:
- 2 portobello mushroom caps, gills removed (see Figure 13-1)
- 1 teaspoon extra-virgin olive oil
- ¼ cup diced onion
- 1 teaspoon minced garlic
- 1 medium zucchini, shredded
- 1 teaspoon dried oregano
- ½ teaspoon black pepper
- ¼ teaspoon salt
- ⅓ cup marinara sauce
- ¼ cup shredded part-skim mozzarella cheese
- ¼ teaspoon red pepper flakes
- 2 tablespoons Parmesan cheese
- 2 tablespoons chopped basil

Directions:
1. Preheat the air fryer to 370°F/185°C.
2. Lightly spray the mushrooms with an olive oil mist and place into the air fryer to cook for 10 minutes, cap side up.
3. Add the olive oil to a pan and sauté the onion and garlic together for about 2 to 4 minutes. Stir in the zucchini, oregano, pepper, and salt, and continue to cook. When the zucchini has cooked down (usually about 4 to 6 minutes), add in the marinara sauce. Remove from the heat and stir in the mozzarella cheese.
4. Remove the mushrooms from the air fryer basket when cooking completes. Reset the temperature to 350°F/175°C.
5. Using a spoon, carefully stuff the mushrooms with the zucchini marinara mixture.
6. Return the stuffed mushrooms to the air fryer basket and cook for 5 to 8 minutes, or until the cheese is lightly browned. You should be able to easily insert a fork into the mushrooms when they're cooked.
7. Remove the mushrooms and sprinkle the red pepper flakes, Parmesan cheese, and fresh basil over the top.
8. Serve warm.

Zucchini & Bell Pepper Stir-fry

Servings: 4
Cooking Time: 25 Minutes
Ingredients:
- 1 zucchini, cut into rounds
- 1 red bell pepper, sliced
- 3 garlic cloves, sliced
- 2 tbsp olive oil
- 1/3 cup vegetable broth
- 1 tbsp lemon juice
- 2 tsp cornstarch
- 1 tsp dried basil
- Salt and pepper to taste

Directions:
1. Preheat the air fryer to 400°F/205°C. Combine the veggies, garlic, and olive oil in a bowl. Put the bowl in the frying basket and Air Fry the zucchini mixture for 5 minutes, stirring once; drain. While the veggies are cooking, whisk the broth, lemon juice, cornstarch, basil, salt, and pepper in a bowl. Pour the broth into the bowl along with the veggies and stir. Air Fry for 5-9 more minutes until the veggies are tender and the sauce is thick. Serve and enjoy!

Tofu & Spinach Lasagna

Servings: 4
Cooking Time: 30 Minutes
Ingredients:
- 8 oz cooked lasagne noodles
- 1 tbsp olive oil
- 2 cups crumbled tofu
- 2 cups fresh spinach
- 2 tbsp cornstarch
- 1 tsp onion powder
- Salt and pepper to taste
- 2 garlic cloves, minced
- 2 cups marinara sauce
- ½ cup shredded mozzarella

Directions:
1. Warm the olive oil in a large pan over medium heat. Add the tofu and spinach and stir-fry for a minute. Add the cornstarch, onion powder, salt, pepper, and garlic. Stir until the spinach wilts. Remove from heat.
2. Preheat air fryer to 390°F/200°C. Pour a thin layer of pasta sauce in a baking pan. Layer 2-3 lasagne noodles on top of the marinara sauce. Top with a little more sauce and some of the tofu mix. Add another 2-3 noodles on top, then another layer of sauce, then another layer of tofu. Finish with a layer of noodles and a final layer of sauce. Sprinkle with mozzarella cheese on top. Place the pan in the air fryer and Bake for 15 minutes or until the noodle edges are browned and the cheese is melted. Cut and serve.

Colorful Vegetable Medley

Servings: 4
Cooking Time: 20 Minutes
Ingredients:
- 1 lb green beans, chopped
- 2 carrots, cubed
- Salt and pepper to taste
- 1 zucchini, cut into chunks
- 1 red bell pepper, sliced

Directions:
1. Preheat air fryer to 390°F/200°C. Combine green beans, carrots, salt and pepper in a large bowl. Spray with cooking oil and transfer to the frying basket. Roast for 6 minutes.
2. Combine zucchini and red pepper in a bowl. Season to taste and spray with cooking oil; set aside. When the cooking time is up, add the zucchini and red pepper to the basket. Cook for another 6 minutes. Serve and enjoy.

Italian Stuffed Bell Peppers

Servings: 4
Cooking Time: 75 Minutes
Ingredients:
- 4 green and red bell peppers, tops and insides discarded
- 2 russet potatoes, scrubbed and perforated with a fork
- 2 tsp olive oil
- 2 Italian sausages, cubed
- 2 tbsp milk
- 2 tbsp yogurt
- 1 tsp olive oil
- 1 tbsp Italian seasoning
- Salt and pepper to taste
- ¼ cup canned corn kernels
- ½ cup mozzarella shreds
- 2 tsp chopped parsley
- 1 cup bechamel sauce

Directions:
1. Preheat air fryer at 400°F/205°C. Rub olive oil over both potatoes and sprinkle with salt and pepper. Place them in the frying basket and Bake for 45 minutes, flipping at 30 minutes mark. Let cool onto a cutting board for 5 minutes until cool enough to handle. Scoop out cooled potato into a bowl. Discard skins.
2. Place Italian sausages in the frying basket and Air Fry for 2 minutes. Using the back of a fork, mash cooked potatoes, yogurt, milk, olive oil, Italian seasoning, salt, and pepper until smooth. Toss in cooked sausages, corn, and mozzarella cheese. Stuff bell peppers with the potato mixture. Place bell peppers in the frying basket and Bake for 10 minutes. Serve immediately sprinkled with parsley and bechamel sauce on side.

Tacos

Servings: 24
Cooking Time: 8 Minutes Per Batch
Ingredients:
- 1 24-count package 4-inch corn tortillas
- 1½ cups refried beans (about ¾ of a 15-ounce can)
- 4 ounces sharp Cheddar cheese, grated
- ½ cup salsa
- oil for misting or cooking spray

Directions:
1. Preheat air fryer to 390°F/200°C.
2. Wrap refrigerated tortillas in damp paper towels and microwave for 30 to 60 seconds to warm. If necessary, rewarm tortillas as you go to keep them soft enough to fold without breaking.
3. Working with one tortilla at a time, top with 1 tablespoon of beans, 1 tablespoon of grated cheese, and 1 teaspoon of salsa. Fold over and press down very gently on the center. Press edges firmly all around to seal. Spray both sides with oil or cooking spray.
4. Cooking in two batches, place half the tacos in the air fryer basket. To cook 12 at a time, you may need to stand them upright and lean some against the sides of basket. It's okay if they're crowded as long as you leave a little room for air to circulate around them.
5. Cook for 8 minutes or until golden brown and crispy.
6. Repeat steps 4 and 5 to cook remaining tacos.

Roasted Vegetable Pita Pizza

Servings: 4
Cooking Time: 20 Minutes
Ingredients:
- 1 medium red bell pepper, seeded and cut into quarters
- 1 teaspoon extra-virgin olive oil
- ⅛ teaspoon black pepper
- ⅛ teaspoon salt
- Two 6-inch whole-grain pita breads
- 6 tablespoons pesto sauce
- ¼ small red onion, thinly sliced
- ½ cup shredded part-skim mozzarella cheese

Directions:
1. Preheat the air fryer to 400°F/205°C.
2. In a small bowl, toss the bell peppers with the olive oil, pepper, and salt.
3. Place the bell peppers in the air fryer and cook for 15 minutes, shaking every 5 minutes to prevent burning.
4. Remove the peppers and set aside. Turn the air fryer temperature down to 350°F/175°C.
5. Lay the pita bread on a flat surface. Cover each with half the pesto sauce; then top with even portions of the red bell peppers and onions. Sprinkle cheese over the top. Spray the air fryer basket with olive oil mist.
6. Carefully lift the pita bread into the air fryer basket with a spatula.
7. Cook for 5 to 8 minutes, or until the outer edges begin to brown and the cheese is melted.
8. Serve warm with desired sides.

Garlicky Brussel Sprouts With Saffron Aioli

Servings: 4
Cooking Time: 20 Minutes
Ingredients:
- 1 lb Brussels sprouts, halved
- 1 tsp garlic powder
- Salt and pepper to taste
- ½ cup mayonnaise
- ½ tbsp olive oil
- 1 tbsp Dijon mustard
- 1 tsp minced garlic
- Salt and pepper to taste
- ½ tsp liquid saffron

Directions:
1. Preheat air fryer to 380°F/195°C. Combine the Brussels sprouts, garlic powder, salt and pepper in a large bowl. Place in the fryer and spray with cooking oil. Bake for 12-14 minutes, shaking once, until just brown.
2. Meanwhile, in a small bowl, mix mayonnaise, olive oil, mustard, garlic, saffron, salt and pepper. When the Brussels sprouts are slightly cool, serve with aioli. Enjoy!

Veggie Samosas

Servings: 6
Cooking Time: 30 Minutes
Ingredients:
- 2 tbsp cream cheese, softened
- 3 tbsp minced onion
- 2 garlic cloves, minced
- 2 tbsp grated carrots
- 3 tsp olive oil
- 3 tbsp cooked green lentils
- 6 phyllo dough sheets

Directions:
1. Preheat air fryer to 390°F/200°C. Toss the onion, garlic, carrots, and some oil in a baking pan and stir. Place in the fryer and Air Fry for 2-4 minutes until the veggies are soft. Pour into a bowl. Add the lentils and cream cheese; let chill.
2. To make the dough, first lay a sheet of phyllo on a clean workspace and spritz with some olive oil, then add a second sheet on top. Repeat with the rest of the phyllo sheets until you have 3 stacks of 2 layers. Cut the stacks into 4 lengthwise strips. Add 2 tsp of the veggie mix at the bottom of each strip, then make a triangle by lifting one corner over the filling. Continue the triangle making, like folding a flag, and seal with water. Repeat until all strips are filled and folded. Bake the samosas in the air fryer for 4-7 minutes, until golden and crisp. Serve warm.

Hearty Salad

Servings: 2
Cooking Time: 15 Minutes
Ingredients:
- 5 oz cauliflower, cut into florets
- 2 grated carrots
- 1 tbsp olive oil
- 1 tbsp lemon juice
- 2 tbsp raisins
- 2 tbsp roasted pepitas
- 2 tbsp diced red onion
- ¼ cup mayonnaise
- 1/8 tsp black pepper
- 1 tsp cumin
- ½ tsp chia seeds
- ½ tsp sesame seeds

Directions:
1. Preheat air fryer at 350°F/175°C. Combine the cauliflower, cumin, olive oil, black pepper and lemon juice in a bowl, place it in the frying basket, and Bake for 5 minutes. Transfer it to a serving dish. Toss in the remaining ingredients. Let chill covered in the fridge until ready to use. Serve sprinkled with sesame and chia seeds.

Home-style Cinnamon Rolls

Servings: 4
Cooking Time: 40 Minutes
Ingredients:
- ½ pizza dough
- 1/3 cup dark brown sugar
- ¼ cup butter, softened
- ½ tsp ground cinnamon

Directions:
1. Preheat air fryer to 360°F/180°C. Roll out the dough into a rectangle. Using a knife, spread the brown sugar and butter, covering all the edges, and sprinkle with cinnamon. Fold the long side of the dough into a log, then cut it into 8 equal pieces, avoiding compression. Place the rolls, spiral-side up, onto a parchment-lined sheet. Let rise for 20 minutes. Grease the rolls with cooking spray and Bake for 8 minutes until golden brown. Serve right away.

Vegetarian Paella

Servings: 3
Cooking Time: 50 Minutes
Ingredients:
- ½ cup chopped artichoke hearts
- ½ sliced red bell peppers
- 4 mushrooms, thinly sliced
- ½ cup canned diced tomatoes
- ½ cup canned chickpeas
- 3 tbsp hot sauce
- 2 tbsp lemon juice
- 1 tbsp allspice
- 1 cup rice

Directions:
1. Preheat air fryer to 400°F/205°C. Combine the artichokes, peppers, mushrooms, tomatoes and their juices, chickpeas, hot sauce, lemon juice, and allspice in a baking pan. Roast for 10 minutes. Pour in rice and 2 cups of boiling water, cover with aluminum foil, and Roast for 22 minutes. Discard the foil and Roast for 3 minutes until the top is crisp. Let cool slightly before stirring. Serve.

Spinach And Cheese Calzone

Servings: 2
Cooking Time: 10 Minutes
Ingredients:
- ⅔ cup frozen chopped spinach, thawed
- 1 cup grated mozzarella cheese
- 1 cup ricotta cheese
- ½ teaspoon Italian seasoning
- ½ teaspoon salt
- freshly ground black pepper
- 1 store-bought or homemade pizza dough* (about 12 to 16 ounces)
- 2 tablespoons olive oil
- pizza or marinara sauce (optional)

Directions:
1. Drain and squeeze all the water out of the thawed spinach and set it aside. Mix the mozzarella cheese, ricotta cheese, Italian seasoning, salt and freshly ground black pepper together in a bowl. Stir in the chopped spinach.
2. Divide the dough in half. With floured hands or on a floured surface, stretch or roll one half of the dough into a 10-inch circle. Spread half of the cheese and spinach mixture on half of the dough, leaving about one inch of dough empty around the edge.
3. Fold the other half of the dough over the cheese mixture, almost to the edge of the bottom dough to form a half moon. Fold the bottom edge of dough up over the top edge and crimp the dough around the edges in order to make the crust and seal the calzone. Brush the dough with olive oil. Repeat with the second half of dough to make the second calzone.
4. Preheat the air fryer to 360°F/180°C.
5. Brush or spray the air fryer basket with olive oil. Air-fry the calzones one at a time for 10 minutes, flipping the calzone over half way through. Serve with warm pizza or marinara sauce if desired.

Tex-mex Potatoes With Avocado Dressing

Servings: 2
Cooking Time: 60 Minutes
Ingredients:
- ¼ cup chopped parsley, dill, cilantro, chives
- ¼ cup yogurt
- ½ avocado, diced
- 2 tbsp milk
- 2 tsp lemon juice
- ½ tsp lemon zest
- 1 green onion, chopped
- 2 cloves garlic, quartered
- Salt and pepper to taste
- 2 tsp olive oil
- 2 russet potatoes, scrubbed and perforated with a fork
- 1 cup steamed broccoli florets
- ½ cup canned white beans

Directions:
1. In a food processor, blend the yogurt, avocado, milk, lemon juice, lemon zest, green onion, garlic, parsley, dill, cilantro, chives, salt and pepper until smooth. Transfer it to a small bowl and let chill the dressing covered in the fridge until ready to use.
2. Preheat air fryer at 400°F/205°C. Rub olive oil over both potatoes and sprinkle with salt and pepper. Place them in the frying basket and Bake for 45 minutes, flipping at 30 minutes mark. Let cool onto a cutting board for 5 minutes until cool enough to handle. Cut each potato lengthwise into slices and pinch ends together to open up each slice. Stuff broccoli and beans into potatoes and put them back into the basket, and cook for 3 more minutes. Drizzle avocado dressing over and serve.

Powerful Jackfruit Fritters

Servings: 4
Cooking Time: 30 Minutes
Ingredients:
- 1 can jackfruit, chopped
- 1 egg, beaten
- 1 tbsp Dijon mustard
- 1 tbsp mayonnaise
- 1 tbsp prepared horseradish
- 2 tbsp grated yellow onion
- 2 tbsp chopped parsley
- 2 tbsp chopped nori
- 2 tbsp flour
- 1 tbsp Cajun seasoning
- ¼ tsp garlic powder
- ¼ tsp salt
- 2 lemon wedges

Directions:
1. In a bowl, combine jackfruit, egg, mustard, mayonnaise, horseradish, onion, parsley, nori, flour, Cajun seasoning, garlic, and salt. Let chill in the fridge for 15 minutes. Preheat air fryer to 350°F/175°C. Divide the mixture into 12 balls. Place them in the frying basket and Air Fry for 10 minutes. Serve with lemon wedges.

Honey Pear Chips

Servings: 4
Cooking Time: 30 Minutes
Ingredients:
- 2 firm pears, thinly sliced
- 1 tbsp lemon juice
- ½ tsp ground cinnamon
- 1 tsp honey

Directions:

1. Preheat air fryer to 380°F/195°C. Arrange the pear slices on the parchment-lined cooking basket. Drizzle with lemon juice and honey and sprinkle with cinnamon. Air Fry for 6-8 minutes, shaking the basket once, until golden. Leave to cool. Serve immediately or save for later in an airtight container. Good for 2 days.

Vegan Buddha Bowls(2)
Servings: 4
Cooking Time: 20 Minutes
Ingredients:
- 1 carrot, peeled and julienned
- ½ onion, sliced into half-moons
- ¼ cup apple cider vinegar
- ½ tsp ground ginger
- ⅛ tsp cayenne pepper
- 1 parsnip, diced
- 1 tsp avocado oil
- 4 oz extra-firm tofu, cubed
- ½ tsp five-spice powder
- ½ tsp chili powder
- 2 tsp fresh lime zest
- 1 cup fresh arugula
- ½ cup cooked quinoa
- 2 tbsp canned kidney beans
- 2 tbsp canned sweetcorn
- 1 avocado, diced
- 2 tbsp pine nuts

Directions:
1. Preheat air fryer to 350°F/175°C. Combine carrot, vinegar, ginger, and cayenne in a bowl. In another bowl, combine onion, parsnip, and avocado oil. In a third bowl, mix the tofu, five-spice powder, and chili powder.
2. Place the onion mixture in the greased basket. Air Fry for 6 minutes. Stir in tofu mixture and cook for 8 more minutes. Mix in lime zest. Divide arugula, cooked quinoa, kidney beans, sweetcorn, drained carrots, avocado, pine nuts, and tofu mixture between 2 bowls. Serve.

Spicy Bean Patties
Servings: 4
Cooking Time: 20 Minutes
Ingredients:
- 1 cup canned black beans
- 1 bread slice, torn
- 2 tbsp spicy brown mustard
- 1 tbsp chili powder
- 1 egg white
- 2 tbsp grated carrots
- ¼ diced green bell pepper
- 1-2 jalapeño peppers, diced
- ¼ tsp ground cumin
- ¼ tsp smoked paprika
- 2 tbsp cream cheese
- 1 tbsp olive oil

Directions:
1. Preheat air fryer at 350°F/175°C. Using a fork, mash beans until smooth. Stir in the remaining ingredients, except olive oil. Form mixture into 4 patties. Place bean patties in the greased frying basket and Air Fry for 6 minutes, turning once, and brush with olive oil. Serve immediately.

Lentil Burritos With Cilantro Chutney
Servings: 4
Cooking Time: 30 Minutes
Ingredients:
- 1 cup cilantro chutney
- 1 lb cooked potatoes, mashed
- 2 tsp sunflower oil
- 3 garlic cloves, minced
- 1 ½ tbsp fresh lime juice
- 1 ½ tsp cumin powder
- 1 tsp onion powder
- 1 tsp coriander powder
- Salt to taste
- ½ tsp turmeric
- ¼ tsp cayenne powder
- 4 large flour tortillas
- 1 cup cooked lentils
- ½ cup shredded cabbage
- ¼ cup minced red onions

Directions:
1. Preheat air fryer to 390°F/200°C. Place the mashed potatoes, sunflower oil, garlic, lime, cumin, onion powder, coriander, salt, turmeric, and cayenne in a large bowl. Stir well until combined. Lay the tortillas out flat on the counter. In the middle of each, distribute the potato filling. Add some of the lentils, cabbage, and red onions on top of the potatoes. Close the wraps by folding the bottom of the tortillas up and over the filling, then folding the sides in, then roll the bottom up to form a burrito. Place the wraps in the greased frying basket, seam side down. Air Fry for 6-8 minutes, flipping once until golden and crispy. Serve topped with cilantro chutney.

Farfalle With White Sauce
Servings: 4
Cooking Time: 30 Minutes
Ingredients:
- 4 cups cauliflower florets
- 1 medium onion, chopped
- 8 oz farfalle pasta
- 2 tbsp chives, minced
- ½ cup cashew pieces
- 1 tbsp nutritional yeast
- 2 large garlic cloves, peeled
- 2 tbsp fresh lemon juice
- Salt and pepper to taste

Directions:
1. Preheat air fryer to 390°F/200°C. Put the cauliflower in the fryer, spray with oil, and Bake for 8 minutes. Remove the basket, stir, and add the onion. Roast for 10 minutes or until the cauliflower is golden and the onions soft. Cook the farfalle pasta according to the package directions. Set aside. Put the roasted cauliflower and onions along with the cashews, 1 ½ of cups water, yeast, garlic, lemon, salt, and pepper in a blender. Blend until creamy. Pour a large portion of the sauce on top of the warm pasta and add the minced scallions. Serve.

Effortless Mac 'n' Cheese

Servings: 4
Cooking Time: 15 Minutes
Ingredients:
- 1 cup heavy cream
- 1 cup milk
- ½ cup mozzarella cheese
- 2 tsp grated Parmesan cheese
- 16 oz cooked elbow macaroni

Directions:
1. Preheat air fryer to 400°F/205°C. Whisk the heavy cream, milk, mozzarella cheese, and Parmesan cheese until smooth in a bowl. Stir in the macaroni and pour into a baking dish. Cover with foil and Bake in the air fryer for 6 minutes. Remove foil and Bake until cooked through and bubbly, 3-5 minutes. Serve warm.

Sweet Corn Bread

Servings: 6
Cooking Time: 35 Minutes
Ingredients:
- 2 eggs, beaten
- ½ cup cornmeal
- ½ cup pastry flour
- 1/3 cup sugar
- 1 tsp lemon zest
- ½ tbsp baking powder
- ¼ tsp salt
- ¼ tsp baking soda
- ½ tbsp lemon juice
- ½ cup milk
- ¼ cup sunflower oil

Directions:
1. Preheat air fryer to 350°F/175°C. Add the cornmeal, flour, sugar, lemon zest, baking powder, salt, and baking soda in a bowl. Stir with a whisk until combined. Add the eggs, lemon juice, milk, and oil to another bowl and stir well. Add the wet mixture to the dry mixture and stir gently until combined. Spray a baking pan with oil. Pour the batter in and Bake in the fryer for 25 minutes or until golden and a knife inserted in the center comes out clean. Cut into wedges and serve.

Berbere Eggplant Dip

Servings:4
Cooking Time: 35 Minutes
Ingredients:
- 1 eggplant, halved lengthwise
- 3 tsp olive oil
- 2 tsp pine nuts
- ¼ cup tahini
- 1 tbsp lemon juice
- 2 cloves garlic, minced
- ¼ tsp berbere seasoning
- ⅛ tsp ground cumin
- Salt and pepper to taste
- 1 tbsp chopped parsley

Directions:
1. Preheat air fryer to 370°F/185°C. Brush the eggplant with some olive oil. With a fork, pierce the eggplant flesh a few times. Place them, flat sides-down, in the frying basket. Air Fry for 25 minutes. Transfer the eggplant to a cutting board and let cool for 3 minutes until easy to handle. Place pine nuts in the frying basket and Air Fry for 2 minutes, shaking every 30 seconds. Set aside in a bowl.
2. Scoop out the eggplant flesh and add to a food processor. Add in tahini, lemon juice, garlic, berbere seasoning, cumin, salt, and black pepper and pulse until smooth. Transfer to a serving bowl. Scatter with toasted pine nuts, parsley, and the remaining olive oil. Serve immediately.

Caprese-style Sandwiches

Servings: 2
Cooking Time: 20 Minutes
Ingredients:
- 2 tbsp balsamic vinegar
- 4 sandwich bread slices
- 2 oz mozzarella shreds
- 3 tbsp pesto sauce
- 2 tomatoes, sliced
- 8 basil leaves
- 8 baby spinach leaves
- 2 tbsp olive oil

Directions:
1. Preheat air fryer at 350°F/175°C. Drizzle balsamic vinegar on the bottom of bread slices and smear with pesto sauce. Then, layer mozzarella cheese, tomatoes, baby spinach leaves and basil leaves on top. Add top bread slices. Rub the outside top and bottom of each sandwich with olive oil. Place them in the frying basket and Bake for 5 minutes, flipping once. Serve right away.

Vegetable Couscous

Servings: 4
Cooking Time: 10 Minutes
Ingredients:
- 4 ounces white mushrooms, sliced
- ½ medium green bell pepper, julienned
- 1 cup cubed zucchini
- ¼ small onion, slivered
- 1 stalk celery, thinly sliced
- ¼ teaspoon ground coriander
- ¼ teaspoon ground cumin
- salt and pepper
- 1 tablespoon olive oil
- Couscous
- ¾ cup uncooked couscous
- 1 cup vegetable broth or water
- ½ teaspoon salt (omit if using salted broth)

Directions:
1. Combine all vegetables in large bowl. Sprinkle with coriander, cumin, and salt and pepper to taste. Stir well, add olive oil, and stir again to coat vegetables evenly.
2. Place vegetables in air fryer basket and cook at 390°F/200°C for 5minutes. Stir and cook for 5 more minutes, until tender.
3. While vegetables are cooking, prepare the couscous: Place broth or water and salt in large saucepan. Heat to boiling, stir in couscous, cover, and remove from heat.
4. Let couscous sit for 5minutes, stir in cooked vegetables, and serve hot.

Easy Cheese & Spinach Lasagna

Servings: 6
Cooking Time: 50 Minutes
Ingredients:
- 1 zucchini, cut into strips
- 1 tbsp butter
- 4 garlic cloves, minced
- ½ yellow onion, diced
- 1 tsp dried oregano
- ¼ tsp red pepper flakes
- 1 can diced tomatoes
- 4 oz ricotta
- 3 tbsp grated mozzarella
- ½ cup grated cheddar
- 3 tsp grated Parmesan cheese
- ⅛ cup chopped basil
- 2 tbsp chopped parsley
- Salt and pepper to taste
- ¼ tsp ground nutmeg

Directions:
1. Preheat air fryer to 375°F/190°C. Melt butter in a medium skillet over medium heat. Stir in half of the garlic and onion and cook for 2 minutes. Stir in oregano and red pepper flakes and cook for 1 minute. Reduce the heat to medium-low and pour in crushed tomatoes and their juices. Cover the skillet and simmer for 5 minutes.
2. Mix ricotta, mozzarella, cheddar cheese, rest of the garlic, basil, black pepper, and nutmeg in a large bowl. Arrange a layer of zucchini strips in the baking dish. Scoop 1/3 of the cheese mixture and spread evenly over the zucchini. Spread 1/3 of the tomato sauce over the cheese. Repeat the steps two more times, then top the lasagna with Parmesan cheese. Bake in the frying basket for 25 minutes until the mixture is bubbling and the mozzarella is melted. Allow sitting for 10 minutes before cutting. Serve warm sprinkled with parsley and enjoy!

Smoked Paprika Sweet Potato Fries

Servings: 4
Cooking Time: 35 Minutes
Ingredients:
- 2 sweet potatoes, peeled
- 1 ½ tbsp cornstarch
- 1 tbsp canola oil
- 1 tbsp olive oil
- 1 tsp smoked paprika
- 1 tsp garlic powder
- Salt and pepper to taste
- 1 cup cocktail sauce

Directions:
1. Cut the potatoes lengthwise to form French fries. Put in a resealable plastic bag and add cornstarch. Seal and shake to coat the fries. Combine the canola oil, olive oil, paprika, garlic powder, salt, and pepper fries in a large bowl. Add the sweet potato fries and mix to combine.
2. Preheat air fryer to 380°F/195°C. Place fries in the greased basket and fry for 20-25 minutes, shaking the basket once until crisp. Drizzle with Cocktail sauce to serve.

Curried Potato, Cauliflower And Pea Turnovers

Servings: 4
Cooking Time: 40 Minutes
Ingredients:
- Dough:
- 2 cups all-purpose flour
- ½ teaspoon baking powder
- 1 teaspoon salt
- freshly ground black pepper
- ¼ teaspoon dried thyme
- ¼ cup canola oil
- ½ to ⅔ cup water
- Turnover Filling:
- 1 tablespoon canola or vegetable oil
- 1 onion, finely chopped
- 1 clove garlic, minced
- 1 tablespoon grated fresh ginger
- ½ teaspoon cumin seeds
- ½ teaspoon fennel seeds
- 1 teaspoon curry powder
- 2 russet potatoes, diced
- 2 cups cauliflower florets
- ½ cup frozen peas
- 2 tablespoons chopped fresh cilantro
- salt and freshly ground black pepper
- 2 tablespoons butter, melted
- mango chutney, for serving

Directions:
1. Start by making the dough. Combine the flour, baking powder, salt, pepper and dried thyme in a mixing bowl or the bowl of a stand mixer. Drizzle in the canola oil and pinch it together with your fingers to turn the flour into a crumby mixture. Stir in the water (enough to bring the dough together). Knead the dough for 5 minutes or so until it is smooth. Add a little more water or flour as needed. Let the dough rest while you make the turnover filling.
2. Preheat a large skillet on the stovetop over medium-high heat. Add the oil and sauté the onion until it starts to become tender – about 4 minutes. Add the garlic and ginger and continue to cook for another minute. Add the dried spices and toss everything to coat. Add the potatoes and cauliflower to the skillet and pour in 1½ cups of water. Simmer everything together for 20 to 25 minutes, or until the potatoes are soft and most of the water has evaporated. If the water has evaporated and the vegetables still need more time, just add a little water and continue to simmer until everything is tender. Stir well, crushing the potatoes and cauliflower a little as you do so. Stir in the peas and cilantro, season to taste with salt and freshly ground black pepper and set aside to cool.
3. Divide the dough into 4 balls. Roll the dough balls out into ¼-inch thick circles. Divide the cooled potato filling between the dough circles, placing a mound of the filling on one side of each piece of dough, leaving an empty border around the edge of the dough. Brush the edges of the dough with a little water and fold one edge of circle over the filling to meet the other edge of the circle, creating a half moon. Pinch the edges together with your fingers and then press the edge with the tines of a fork to decorate and seal.
4. Preheat the air fryer to 380°F/195°C.
5. Spray or brush the air fryer basket with oil. Brush the turnovers with the melted butter and place 2 turnovers into the air fryer basket. Air-fry for 15 minutes. Flip the turnovers over and air-fry for another 5 minutes. Repeat with the remaining 2 turnovers.
6. These will be very hot when they come out of the air fryer. Let them cool for at least 20 minutes before serving warm with mango chutney.

Roasted Vegetable, Brown Rice And Black Bean Burrito

Servings: 2
Cooking Time: 20 Minutes
Ingredients:
- ½ zucchini, sliced ¼-inch thick
- ½ red onion, sliced
- 1 yellow bell pepper, sliced
- 2 teaspoons olive oil
- salt and freshly ground black pepper
- 2 burrito size flour tortillas
- 1 cup grated pepper jack cheese
- ½ cup cooked brown rice
- ½ cup canned black beans, drained and rinsed
- ¼ teaspoon ground cumin
- 1 tablespoon chopped fresh cilantro
- fresh salsa, guacamole and sour cream, for serving

Directions:
1. Preheat the air fryer to 400°F/205°C.
2. Toss the vegetables in a bowl with the olive oil, salt and freshly ground black pepper. Air-fry at 400°F/205°C for 12 to 15 minutes, shaking the basket a few times during the cooking process. The vegetables are done when they are cooked to your liking.
3. In the meantime, start building the burritos. Lay the tortillas out on the counter. Sprinkle half of the cheese in the center of the tortillas. Combine the rice, beans, cumin and cilantro in a bowl, season to taste with salt and freshly ground black pepper and then divide the mixture between the two tortillas. When the vegetables have finished cooking, transfer them to the two tortillas, placing the vegetables on top of the rice and beans. Sprinkle the remaining cheese on top and then roll the burritos up, tucking in the sides of the tortillas as you roll. Brush or spray the outside of the burritos with olive oil and transfer them to the air fryer.
4. Air-fry at 360°F/180°C for 8 minutes, turning them over when there are about 2 minutes left. The burritos will have slightly brown spots, but will still be pliable.
5. Serve with some fresh salsa, guacamole and sour cream.

Chili Tofu & Quinoa Bowls

Servings: 2
Cooking Time: 30 Minutes
Ingredients:
- 1 cup diced peeled sweet potatoes
- ¼ cup chopped mixed bell peppers
- 1/8 cup sprouted green lentils
- ½ onion, sliced
- 1 tsp avocado oil
- 1/8 cup chopped carrots
- 8 oz extra-firm tofu, cubed
- ½ tsp smoked paprika
- ½ tsp chili powder
- ¼ tsp salt
- 2 tsp lime zest
- 1 cup cooked quinoa
- 2 lime wedges

Directions:
1. Preheat air fryer at 350ºF/175°C. Combine the onion, carrots, bell peppers, green lentils, sweet potato, and avocado oil in a bowl. In another bowl, mix the tofu, paprika, chili powder, and salt. Add veggie mixture to the frying basket and Air Fry for 8 minutes. Stir in tofu mixture and cook for 8 more minutes. Combine lime zest and quinoa. Divide into 2 serving bowls. Top each with the tofu mixture and squeeze a lime wedge over. Serve warm.

Bengali Samosa With Mango Chutney

Servings: 4
Cooking Time: 65 Minutes
Ingredients:
- ¼ tsp ground fenugreek seeds
- 1 cup diced mango
- 1 tbsp minced red onion
- 2 tsp honey
- 1 tsp minced ginger
- 1 tsp apple cider vinegar
- 1 phyllo dough sheet
- 2 tbsp olive oil
- 1 potato, mashed
- ½ tsp garam masala
- ¼ tsp ground turmeric
- 1/8 tsp chili powder
- ¼ tsp ground cumin
- ½ cup green peas
- 2 scallions, chopped

Directions:
1. Mash mango in a small bowl until chunky. Stir in onion, ginger, honey, and vinegar. Save in the fridge until ready to use. Place the mashed potato in a bowl. Add half of the olive oil, garam masala, turmeric, chili powder, ground fenugreek seeds, cumin, and salt and stir until mostly smooth. Stir in peas and scallions.
2. Preheat air fryer to 425°F/220°C. Lightly flour a flat work surface and transfer the phyllo dough. Cut into 8 equal portions and roll each portion to ¼-inch thick rounds. Divide the potato filling between the dough rounds. Fold in three sides and pinch at the meeting point, almost like a pyramid. Arrange the samosas in the frying basket and brush with the remaining olive oil. Bake for 10 minutes, then flip the samosas. Bake for another 4-6 minutes until the crust is crisp and golden. Serve with mango chutney.

Sicilian-style Vegetarian Pizza

Servings: 2
Cooking Time: 20 Minutes
Ingredients:
- 1 pizza pie crust
- ¼ cup ricotta cheese
- ½ tbsp tomato paste
- ½ white onion, sliced
- ½ tsp dried oregano
- ¼ cup Sicilian olives, sliced
- ¼ cup grated mozzarella

Directions:
1. Preheat air fryer to 350°F/175°C. Lay the pizza dough on a parchment paper sheet. Spread the tomato paste evenly over the pie crust, allowing at least ½ inch border. Sprinkle with oregano and scatter the ricotta cheese on top. Cover with onion and Sicilian olive slices and finish with a layer of mozzarella cheese. Bake for 10 minutes until the cheese has melted and lightly crisped, and the crust is golden brown. Serve sliced and enjoy!

Crispy Apple Fries With Caramel Sauce

Servings: 4
Cooking Time: 15 Minutes
Ingredients:
- 4 medium apples, cored
- ¼ tsp cinnamon
- ¼ tsp nutmeg
- 1 cup caramel sauce

Directions:
1. Preheat air fryer to 350°F/175°C. Slice the apples to a 1/3-inch thickness for a crunchy chip. Place in a large bowl and sprinkle with cinnamon and nutmeg. Place the slices in the air fryer basket. Bake for 6 minutes. Shake the basket, then cook for another 4 minutes or until crunchy. Serve drizzled with caramel sauce and enjoy!

Cheddar Stuffed Portobellos With Salsa

Servings: 4
Cooking Time: 20 Minutes
Ingredients:
- 8 portobello mushrooms
- 1/3 cup salsa
- ½ cup shredded cheddar
- 2 tbsp cilantro, chopped

Directions:
1. Preheat air fryer to 370°F/185°C. Remove the mushroom stems. Divide the salsa between the caps. Top with cheese and sprinkle with cilantro. Place the mushrooms in the greased frying basket and Bake for 8-10 minutes. Let cool slightly, then serve.

Zucchini Tacos

Servings: 3
Cooking Time: 20 Minutes
Ingredients:
- 1 small zucchini, sliced
- 1 yellow onion, sliced
- ¼ tsp garlic powder
- Salt and pepper to taste
- 1 can refried beans
- 6 corn tortillas, warm
- 1 cup guacamole
- 1 tbsp cilantro, chopped

Directions:
1. Preheat air fryer to 390°F/200°C. Place the zucchini and onion in the greased frying basket. Spray with more oil and sprinkle with garlic, salt, and pepper to taste. Roast for 6 minutes. Remove, shake, or stir, then cook for another 6 minutes, until the veggies are golden and tender.
2. In a pan, heat the refried beans over low heat. Stir often. When warm enough, remove from heat and set aside. Place a corn tortilla on a plate and fill it with beans, roasted vegetables, and guacamole. Top with cilantro to serve.

Fennel Tofu Bites

Servings: 4
Cooking Time: 35 Minutes
Ingredients:
- 1/3 cup vegetable broth
- 2 tbsp tomato sauce
- 2 tsp soy sauce
- 1 tbsp nutritional yeast
- 1 tsp Italian seasoning
- 1 tsp granulated sugar
- 1 tsp ginger grated
- ½ tsp fennel seeds
- ½ tsp garlic powder
- Salt and pepper to taste
- 14 oz firm tofu, cubed
- 2/3 cup bread crumbs
- 1 tsp Italian seasoning
- 2 tsp toasted sesame seeds
- 1 cup marinara sauce, warm

Directions:
1. In a large bowl, whisk the vegetable broth, soy sauce, ginger, tomato sauce, nutritional yeast, Italian seasoning, sugar, fennel seeds, garlic powder, salt and black pepper. Toss in tofu to coat. Let marinate covered in the fridge for 30 minutes, tossing once.
2. Preheat air fryer at 350°F/175°C. Mix the breadcrumbs, Italian seasoning, and salt in a bowl. Strain marinade from tofu cubes and dredge them in the breadcrumb mixture. Place tofu cubes in the greased frying basket and Air Fry for 10 minutes, turning once. Serve sprinkled with sesame seeds and marinara sauce on the side.

Breaded Avocado Tacos

Servings: 3
Cooking Time: 20 Minutes
Ingredients:
- 2 tomatoes, diced
- ¼ cup diced red onion
- 1 jalapeño, finely diced
- 1 tbsp lime juice
- 1 tsp lime zest
- ¼ cup chopped cilantro
- 1 tsp salt
- 1 egg
- 2 tbsp milk
- 1 cup crumbs
- ¼ cup of almond flour
- 1 avocado, sliced into fries
- 6 flour tortillas
- 1 cup coleslaw mix

Directions:
1. In a bowl, combine the tomatoes, jalapeño, red onion, lime juice, lime zest, cilantro, and salt. Let chill the pico de gallo covered in the fridge until ready to use.
2. Preheat air fryer at 375ºF/190°C. In a small bowl, beat egg and milk. In another bowl, add breadcrumbs. Dip avocado slices in the egg mixture, then dredge them in the mixed almond flour and breadcrumbs. Place avocado slices in the greased frying basket and Air Fry for 5 minutes. Add 2 avocado fries to each tortilla. Top each with coleslaw mix. Serve immediately.

Egg Rolls

Servings: 4
Cooking Time: 8 Minutes
Ingredients:
- 1 clove garlic, minced
- 1 teaspoon sesame oil
- 1 teaspoon olive oil
- ½ cup chopped celery
- ½ cup grated carrots

- 2 green onions, chopped
- 2 ounces mushrooms, chopped
- 2 cups shredded Napa cabbage
- 1 teaspoon low-sodium soy sauce
- 1 teaspoon cornstarch
- salt
- 1 egg
- 1 tablespoon water
- 4 egg roll wraps
- olive oil for misting or cooking spray

Directions:
1. In a large skillet, sauté garlic in sesame and olive oils over medium heat for 1 minute.
2. Add celery, carrots, onions, and mushrooms to skillet. Cook 1 minute, stirring.
3. Stir in cabbage, cover, and cook for 1 minute or just until cabbage slightly wilts.
4. In a small bowl, mix soy sauce and cornstarch. Stir into vegetables to thicken. Remove from heat. Salt to taste if needed.
5. Beat together egg and water in a small bowl.
6. Divide filling into 4 portions and roll up in egg roll wraps. Brush all over with egg wash to seal.
7. Mist egg rolls very lightly with olive oil or cooking spray and place in air fryer basket.
8. Cook at 390°F/200°C for 4minutes. Turn over and cook 4 more minutes, until golden brown and crispy.

Falafel
Servings: 4
Cooking Time: 10 Minutes
Ingredients:
- 1 cup dried chickpeas
- ½ onion, chopped
- 1 clove garlic
- ¼ cup fresh parsley leaves
- 1 teaspoon salt
- ¼ teaspoon crushed red pepper flakes
- 1 teaspoon ground cumin
- ½ teaspoon ground coriander
- 1 to 2 tablespoons flour
- olive oil
- Tomato Salad
- 2 tomatoes, seeds removed and diced
- ½ cucumber, finely diced
- ¼ red onion, finely diced and rinsed with water
- 1 teaspoon red wine vinegar
- 1 tablespoon olive oil
- salt and freshly ground black pepper
- 2 tablespoons chopped fresh parsley

Directions:
1. Cover the chickpeas with water and let them soak overnight on the counter. Then drain the chickpeas and put them in a food processor, along with the onion, garlic, parsley, spices and 1 tablespoon of flour. Pulse in the food processor until the mixture has broken down into a coarse paste consistency. The mixture should hold together when you pinch it. Add more flour as needed, until you get this consistency.
2. Scoop portions of the mixture (about 2 tablespoons in size) and shape into balls. Place the balls on a plate and refrigerate for at least 30 minutes. You should have between 12 and 14 balls.
3. Preheat the air fryer to 380°F/195°C.
4. Spray the falafel balls with oil and place them in the air fryer. Air-fry for 10 minutes, rolling them over and spraying them with oil again halfway through the cooking time so that they cook and brown evenly.
5. Serve with pita bread, hummus, cucumbers, hot peppers, tomatoes or any other fillings you might like.

Vegetarian Shepherd's Pie
Servings: 4
Cooking Time: 40 Minutes
Ingredients:
- 1 russet potato, peeled and diced
- 1 tbsp olive oil
- 2 tbsp balsamic vinegar
- ¼ cup cheddar shreds
- 2 tbsp milk
- Salt and pepper to taste
- 2 tsp avocado oil
- 1 cup beefless grounds
- ½ onion, diced
- 3 cloves garlic
- 1 carrot, diced
- ¼ diced green bell peppers
- 1 celery stalk, diced
- 2/3 cup tomato sauce
- 1 tsp chopped rosemary
- 1 tbsp sesame seeds
- 1 tsp thyme leaves
- 1 lemon

Directions:
1. Add salted water to a pot over high heat and bring it to a boil. Add in diced potatoes and cook for 5 minutes until fork tender. Drain and transfer it to a bowl. Add in the olive oil cheddar shreds, milk, salt, and pepper and mash it until smooth. Set the potato topping aside.
2. Preheat air fryer at 350°F/175°C. Place avocado oil, beefless grounds, garlic, onion, carrot, bell pepper, and celery in a skillet over medium heat and cook for 4 minutes until the veggies are tender. Stir in the remaining ingredients and turn the heat off. Spoon the filling into a greased cake pan. Top with the potato topping.
3. Using tines of a fork, create shallow lines along the top of mashed potatoes. Place cake pan in the frying basket and Bake for 12 minutes. Let rest for 10 minutes before serving sprinkled with sesame seeds and squeezed lemon.

Mushroom, Zucchini And Black Bean Burgers
Servings: 4
Cooking Time: 18 Minutes
Ingredients:
- 1 cup diced zucchini, (about ½ medium zucchini)
- 1 tablespoon olive oil
- salt and freshly ground black pepper
- 1 cup chopped brown mushrooms (about 3 ounces)
- 1 small clove garlic
- 1 (15-ounce) can black beans, drained and rinsed
- 1 teaspoon lemon zest
- 1 tablespoon chopped fresh cilantro
- ½ cup plain breadcrumbs
- 1 egg, beaten
- ½ teaspoon salt

- freshly ground black pepper
- whole-wheat pita bread, burger buns or brioche buns
- mayonnaise, tomato, avocado and lettuce, for serving

Directions:
1. Preheat the air fryer to 400°F/205°C.
2. Toss the zucchini with the olive oil, season with salt and freshly ground black pepper and air-fry for 6 minutes, shaking the basket once or twice while it cooks.
3. Transfer the zucchini to a food processor with the mushrooms, garlic and black beans and process until still a little chunky but broken down and pasty. Transfer the mixture to a bowl. Add the lemon zest, cilantro, breadcrumbs and egg and mix well. Season again with salt and freshly ground black pepper. Shape the mixture into four burger patties and refrigerate for at least 15 minutes.
4. Preheat the air fryer to 370°F/185°C. Transfer two of the veggie burgers to the air fryer basket and air-fry for 12 minutes, flipping the burgers gently halfway through the cooking time. Keep the burgers warm by loosely tenting them with foil while you cook the remaining two burgers. Return the first batch of burgers back into the air fryer with the second batch for the last two minutes of cooking to re-heat.
5. Serve on toasted whole-wheat pita bread, burger buns or brioche buns with some mayonnaise, tomato, avocado and lettuce.

Cheesy Enchilada Stuffed Baked Potatoes

Servings: 4
Cooking Time: 37 Minutes
Ingredients:
- 2 medium russet potatoes, washed
- One 15-ounce can mild red enchilada sauce
- One 15-ounce can low-sodium black beans, rinsed and drained
- 1 teaspoon taco seasoning
- ½ cup shredded cheddar cheese
- 1 medium avocado, halved
- ½ teaspoon garlic powder
- ¼ teaspoon black pepper
- ¼ teaspoon salt
- 2 teaspoons fresh lime juice
- 2 tablespoon chopped red onion
- ¼ cup chopped cilantro

Directions:
1. Preheat the air fryer to 390°F/200°C.
2. Puncture the outer surface of the potatoes with a fork.
3. Set the potatoes inside the air fryer basket and cook for 20 minutes, rotate, and cook another 10 minutes.
4. In a large bowl, mix the enchilada sauce, black beans, and taco seasoning.
5. When the potatoes have finished cooking, carefully remove them from the air fryer basket and let cool for 5 minutes.
6. Using a pair of tongs to hold the potato if it's still too hot to touch, slice the potato in half lengthwise. Use a spoon to scoop out the potato flesh and add it into the bowl with the enchilada sauce. Mash the potatoes with the enchilada sauce mixture, creating a uniform stuffing.
7. Place the potato skins into an air-fryer-safe pan and stuff the halves with the enchilada stuffing. Sprinkle the cheese over the top of each potato.
8. Set the air fryer temperature to 350°F/175°C, return the pan to the air fryer basket, and cook for another 5 to 7 minutes to heat the potatoes and melt the cheese.
9. While the potatoes are cooking, take the avocado and scoop out the flesh into a small bowl. Mash it with the back of a fork; then mix in the garlic powder, pepper, salt, lime juice, and onion. Set aside.
10. When the potatoes have finished cooking, remove the pan from the air fryer and place the potato halves on a plate. Top with avocado mash and fresh cilantro. Serve immediately.

Poultry Recipes

Chicken Souvlaki Gyros

Servings: 4
Cooking Time: 18 Minutes
Ingredients:
- ¼ cup extra-virgin olive oil
- 1 clove garlic, crushed
- 1 tablespoon Italian seasoning
- ½ teaspoon paprika
- ½ lemon, sliced
- ¼ teaspoon salt
- 1 pound boneless, skinless chicken breasts
- 4 whole-grain pita breads
- 1 cup shredded lettuce
- ½ cup chopped tomatoes
- ¼ cup chopped red onion
- ¼ cup cucumber yogurt sauce

Directions:
1. In a large resealable plastic bag, combine the olive oil, garlic, Italian seasoning, paprika, lemon, and salt. Add the chicken to the bag and secure shut. Vigorously shake until all the ingredients are combined. Set in the fridge for 2 hours to marinate.
2. When ready to cook, preheat the air fryer to 360°F/180°C.
3. Liberally spray the air fryer basket with olive oil mist. Remove the chicken from the bag and discard the leftover marinade. Place the chicken into the air fryer basket, allowing enough room between the chicken breasts to flip.
4. Cook for 10 minutes, flip, and cook another 8 minutes.
5. Remove the chicken from the air fryer basket when it has cooked (or the internal temperature of the chicken reaches 165°F/75°C). Let rest 5 minutes. Then thinly slice the chicken into strips.
6. Assemble the gyros by placing the pita bread on a flat surface and topping with chicken, lettuce, tomatoes, onion, and a drizzle of yogurt sauce.
7. Serve warm.

Teriyaki Chicken Legs

Servings: 2
Cooking Time: 20 Minutes
Ingredients:
- 4 tablespoons teriyaki sauce
- 1 tablespoon orange juice
- 1 teaspoon smoked paprika
- 4 chicken legs
- cooking spray

Directions:
1. Mix together the teriyaki sauce, orange juice, and smoked paprika. Brush on all sides of chicken legs.
2. Spray air fryer basket with nonstick cooking spray and place chicken in basket.
3. Cook at 360°F/180°C for 6minutes. Turn and baste with sauce. Cook for 6 moreminutes, turn and baste. Cook for 8 minutes more, until juices run clear when chicken is pierced with a fork.

Christmas Chicken & Roasted Grape Salad

Servings: 4
Cooking Time: 40 Minutes
Ingredients:
- 3 chicken breasts, pat-dried
- 1 tsp paprika
- Salt and pepper to taste
- 2 cups seedless red grapes
- ½ cup mayonnaise
- ½ cup plain yogurt
- 2 tbsp honey mustard
- 2 tbsp fresh lemon juice
- 1 cup chopped celery
- 2 scallions, chopped
- 2 tbsp walnuts, chopped

Directions:
1. Preheat the air fryer to 370°F/185°C. Sprinkle the chicken breasts with paprika, salt, and pepper. Transfer to the greased frying basket and Air Fry for 16-19 minutes, flipping once. Remove and set on a cutting board. Put the grapes in the fryer and spray with cooking oil. Fry for 4 minutes or until the grapes are hot and tender.Mix the mayonnaise, yogurt, honey mustard, and lemon juice in a bowl and whisk. Cube the chicken and add to the dressing along with the grapes, walnuts, celery, and scallions. Toss gently and serve.

Chicken Cordon Bleu

Servings: 2
Cooking Time: 16 Minutes
Ingredients:
- 2 boneless, skinless chicken breasts
- ¼ teaspoon salt
- 2 teaspoons Dijon mustard
- 2 ounces deli ham
- 2 ounces Swiss, fontina, or Gruyère cheese
- ⅓ cup all-purpose flour
- 1 egg
- ½ cup breadcrumbs

Directions:
1. Pat the chicken breasts with a paper towel. Season the chicken with the salt. Pound the chicken breasts to 1½ inches thick. Create a pouch by slicing the side of each chicken breast. Spread 1 teaspoon Dijon mustard inside the pouch of each chicken breast. Wrap a 1-ounce slice of ham around a 1-ounce slice of cheese and place into the pouch. Repeat with the remaining ham and cheese.
2. In a medium bowl, place the flour.
3. In a second bowl, whisk the egg.
4. In a third bowl, place the breadcrumbs.
5. Dredge the chicken in the flour and shake off the excess. Next, dip the chicken into the egg and then in the breadcrumbs. Set the chicken on a plate and repeat with the remaining chicken piece.
6. Preheat the air fryer to 360°F/180°C.

Tower Air Fryer Cookbook

7. Place the chicken in the air fryer basket and spray liberally with cooking spray. Cook for 8 minutes, turn the chicken breasts over, and liberally spray with cooking spray again; cook another 6 minutes. Once golden brown, check for an internal temperature of 165°F/75°C.

Country Chicken Hoagies

Servings: 2
Cooking Time: 30 Minutes
Ingredients:
- ¼ cup button mushrooms, sliced
- 1 hoagie bun, halved
- 1 chicken breast, cubed
- ½ white onion, sliced
- 1 cup bell pepper strips
- 2 cheddar cheese slices

Directions:
1. Preheat air fryer to 320°F/160°C. Place the chicken pieces, onions, bell pepper strips, and mushroom slices on one side of the frying basket. Lay the hoagie bun halves, crusty side up and soft side down, on the other half of the air fryer. Bake for 10 minutes. Flip the hoagie buns and cover with cheddar cheese. Stir the chicken and vegetables. Cook for another 6 minutes until the cheese is melted and the chicken is juicy on the inside and crispy on the outside. Place the cheesy hoagie halves on a serving plate and cover one half with the chicken and veggies. Close with the other cheesy hoagie half. Serve.

Basic Chicken Breasts(2)

Servings: 4
Cooking Time: 15 Minutes
Ingredients:
- 2 tsp olive oil
- 2 chicken breasts
- Salt and pepper to taste
- ½ tsp garlic powder
- ½ tsp rosemary

Directions:
1. Preheat air fryer to 350°F/175°C. Rub the chicken breasts with olive oil over tops and bottom and sprinkle with garlic powder, rosemary, salt, and pepper. Place the chicken in the frying basket and Air Fry for 9 minutes, flipping once. Let rest onto a serving plate for 5 minutes before cutting into cubes. Serve and enjoy!

Spicy Honey Mustard Chicken

Servings: 4
Cooking Time: 30 Minutes
Ingredients:
- 1/3 cup tomato sauce
- 2 tbsp yellow mustard
- 2 tbsp apple cider vinegar
- 1 tbsp honey
- 2 garlic cloves, minced
- 1 Fresno pepper, minced
- 1 tsp onion powder
- 4 chicken breasts

Directions:
1. Preheat air fryer to 370°F/185°C. Mix the tomato sauce, mustard, apple cider vinegar, honey, garlic, Fresno pepper, and onion powder in a bowl, then use a brush to rub the mix over the chicken breasts. Put the chicken in the air fryer and Grill for 10 minutes. Remove it, turn it, and rub with more sauce. Cook further for about 5 minutes. Remove the basket and flip the chicken. Add more sauce, return to the fryer, and cook for 3-5 more minutes or until the chicken is cooked through. Serve warm.

Chicken & Rice Sautée

Servings: 4
Cooking Time: 25 Minutes
Ingredients:
- 1 can pineapple chunks, drained, ¼ cup juice reserved
- 1 cup cooked long-grain rice
- 1 lb chicken breasts, cubed
- 1 red onion, chopped
- 1 tbsp peanut oil
- 1 peeled peach, cubed
- 1 tbsp cornstarch
- ½ tsp ground ginger
- ¼ tsp chicken seasoning

Directions:
1. Preheat air fryer to 400°F/205°C. Combine the chicken, red onion, pineapple, and peanut oil in a metal bowl, then put the bowl in the fryer. Air Fry for 9 minutes, remove and stir. Toss the peach in and put the bowl back into the fryer for 3 minutes. Slide out and stir again. Mix the reserved pineapple juice, corn starch, ginger, and chicken seasoning in a bowl, then pour over the chicken mixture and stir well. Put the bowl back into the fryer and cook for 3 more minutes or until the chicken is cooked through and the sauce is thick. Serve over cooked rice.

Guajillo Chile Chicken Meatballs

Servings: 4
Cooking Time: 30 Minutes
Ingredients:
- 1 lb ground chicken
- 1 large egg
- ½ cup bread crumbs
- 1 tbsp sour cream
- 2 tsp brown mustard
- 2 tbsp grated onion
- 2 tbsp tomato paste
- 1 tsp ground cumin
- 1 tsp guajillo chile powder
- 2 tbsp olive oil

Directions:
1. Preheat air fryer to 350°F/175°C. Mix the ground chicken, egg, bread crumbs, sour cream, mustard, onion, tomato paste, cumin, and chili powder in a bowl. Form into 16 meatballs. Place the meatballs in the greased frying basket and Air Fry for 8-10 minutes, shaking once until browned and cooked through. Serve immediately.

Katsu Chicken Thighs

Servings: 4
Cooking Time: 35 Minutes
Ingredients:
- 1 ½ lb boneless, skinless chicken thighs
- 3 tbsp tamari sauce
- 3 tbsp lemon juice
- ½ tsp ground ginger
- Black pepper to taste
- 6 tbsp cornstarch
- 1 cup chicken stock
- 2 tbsp hoisin sauce

- 2 tbsp light brown sugar
- 2 tbsp sesame seeds

Directions:
1. Preheat the air fryer to 400°F/205°C. After cubing the chicken thighs, put them in a cake pan. Add a tbsp of tamari sauce, a tbsp of lemon juice, ginger, and black pepper. Mix and let marinate for 10 minutes. Remove the chicken and coat it in 4 tbsp of cornstarch; set aside. Add the rest of the marinade to the pan and add the stock, hoisin sauce, brown sugar, and the remaining tamari sauce, lemon juice, and cornstarch. Mix well. Put the pan in the frying basket and Air Fry for 5-8 minutes or until bubbling and thick, stirring once. Remove and set aside. Put the chicken in the frying basket and Fry for 15-18 minutes, shaking the basket once. Remove the chicken to the sauce in the pan and return to the fryer to reheat for 2 minutes. Sprinkle with the sesame seeds and serve.

Intense Buffalo Chicken Wings
Servings: 2
Cooking Time: 40 Minutes
Ingredients:
- 8 chicken wings
- ½ cup melted butter
- 2 tbsp Tabasco sauce
- ½ tbsp lemon juice
- 1 tbsp Worcestershire sauce
- 2 tsp cayenne pepper
- 1 tsp garlic powder
- 1 tsp lemon zest
- Salt and pepper to taste

Directions:
1. Preheat air fryer to 350°F/175°C. Place the melted butter, Tabasco, lemon juice, Worcestershire sauce, cayenne, garlic powder, lemon zest, salt, and pepper in a bowl and stir to combine. Dip the chicken wings into the mixture, coating thoroughly. Lay the coated chicken wings on the foil-lined frying basket in an even layer. Air Fry for 16-18 minutes. Shake the basket several times during cooking until the chicken wings are crispy brown. Serve.

Japanese-style Turkey Meatballs
Servings: 4
Cooking Time: 25 Minutes
Ingredients:
- 1 1/3 lb ground turkey
- ¼ cup panko bread crumbs
- 4 chopped scallions
- ¼ cup chopped cilantro
- 1 egg
- 1 tbsp grated ginger
- 1 garlic clove, minced
- 3 tbsp shoyu
- 2 tsp toasted sesame oil
- ¾ tsp salt
- 2 tbsp oyster sauce sauce
- 2 tbsp fresh orange juice

Directions:
1. Add ground turkey, panko, 3 scallions, cilantro, egg, ginger, garlic, 1 tbsp of shoyu sauce, sesame oil, and salt in a bowl. Mix with hands until combined. Divide the mixture into 12 equal parts and roll into balls. Preheat air fryer to 380°F/195°C. Place the meatballs in the greased frying basket. Bake for about 9-11 minutes, flipping once until browned and cooked through. Repeat for all meatballs.
2. In a small saucepan over medium heat, add oyster sauce, orange juice and remaining shoyu sauce. Bring to a boil, then reduce the heat to low. Cook until the sauce is slightly reduced, 3 minutes. Serve the meatballs with the oyster sauce drizzled over them and topped with the remaining scallions.

Spinach & Turkey Meatballs
Servings: 4
Cooking Time: 45 Minutes
Ingredients:
- ¼ cup grated Parmesan cheese
- 2 scallions, chopped
- 1 garlic clove, minced
- 1 egg, beaten
- 1 cup baby spinach
- ¼ cup bread crumbs
- 1 tsp dried oregano
- Salt and pepper to taste
- 1 ¼ lb ground turkey

Directions:
1. Preheat the air fryer to 400°F/205°C and preheat the oven to 250°F/120°C. Combine the scallions, garlic, egg, baby spinach, breadcrumbs, Parmesan, oregano, salt, and pepper in a bowl and mix well. Add the turkey and mix, then form into 1½-inch balls. Add as many meatballs as will fit in a single layer in the frying basket and Air Fry for 10-15 minutes, shaking once around minute 7. Put the cooked meatballs on a tray in the oven and cover with foil to keep warm. Repeat with the remaining balls.

Boss Chicken Cobb Salad
Servings: 2
Cooking Time: 30 Minutes
Ingredients:
- 4 oz cooked bacon, crumbled
- ¼ cup diced peeled red onion
- ½ cup crumbled blue cheese
- 1 egg
- 1 tbsp honey
- 1 tbsp Dijon mustard
- ½ tsp apple cider vinegar
- 2 chicken breasts, cubed
- 3/4 cup bread crumbs
- Salt and pepper to taste
- 3 cups torn iceberg lettuce
- 2 cups baby spinach
- ½ cup ranch dressing
- ½ avocado, diced
- 1 beefsteak tomato, diced
- 1 hard-boiled egg, diced
- 2 tbsp parsley

Directions:
1. Preheat air fryer at 350°F/175°C. Mix the egg, honey, mustard, and vinegar in a bowl. Toss in chicken cubes to coat. Shake off excess marinade of chicken. In another bowl, combine breadcrumbs, salt, and pepper. Dredge chicken cubes in the mixture. Place chicken cubes in the greased frying basket. Air Fry for 8-10 minutes, tossing once. In a salad bowl, combine lettuce, baby spinach, and ranch dressing and toss to coat. Add in the cooked chicken and the remaining ingredients. Serve immediately.

Garlic Chicken

Servings: 4
Cooking Time: 30 Minutes
Ingredients:
- 4 bone-in skinless chicken thighs
- 1 tbsp olive oil
- 1 tbsp lemon juice
- 3 tbsp cornstarch
- 1 tsp dried sage
- Black pepper to taste
- 20 garlic cloves, unpeeled

Directions:
1. Preheat air fryer to 370°F/185°C. Brush the chicken with olive oil and lemon juice, then drizzle cornstarch, sage, and pepper. Put the chicken in the frying basket and scatter the garlic cloves on top. Roast for 25 minutes or until the garlic is soft, and the chicken is cooked through. Serve.

Glazed Chicken Thighs

Servings: 4
Cooking Time: 25 Minutes
Ingredients:
- 1 lb boneless, skinless chicken thighs
- ¼ cup balsamic vinegar
- 3 tbsp honey
- 2 tbsp brown sugar
- 1 tsp whole-grain mustard
- ¼ cup soy sauce
- 3 garlic cloves, minced
- Salt and pepper to taste
- ½ tsp smoked paprika
- 2 tbsp chopped shallots

Directions:
1. Preheat air fryer to 375°F/190°C. Whisk vinegar, honey, sugar, soy sauce, mustard, garlic, salt, pepper, and paprika in a small bowl. Arrange the chicken in the frying basket and brush the top of each with some of the vinegar mixture. Air Fry for 7 minutes, then flip the chicken. Brush the tops with the rest of the vinegar mixture and Air Fry for another 5 to 8 minutes. Allow resting for 5 minutes before slicing. Serve warm sprinkled with shallots.

Sunday Chicken Skewers

Servings: 4
Cooking Time: 25 Minutes
Ingredients:
- 1 green bell pepper, cut into chunks
- 1 red bell pepper, cut into chunks
- 4 chicken breasts, cubed
- 1 tbsp chicken seasoning
- Salt and pepper to taste
- 16 cherry tomatoes
- 8 pearl onions, peeled

Directions:
1. Preheat air fryer to 360°F/180°C. Season the cubes with chicken seasoning, salt, and pepper. Thread metal skewers with chicken, bell pepper chunks, cherry tomatoes, and pearl onions. Put the kabobs in the greased frying basket. Bake for 14-16 minutes, flipping once until cooked through. Let cool slightly. Serve.

Peanut Butter-barbeque Chicken

Servings: 4
Cooking Time: 20 Minutes
Ingredients:
- 1 pound boneless, skinless chicken thighs
- salt and pepper
- 1 large orange
- ½ cup barbeque sauce
- 2 tablespoons smooth peanut butter
- 2 tablespoons chopped peanuts for garnish (optional)
- cooking spray

Directions:
1. Season chicken with salt and pepper to taste. Place in a shallow dish or plastic bag.
2. Grate orange peel, squeeze orange and reserve 1 tablespoon of juice for the sauce.
3. Pour remaining juice over chicken and marinate for 30minutes.
4. Mix together the reserved 1 tablespoon of orange juice, barbeque sauce, peanut butter, and 1 teaspoon grated orange peel.
5. Place ¼ cup of sauce mixture in a small bowl for basting. Set remaining sauce aside to serve with cooked chicken.
6. Preheat air fryer to 360°F/180°C. Spray basket with nonstick cooking spray.
7. Remove chicken from marinade, letting excess drip off. Place in air fryer basket and cook for 5minutes. Turn chicken over and cook 5minutes longer.
8. Brush both sides of chicken lightly with sauce.
9. Cook chicken 5minutes, then turn thighs one more time, again brushing both sides lightly with sauce. Cook for 5 moreminutes or until chicken is done and juices run clear.
10. Serve chicken with remaining sauce on the side and garnish with chopped peanuts if you like.

Korean-style Chicken Bulgogi

Servings: 4
Cooking Time: 30 Minutes
Ingredients:
- 6 boneless, skinless chicken thighs, cubed
- 3 scallions, sliced, whites and green separated
- 2 carrots, grated
- ½ cup rice vinegar
- 2 tsp granulated sugar
- Salt to taste
- 2 tbsp tamari
- 2 tsp sesame oil
- 1 tbsp light brown sugar
- 1 tbsp lime juice
- 1 tbsp soy sauce
- 2 cloves garlic, minced
- ½ Asian pear
- 2 tsp minced ginger
- 4 cups cooked white rice
- 2 tsp sesame seeds

Directions:
1. In a bowl, combine the carrots, half of the rice vinegar, sugar, and salt. Let chill covered in the fridge until ready to use. Mix the tamari, sesame oil, soy sauce, brown sugar, remaining rice vinegar, lime juice, garlic, Asian pear, ginger, and scallion whites in a bowl. Toss in chicken thighs and let marinate for 10 minutes.
2. Preheat air fryer at 350°F/175°C. Using a slotted spoon, transfer chicken thighs to the frying basket, reserve marinade, and Air Fry for 10-12 minutes, shaking once. Place chicken over a rice bed on serving plates and scatter with scallion greens and sesame seeds. Serve with pickled carrots.

Sweet-and-sour Chicken

Servings: 6
Cooking Time: 10 Minutes
Ingredients:
- 1 cup pineapple juice
- 1 cup plus 3 tablespoons cornstarch, divided
- ¼ cup sugar
- ¼ cup ketchup
- ¼ cup apple cider vinegar
- 2 tablespoons soy sauce or tamari
- 1 teaspoon garlic powder, divided
- ¼ cup flour
- 1 tablespoon sesame seeds
- ½ teaspoon salt
- ¼ teaspoon ground black pepper
- 2 large eggs
- 2 pounds chicken breasts, cut into 1-inch cubes
- 1 red bell pepper, cut into 1-inch pieces
- 1 carrot, sliced into ¼-inch-thick rounds

Directions:
1. In a medium saucepan, whisk together the pineapple juice, 3 tablespoons of the cornstarch, the sugar, the ketchup, the apple cider vinegar, the soy sauce or tamari, and ½ teaspoon of the garlic powder. Cook over medium-low heat, whisking occasionally as the sauce thickens, about 6 minutes. Stir and set aside while preparing the chicken.
2. Preheat the air fryer to 370°F/185°C.
3. In a medium bowl, place the remaining 1 cup of cornstarch, the flour, the sesame seeds, the salt, the remaining ½ teaspoon of garlic powder, and the pepper.
4. In a second medium bowl, whisk the eggs.
5. Working in batches, place the cubed chicken in the cornstarch mixture to lightly coat; then dip it into the egg mixture, and return it to the cornstarch mixture. Shake off the excess and place the coated chicken in the air fryer basket. Spray with cooking spray and cook for 5 minutes, shake the basket, and spray with more cooking spray. Cook an additional 3 to 5 minutes, or until completely cooked and golden brown.
6. On the last batch of chicken, add the bell pepper and carrot to the basket and cook with the chicken.
7. Place the cooked chicken and vegetables into a serving bowl and toss with the sweet-and-sour sauce to serve.

Chicken Hand Pies

Servings: 8
Cooking Time: 10 Minutes Per Batch
Ingredients:
- ¾ cup chicken broth
- ¾ cup frozen mixed peas and carrots
- 1 cup cooked chicken, chopped
- 1 tablespoon cornstarch
- 1 tablespoon milk
- salt and pepper
- 1 8-count can organic flaky biscuits
- oil for misting or cooking spray

Directions:
1. In a medium saucepan, bring chicken broth to a boil. Stir in the frozen peas and carrots and cook for 5minutes over medium heat. Stir in chicken.
2. Mix the cornstarch into the milk until it dissolves. Stir it into the simmering chicken broth mixture and cook just until thickened.
3. Remove from heat, add salt and pepper to taste, and let cool slightly.
4. Lay biscuits out on wax paper. Peel each biscuit apart in the middle to make 2 rounds so you have 16 rounds total. Using your hands or a rolling pin, flatten each biscuit round slightly to make it larger and thinner.
5. Divide chicken filling among 8 of the biscuit rounds. Place remaining biscuit rounds on top and press edges all around. Use the tines of a fork to crimp biscuit edges and make sure they are sealed well.
6. Spray both sides lightly with oil or cooking spray.
7. Cook in a single layer, 4 at a time, at 330°F/165°C for 10minutes or until biscuit dough is cooked through and golden brown.

Punjabi-inspired Chicken

Servings: 4
Cooking Time: 35 Minutes
Ingredients:
- 2/3 cup plain yogurt
- 2 tbsp lemon juice
- 2 tsp curry powder
- ½ tsp ground cinnamon
- 2 garlic cloves, minced
- ½-inch piece ginger, grated
- 2 tsp olive oil
- 4 chicken breasts

Directions:
1. Mix the yogurt, lemon juice, curry powder, cinnamon, garlic, ginger, and olive oil in a bowl. Slice the chicken, without cutting, all the way through, by making thin slits, then toss it into the yogurt mix. Coat well and let marinate for 10 minutes.
2. Preheat air fryer to 360°F/180°C. Take the chicken out of the marinade, letting the extra liquid drip off. Toss the rest of the marinade away. Air Fry the chicken for 10 minutes. Turn each piece, then cook for 8-13 minutes more until cooked through and no pink meat remains. Serve warm.

Easy Turkey Meatballs

Servings: 4
Cooking Time: 20 Minutes
Ingredients:
- 1 lb ground turkey
- ½ celery stalk, chopped
- 1 egg
- ¼ tsp red pepper flakes
- ¼ cup bread crumbs
- Salt and pepper to taste
- ½ tsp garlic powder
- ½ tsp onion powder
- ½ tsp cayenne pepper

Directions:
1. Preheat air fryer to 360°F/180°C. Add all of the ingredients to a bowl and mix well. Shape the mixture into 12 balls and arrange them on the greased frying basket. Air Fry for 10-12 minutes or until the meatballs are cooked through and browned. Serve and enjoy!

Italian Roasted Chicken Thighs

Servings: 6
Cooking Time: 14 Minutes
Ingredients:
- 6 boneless chicken thighs
- ½ teaspoon dried oregano

- ½ teaspoon garlic powder
- ½ teaspoon sea salt
- ½ teaspoon black pepper
- ¼ teaspoon crushed red pepper flakes

Directions:
1. Pat the chicken thighs with paper towel.
2. In a small bowl, mix the oregano, garlic powder, salt, pepper, and crushed red pepper flakes. Rub the spice mixture onto the chicken thighs.
3. Preheat the air fryer to 400°F/205°C.
4. Place the chicken thighs in the air fryer basket and spray with cooking spray. Cook for 10 minutes, turn over, and cook another 4 minutes. When cooking completes, the internal temperature should read 165°F/75°C.

Gluten-free Nutty Chicken Fingers

Servings: 4
Cooking Time: 10 Minutes
Ingredients:
- ½ cup gluten-free flour
- ½ teaspoon garlic powder
- ¼ teaspoon onion powder
- ¼ teaspoon black pepper
- ¼ teaspoon salt
- 1 cup walnuts, pulsed into coarse flour
- ½ cup gluten-free breadcrumbs
- 2 large eggs
- 1 pound boneless, skinless chicken tenders

Directions:
1. Preheat the air fryer to 400°F/205°C.
2. In a medium bowl, mix the flour, garlic, onion, pepper, and salt. Set aside.
3. In a separate bowl, mix the walnut flour and breadcrumbs.
4. In a third bowl, whisk the eggs.
5. Liberally spray the air fryer basket with olive oil spray.
6. Pat the chicken tenders dry with a paper towel. Dredge the tenders one at a time in the flour, then dip them in the egg, and toss them in the breadcrumb coating. Repeat until all tenders are coated.
7. Set each tender in the air fryer, leaving room on each side of the tender to allow for flipping.
8. When the basket is full, cook 5 minutes, flip, and cook another 5 minutes. Check the internal temperature after cooking completes; it should read 165°F. If it does not, cook another 2 to 4 minutes.
9. Remove the tenders and let cool 5 minutes before serving. Repeat until all the tenders are cooked.

Farmer's Fried Chicken

Servings: 4
Cooking Time: 55 Minutes
Ingredients:
- 3 lb whole chicken, cut into breasts, drumsticks, and thighs
- 2 cups flour
- 4 tsp salt
- 4 tsp dried basil
- 4 tsp dried thyme
- 2 tsp dried shallot powder
- 2 tsp smoked paprika
- 1 tsp mustard powder
- 1 tsp celery salt
- 1 cup kefir
- ¼ cup honey

Directions:
1. Preheat the air fryer to 370°F/185°C. Combine the flour, salt, basil, thyme, shallot, paprika, mustard powder, and celery salt in a bowl. Pour into a glass jar. Mix the kefir and honey in a large bowl and add the chicken, stir to coat. Marinate for 15 minutes at room temperature. Remove the chicken from the kefir mixture; discard the rest. Put 2/3 cup of the flour mix onto a plate and dip the chicken. Shake gently and put on a wire rack for 10 minutes. Line the frying basket with round parchment paper with holes punched in it. Place the chicken in a single layer and spray with cooking oil. Air Fry for 18-25 minutes, flipping once around minute 10. Serve hot.

Chicken Burgers With Blue Cheese Sauce

Servings: 4
Cooking Time: 40 Minutes
Ingredients:
- ¼ cup crumbled blue cheese
- ¼ cup sour cream
- 2 tbsp mayonnaise
- 1 tbsp red hot sauce
- Salt to taste
- 3 tbsp buffalo wing sauce
- 1 lb ground chicken
- 2 tbsp grated carrot
- 2 tbsp diced celery
- 1 egg white

Directions:
1. Whisk the blue cheese, sour cream, mayonnaise, red hot sauce, salt, and 1 tbsp of buffalo sauce in a bowl. Let sit covered in the fridge until ready to use.
2. Preheat air fryer at 350°F/175°C. In another bowl, combine the remaining ingredients. Form mixture into 4 patties, making a slight indentation in the middle of each. Place patties in the greased frying basket and Air Fry for 13 minutes until you reach your desired doneness, flipping once. Serve with the blue cheese sauce.

Buttered Turkey Breasts

Servings: 6
Cooking Time: 65 Minutes
Ingredients:
- ½ cup butter, melted
- 6 garlic cloves, minced
- 1 tsp dried oregano
- ½ tsp dried thyme
- ½ tsp dried rosemary
- Salt and pepper to taste
- 4 lb bone-in turkey breast
- 1 tbsp chopped cilantro

Directions:
1. Preheat air fryer to 350°F/175°C. Combine butter, garlic, oregano, salt, and pepper in a small bowl. Place the turkey breast on a plate and coat the entire turkey with the butter mixture. Put the turkey breast-side down in the frying basket and scatter with thyme and rosemary. Bake for 20 minutes. Flip the turkey so that the breast side is up, then bake for another 20-30 minutes until it has an internal temperature of 165°F/75°C. Allow to rest for 10 minutes before carving. Serve sprinkled with cilantro.

Parmesan Chicken Meatloaf

Servings: 4
Cooking Time: 45 Minutes
Ingredients:
- 1 ½ tsp evaporated cane sugar
- 1 lb ground chicken
- 4 garlic cloves, minced
- 2 tbsp grated Parmesan
- ¼ cup heavy cream
- ¼ cup minced onion
- 2 tbsp chopped basil
- 2 tbsp chopped parsley
- Salt and pepper to taste
- ½ tsp onion powder
- ½ cup bread crumbs
- ¼ tsp red pepper flakes
- 1 egg
- 1 cup tomato sauce
- ½ tsp garlic powder
- ½ tsp dried thyme
- ½ tsp dried oregano
- 1 tbsp coconut aminos

Directions:
1. Preheat air fryer to 400°F/205°C. Combine chicken, garlic, minced onion, oregano, thyme, basil, salt, pepper, onion powder, Parmesan cheese, red pepper flakes, bread crumbs, egg, and cream in a large bowl. Transfer the chicken mixture to a prepared baking dish. Stir together tomato sauce, garlic powder, coconut aminos, and sugar in a small bowl. Spread over the meatloaf. Loosely cover with foil. Place the pan in the frying basket and bake for 15 minutes. Take the foil off and bake for another 15 minutes. Allow resting for 10 minutes before slicing. Serve sprinkled with parsley.

Jerk Chicken Drumsticks

Servings: 2
Cooking Time: 20 Minutes
Ingredients:
- 1 or 2 cloves garlic
- 1 inch of fresh ginger
- 2 serrano peppers, (with seeds if you like it spicy, seeds removed for less heat)
- 1 teaspoon ground allspice
- 1 teaspoon ground nutmeg
- 1 teaspoon chili powder
- ½ teaspoon dried thyme
- ½ teaspoon ground cinnamon
- ½ teaspoon paprika
- 1 tablespoon brown sugar
- 1 teaspoon soy sauce
- 2 tablespoons vegetable oil
- 6 skinless chicken drumsticks

Directions:
1. Combine all the ingredients except the chicken in a small chopper or blender and blend to a paste. Make slashes into the meat of the chicken drumsticks and rub the spice blend all over the chicken (a pair of plastic gloves makes this really easy). Transfer the rubbed chicken to a non-reactive covered container and let the chicken marinate for at least 30 minutes or overnight in the refrigerator.
2. Preheat the air fryer to 400°F/205°C.
3. Transfer the drumsticks to the air fryer basket. Air-fry for 10 minutes. Turn the drumsticks over and air-fry for another 10 minutes. Serve warm with some rice and vegetables or a green salad.

Chicken Chimichangas

Servings: 4
Cooking Time: 10 Minutes
Ingredients:
- 2 cups cooked chicken, shredded
- 2 tablespoons chopped green chiles
- ½ teaspoon oregano
- ½ teaspoon cumin
- ½ teaspoon onion powder
- ¼ teaspoon garlic powder
- salt and pepper
- 8 flour tortillas (6- or 7-inch diameter)
- oil for misting or cooking spray
- Chimichanga Sauce
- 2 tablespoons butter
- 2 tablespoons flour
- 1 cup chicken broth
- ¼ cup light sour cream
- ¼ teaspoon salt
- 2 ounces Pepper Jack or Monterey Jack cheese, shredded

Directions:
1. Make the sauce by melting butter in a saucepan over medium-low heat. Stir in flour until smooth and slightly bubbly. Gradually add broth, stirring constantly until smooth. Cook and stir 1 minute, until the mixture slightly thickens. Remove from heat and stir in sour cream and salt. Set aside.
2. In a medium bowl, mix together the chicken, chiles, oregano, cumin, onion powder, garlic, salt, and pepper. Stir in 3 to 4 tablespoons of the sauce, using just enough to make the filling moist but not soupy.
3. Divide filling among the 8 tortillas. Place filling down the center of tortilla, stopping about 1 inch from edges. Fold one side of tortilla over filling, fold the two sides in, and then roll up. Mist all sides with oil or cooking spray.
4. Place chimichangas in air fryer basket seam side down. To fit more into the basket, you can stand them on their sides with the seams against the sides of the basket.
5. Cook at 360°F/180°C for 10 minutes or until heated through and crispy brown outside.
6. Add the shredded cheese to the remaining sauce. Stir over low heat, warming just until the cheese melts. Don't boil or sour cream may curdle.
7. Drizzle the sauce over the chimichangas.

Simple Buttermilk Fried Chicken

Servings: 4
Cooking Time: 27 Minutes
Ingredients:
- 1 (4-pound) chicken, cut into 8 pieces
- 2 cups buttermilk
- hot sauce (optional)
- 1½ cups flour*
- 2 teaspoons paprika
- 1 teaspoon salt
- freshly ground black pepper
- 2 eggs, lightly beaten
- vegetable oil, in a spray bottle

Directions:
1. Cut the chicken into 8 pieces and submerge them in the buttermilk and hot sauce, if using. A zipper-sealable plastic bag works well for this. Let the chicken soak in the

buttermilk for at least one hour or even overnight in the refrigerator.
2. Set up a dredging station. Mix the flour, paprika, salt and black pepper in a clean zipper-sealable plastic bag. Whisk the eggs and place them in a shallow dish. Remove four pieces of chicken from the buttermilk and transfer them to the bag with the flour. Shake them around to coat on all sides. Remove the chicken from the flour, shaking off any excess flour, and dip them into the beaten egg. Return the chicken to the bag of seasoned flour and shake again. Set the coated chicken aside and repeat with the remaining four pieces of chicken.
3. Preheat the air fryer to 370°F/185°C.
4. Spray the chicken on all sides with the vegetable oil and then transfer one batch to the air fryer basket. Air-fry the chicken at 370°F/185°C for 20 minutes, flipping the pieces over halfway through the cooking process, taking care not to knock off the breading. Transfer the chicken to a plate, but do not cover. Repeat with the second batch of chicken.
5. Lower the temperature on the air fryer to 340°F/170°C. Flip the chicken back over and place the first batch of chicken on top of the second batch already in the basket. Air-fry for another 7 minutes and serve warm.

Rich Turkey Burgers
Servings: 4
Cooking Time: 30 Minutes
Ingredients:
- 2 tbsp finely grated Emmental
- 1/3 cup minced onions
- ¼ cup grated carrots
- 2 garlic cloves, minced
- 2 tsp olive oil
- 1 tsp dried marjoram
- 1 egg
- 1 lb ground turkey

Directions:
1. Preheat air fryer to 400°F/205°C. Mix the onions, carrots, garlic, olive oil, marjoram, Emmental, and egg in a bowl, then add the ground turkey. Use your hands to mix the ingredients together. Form the mixture into 4 patties. Set them in the air fryer and Air Fry for 18-20 minutes, flipping once until cooked through and golden. Serve.

Chicken Pasta Pie
Servings: 4
Cooking Time: 40 Minutes
Ingredients:
- 1/3 cup green bell peppers, diced
- ¼ cup yellow bell peppers, diced
- ½ cup mozzarella cheese, grated
- 3/4 cup grated Parmesan cheese
- 2/3 cup ricotta cheese
- 2 tbsp butter, melted
- 1 egg
- ¼ tsp salt
- 6 oz cooked spaghetti
- 2 tsp olive oil
- 1/3 cup diced onions
- 2 cloves minced garlic
- ¼ lb ground chicken
- 1 cup marinara sauce
- ½ tsp dried oregano

Directions:
1. Combine the ricotta cheese, 1 tbsp of Parmesan cheese, minced garlic, and salt in a bowl. Whisk the melted butter and egg in another bowl. Add the remaining Parmesan cheese and cooked spaghetti and mix well. Set aside. Warm the olive oil in a skillet over medium heat. Add in onions, green bell peppers, yellow bell peppers and cook for 3 minutes until the onions tender. Stir in ground chicken and cook for 5 minutes until no longer pink.
2. Preheat air fryer at 350°F/175°C. Press spaghetti mixture into a greased baking pan, then spread ricotta mixture on top, and finally top with the topping mixture, followed by the marinara sauce. Place baking pan in the frying basket and Bake for 10 minutes. Scatter with mozzarella cheese on top and cook for 4 more minutes. Let rest for 20 minutes before releasing the sides of the baking pan. Cut into slices and serve sprinkled with oregano.

Gingery Turkey Meatballs
Servings: 4
Cooking Time: 25 Minutes
Ingredients:
- ¼ cup water chestnuts, chopped
- ¼ cup panko bread crumbs
- 1 lb ground turkey
- ½ tsp ground ginger
- 2 tbsp fish sauce
- 1 tbsp sesame oil
- 1 small onion, minced
- 1 egg, beaten

Directions:
1. Preheat air fryer to 400°F/205°C. Place the ground turkey, water chestnuts, ground ginger, fish sauce, onion, egg, and bread crumbs in a bowl and stir to combine. Form the turkey mixture into 1-inch meatballs. Arrange the meatballs in the baking pan. Drizzle with sesame oil. Bake until the meatballs are cooked through, 10-12 minutes, flipping once. Serve and enjoy!

Gruyère Asparagus & Chicken Quiche
Servings: 4
Cooking Time: 30 Minutes
Ingredients:
- 1 grilled chicken breasts, diced
- ½ cup shredded Gruyère cheese
- 1 premade pie crust
- 2 eggs, beaten
- ¼ cup milk
- Salt and pepper to taste
- ½ lb asparagus, sliced
- 1 lemon, zested

Directions:
1. Preheat air fryer to 360°F/180°C. Carefully press the crust into a baking dish, trimming the edges. Prick the dough with a fork a few times. Add the eggs, milk, asparagus, salt, pepper, chicken, lemon zest, and half of Gruyère cheese to a mixing bowl and stir until completely blended. Pour the mixture into the pie crust. Bake in the air fryer for 15 minutes. Sprinkle the remaining Gruyère cheese on top of the quiche filling. Bake for 5 more minutes until the quiche is golden brown. Remove and allow to cool for a few minutes before cutting. Serve sliced and enjoy!

Poblano Bake

Servings: 4
Cooking Time: 11 Minutes Per Batch
Ingredients:
- 2 large poblano peppers (approx. 5½ inches long excluding stem)
- ¾ pound ground turkey, raw
- ¾ cup cooked brown rice
- 1 teaspoon chile powder
- ½ teaspoon ground cumin
- ½ teaspoon garlic powder
- 4 ounces sharp Cheddar cheese, grated
- 1 8-ounce jar salsa, warmed

Directions:
1. Slice each pepper in half lengthwise so that you have four wide, flat pepper halves.
2. Remove seeds and membrane and discard. Rinse inside and out.
3. In a large bowl, combine turkey, rice, chile powder, cumin, and garlic powder. Mix well.
4. Divide turkey filling into 4 portions and stuff one into each of the 4 pepper halves. Press lightly to pack down.
5. Place 2 pepper halves in air fryer basket and cook at 390°F/200°C for 10minutes or until turkey is well done.
6. Top each pepper half with ¼ of the grated cheese. Cook 1 more minute or just until cheese melts.
7. Repeat steps 5 and 6 to cook remaining pepper halves.
8. To serve, place each pepper half on a plate and top with ¼ cup warm salsa.

Greek Chicken Wings

Servings: 4
Cooking Time: 30 Minutes
Ingredients:
- 8 whole chicken wings
- ½ lemon, juiced
- ½ tsp garlic powder
- 1 tsp shallot powder
- ½ tsp Greek seasoning
- Salt and pepper to taste
- ¼ cup buttermilk
- ½ cup all-purpose flour

Directions:
1. Preheat air fryer to 400°F/205°C. Put the wings in a resealable bag along with lemon juice, garlic, shallot, Greek seasoning, salt and pepper. Seal the bag and shake to coat. Set up bowls large enough to fit the wings.
2. In one bowl, pour the buttermilk. In the other, add flour. Using tongs, dip the wings into the buttermilk, then dredge in flour. Transfer the wings in the greased frying basket, spraying lightly with cooking oil. Air Fry for 25 minutes, shaking twice, until golden and cooked through. Allow to cool slightly, and serve.

Cheesy Chicken-avocado Paninis

Servings: 2
Cooking Time: 25 Minutes
Ingredients:
- 2 tbsp mayonnaise
- 4 tsp yellow mustard
- 4 sandwich bread slices
- 4 oz sliced deli chicken ham
- 2 oz sliced provolone cheese
- 2 oz sliced mozzarella
- 1 avocado, sliced
- 1 tomato, sliced
- Salt and pepper to taste
- 1 tsp sesame seeds
- 2 tbsp butter, melted

Directions:
1. Preheat air fryer at 350ºF/175°C. Rub mayonnaise and mustard on the inside of each bread slice. Top 2 bread slices with chicken ham, provolone and mozzarella cheese, avocado, sesame seeds, and tomato slices. Season with salt and pepper. Then, close sandwiches with the remaining bread slices. Brush the top and bottom of each sandwich lightly with melted butter. Place sandwiches in the frying basket and Bake for 6 minutes, flipping once. Serve.

Southern-style Chicken Legs

Servings: 6
Cooking Time: 20 Minutes
Ingredients:
- 2 cups buttermilk
- 1 tablespoon hot sauce
- 12 chicken legs
- ½ teaspoon salt
- ½ teaspoon pepper
- 1 teaspoon paprika
- ½ teaspoon onion powder
- 1 teaspoon garlic powder
- 1 cup all-purpose flour

Directions:
1. In an airtight container, place the buttermilk, hot sauce, and chicken legs and refrigerate for 4 to 8 hours.
2. In a medium bowl, whisk together the salt, pepper, paprika, onion powder, garlic powder, and flour. Drain the chicken legs from the buttermilk and dip the chicken legs into the flour mixture, stirring to coat well.
3. Preheat the air fryer to 390°F/200°C.
4. Place the chicken legs in the air fryer basket and spray with cooking spray. Cook for 10 minutes, turn the chicken legs over, and cook for another 8 to 10 minutes. Check for an internal temperature of 165°F/75°C.

Mexican Turkey Meatloaves

Servings: 4
Cooking Time: 30 Minutes
Ingredients:
- ¼ cup jarred chunky mild salsa
- 1 lb ground turkey
- 1/3 cup bread crumbs
- 1/3 cup canned black beans
- 1/3 cup frozen corn
- ¼ cup minced onion
- ¼ cup chopped scallions
- 2 tbsp chopped cilantro
- 1 egg, beaten
- 1 tbsp tomato puree
- 1 tsp salt
- ½ tsp ground cumin
- 1 tsp Mulato chile powder
- ½ tsp ground aniseed
- ¼ tsp ground cloves
- 2 tbsp ketchup
- 2 tbsp jarred mild salsa

Tower Air Fryer Cookbook

Directions:
1. In a bowl, use your hands to mix the turkey, bread crumbs, beans, corn, salsa, onion, scallions, cilantro, egg, tomato puree, salt, chile powder, aniseed, cloves, and cumin. Shape into 4 patties about 1-inch in thickness.
2. Preheat air fryer to 350°F/175°C. Put the meatloaves in the greased frying basket and Bake for about 18-20 minutes, flipping once until cooked through. Stir together the ketchup and salsa in a small bowl. When all loaves are cooked, brush them with the glaze and return to the fryer to heat up for 2 minutes. Serve immediately.

Cajun Chicken Livers
Servings: 2
Cooking Time: 45 Minutes
Ingredients:
- 1 lb chicken livers, rinsed, connective tissue discarded
- 1 cup whole milk
- ½ cup cornmeal
- 3/4 cup flour
- 1 tsp salt and black pepper
- 1 tsp Cajun seasoning
- 2 eggs
- 1 ½ cups bread crumbs
- 1 tbsp olive oil
- 2 tbsp chopped parsley

Directions:
1. Pat chicken livers dry with paper towels, then transfer them to a small bowl and pour in the milk and black pepper. Let sit covered in the fridge for 2 hours.
2. Preheat air fryer at 375°F/190°C. In a bowl, combine cornmeal, flour, salt, and Cajun seasoning. In another bowl, beat the eggs, and in a third bowl, add bread crumbs. Dip chicken livers first in the cornmeal mixture, then in the egg, and finally in the bread crumbs. Place chicken livers in the greased frying basket, brush the tops lightly with olive oil, and Air Fry for 16 minutes, turning once. Serve right away sprinkled with parsley.

Pulled Turkey Quesadillas
Servings: 4
Cooking Time: 15 Minutes
Ingredients:
- ¾ cup pulled cooked turkey breast
- 6 tortilla wraps
- 1/3 cup grated Swiss cheese
- 1 small red onion, sliced
- 2 tbsp Mexican chili sauce

Directions:
1. Preheat air fryer to 400°F/205°C. Lay 3 tortilla wraps on a clean workspace, then spoon equal amounts of Swiss cheese, turkey, Mexican chili sauce, and red onion on the tortillas. Spritz the exterior of the tortillas with cooking spray. Air Fry the quesadillas, one at a time, for 5-8 minutes. The cheese should be melted and the outsides crispy. Serve.

Honey Lemon Thyme Glazed Cornish Hen
Servings: 2
Cooking Time: 20 Minutes
Ingredients:
- 1 (2-pound) Cornish game hen, split in half
- olive oil
- salt and freshly ground black pepper
- ¼ teaspoon dried thyme
- ¼ cup honey
- 1 tablespoon lemon zest
- juice of 1 lemon
- 1½ teaspoons chopped fresh thyme leaves
- ½ teaspoon soy sauce
- freshly ground black pepper

Directions:
1. Split the game hen in half by cutting down each side of the backbone and then cutting through the breast. Brush or spray both halves of the game hen with the olive oil and then season with the salt, pepper and dried thyme.
2. Preheat the air fryer to 390°F/200°C.
3. Place the game hen, skin side down, into the air fryer and air-fry for 5 minutes. Turn the hen halves over and air-fry for 10 minutes.
4. While the hen is cooking, combine the honey, lemon zest and juice, fresh thyme, soy sauce and pepper in a small bowl.
5. When the air fryer timer rings, brush the honey glaze onto the game hen and continue to air-fry for another 3 to 5 minutes, just until the hen is nicely glazed, browned and has an internal temperature of 165°F/75°C.
6. Let the hen rest for 5 minutes and serve warm.

Chicken Adobo
Servings: 6
Cooking Time: 12 Minutes
Ingredients:
- 6 boneless chicken thighs
- ¼ cup soy sauce or tamari
- ½ cup rice wine vinegar
- 4 cloves garlic, minced
- ⅛ teaspoon crushed red pepper flakes
- ½ teaspoon black pepper

Directions:
1. Place the chicken thighs into a resealable plastic bag with the soy sauce or tamari, the rice wine vinegar, the garlic, and the crushed red pepper flakes. Seal the bag and let the chicken marinate at least 1 hour in the refrigerator.
2. Preheat the air fryer to 400°F/205°C.
3. Drain the chicken and pat dry with a paper towel. Season the chicken with black pepper and liberally spray with cooking spray.
4. Place the chicken in the air fryer basket and cook for 9 minutes, turn over at 9 minutes and check for an internal temperature of 165°F, and cook another 3 minutes.

Fantasy Sweet Chili Chicken Strips
Servings: 2
Cooking Time: 20 Minutes
Ingredients:
- 1 lb chicken strips
- 1 cup sweet chili sauce
- ½ cup bread crumbs
- ½ cup cornmeal

Directions:
1. Preheat air fryer at 350°F/175°C. Combine chicken strips and sweet chili sauce in a bowl until fully coated. In another bowl, mix the remaining ingredients. Dredge strips in the mixture. Shake off any excess. Place chicken strips in the greased frying basket and Air Fry for 10 minutes, tossing once. Serve right away.

Chicken Tenders With Basil-strawberry Glaze

Servings: 4
Cooking Time: 20 Minutes
Ingredients:
- 1 lb chicken tenderloins
- ¼ cup strawberry preserves
- 3 tbsp chopped basil
- 1 tsp orange juice
- ½ tsp orange zest
- Salt and pepper to taste

Directions:
1. Combine all ingredients, except for 1 tbsp of basil, in a bowl. Marinade in the fridge covered for 30 minutes.
2. Preheat air fryer to 350°F/175°C. Place the chicken tenders in the frying basket and Air Fry for 4-6 minutes. Shake gently the basket and turn over the chicken. Cook for 5 more minutes. Top with the remaining basil to serve.

Southern-fried Chicken Livers

Servings: 4
Cooking Time: 12 Minutes
Ingredients:
- 2 eggs
- 2 tablespoons water
- ¾ cup flour
- 1½ cups panko breadcrumbs
- ½ cup plain breadcrumbs
- 1 teaspoon salt
- ½ teaspoon black pepper
- 20 ounces chicken livers, salted to taste
- oil for misting or cooking spray

Directions:
1. Beat together eggs and water in a shallow dish. Place the flour in a separate shallow dish.
2. In the bowl of a food processor, combine the panko, plain breadcrumbs, salt, and pepper. Process until well mixed and panko crumbs are finely crushed. Place crumbs in a third shallow dish.
3. Dip livers in flour, then egg wash, and then roll in panko mixture to coat well with crumbs.
4. Spray both sides of livers with oil or cooking spray. Cooking in two batches, place livers in air fryer basket in single layer.
5. Cook at 390°F/200°C for 7minutes. Spray livers, turn over, and spray again. Cook for 5 more minutes, until done inside and coating is golden brown.
6. Repeat to cook remaining livers.

Japanese-inspired Glazed Chicken

Servings: 4
Cooking Time: 25 Minutes
Ingredients:
- 4 chicken breasts
- Chicken seasoning to taste
- Salt and pepper to taste
- 2 tsp grated fresh ginger
- 2 garlic cloves, minced
- ¼ cup molasses
- 2 tbsp tamari sauce

Directions:
1. Preheat air fryer to 400°F/205°C. Season the chicken with seasoning, salt, and pepper. Place the chicken in the greased frying basket and Air Fry for 7 minutes, then flip the chicken. Cook for another 3 minutes.
2. While the chicken is cooking, combine ginger, garlic, molasses, and tamari sauce in a saucepan over medium heat. Cook for 4 minutes or until the sauce thickens. Transfer all of the chicken to a serving dish. Drizzle with ginger-tamari glaze and serve.

Chicken Wellington

Servings: 2
Cooking Time: 31 Minutes
Ingredients:
- 2 (5-ounce) boneless, skinless chicken breasts
- ½ cup White Worcestershire sauce
- 3 tablespoons butter
- ½ cup finely diced onion (about ½ onion)
- 8 ounces button mushrooms, finely chopped
- ¼ cup chicken stock
- 2 tablespoons White Worcestershire sauce (or white wine)
- salt and freshly ground black pepper
- 1 tablespoon chopped fresh tarragon
- 2 sheets puff pastry, thawed
- 1 egg, beaten
- vegetable oil

Directions:
1. Place the chicken breasts in a shallow dish. Pour the White Worcestershire sauce over the chicken coating both sides and marinate for 30 minutes.
2. While the chicken is marinating, melt the butter in a large skillet over medium-high heat on the stovetop. Add the onion and sauté for a few minutes, until it starts to soften. Add the mushrooms and sauté for 5 minutes until the vegetables are brown and soft. Deglaze the skillet with the chicken stock, scraping up any bits from the bottom of the pan. Add the White Worcestershire sauce and simmer for 3 minutes until the mixture reduces and starts to thicken. Season with salt and freshly ground black pepper. Remove the mushroom mixture from the heat and stir in the fresh tarragon. Let the mushroom mixture cool.
3. Preheat the air fryer to 360°F.
4. Remove the chicken from the marinade and transfer it to the air fryer basket. Tuck the small end of the chicken breast under the thicker part to shape it into a circle rather than an oval. Pour the marinade over the chicken and air-fry for 10 minutes.
5. Roll out the puff pastry and cut out two 6-inch squares. Brush the perimeter of each square with the egg wash. Place half of the mushroom mixture in the center of each puff pastry square. Place the chicken breasts, top side down on the mushroom mixture. Starting with one corner of puff pastry and working in one direction, pull the pastry up over the chicken to enclose it and press the ends of the pastry together in the middle. Brush the pastry with the egg wash to seal the edges. Turn the Wellingtons over and set aside.
6. To make a decorative design with the remaining puff pastry, cut out four 10-inch strips. For each Wellington, twist two of the strips together, place them over the chicken breast wrapped in puff pastry, and tuck the ends underneath to seal it. Brush the entire top and sides of the Wellingtons with the egg wash.
7. Preheat the air fryer to 350°F/175°C.
8. Spray or brush the air fryer basket with vegetable oil. Air-fry the chicken Wellingtons for 13 minutes. Carefully turn the Wellingtons over. Air-fry for another 8 minutes. Transfer to serving plates, light a candle and enjoy!

Chicken Cutlets With Broccoli Rabe And Roasted Peppers

Servings: 2
Cooking Time: 10 Minutes
Ingredients:
- ½ bunch broccoli rabe
- olive oil, in a spray bottle
- salt and freshly ground black pepper
- ⅔ cup roasted red pepper strips
- 2 (4-ounce) boneless, skinless chicken breasts
- 2 tablespoons all-purpose flour*
- 1 egg, beaten
- ⅓ cup seasoned breadcrumbs*
- 2 slices aged provolone cheese

Directions:
1. Bring a medium saucepot of salted water to a boil on the stovetop. Blanch the broccoli rabe for 3 minutes in the boiling water and then drain. When it has cooled a little, squeeze out as much water as possible, drizzle a little olive oil on top, season with salt and black pepper and set aside. Dry the roasted red peppers with a clean kitchen towel and set them aside as well.
2. Place each chicken breast between 2 pieces of plastic wrap. Use a meat pounder to flatten the chicken breasts to about ½-inch thick. Season the chicken on both sides with salt and pepper.
3. Preheat the air fryer to 400°F/205°C.
4. Set up a dredging station with three shallow dishes. Place the flour in one dish, the egg in a second dish and the breadcrumbs in a third dish. Coat the chicken on all sides with the flour. Shake off any excess flour and dip the chicken into the egg. Let the excess egg drip off and coat both sides of the chicken in the breadcrumbs. Spray the chicken with olive oil on both sides and transfer to the air fryer basket.
5. Air-fry the chicken at 400°F/205°C for 5 minutes. Turn the chicken over and air-fry for another minute. Then, top the chicken breast with the broccoli rabe and roasted peppers. Place a slice of the provolone cheese on top and secure it with a toothpick or two.
6. Air-fry at 360°F/180°C for 3 to 4 minutes to melt the cheese and warm everything together.

Mexican-inspired Chicken Breasts

Servings: 4
Cooking Time: 20 Minutes
Ingredients:
- ⅛ tsp crushed red pepper flakes
- 1 red pepper, deseeded and diced
- Salt to taste
- 4 chicken breasts
- ¾ tsp garlic powder
- ½ tsp onion powder
- ½ tsp ground cumin
- ½ tsp ancho chile powder
- ½ tsp sweet paprika
- ½ tsp Mexican oregano
- 1 tomato, chopped
- ½ diced red onion
- 3 tbsp fresh lime juice
- 10 ounces avocado, diced
- 1 tbsp chopped cilantro

Directions:
1. Preheat air fryer to 380°F/195°C. Stir together salt, garlic and onion powder, cumin, ancho chili powder, paprika, Mexican oregano, and pepper flakes in a bowl. Spray the chicken with cooking oil and rub with the spice mix. Air Fry the chicken for 10 minutes, flipping once until browned and fully cooked. Repeat for all of the chicken. Mix the onion and lime juice in a bowl. Fold in the avocado, cilantro, red pepper, salt, and tomato and coat gently. To serve, top the chicken with guacamole salsa.

Greek Gyros With Chicken & Rice

Servings: 4
Cooking Time: 25 Minutes
Ingredients:
- 1 lb chicken breasts, cubed
- ¼ cup cream cheese
- 2 tbsp olive oil
- 1 tsp dried oregano
- 1 tsp ground cumin
- 1 tsp ground cinnamon
- ¼ tsp ground nutmeg
- Salt and pepper to taste
- ¼ tsp ground turmeric
- 2 cups cooked rice
- 1 cup Tzatziki sauce

Directions:
1. Preheat air fryer to 380°F/195°C. Put all ingredients in a bowl and mix together until the chicken is coated well. Spread the chicken mixture in the frying basket, then Bake for 10 minutes. Stir the chicken mixture and Bake for an additional 5 minutes. Serve with rice and tzatziki sauce.

Chicken Nuggets

Servings: 20
Cooking Time: 14 Minutes Per Batch
Ingredients:
- 1 pound boneless, skinless chicken thighs, cut into 1-inch chunks
- ¾ teaspoon salt
- ½ teaspoon black pepper
- ½ teaspoon garlic powder
- ½ teaspoon onion powder
- ½ cup flour
- 2 eggs, beaten
- ½ cup panko breadcrumbs
- 3 tablespoons plain breadcrumbs
- oil for misting or cooking spray

Directions:
1. In the bowl of a food processor, combine chicken, ½ teaspoon salt, pepper, garlic powder, and onion powder. Process in short pulses until chicken is very finely chopped and well blended.
2. Place flour in one shallow dish and beaten eggs in another. In a third dish or plastic bag, mix together the panko crumbs, plain breadcrumbs, and ¼ teaspoon salt.
3. Shape chicken mixture into small nuggets. Dip nuggets in flour, then eggs, then panko crumb mixture.
4. Spray nuggets on both sides with oil or cooking spray and place in air fryer basket in a single layer, close but not overlapping.
5. Cook at 360°F/180°C for 10minutes. Spray with oil and cook 4 minutes, until chicken is done and coating is golden brown.
6. Repeat step 5 to cook remaining nuggets.

Harissa Chicken Wings
Servings: 4
Cooking Time: 25 Minutes
Ingredients:
- 8 whole chicken wings
- 1 tsp garlic powder
- ¼ tsp dried oregano
- 1 tbsp harissa seasoning

Directions:
1. Preheat air fryer to 400°F/205°C. Season the wings with garlic, harissa seasoning, and oregano. Place them in the greased frying basket and spray with cooking oil spray. Air Fry for 10 minutes, shake the basket, and cook for another 5-7 minutes until golden and crispy. Serve warm.

Asian Meatball Tacos
Servings: 4
Cooking Time: 10 Minutes
Ingredients:
- 1 pound lean ground turkey
- 3 tablespoons soy sauce
- 1 tablespoon brown sugar
- ½ teaspoon onion powder
- ½ teaspoon garlic powder
- 1 tablespoon sesame seeds
- 1 English cucumber
- 4 radishes
- 2 tablespoons white wine vinegar
- 1 lime, juiced and divided
- 1 tablespoon avocado oil
- Salt, to taste
- ½ cup Greek yogurt
- 1 to 3 teaspoons Sriracha, based on desired spiciness
- 1 cup shredded cabbage
- ¼ cup chopped cilantro
- Eight 6-inch flour tortillas

Directions:
1. Preheat the air fryer to 360°F/180°C.
2. In a large bowl, mix the ground turkey, soy sauce, brown sugar, onion powder, garlic powder, and sesame seeds. Form the meat into 1-inch meatballs and place in the air fryer basket. Cook for 5 minutes, shake the basket, and cook another 5 minutes. Using a food thermometer, make sure the internal temperature of the meatballs is 165°F/75°C.
3. Meanwhile, dice the cucumber and radishes and place in a medium bowl. Add the white wine vinegar, 1 teaspoon of the lime juice, and the avocado oil, and stir to coat. Season with salt to desired taste.
4. In a large bowl, mix the Greek yogurt, Sriracha, and the remaining lime juice, and stir. Add in the cabbage and cilantro; toss well to create a slaw.
5. In a heavy skillet, heat the tortillas over medium heat for 1 to 2 minutes on each side, or until warmed.
6. To serve, place a tortilla on a plate, top with 5 meatballs, then with cucumber and radish salad, and finish with 2 tablespoons of cabbage slaw.

Herb-marinated Chicken
Servings: 4
Cooking Time: 25 Minutes
Ingredients:
- 4 chicken breasts
- 2 tsp rosemary, minced
- 2 tsp thyme, minced
- Salt and pepper to taste
- ½ cup chopped cilantro
- 1 lime, juiced

Directions:
1. Place chicken in a resealable bag. Add rosemary, thyme, salt, pepper, cilantro, and lime juice. Seal the bag and toss to coat, then place in the refrigerator for 2 hours.
2. Preheat air fryer to 400°F/205°C. Arrange the chicken in a single layer in the greased frying basket. Spray the chicken with cooking oil. Air Fry for 6-7 minutes, then flip the chicken. Cook for another 3 minutes. Serve and enjoy!

Kale & Rice Chicken Rolls
Servings: 4
Cooking Time: 35 Minutes
Ingredients:
- 4 boneless, skinless chicken thighs
- ½ tsp ground fenugreek seeds
- 1 cup cooked wild rice
- 2 sundried tomatoes, diced
- ½ cup chopped kale
- 2 garlic cloves, minced
- 1 tsp salt
- 1 lemon, juiced
- ½ cup crumbled feta
- 1 tbsp olive oil

Directions:
1. Preheat air fryer to 380°F/195°C. Put the chicken thighs between two pieces of plastic wrap, and using a meat mallet or a rolling pin, pound them out to about ¼-inch thick. Combine the rice, tomatoes, kale, garlic, salt, fenugreek seeds and lemon juice in a bowl and mix well.
2. Divide the rice mixture among the chicken thighs and sprinkle with feta. Fold the sides of the chicken thigh over the filling, and then gently place each of them seam-side down into the greased air frying basket. Drizzle the stuffed chicken thighs with olive oil. Roast the stuffed chicken thighs for 12 minutes, then turn them over and cook for an additional 10 minutes. Serve and enjoy!

Chicken Parmigiana
Servings: 2
Cooking Time: 35 Minutes
Ingredients:
- 2 chicken breasts
- 1 cup breadcrumbs
- 2 eggs, beaten
- Salt and pepper to taste
- 1 tbsp dried basil
- 1 cup passata
- 2 provolone cheese slices
- 1 tbsp Parmesan cheese

Directions:
1. Preheat air fryer to 350°F/175°C. Mix the breadcrumbs, basil, salt, and pepper in a mixing bowl. Coat the chicken breasts with the crumb mixture, then dip in the beaten eggs. Finally, coat again with the dry ingredients. Arrange the coated chicken breasts on the greased frying basket and Air Fry for 20 minutes. At the 10-minutes mark, turn the breasts over and cook for the remaining 10 minutes.
2. Pour half of the passata into a baking pan. When the chicken is ready, remove it to the passata-covered pan. Pour the remaining passata over the fried chicken and arrange the provolone cheese slices on top and sprinkle with Parmesan cheese. Bake for 5 minutes until the chicken is crisped and the cheese melted and lightly toasted. Serve.

Mustardy Chicken Bites

Servings: 4
Cooking Time: 20 Minutes + Chilling Time
Ingredients:
- 2 tbsp horseradish mustard
- 1 tbsp mayonnaise
- 1 tbsp olive oil
- 2 chicken breasts, cubes
- 1 tbsp parsley

Directions:
1. Combine all ingredients, excluding parsley, in a bowl. Let marinate covered in the fridge for 30 minutes. Preheat air fryer at 350ºF/175°C. Place chicken cubes in the greased frying basket and Air Fry for 9 minutes, tossing once. Serve immediately sprinkled with parsley.

Restaurant-style Chicken Thighs

Servings: 4
Cooking Time: 30 Minutes
Ingredients:
- 1 lb boneless, skinless chicken thighs
- ¼ cup barbecue sauce
- 2 cloves garlic, minced
- 1 tsp lemon zest
- 2 tbsp parsley, chopped
- 2 tbsp lemon juice

Directions:
1. Coat the chicken with barbecue sauce, garlic, and lemon juice in a medium bowl. leave to marinate for 10 minutes.
2. Preheat air fryer to 380°F/195°C. When ready to cook, remove the chicken from the bowl and shake off any drips. Arrange the chicken in the air fryer and Bake for 16-18 minutes, until golden and cooked through. Serve topped with lemon zest and parsley. Enjoy!

Chicken & Fruit Biryani

Servings: 4
Cooking Time: 30 Minutes
Ingredients:
- 3 chicken breasts, cubed
- 2 tsp olive oil
- 2 tbsp cornstarch
- 1 tbsp curry powder
- 1 apple, chopped
- ½ cup chicken broth
- 1/3 cup dried cranberries
- 1 cooked basmati rice

Directions:
1. Preheat air fryer to 380°F/195°C. Combine the chicken and olive oil, then add some corn starch and curry powder. Mix to coat, then add the apple and pour the mix in a baking pan. Put the pan in the air fryer and Bake for 8 minutes, stirring once. Add the chicken broth, cranberries, and 2 tbsp of water and continue baking for 10 minutes, letting the sauce thicken. The chicken should be lightly charred and cooked through. Serve warm with basmati rice.

Cal-mex Turkey Patties

Servings: 4
Cooking Time: 30 Minutes
Ingredients:
- 1/3 cup crushed corn tortilla chips
- 1/3 cup grated American cheese
- 1 egg, beaten
- ¼ cup salsa
- Salt and pepper to taste
- 1 lb ground turkey
- 1 tbsp olive oil
- 1 tsp chili powder

Directions:
1. Preheat air fryer to 330°F/165°C. Mix together egg, tortilla chips, salsa, cheese, salt, and pepper in a bowl. Using your hands, add the ground turkey and mix gently until just combined. Divide the meat into 4 equal portions and shape into patties about ½ inch thick. Brush the patties with olive oil and sprinkle with chili powder. Air Fry the patties for 14-16 minutes, flipping once until cooked through and golden. Serve and enjoy!

Chipotle Chicken Drumsticks

Servings: 4
Cooking Time: 40 Minutes
Ingredients:
- 1 can chipotle chilies packed in adobe sauce
- 2 tbsp grated Mexican cheese
- 6 chicken drumsticks
- 1 egg, beaten
- ½ cup bread crumbs
- 1 tbsp corn flakes
- Salt and pepper to taste

Directions:
1. Preheat air fryer to 350°F/175°C. Place the chilies in the sauce in your blender and pulse until a fine paste is formed. Transfer to a bowl and add the beaten egg. Combine thoroughly. Mix the breadcrumbs, Mexican cheese, corn flakes, salt, and pepper in a separate bowl, and set aside.
2. Coat the chicken drumsticks with the crumb mixture, then dip into the bowl with wet ingredients, then dip again into the dry ingredients. Arrange the chicken drumsticks on the greased frying basket in a single flat layer. Air Fry for 14-16 minutes, turning each chicken drumstick over once. Serve warm.

Mom's Chicken Wings

Servings: 4
Cooking Time: 35 Minutes
Ingredients:
- 2 lb chicken wings, split at the joint
- 1 tbsp water
- 1 tbsp sesame oil
- 2 tbsp Dijon mustard
- ¼ tsp chili powder
- 1 tbsp tamari
- 1 tsp honey
- 1 tsp white wine vinegar

Directions:
1. Preheat air fryer to 400ºF/205°C. Coat the wings with sesame oil. Place them in the frying basket and Air Fry for 16-18 minutes, tossing once or twice. Whisk the remaining ingredients in a bowl. Reserve. When ready, transfer the wings to a serving bowl. Pour the previously prepared sauce over and toss to coat. Serve immediately.

Family Chicken Fingers

Servings: 4
Cooking Time: 30 Minutes
Ingredients:
- 1 lb chicken breast fingers
- 1 tbsp chicken seasoning
- ½ tsp mustard powder
- Salt and pepper to taste
- 2 eggs
- 1 cup bread crumbs

Directions:
1. Preheat air fryer to 400°F/205°C. Add the chicken fingers to a large bowl along with chicken seasoning, mustard, salt, and pepper; mix well. Set up two small bowls. In one bowl, beat the eggs. In the second bowl, add the bread crumbs. Dip the chicken in the egg, then dredge in breadcrumbs. Place the nuggets in the air fryer. Lightly spray with cooking oil, then Air Fry for 8 minutes, shaking the basket once until crispy and cooked through. Serve warm.

Crispy Cordon Bleu

Servings: 4
Cooking Time: 25 Minutes
Ingredients:
- 4 deli ham slices, halved lengthwise
- 2 tbsp grated Parmesan
- 4 chicken breast halves
- Salt and pepper to taste
- 8 Swiss cheese slices
- 1 egg
- 2 egg whites
- ¾ cup bread crumbs
- 1 tsp garlic powder
- 1 tsp onion powder
- 1 tsp mustard powder

Directions:
1. Preheat air fryer to 400°F/205°C. Season the chicken cutlets with salt and pepper. On one cutlet, put a half slice of ham and cheese on the top. Roll the chicken tightly, then set aside. Beat the eggs and egg whites in a shallow bowl. Put the crumbs, Parmesan, garlic, onion, and mustard powder, in a second bowl. Dip the cutlet in the egg bowl and then in the crumb mix. Press so that they stick to the chicken. Put the rolls of chicken seam side down in the greased frying basket and Air Fry for 12-14 minutes, flipping once until golden and cooked through. Serve.

Chicken Wings Al Ajillo

Servings: 4
Cooking Time: 35 Minutes
Ingredients:
- 2 lb chicken wings, split at the joint
- 2 tbsp melted butter
- 2 tbsp grated Cotija cheese
- 4 cloves garlic, minced
- ½ tbsp hot paprika
- ¼ tsp salt

Directions:
1. Preheat air fryer to 250°F/120°C. Coat the chicken wings with 1 tbsp of butter. Place them in the basket and Air Fry for 12 minutes, tossing once. In another bowl, whisk 1 tbsp of butter, Cotija cheese, garlic, hot paprika, and salt. Reserve. Increase temperature to 400°F/205°C. Air Fry wings for 10 more minutes, tossing twice. Transfer them to the bowl with the sauce, and toss to coat. Serve immediately.

Chicken Breast Burgers

Servings: 4
Cooking Time: 35 Minutes
Ingredients:
- 2 chicken breasts
- 1 cup dill pickle juice
- 1 cup buttermilk
- 1 egg
- ½ cup flour
- Salt and pepper to taste
- 4 buns
- 2 pickles, sliced

Directions:
1. Cut the chicken into cutlets by cutting them in half horizontally on a cutting board. Transfer them to a large bowl along with pickle juice and ½ cup of buttermilk. Toss to coat, then marinate for 30 minutes in the fridge.
2. Preheat air fryer to 370°F/185°C. In a shallow bowl, beat the egg and the rest of the buttermilk to combine. In another shallow bowl, mix flour, salt, and pepper. Dip the marinated cutlet in the egg mixture, then dredge in flour. Place the cutlets in the greased frying basket and Air Fry for 12 minutes, flipping once halfway through. Remove the cutlets and pickles on buns and serve.

Sage & Paprika Turkey Cutlets

Servings: 4
Cooking Time: 15 Minutes
Ingredients:
- ½ cup bread crumbs
- ¼ tsp paprika
- Salt and pepper to taste
- ⅛ tsp dried sage
- ⅛ tsp garlic powder
- ¼ tsp ground cumin
- 1 egg
- 4 turkey breast cutlets
- 2 tbsp chopped chervil

Directions:
1. Preheat air fryer to 380°F/195°C. Combine the bread crumbs, paprika, salt, black pepper, sage, cumin, and garlic powder in a bowl and mix well. Beat the egg in another bowl until frothy. Dip the turkey cutlets into the egg mixture, then coat them in the bread crumb mixture. Put the breaded turkey cutlets in the frying basket. Bake for 4 minutes. Turn the cutlets over, then Bake for 4 more minutes. Decorate with chervil and serve.

Fish And Seafood Recipes

Coconut-shrimp Po' Boys

Servings: 4
Cooking Time: 5 Minutes
Ingredients:
- ½ cup cornstarch
- 2 eggs
- 2 tablespoons milk
- ¾ cup shredded coconut
- ½ cup panko breadcrumbs
- 1 pound (31–35 count) shrimp, peeled and deveined
- Old Bay Seasoning
- oil for misting or cooking spray
- 2 large hoagie rolls
- honey mustard or light mayonnaise
- 1½ cups shredded lettuce
- 1 large tomato, thinly sliced

Directions:
1. Place cornstarch in a shallow dish or plate.
2. In another shallow dish, beat together eggs and milk.
3. In a third dish mix the coconut and panko crumbs.
4. Sprinkle shrimp with Old Bay Seasoning to taste.
5. Dip shrimp in cornstarch to coat lightly, dip in egg mixture, shake off excess, and roll in coconut mixture to coat well.
6. Spray both sides of coated shrimp with oil or cooking spray.
7. Cook half the shrimp in a single layer at 390°F/200°C for 5minutes.
8. Repeat to cook remaining shrimp.
9. To Assemble
10. Split each hoagie lengthwise, leaving one long edge intact.
11. Place in air fryer basket and cook at 390°F for 1 to 2minutes or until heated through.
12. Remove buns, break apart, and place on 4 plates, cut side up.
13. Spread with honey mustard and/or mayonnaise.
14. Top with shredded lettuce, tomato slices, and coconut shrimp.

Hot Calamari Rings

Servings: 4
Cooking Time: 25 Minutes
Ingredients:
- ½ cup all-purpose flour
- 2 tsp hot chili powder
- 2 eggs
- 1 tbsp milk
- 1 cup bread crumbs
- Salt and pepper to taste
- 1 lb calamari rings
- 1 lime, quartered
- ½ cup aioli sauce

Directions:
1. Preheat air fryer at 400°F/205°C. In a shallow bowl, add flour and hot chili powder. In another bowl, mix the eggs and milk. In a third bowl, mix the breadcrumbs, salt and pepper. Dip calamari rings in flour mix first, then in eggs mix and shake off excess. Then, roll ring through breadcrumb mixture. Place calamari rings in the greased frying basket and Air Fry for 4 minutes, tossing once. Squeeze lime quarters over calamari. Serve with aioli sauce.

Almond-crusted Fish

Servings: 4
Cooking Time: 10 Minutes
Ingredients:
- 4 4-ounce fish fillets
- ¾ cup breadcrumbs
- ¼ cup sliced almonds, crushed
- 2 tablespoons lemon juice
- ⅛ teaspoon cayenne
- salt and pepper
- ¾ cup flour
- 1 egg, beaten with 1 tablespoon water
- oil for misting or cooking spray

Directions:
1. Split fish fillets lengthwise down the center to create 8 pieces.
2. Mix breadcrumbs and almonds together and set aside.
3. Mix the lemon juice and cayenne together. Brush on all sides of fish.
4. Season fish to taste with salt and pepper.
5. Place the flour on a sheet of wax paper.
6. Roll fillets in flour, dip in egg wash, and roll in the crumb mixture.
7. Mist both sides of fish with oil or cooking spray.
8. Spray air fryer basket and lay fillets inside.
9. Cook at 390°F/200°C for 5minutes, turn fish over, and cook for an additional 5minutes or until fish is done and flakes easily.

Garlicky Sea Bass With Root Veggies

Servings: 4
Cooking Time: 25 Minutes
Ingredients:
- 1 carrot, diced
- 1 parsnip, diced
- ½ rutabaga, diced
- ½ turnip, diced
- ¼ cup olive oil
- Celery salt to taste
- 4 sea bass fillets
- ½ tsp onion powder
- 2 garlic cloves, minced
- 1 lemon, sliced

Directions:
1. Preheat air fryer to 380°F/195°C. Coat the carrot, parsnip, turnip and rutabaga with olive oil and salt in a small bowl. Lightly season the sea bass with and onion powder, then place into the frying basket. Spread the garlic over the top of the fillets, then cover with lemon slices. Pour the prepared vegetables into the basket around and on top of the fish. Roast for 15 minutes. Serve and enjoy!

Breaded Parmesan Perch

Servings: 5
Cooking Time: 15 Minutes
Ingredients:
- ¼ cup grated Parmesan
- ½ tsp salt
- ¼ tsp paprika
- 1 tbsp chopped dill
- 1 tsp dried thyme
- 2 tsp Dijon mustard
- 2 tbsp bread crumbs
- 4 ocean perch fillets
- 1 lemon, quartered
- 2 tbsp chopped cilantro

Directions:
1. Preheat air fryer to 400°F/205°C. Combine salt, paprika, pepper, dill, mustard, thyme, Parmesan, and bread crumbs in a wide bowl. Coat all sides of the fillets in the breading, then transfer to the greased frying basket. Air Fry for 8 minutes until outside is golden and the inside is cooked through. Garnish with lemon wedges and sprinkle with cilantro. Serve and enjoy!

Fish Tacos With Jalapeño-lime Sauce

Servings: 4
Cooking Time: 7 Minutes
Ingredients:
- Fish Tacos
- 1 pound fish fillets
- ¼ teaspoon cumin
- ¼ teaspoon coriander
- ⅛ teaspoon ground red pepper
- 1 tablespoon lime zest
- ¼ teaspoon smoked paprika
- 1 teaspoon oil
- cooking spray
- 6–8 corn or flour tortillas (6-inch size)
- Jalapeño-Lime Sauce
- ½ cup sour cream
- 1 tablespoon lime juice
- ¼ teaspoon grated lime zest
- ½ teaspoon minced jalapeño (flesh only)
- ¼ teaspoon cumin
- Napa Cabbage Garnish
- 1 cup shredded Napa cabbage
- ¼ cup slivered red or green bell pepper
- ¼ cup slivered onion

Directions:
1. Slice the fish fillets into strips approximately ½-inch thick.
2. Put the strips into a sealable plastic bag along with the cumin, coriander, red pepper, lime zest, smoked paprika, and oil. Massage seasonings into the fish until evenly distributed.
3. Spray air fryer basket with nonstick cooking spray and place seasoned fish inside.
4. Cook at 390°F/200°C for approximately 5minutes. Shake basket to distribute fish. Cook an additional 2 minutes, until fish flakes easily.
5. While the fish is cooking, prepare the Jalapeño-Lime Sauce by mixing the sour cream, lime juice, lime zest, jalapeño, and cumin together to make a smooth sauce. Set aside.
6. Mix the cabbage, bell pepper, and onion together and set aside.
7. To warm refrigerated tortillas, wrap in damp paper towels and microwave for 30 to 60 seconds.
8. To serve, spoon some of fish into a warm tortilla. Add one or two tablespoons Napa Cabbage Garnish and drizzle with Jalapeño-Lime Sauce.

King Prawns Al Ajillo

Servings: 4
Cooking Time: 15 Minutes
Ingredients:
- 1 ¼ lb peeled king prawns, deveined
- ½ cup grated Parmesan
- 1 tbsp olive oil
- 1 tbsp lemon juice
- ½ tsp garlic powder
- 2 garlic cloves, minced

Directions:
1. Preheat the air fryer to 350°F/175°C. In a large bowl, add the prawns and sprinkle with olive oil, lemon juice, and garlic powder. Toss in the minced garlic and Parmesan, then toss to coat. Put the prawns in the frying basket and Air Fry for 10-15 minutes or until the prawns cook through. Shake the basket once while cooking. Serve immediately.

Filled Mushrooms With Crab & Cheese

Servings:6
Cooking Time: 30 Minutes
Ingredients:
- 16 oz baby bella mushrooms, stems removed
- ½ cup lump crabmeat, shells discarded
- 2 oz feta cheese, crumbled
- 1 tsp prepared horseradish
- 1 tsp lemon juice
- Salt and pepper to taste
- 2 tbsp bread crumbs
- 2 tbsp butter, melted
- ¼ cup chopped dill

Directions:
1. Preheat air fryer to 350ºF/175°C. Combine the feta, crabmeat, horseradish, lemon juice, salt, and pepper in a bowl. Evenly stuff the crab mixture into mushroom caps, scatter bread crumbs over and drizzle with melted butter over the crumbs. Place the stuffed mushrooms in the frying basket. Bake for 10 minutes. Scatter with dill to serve.

Stuffed Shrimp

Servings: 4
Cooking Time: 12 Minutes Per Batch
Ingredients:
- 16 tail-on shrimp, peeled and deveined (last tail section intact)
- ¾ cup crushed panko breadcrumbs
- oil for misting or cooking spray
- Stuffing
- 2 6-ounce cans lump crabmeat
- 2 tablespoons chopped shallots
- 2 tablespoons chopped green onions
- 2 tablespoons chopped celery
- 2 tablespoons chopped green bell pepper

- ½ cup crushed saltine crackers
- 1 teaspoon Old Bay Seasoning
- 1 teaspoon garlic powder
- ¼ teaspoon ground thyme
- 2 teaspoons dried parsley flakes
- 2 teaspoons fresh lemon juice
- 2 teaspoons Worcestershire sauce
- 1 egg, beaten

Directions:
1. Rinse shrimp. Remove tail section (shell) from 4 shrimp, discard, and chop the meat finely.
2. To prepare the remaining 12 shrimp, cut a deep slit down the back side so that the meat lies open flat. Do not cut all the way through.
3. Preheat air fryer to 360°F/180°C.
4. Place chopped shrimp in a large bowl with all of the stuffing ingredients and stir to combine.
5. Divide stuffing into 12 portions, about 2 tablespoons each.
6. Place one stuffing portion onto the back of each shrimp and form into a ball or oblong shape. Press firmly so that stuffing sticks together and adheres to shrimp.
7. Gently roll each stuffed shrimp in panko crumbs and mist with oil or cooking spray.
8. Place 6 shrimp in air fryer basket and cook at 360°F/180°C for 10 minutes. Mist with oil or spray and cook 2 minutes longer or until stuffing cooks through inside and is crispy outside.
9. Repeat step 8 to cook remaining shrimp.

Saucy Shrimp

Servings: 4
Cooking Time: 30 Minutes
Ingredients:
- 1 lb peeled shrimp, deveined
- ½ cup grated coconut
- ¼ cup bread crumbs
- ¼ cup flour
- ¼ tsp smoked paprika
- Salt and pepper to taste
- 1 egg
- 2 tbsp maple syrup
- ½ tsp rice vinegar
- 1 tbsp hot sauce
- ⅛ tsp red pepper flakes
- ¼ cup orange juice
- 1 tsp cornstarch
- ½ cup banana ketchup
- 1 lemon, sliced

Directions:
1. Preheat air fryer to 350°F/175°C. Combine coconut, bread crumbs, flour, paprika, black pepper, and salt in a bowl. In a separate bowl, whisk egg and 1 teaspoon water. Dip one shrimp into the egg bowl and shake off excess drips. Dip the shrimp in the bread crumb mixture and coat it completely. Continue the process for all of the shrimp. Arrange the shrimp on the greased frying basket. Air Fry for 5 minutes, then use tongs to flip the shrimp. Cook for another 2-3 minutes.
2. To make the sauce, add maple syrup, banana ketchup, hot sauce, vinegar, and red pepper flakes in a small saucepan over medium heat. Make a slurry in a small bowl with orange juice and cornstarch. Stir in slurry and continue stirring. Bring the sauce to a boil and cook for 5 minutes. When the sauce begins to thicken, remove from heat and allow to sit for 5 minutes. Serve shrimp warm along with sauce and lemon slices on the side.

Shrimp Patties

Servings: 4
Cooking Time: 10 Minutes
Ingredients:
- ½ pound shelled and deveined raw shrimp
- ¼ cup chopped red bell pepper
- ¼ cup chopped green onion
- ¼ cup chopped celery
- 2 cups cooked sushi rice
- ½ teaspoon garlic powder
- ½ teaspoon Old Bay Seasoning
- ½ teaspoon salt
- 2 teaspoons Worcestershire sauce
- ½ cup plain breadcrumbs
- oil for misting or cooking spray

Directions:
1. Finely chop the shrimp. You can do this in a food processor, but it takes only a few pulses. Be careful not to overprocess into mush.
2. Place shrimp in a large bowl and add all other ingredients except the breadcrumbs and oil. Stir until well combined.
3. Preheat air fryer to 390°F/200°C.
4. Shape shrimp mixture into 8 patties, no more than ½-inch thick. Roll patties in breadcrumbs and mist with oil or cooking spray.
5. Place 4 shrimp patties in air fryer basket and cook at 390°F/200°C for 10 minutes, until shrimp cooks through and outside is crispy.
6. Repeat step 5 to cook remaining shrimp patties.

Mom's Tuna Melt Toastie

Servings: 4
Cooking Time: 30 Minutes
Ingredients:
- 4 white bread slices
- 2 oz canned tuna
- 2 tbsp mayonnaise
- ½ lemon, zested and juiced
- Salt and pepper to taste
- ½ red onion, finely sliced
- 1 red tomato, sliced
- 4 cheddar cheese slices
- 2 tbsp butter, melted

Directions:
1. Preheat air fryer to 360°F/180°C. Put the butter-greased bread slices in the frying basket. Toast for 6 minutes. Meanwhile, mix the tuna, lemon juice and zest, salt, pepper, and mayonnaise in a small bowl. When the time is over, slide the frying basket out, flip the bread slices, and spread the tuna mixture evenly all over them. Cover with tomato slices, red onion, and cheddar cheese. Toast for 10 minutes or until the cheese is melted and lightly bubbling. Serve and enjoy!

Californian Tilapia

Servings: 4
Cooking Time: 15 Minutes
Ingredients:
- Salt and pepper to taste
- ¼ tsp garlic powder
- ¼ tsp chili powder
- ¼ tsp dried oregano
- ¼ tsp smoked paprika
- 1 tbsp butter, melted
- 4 tilapia fillets
- 2 tbsp lime juice
- 1 lemon, sliced

Directions:
1. Preheat air fryer to 400°F/205°C. Combine salt, pepper, oregano, garlic powder, chili powder, and paprika in a small bowl. Place tilapia in a pie pan, then pour lime juice and butter over the fish. Season both sides of the fish with the spice blend. Arrange the tilapia in a single layer of the parchment-lined frying basket without touching each other. Air Fry for 4 minutes, then carefully flip the fish. Air Fry for another 4 to 5 minutes until the fish is cooked and the outside is crispy. Serve immediately with lemon slices on the side and enjoy.

Five Spice Red Snapper With Green Onions And Orange Salsa

Servings: 2
Cooking Time: 8 Minutes
Ingredients:
- 2 oranges, peeled, segmented and chopped
- 1 tablespoon minced shallot
- 1 to 3 teaspoons minced red Jalapeño or Serrano pepper
- 1 tablespoon chopped fresh cilantro
- lime juice, to taste
- salt, to taste
- 2 (5- to 6-ounce) red snapper fillets
- ½ teaspoon Chinese five spice powder
- salt and freshly ground black pepper
- vegetable or olive oil, in a spray bottle
- 4 green onions, cut into 2-inch lengths

Directions:
1. Start by making the salsa. Cut the peel off the oranges, slicing around the oranges to expose the flesh. Segment the oranges by cutting in between the membranes of the orange. Chop the segments roughly and combine in a bowl with the shallot, Jalapeño or Serrano pepper, cilantro, lime juice and salt. Set the salsa aside.
2. Preheat the air fryer to 400°F/205°C.
3. Season the fish fillets with the five-spice powder, salt and freshly ground black pepper. Spray both sides of the fish fillets with oil. Toss the green onions with a little oil.
4. Transfer the fish to the air fryer basket and scatter the green onions around the fish. Air-fry at 400°F/205°C for 8 minutes.
5. Remove the fish from the air fryer, along with the fried green onions. Serve with white rice and a spoonful of the salsa on top.

Fish Sticks With Tartar Sauce

Servings: 2
Cooking Time: 6 Minutes
Ingredients:
- 12 ounces cod or flounder
- ½ cup flour
- ½ teaspoon paprika
- 1 teaspoon salt
- lots of freshly ground black pepper
- 2 eggs, lightly beaten
- 1½ cups panko breadcrumbs
- 1 teaspoon salt
- vegetable oil
- Tartar Sauce:
- ¼ cup mayonnaise
- 2 teaspoons lemon juice
- 2 tablespoons finely chopped sweet pickles
- salt and freshly ground black pepper

Directions:
1. Cut the fish into ¾-inch wide sticks or strips. Set up a dredging station. Combine the flour, paprika, salt and pepper in a shallow dish. Beat the eggs lightly in a second shallow dish. Finally, mix the breadcrumbs and salt in a third shallow dish. Coat the fish sticks by dipping the fish into the flour, then the egg and finally the breadcrumbs, coating on all sides in each step and pressing the crumbs firmly onto the fish. Place the finished sticks on a plate or baking sheet while you finish all the sticks.
2. Preheat the air fryer to 400°F/205°C.
3. Spray the fish sticks with the oil and spray or brush the bottom of the air fryer basket. Place the fish into the basket and air-fry at 400°F/205°C for 4 minutes, turn the fish sticks over, and air-fry for another 2 minutes.
4. While the fish is cooking, mix the tartar sauce ingredients together.
5. Serve the fish sticks warm with the tartar sauce and some French fries on the side.

Family Fish Nuggets With Tartar Sauce

Servings: 4
Cooking Time: 30 Minutes
Ingredients:
- ½ cup mayonnaise
- 1 tbsp yellow mustard
- ½ cup diced dill pickles
- Salt and pepper to taste
- 1 egg, beaten
- ¼ cup cornstarch
- ¼ cup flour
- 1 lb cod, cut into sticks

Directions:
1. In a bowl, whisk the mayonnaise, mustard, pickles, salt, and pepper. Set aside the resulting tarter sauce.
2. Preheat air fryer to 350°F/175°C. Add the beaten egg to a bowl. In another bowl, combine cornstarch, flour, salt, and pepper. Dip fish nuggets in the egg and roll them in the flour mixture. Place fish nuggets in the lightly greased frying basket and Air Fry for 10 minutes, flipping once. Serve with the sauce on the side.

Cajun-seasoned Shrimp

Servings: 2
Cooking Time: 15 Minutes
Ingredients:
- 1 lb shelled tail on shrimp, deveined
- 2 tsp grated Parmesan cheese

- 2 tbsp butter, melted
- 1 tsp cayenne pepper
- 1 tsp garlic powder
- 2 tsp Cajun seasoning
- 1 tbsp lemon juice

Directions:
1. Preheat air fryer at 350°F/175°C. Toss the shrimp, melted butter, cayenne pepper, garlic powder and cajun seasoning in a bowl, place them in the greased frying basket, and Air Fry for 6 minutes, flipping once. Transfer it to a plate. Squeeze lemon juice over shrimp and stir in Parmesan cheese. Serve immediately.

Easy Asian-style Tuna
Servings: 4
Cooking Time: 25 Minutes
Ingredients:
- 1 jalapeño pepper, minced
- ½ tsp Chinese five-spice
- 4 tuna steaks
- ½ tsp toasted sesame oil
- 2 garlic cloves, grated
- 1 tbsp grated fresh ginger
- Black pepper to taste
- 2 tbsp lemon juice

Directions:
1. Preheat air fryer to 380°F/195°C. Pour sesame oil over the tuna steaks and let them sit while you make the marinade. Combine the jalapeño, garlic, ginger, five-spice powder, black pepper, and lemon juice in a bowl, then brush the mix on the fish. Let it sit for 10 minutes. Air Fry the tuna in the fryer for 6-11 minutes until it is cooked through and flakes easily when pressed with a fork. Serve warm.

Sardinas Fritas
Servings: 2
Cooking Time: 15 Minutes
Ingredients:
- 2 cans boneless, skinless sardines in mustard sauce
- Salt and pepper to taste
- ½ cup bread crumbs
- 2 lemon wedges
- 1 tsp chopped parsley

Directions:
1. Preheat air fryer at 350°F/175°C. Add breadcrumbs, salt and black pepper to a bowl. Roll sardines in the breadcrumbs to coat. Place them in the greased frying basket and Air Fry for 6 minutes, flipping once. Transfer them to a serving dish. Serve topped with parsley and lemon wedges.

Shrimp Al Pesto
Servings: 4
Cooking Time: 10 Minutes
Ingredients:
- 1 lb peeled shrimp, deveined
- ¼ cup pesto sauce
- 1 lime, sliced
- 2 cups cooked farro

Directions:
1. Preheat air fryer to 360°F/180°C. Coat the shrimp with the pesto sauce in a bowl. Put the shrimp in a single layer in the frying basket. Put the lime slices over the shrimp and Roast for 5 minutes. Remove lime and discard. Serve the shrimp over a bed of farro pilaf. Enjoy!

Crab Cakes On A Budget
Servings: 4
Cooking Time: 12 Minutes
Ingredients:
- 8 ounces imitation crabmeat
- 4 ounces leftover cooked fish (such as cod, pollock, or haddock)
- 2 tablespoons minced green onion
- 2 tablespoons minced celery
- ¾ cup crushed saltine cracker crumbs
- 2 tablespoons light mayonnaise
- 1 teaspoon prepared yellow mustard
- 1 tablespoon Worcestershire sauce, plus 2 teaspoons
- 2 teaspoons dried parsley flakes
- ½ teaspoon dried dill weed, crushed
- ½ teaspoon garlic powder
- ½ teaspoon Old Bay Seasoning
- ½ cup panko breadcrumbs
- oil for misting or cooking spray

Directions:
1. Use knives or a food processor to finely shred crabmeat and fish.
2. In a large bowl, combine all ingredients except panko and oil. Stir well.
3. Shape into 8 small, fat patties.
4. Carefully roll patties in panko crumbs to coat. Spray both sides with oil or cooking spray.
5. Place patties in air fryer basket and cook at 390°F/200°C for 12 minutes or until golden brown and crispy.

Catalan Sardines With Romesco Sauce
Servings: 2
Cooking Time: 15 Minutes
Ingredients:
- 2 cans skinless, boneless sardines in oil, drained
- ½ cup warmed romesco sauce
- ½ cup bread crumbs

Directions:
1. Preheat air fryer to 350°F/175°C. In a shallow dish, add bread crumbs. Roll in sardines to coat. Place sardines in the greased frying basket and Air Fry for 6 minutes, turning once. Serve with romesco sauce.

Shrimp Teriyaki
Servings: 10
Cooking Time: 6 Minutes
Ingredients:
- 1 tablespoon Regular or low-sodium soy sauce or gluten-free tamari sauce
- 1 tablespoon Mirin or a substitute (see here)
- 1 teaspoon Ginger juice (see the headnote)
- 10 Large shrimp (20–25 per pound), peeled and deveined
- ⅔ cup Plain panko bread crumbs (gluten-free, if a concern)
- 1 Large egg
- Vegetable oil spray

Directions:
1. Whisk the soy or tamari sauce, mirin, and ginger juice in an 8- or 9-inch square baking pan until uniform. Add the

Tower Air Fryer Cookbook

shrimp and toss well to coat. Cover and refrigerate for 1 hour, tossing the shrimp in the marinade at least twice.
2. Preheat the air fryer to 400°F/205°C.
3. Thread a marinated shrimp on a 4-inch bamboo skewer by inserting the pointy tip at the small end of the shrimp, then guiding the skewer along the shrimp so that the tip comes out the thick end and the shrimp is flat along the length of the skewer. Repeat with the remaining shrimp. (You'll need eight 4-inch skewers for the small batch, 10 skewers for the medium batch, and 12 for the large.)
4. Pour the bread crumbs onto a dinner plate. Whisk the egg in the baking pan with any marinade that stayed behind. Lay the skewers in the pan, in as close to a single layer as possible. Turn repeatedly to make sure the shrimp is coated in the egg mixture.
5. One at a time, take a skewered shrimp out of the pan and set it in the bread crumbs, turning several times and pressing gently until the shrimp is evenly coated on all sides. Coat the shrimp with vegetable oil spray and set the skewer aside. Repeat with the remainder of the shrimp.
6. Set the skewered shrimp in the basket in one layer. Air-fry undisturbed for 6 minutes, or until pink and firm.
7. Transfer the skewers to a wire rack. Cool for only a minute or two before serving.

Coconut Shrimp
Servings: 4
Cooking Time: 12 Minutes
Ingredients:
- 1 pound large shrimp (about 16 to 20), peeled and deveined
- ½ cup flour
- salt and freshly ground black pepper
- 2 egg whites
- ½ cup fine breadcrumbs
- ½ cup shredded unsweetened coconut
- zest of one lime
- ½ teaspoon salt
- ⅛ to ¼ teaspoon ground cayenne pepper
- vegetable or canola oil
- sweet chili sauce or duck sauce (for serving)

Directions:
1. Set up a dredging station. Place the flour in a shallow dish and season well with salt and freshly ground black pepper. Whisk the egg whites in a second shallow dish. In a third shallow dish, combine the breadcrumbs, coconut, lime zest, salt and cayenne pepper.
2. Preheat the air fryer to 400°F/205°C.
3. Dredge each shrimp first in the flour, then dip it in the egg mixture, and finally press it into the breadcrumb-coconut mixture to coat all sides. Place the breaded shrimp on a plate or baking sheet and spray both sides with vegetable oil.
4. Air-fry the shrimp in two batches, being sure not to over-crowd the basket. Air-fry for 5 minutes, turning the shrimp over for the last minute or two. Repeat with the second batch of shrimp.
5. Lower the temperature of the air fryer to 340°F/170°C. Return the first batch of shrimp to the air fryer basket with the second batch and air-fry for an additional 2 minutes, just to re-heat everything.
6. Serve with sweet chili sauce, duck sauce or just eat them plain!

Lime Flaming Halibut
Servings: 2
Cooking Time: 20 Minutes
Ingredients:
- 2 tbsp butter, melted
- ½ tsp chili powder
- ½ cup bread crumbs
- 2 halibut fillets

Directions:
1. Preheat air fryer to 350ºF/175°C. In a bowl, mix the butter, chili powder and bread crumbs. Press mixture onto tops of halibut fillets. Place halibut in the greased frying basket and Air Fry for 10 minutes or until the fish is opaque and flake easily with a fork. Serve right away.

Sweet Potato - wrapped Shrimp
Servings: 3
Cooking Time: 6 Minutes
Ingredients:
- 24 Long spiralized sweet potato strands
- Olive oil spray
- ¼ teaspoon Garlic powder
- ¼ teaspoon Table salt
- Up to a ⅛ teaspoon Cayenne
- 12 Large shrimp (20–25 per pound), peeled and deveined

Directions:
1. Preheat the air fryer to 400°F/205°C.
2. Lay the spiralized sweet potato strands on a large swath of paper towels and straighten out the strands to long ropes. Coat them with olive oil spray, then sprinkle them with the garlic powder, salt, and cayenne.
3. Pick up 2 strands and wrap them around the center of a shrimp, with the ends tucked under what now becomes the bottom side of the shrimp. Continue wrapping the remainder of the shrimp.
4. Set the shrimp bottom side down in the basket with as much air space between them as possible. Air-fry undisturbed for 6 minutes, or until the sweet potato strands are crisp and the shrimp are pink and firm.
5. Use kitchen tongs to transfer the shrimp to a wire rack. Cool for only a minute or two before serving.

Mojo Sea Bass
Servings: 2
Cooking Time: 15 Minutes
Ingredients:
- 1 tbsp butter, melted
- ¼ tsp chili powder
- 2 cloves garlic, minced
- 1 tbsp lemon juice
- ¼ tsp salt
- 2 sea bass fillets
- 2 tsp chopped cilantro

Directions:
1. Preheat air fryer to 370ºF/185°C. Whisk the butter, chili powder, garlic, lemon juice, and salt in a bowl. Rub mixture over the tops of each fillet. Place the fillets in the frying basket and Air Fry for 7 minutes. Let rest for 5 minutes. Divide between 2 plates and garnish with cilantro to serve.

Tower Air Fryer Cookbook

Shrimp-jalapeño Poppers In Prosciutto

Servings: 4
Cooking Time: 30 Minutes
Ingredients:
- 1 lb shelled tail on shrimp, deveined, sliced down the spine
- 2 jalapeños, diced
- 2 tbsp grated cheddar
- 3 tbsp mascarpone cheese
- ¼ tsp garlic powder
- 1 tbsp mayonnaise
- ¼ tsp ground black pepper
- 20 prosciutto slices
- ¼ cup chopped parsley
- 1 lemon

Directions:
1. Preheat air fryer at 400°F/205°C. Combine the mascarpone and cheddar cheeses, jalapeños, garlic, mayonnaise, and black pepper in a bowl. Press cheese mixture into shrimp. Wrap 1 piece of prosciutto around each shrimp to hold in the cheese mixture. Place wrapped shrimp in the frying basket and Air Fry for 8-10 minutes, flipping once. To serve, scatter with parsley and squeeze lemon.

The Best Shrimp Risotto

Servings: 4
Cooking Time: 50 Minutes + 5 Minutes To Sit
Ingredients:
- 1/3 cup grated Parmesan
- 2 tbsp olive oil
- 1 lb peeled shrimp, deveined
- 1 onion, chopped
- 1 red bell pepper, chopped
- Salt and pepper to taste
- 1 cup Carnaroli rice
- 21/3 cups vegetable stock
- 2 tbsp butter
- 1 tbsp heavy cream

Directions:
1. Preheat the air fryer to 380°F/195°C. Add a tbsp of olive oil to a cake pan, then toss in the shrimp. Put the pan in the frying basket and cook the shrimp for 4-7 minutes or until they curl and pinken. Remove the shrimp and set aside. Add the other tbsp of olive oil to the cake pan, then add the onion, bell pepper, salt, and pepper and Air Fry for 3 minutes. Add the rice to the cake pan, stir, and cook for 2 minutes. Add the stock, stir again, and cover the pan with foil. Bake for another 18-22 minutes, stirring twice until the rice is tender. Remove the foil. Return the shrimp to the pan along with butter, heavy cream, and Parmesan, then cook for another minute. Stir and serve.

Stuffed Shrimp Wrapped In Bacon

Servings: 4
Cooking Time: 30 Minutes
Ingredients:
- 1 lb shrimp, deveined and shelled
- 3 tbsp crumbled goat cheese
- 2 tbsp panko bread crumbs
- ¼ tsp soy sauce
- ½ tsp prepared horseradish
- ¼ tsp garlic powder
- ½ tsp chili powder
- 2 tsp mayonnaise
- Black pepper to taste
- 5 slices bacon, quartered
- ¼ cup chopped parsley

Directions:
1. Preheat air fryer to 400°F/205°C. Butterfly shrimp by cutting down the spine of each shrimp without going all the way through. Combine the goat cheese, bread crumbs, soy sauce, horseradish, garlic powder, chili powder, mayonnaise, and black pepper in a bowl. Evenly press goat cheese mixture into shrimp. Wrap a piece of bacon around each piece of shrimp to hold in the cheese mixture. Place them in the frying basket and Air Fry for 8-10 minutes, flipping once. Top with parsley to serve.

Buttered Swordfish Steaks

Servings: 4
Cooking Time: 30 Minutes
Ingredients:
- 4 swordfish steaks
- 2 eggs, beaten
- 3 oz melted butter
- ½ cup breadcrumbs
- Black pepper to taste
- 1 tsp dried rosemary
- 1 tsp dried marjoram
- 1 lemon, cut into wedges

Directions:
1. Preheat air fryer to 350°F/175°C. Place the eggs and melted butter in a bowl and stir thoroughly. Combine the breadcrumbs, rosemary, marjoram, and black pepper in a separate bowl. Dip the swordfish steaks in the beaten eggs, then coat with the crumb mixture. Place the coated fish in the frying basket. Air Fry for 12-14 minutes, turning once until the fish is cooked through and the crust is toasted and crispy. Serve with lemon wedges.

Lemon-roasted Salmon Fillets

Servings: 3
Cooking Time: 7 Minutes
Ingredients:
- 3 6-ounce skin-on salmon fillets
- Olive oil spray
- 9 Very thin lemon slices
- ¾ teaspoon Ground black pepper
- ¼ teaspoon Table salt

Directions:
1. Preheat the air fryer to 400°F/205°C.
2. Generously coat the skin of each of the fillets with olive oil spray. Set the fillets skin side down on your work surface. Place three overlapping lemon slices down the length of each salmon fillet. Sprinkle them with the pepper and salt. Coat lightly with olive oil spray.
3. Use a nonstick-safe spatula to transfer the fillets one by one to the basket, leaving as much air space between them as possible. Air-fry undisturbed for 7 minutes, or until cooked through.
4. Use a nonstick-safe spatula to transfer the fillets to serving plates. Cool for only a minute or two before serving.

Sea Scallops

Servings: 4
Cooking Time: 8 Minutes
Ingredients:
- 1½ pounds sea scallops
- salt and pepper
- 2 eggs
- ½ cup flour
- ½ cup plain breadcrumbs
- oil for misting or cooking spray

Directions:
1. Rinse scallops and remove the tough side muscle. Sprinkle to taste with salt and pepper.
2. Beat eggs together in a shallow dish. Place flour in a second shallow dish and breadcrumbs in a third.
3. Preheat air fryer to 390°F/200°C.
4. Dip scallops in flour, then eggs, and then roll in breadcrumbs. Mist with oil or cooking spray.
5. Place scallops in air fryer basket in a single layer, leaving some space between. You should be able to cook about a dozen at a time.
6. Cook at 390°F/200°C for 8 minutes, watching carefully so as not to overcook. Scallops are done when they turn opaque all the way through. They will feel slightly firm when pressed with tines of a fork.
7. Repeat step 6 to cook remaining scallops.

Dilly Red Snapper

Servings: 4
Cooking Time: 40 Minutes
Ingredients:
- Salt and pepper to taste
- ½ tsp ground cumin
- ¼ tsp cayenne
- ¼ teaspoon paprika
- 1 whole red snapper
- 2 tbsp butter
- 2 garlic cloves, minced
- ¼ cup dill
- 4 lemon wedges

Directions:
1. Preheat air fryer to 360°F/180°C. Combine salt, pepper, cumin, paprika and cayenne in a bowl. Brush the fish with butter, then rub with the seasoning mix. Stuff the minced garlic and dill inside the cavity of the fish. Put the snapper into the basket of the air fryer and Roast for 20 minutes. Flip the snapper over and Roast for 15 more minutes. Serve with lemon wedges and enjoy!

Seared Scallops In Beurre Blanc

Servings: 4
Cooking Time: 15 Minutes
Ingredients:
- 1 lb sea scallops
- Salt and pepper to taste
- 2 tbsp butter, melted
- 1 lemon, zested and juiced
- 2 tbsp dry white wine

Directions:
1. Preheat the air fryer to 400°F/205°C. Sprinkle the scallops with salt and pepper, then set in a bowl. Combine the butter, lemon zest, lemon juice, and white wine in another bowl; mix well. Put the scallops in a baking pan and drizzle over them the mixture. Air Fry for 8-11 minutes, flipping over at about 5 minutes until opaque. Serve and enjoy!

Holliday Lobster Salad

Servings: 2
Cooking Time: 20 Minutes
Ingredients:
- 2 lobster tails
- ¼ cup mayonnaise
- 2 tsp lemon juice
- 1 stalk celery, sliced
- 2 tsp chopped chives
- 2 tsp chopped tarragon
- Salt and pepper to taste
- 2 tomato slices
- 4 cucumber slices
- 1 avocado, diced

Directions:
1. Preheat air fryer to 400°F/205°C. Using kitchen shears, cut down the middle of each lobster tail on the softer side. Carefully run your finger between the lobster meat and the shell to loosen meat. Place lobster tails, cut sides up, in the frying basket, and Air Fry for 8 minutes. Transfer to a large plate and let cool for 3 minutes until easy to handle, then pull lobster meat from the shell and roughly chop it. Combine chopped lobster, mayonnaise, lemon juice, celery, chives, tarragon, salt, and pepper in a bowl. Divide between 2 medium plates and top with tomato slices, cucumber and avocado cubes. Serve immediately.

Buttery Lobster Tails

Servings: 4
Cooking Time: 6 Minutes
Ingredients:
- 4 6- to 8-ounce shell-on raw lobster tails
- 2 tablespoons Butter, melted and cooled
- 1 teaspoon Lemon juice
- ½ teaspoon Finely grated lemon zest
- ½ teaspoon Garlic powder
- ½ teaspoon Table salt
- ½ teaspoon Ground black pepper

Directions:
1. Preheat the air fryer to 375°F/190°C.
2. To give the tails that restaurant look, you need to butterfly the meat. To do so, place a tail on a cutting board so that the shell is convex. Use kitchen shears to cut a line down the middle of the shell from the larger end to the smaller, cutting only the shell and not the meat below, and stopping before the back fins. Pry open the shell, leaving it intact. Use your clean fingers to separate the meat from the shell's sides and bottom, keeping it attached to the shell at the back near the fins. Pull the meat up and out of the shell through the cut line, laying the meat on top of the shell and closing the shell (as well as you can) under the meat. Make two equidistant cuts down the meat from the larger end to near the smaller end, each about ¼ inch deep, for the classic restaurant look on the plate. Repeat this procedure with the remaining tail(s).
3. Stir the butter, lemon juice, zest, garlic powder, salt, and pepper in a small bowl until well combined. Brush this mixture over the lobster meat set atop the shells.
4. When the machine is at temperature, place the tails shell side down in the basket with as much air space between them as possible. Air-fry undisturbed for 6 minutes, or until the lobster meat has pink streaks over it and is firm.
5. Use kitchen tongs to transfer the tails to a wire rack. Cool for only a minute or two before serving.

Shrimp "scampi"

Servings: 4
Cooking Time: 5 Minutes
Ingredients:
- 1½ pounds Large shrimp (20–25 per pound), peeled and deveined
- ¼ cup Olive oil
- 2 tablespoons Minced garlic
- 1 teaspoon Dried oregano
- Up to 1 teaspoon Red pepper flakes
- ½ teaspoon Table salt
- 2 tablespoons White balsamic vinegar (see here)

Directions:
1. Preheat the air fryer to 400°F/205°C.
2. Stir the shrimp, olive oil, garlic, oregano, red pepper flakes, and salt in a large bowl until the shrimp are well coated.
3. When the machine is at temperature, transfer the shrimp to the basket. They will overlap and even sit on top of each other. Air-fry for 5 minutes, tossing and rearranging the shrimp twice to make sure the covered surfaces are exposed, until pink and firm.
4. Pour the contents of the basket into a serving bowl. Pour the vinegar over the shrimp while hot and toss to coat.

Chinese Fish Noodle Bowls

Servings: 4
Cooking Time: 40 Minutes
Ingredients:
- 1 can crushed pineapple, drained
- 1 shallot, minced
- 2 tbsp chopped cilantro
- 2 ½ tsp lime juice
- 1 tbsp honey
- Salt and pepper to taste
- 1 ½ cups grated red cabbage
- ¼ chopped green beans
- 2 grated baby carrots
- ½ tsp granulated sugar
- 2 tbsp mayonnaise
- 1 clove garlic, minced
- 8 oz cooked rice noodles
- 2 tsp sesame oil
- 1 tsp sesame seeds
- 4 cod fillets
- 1 tsp Chinese five-spice

Directions:
1. Preheat air fryer at 350°F/175°C. Combine the pineapple, shallot, 1 tbsp of cilantro, honey, 2 tsp of lime juice, salt, and black pepper in a bowl. Let chill the salsa covered in the fridge until ready to use. Mix the cabbage, green beans, carrots, sugar, remaining lime juice, mayonnaise, garlic, salt, and pepper in a bowl. Let chill covered in the fridge until ready to use. In a bowl, toss cooked noodles and sesame oil, stirring occasionally to avoid sticking.
2. Sprinkle cod fillets with salt and five-spice. Place them in the greased frying basket and Air Fry for 10 minutes until the fish is opaque and flakes easily with a fork. Divide noodles into 4 bowls, top each with salsa, slaw, and fish. Serve right away sprinkled with another tbsp of cilantro and sesame seeds.

Peppery Tilapia Roulade

Servings: 4
Cooking Time: 25 Minutes

Ingredients:
- 4 jarred roasted red pepper slices
- 1 egg
- ½ cup breadcrumbs
- Salt and pepper to taste
- 4 tilapia fillets
- 2 tbsp butter, melted
- 4 lime wedges
- 1 tsp dill

Directions:
1. Preheat air fryer at 350°F/175°C. Beat the egg and 2 tbsp of water in a bowl. In another bowl, mix the breadcrumbs, salt, and pepper. Place a red pepper slice and sprinkle with dill on each fish fillet. Tightly roll tilapia fillets from one short end to the other. Secure with toothpicks. Roll each fillet in the egg mixture, then dredge them in the breadcrumbs. Place fish rolls in the greased frying basket and drizzle the tops with melted butter. Roast for 6 minutes. Let rest in a serving dish for 5 minutes before removing the toothpicks. Serve with lime wedges. Enjoy!

Shrimp & Grits

Servings: 4
Cooking Time: 5 Minutes
Ingredients:
- 1 pound raw shelled shrimp, deveined (26–30 count or smaller)
- Marinade
- 2 tablespoons lemon juice
- 2 tablespoons Worcestershire sauce
- 1 tablespoon olive oil
- 1 teaspoon Old Bay Seasoning
- ½ teaspoon hot sauce
- Grits
- ¾ cup quick cooking grits (not instant)
- 3 cups water
- ½ teaspoon salt
- 1 tablespoon butter
- ½ cup chopped green bell pepper
- ½ cup chopped celery
- ½ cup chopped onion
- ½ teaspoon oregano
- ¼ teaspoon Old Bay Seasoning
- 2 ounces sharp Cheddar cheese, grated

Directions:
1. Stir together all marinade ingredients. Pour marinade over shrimp and set aside.
2. For grits, heat water and salt to boil in saucepan on stovetop. Stir in grits, lower heat to medium-low, and cook about 5 minutes or until thick and done.
3. Place butter, bell pepper, celery, and onion in air fryer baking pan. Cook at 390°F/200°C for 2 minutes and stir. Cook 6 or 7 minutes longer, until crisp tender.
4. Add oregano and 1 teaspoon Old Bay to cooked vegetables. Stir in grits and cheese and cook at 390°F/200°C for 1 minute. Stir and cook 1 to 2 minutes longer to melt cheese.
5. Remove baking pan from air fryer. Cover with plate to keep warm while shrimp cooks.
6. Drain marinade from shrimp. Place shrimp in air fryer basket and cook at 360°F/180°C for 3 minutes. Stir or shake basket. Cook 2 more minutes, until done.
7. To serve, spoon grits onto plates and top with shrimp.

Fried Shrimp

Servings: 3
Cooking Time: 7 Minutes
Ingredients:
- 1 Large egg white
- 2 tablespoons Water
- 1 cup Plain dried bread crumbs (gluten-free, if a concern)
- ¼ cup All-purpose flour or almond flour
- ¼ cup Yellow cornmeal
- 1 teaspoon Celery salt
- 1 teaspoon Mild paprika
- Up to ½ teaspoon Cayenne (optional)
- ¾ pound Large shrimp (20–25 per pound), peeled and deveined
- Vegetable oil spray

Directions:
1. Preheat the air fryer to 400°F/205°C.
2. Set two medium or large bowls on your counter. In the first, whisk the egg white and water until foamy. In the second, stir the bread crumbs, flour, cornmeal, celery salt, paprika, and cayenne (if using) until well combined.
3. Pour all the shrimp into the egg white mixture and stir gently until all the shrimp are coated. Use kitchen tongs to pick them up one by one and transfer them to the bread-crumb mixture. Turn each in the bread-crumb mixture to coat it evenly and thoroughly on all sides before setting it on a cutting board. When you're done coating the shrimp, coat them all on both sides with the vegetable oil spray.
4. Set the shrimp in as close to one layer in the basket as you can. Some may overlap. Air-fry for 7 minutes, gently rearranging the shrimp at the 4-minute mark to get covered surfaces exposed, until golden brown and firm but not hard.
5. Use kitchen tongs to gently transfer the shrimp to a wire rack. Cool for only a minute or two before serving.

Bbq Fried Oysters

Servings: 2
Cooking Time: 30 Minutes
Ingredients:
- ½ cup all-purpose flour
- ½ cup barbecue sauce
- 1 cup bread crumbs
- ½ lb shelled raw oysters
- 1 lemon
- 1 tbsp chopped parsley

Directions:
1. Preheat air fryer at 400ºF/205°C. In a bowl, add flour. In another bowl, pour barbecue sauce and in a third bowl, add breadcrumbs. Roll the oysters in the flour, shake off excess flour. Then, dip them in the sauce, shake off excess sauce. Finally, dredge them in the breadcrumbs. Place oysters in the greased frying basket and Air Fry for 8 minutes, flipping once. Sprinkle with parsley and squeeze lemon to serve.

Holiday Shrimp Scampi

Servings: 4
Cooking Time: 25 Minutes
Ingredients:
- 1 ½ lb peeled shrimp, deveined
- ¼ tsp lemon pepper seasoning
- 6 garlic cloves, minced
- 1 tsp salt
- ½ tsp grated lemon zest
- 3 tbsp fresh lemon juice
- 3 tbsp sunflower oil
- 3 tbsp butter
- 2 tsp fresh thyme leaves
- 1 lemon, cut into wedges

Directions:
1. Preheat the air fryer to 400°F/205°C. Combine the shrimp and garlic in a cake pan, then sprinkle with salt and lemon pepper seasoning. Toss to coat, then add the lemon zest, lemon juice, oil, and butter. Place the cake pan in the frying basket and Bake for 10-13 minutes, stirring once until no longer pink. Sprinkle with thyme leaves. Serve hot with lemon wedges on the side.

Crunchy Clam Strips

Servings: 3
Cooking Time: 8 Minutes
Ingredients:
- ½ pound Clam strips, drained
- 1 Large egg, well beaten
- ½ cup All-purpose flour
- ½ cup Yellow cornmeal
- 1½ teaspoons Table salt
- 1½ teaspoons Ground black pepper
- Up to ¾ teaspoon Cayenne
- Vegetable oil spray

Directions:
1. Preheat the air fryer to 400°F/205°C.
2. Toss the clam strips and beaten egg in a bowl until the clams are well coated.
3. Mix the flour, cornmeal, salt, pepper, and cayenne in a large zip-closed plastic bag until well combined. Using a flatware fork or small kitchen tongs, lift the clam strips one by one out of the egg, letting any excess egg slip back into the rest. Put the strips in the bag with the flour mixture. Once all the strips are in the bag, seal it and shake gently until the strips are well coated.
4. Use kitchen tongs to pick out the clam strips and lay them on a cutting board (leaving any extra flour mixture in the bag to be discarded). Coat the strips on both sides with vegetable oil spray.
5. When the machine is at temperature, spread the clam strips in the basket in one layer. They may touch in places, but try to leave as much air space as possible around them. Air-fry undisturbed for 8 minutes, or until brown and crunchy.
6. Gently dump the contents of the basket onto a serving platter. Cool for just a minute or two before serving hot.

Tilapia Al Pesto

Servings: 4
Cooking Time: 25 Minutes
Ingredients:
- 4 tilapia fillets
- 1 egg
- 2 tbsp buttermilk
- 1 cup crushed cornflakes
- Salt and pepper to taste
- 4 tsp pesto
- 2 tbsp butter, melted
- 4 lemon wedges

Directions:
1. Preheat air fryer to 350°F/175°C. Whisk egg and buttermilk in a bowl. In another bowl, combine cornflakes,

salt, and pepper. Spread 1 tsp of pesto on each tilapia fillet, then tightly roll the fillet from one short end to the other. Secure with a toothpick. Dip each fillet in the egg mixture and dredge in the cornflake mixture. Place fillets in the greased frying basket, drizzle with melted butter, and Air Fry for 6 minutes. Let rest onto a serving dish for 5 minutes before removing the toothpicks. Serve with lemon wedges.

Mojito Fish Tacos

Servings: 4
Cooking Time: 30 Minutes
Ingredients:
- 1 ½ cups chopped red cabbage
- 1 lb cod fillets
- 2 tsp olive oil
- 3 tbsp lemon juice
- 1 large carrot, grated
- 1 tbsp white rum
- ½ cup salsa
- 1/3 cup Greek yogurt
- 4 soft tortillas

Directions:
1. Preheat air fryer to 390°F/200°C. Rub the fish with olive oil, then a splash with a tablespoon of lemon juice. Place in the fryer and Air Fry for 9-12 minutes. The fish should flake when done. Mix the remaining lemon juice, red cabbage, carrots, salsa, rum, and yogurt in a bowl. Take the fish out of the fryer and tear into large pieces. Serve with tortillas and cabbage mixture. Enjoy!

Cajun Flounder Fillets

Servings: 2
Cooking Time: 5 Minutes
Ingredients:
- 2 4-ounce skinless flounder fillet(s)
- 2 teaspoons Peanut oil
- 1 teaspoon Purchased or homemade Cajun dried seasoning blend (see the headnote)

Directions:
1. Preheat the air fryer to 400°F/205°C.
2. Oil the fillet(s) by drizzling on the peanut oil, then gently rubbing in the oil with your clean, dry fingers. Sprinkle the seasoning blend evenly over both sides of the fillet(s).
3. When the machine is at temperature, set the fillet(s) in the basket. If working with more than one fillet, they should not touch, although they may be quite close together, depending on the basket's size. Air-fry undisturbed for 5 minutes, or until lightly browned and cooked through.
4. Use a nonstick-safe spatula to transfer the fillets to a serving platter or plate(s). Serve at once.

Crabmeat-stuffed Flounder

Servings: 3
Cooking Time: 12 Minutes
Ingredients:
- 4½ ounces Purchased backfin or claw crabmeat, picked over for bits of shell and cartilage
- 6 Saltine crackers, crushed into fine crumbs
- 2 tablespoons plus 1 teaspoon Regular or low-fat mayonnaise (not fat-free)
- ¾ teaspoon Yellow prepared mustard
- 1½ teaspoons Worcestershire sauce
- ⅛ teaspoon Celery salt
- 3 5- to 6-ounce skinless flounder fillets
- Vegetable oil spray
- Mild paprika

Directions:
1. Preheat the air fryer to 400°F/205°C.
2. Gently mix the crabmeat, crushed saltines, mayonnaise, mustard, Worcestershire sauce, and celery salt in a bowl until well combined.
3. Generously coat the flat side of a fillet with vegetable oil spray. Set the fillet sprayed side down on your work surface. Cut the fillet in half widthwise, then cut one of the halves in half lengthwise. Set a scant ⅓ cup of the crabmeat mixture on top of the undivided half of the fish fillet, mounding the mixture to make an oval that somewhat fits the shape of the fillet with at least a ¼-inch border of fillet beyond the filling all around.
4. Take the two thin divided quarters (that is, the halves of the half) and lay them lengthwise over the filling, overlapping at each end and leaving a little space in the middle where the filling peeks through. Coat the top of the stuffed flounder piece with vegetable oil spray, then sprinkle paprika over the stuffed flounder fillet. Set aside and use the remaining fillet(s) to make more stuffed flounder "packets," repeating steps 3 and
5. Use a nonstick-safe spatula to transfer the stuffed flounder fillets to the basket. Leave as much space between them as possible. Air-fry undisturbed for 12 minutes, or until lightly brown and firm (but not hard).
6. Use that same spatula, plus perhaps another one, to transfer the fillets to a serving platter or plates. Cool for a minute or two, then serve hot.

Catfish Nuggets

Servings: 4
Cooking Time: 7 Minutes Per Batch
Ingredients:
- 2 medium catfish fillets, cut in chunks (approximately 1 x 2 inch)
- salt and pepper
- 2 eggs
- 2 tablespoons skim milk
- ½ cup cornstarch
- 1 cup panko breadcrumbs, crushed
- oil for misting or cooking spray

Directions:
1. Season catfish chunks with salt and pepper to your liking.
2. Beat together eggs and milk in a small bowl.
3. Place cornstarch in a second small bowl.
4. Place breadcrumbs in a third small bowl.
5. Dip catfish chunks in cornstarch, dip in egg wash, shake off excess, then roll in breadcrumbs.
6. Spray all sides of catfish chunks with oil or cooking spray.
7. Place chunks in air fryer basket in a single layer, leaving space between for air circulation.
8. Cook at 390°F/200°C for 4 minutes, turn, and cook an additional 3 minutes, until fish flakes easily and outside is crispy brown.
9. Repeat steps 7 and 8 to cook remaining catfish nuggets.

Crunchy And Buttery Cod With Ritz® Cracker Crust

Servings: 2
Cooking Time: 10 Minutes
Ingredients:
- 4 tablespoons butter, melted
- 8 to 10 RITZ® crackers, crushed into crumbs
- 2 (6-ounce) cod fillets
- salt and freshly ground black pepper
- 1 lemon

Directions:
1. Preheat the air fryer to 380°F/195°C.
2. Melt the butter in a small saucepan on the stovetop or in a microwavable dish in the microwave, and then transfer the butter to a shallow dish. Place the crushed RITZ® crackers into a second shallow dish.
3. Season the fish fillets with salt and freshly ground black pepper. Dip them into the butter and then coat both sides with the RITZ® crackers.
4. Place the fish into the air fryer basket and air-fry at 380°F/195°C for 10 minutes, flipping the fish over halfway through the cooking time.
5. Serve with a wedge of lemon to squeeze over the top.

Tuscan Salmon

Servings: 4
Cooking Time: 15 Minutes
Ingredients:
- 2 tbsp olive oil
- 4 salmon fillets
- ½ tsp salt
- ¼ tsp red pepper flakes
- 1 tsp chopped dill
- 2 tomatoes, diced
- ¼ cup sliced black olives
- 4 lemon slices

Directions:
1. Preheat air fryer to 380°F/195°C. Lightly brush the olive oil on both sides of the salmon fillets and season them with salt, red flakes, and dill. Put the fillets in a single layer in the frying basket, then layer the tomatoes and black olives over the top. Top each fillet with a lemon slice. Bake for 8 minutes. Serve and enjoy!

Mahi-mahi "burrito" Fillets

Servings: 3
Cooking Time: 10 Minutes
Ingredients:
- 1 Large egg white
- 1½ cups (6 ounces) Crushed corn tortilla chips (gluten-free, if a concern)
- 1 tablespoon Chile powder
- 3 5-ounce skinless mahi-mahi fillets
- 6 tablespoons Canned refried beans
- Vegetable oil spray

Directions:
1. Preheat the air fryer to 400°F/205°C.
2. Set up and fill two shallow soup plates or small pie plates on your counter: one with the egg white, beaten until foamy; and one with the crushed tortilla chips.
3. Gently rub ½ teaspoon chile powder on each side of each fillet.
4. Spread (or maybe smear) 1 tablespoon refried beans over both sides and the edges of a fillet. Dip the fillet in the egg white, turning to coat it on both sides. Let any excess egg white slip back into the rest, then set the fillet in the crushed tortilla chips. Turn several times, pressing gently to coat it evenly. Coat the fillet on all sides with the vegetable oil spray, then set it aside. Prepare the remaining fillet(s) in the same way.
5. When the machine is at temperature, set the fillets in the basket with as much air space between them as possible. Air-fry undisturbed for 10 minutes, or until crisp and browned.
6. Use a nonstick-safe spatula to transfer the fillets to a serving platter or plates. Cool for only a minute or so, then serve hot.

Horseradish-crusted Salmon Fillets

Servings: 3
Cooking Time: 8 Minutes
Ingredients:
- ½ cup Fresh bread crumbs (see the headnote)
- 4 tablespoons (¼ cup/½ stick) Butter, melted and cooled
- ¼ cup Jarred prepared white horseradish
- Vegetable oil spray
- 4 6-ounce skin-on salmon fillets (for more information, see here)

Directions:
1. Preheat the air fryer to 400°F/205°C.
2. Mix the bread crumbs, butter, and horseradish in a bowl until well combined.
3. Take the basket out of the machine. Generously spray the skin side of each fillet. Pick them up one by one with a nonstick-safe spatula and set them in the basket skin side down with as much air space between them as possible. Divide the bread-crumb mixture between the fillets, coating the top of each fillet with an even layer. Generously coat the bread-crumb mixture with vegetable oil spray.
4. Return the basket to the machine and air-fry undisturbed for 8 minutes, or until the topping has lightly browned and the fish is firm but not hard.
5. Use a nonstick-safe spatula to transfer the salmon fillets to serving plates. Cool for 5 minutes before serving. Because of the butter in the topping, it will stay very hot for quite a while. Take care, especially if you're serving these fillets to children.

Garlic And Dill Salmon

Servings: 2
Cooking Time: 8 Minutes
Ingredients:
- 12 ounces salmon filets with skin
- 2 tablespoons melted butter
- 1 tablespoon extra-virgin olive oil
- 2 garlic cloves, minced
- 1 tablespoon fresh dill
- ½ teaspoon sea salt
- ½ lemon

Directions:
1. Pat the salmon dry with paper towels.
2. In a small bowl, mix together the melted butter, olive oil, garlic, and dill.
3. Sprinkle the top of the salmon with sea salt. Brush all sides of the salmon with the garlic and dill butter.
4. Preheat the air fryer to 350°F/175°C.

5. Place the salmon, skin side down, in the air fryer basket. Cook for 6 to 8 minutes, or until the fish flakes in the center.
6. Remove the salmon and plate on a serving platter. Squeeze fresh lemon over the top of the salmon. Serve immediately.

Southeast Asian-style Tuna Steaks

Servings: 4
Cooking Time: 20 Minutes
Ingredients:
- 1 stalk lemongrass, bent in half
- 4 tuna steaks
- 2 tbsp soy sauce
- 2 tsp sesame oil
- 2 tsp rice wine vinegar
- 1 tsp grated fresh ginger
- ⅛ tsp pepper
- 3 tbsp lemon juice
- 2 tbsp chopped cilantro
- 1 sliced red chili

Directions:
1. Preheat air fryer to 390°F/200°C. Place the tuna steak on a shallow plate. Mix together soy sauce, sesame oil, rice wine vinegar, and ginger in a small bowl. Pour over the tuna, rubbing the marinade gently into both sides of the fish. Marinate for about 10 minutes. Then sprinkle with pepper. Place the lemongrass in the frying basket and top with tuna steaks. Add the remaining lemon juice and 1 tablespoon of water in the pan below the basket. Bake until the tuna is cooked through, 8-10 minutes. Discard the lemongrass before topping with cilantro and red chili. Serve and enjoy!

Cheese & Crab Stuffed Mushrooms

Servings: 2
Cooking Time: 30 Minutes
Ingredients:
- 6 oz lump crabmeat, shells discarded
- 6 oz mascarpone cheese, softened
- 2 jalapeño peppers, minced
- ¼ cup diced red onions
- 2 tsp grated Parmesan cheese
- 2 portobello mushroom caps
- 2 tbsp butter, divided
- ½ tsp prepared horseradish
- ¼ tsp Worcestershire sauce
- ¼ tsp smoked paprika
- Salt and pepper to taste
- ¼ cup bread crumbs

Directions:
1. Melt 1 tbsp of butter in a skillet over heat for 30 seconds. Add in onion and cook for 3 minutes until tender. Stir in mascarpone cheese, Parmesan cheese, horseradish, jalapeño peppers, Worcestershire sauce, paprika, salt and pepper and cook for 2 minutes until smooth. Fold in crabmeat. Spoon mixture into mushroom caps. Set aside.
2. Preheat air fryer at 350°F/175°C. Microwave the remaining butter until melted. Stir in breadcrumbs. Scatter over stuffed mushrooms. Place mushrooms in the greased frying basket and Bake for 8 minutes. Serve immediately.

Easy-peasy Shrimp

Servings: 2
Cooking Time: 15 Minutes
Ingredients:
- 1 lb tail-on shrimp, deveined
- 2 tbsp butter, melted
- 1 tbsp lemon juice
- 1 tbsp dill, chopped

Directions:
1. Preheat air fryer to 350°F/175°C. Combine shrimp and butter in a bowl. Place shrimp in the greased frying basket and Air Fry for 6 minutes, flipping once. Squeeze lemon juice over and top with dill. Serve hot.

Fish Tortillas With Coleslaw

Servings: 4
Cooking Time: 30 Minutes
Ingredients:
- 1 tbsp olive oil
- 1 lb cod fillets
- 3 tbsp lemon juice
- 2 cups chopped red cabbage
- ½ cup salsa
- 1/3 cup sour cream
- 6 taco shells, warm
- 1 avocado, chopped

Directions:
1. Preheat air fryer to 400°F/205°C. Brush oil on the cod and sprinkle with some lemon juice. Place in the frying basket and Air Fry until the fish flakes with a fork, 9-12 minutes.
2. Meanwhile, mix together the remaining lemon juice, red cabbage, salsa, and sour cream in a medium bowl. Put the cooked fish in a bowl, breaking it into large pieces. Then add the cabbage mixture, avocados, and warmed tortilla shells ready for assembly. Enjoy!

Summer Sea Scallops

Servings: 4
Cooking Time: 30 Minutes
Ingredients:
- 1 cup asparagus
- 1 cup peas
- 1 cup chopped broccoli
- 2 tsp olive oil
- ½ tsp dried oregano
- 12 oz sea scallops

Directions:
1. Preheat air fryer to 400°F/205°C. Add the asparagus, peas, and broccoli to a bowl and mix with olive oil. Put the bowl in the fryer and Air Fry for 4-6 minutes until crispy and soft. Take the veggies out and add the herbs; let sit. Add the scallops to the fryer and Air Fry for 4-5 minutes until the scallops are springy to the touch. Serve immediately with the vegetables. Enjoy!

Rich Salmon Burgers With Broccoli Slaw

Servings: 4
Cooking Time: 25 Minutes
Ingredients:
- 1 lb salmon fillets
- 1 egg
- ¼ cup dill, chopped
- 1 cup bread crumbs
- Salt to taste

- ½ tsp cayenne pepper
- 1 lime, zested
- 1 tsp fish sauce
- 4 buns
- 3 cups chopped broccoli
- ½ cup shredded carrots
- ¼ cup sunflower seeds
- 2 garlic cloves, minced
- 1 cup Greek yogurt

Directions:
1. Preheat air fryer to 360°F/180°C. Blitz the salmon fillets in your food processor until they are finely chopped. Remove to a large bowl and add egg, dill, bread crumbs, salt, and cayenne. Stir to combine. Form the mixture into 4 patties. Put them into the frying basket and Bake for 10 minutes, flipping once. Combine broccoli, carrots, sunflower seeds, garlic, salt, lime, fish sauce, and Greek yogurt in a bowl. Serve the salmon burgers onto buns with broccoli slaw. Enjoy!

The Best Oysters Rockefeller
Servings: 2
Cooking Time: 30 Minutes
Ingredients:
- 4 tsp grated Parmesan
- 2 tbsp butter
- 1 sweet onion, minced
- 1 clove garlic, minced
- 1 cup baby spinach
- ⅛ tsp Tabasco hot sauce
- ½ tsp lemon juice
- ½ tsp lemon zest
- ¼ cup bread crumbs
- 12 oysters, on the half shell

Directions:
1. Melt butter in a skillet over medium heat. Stir in onion, garlic, and spinach and stir-fry for 3 minutes until the onion is translucent. Mix in Parmesan cheese, hot sauce, lemon juice, lemon zest, and bread crumbs. Divide this mixture between the tops of oysters.
2. Preheat air fryer to 400°F/205°C. Place oysters in the frying basket and Air Fry for 6 minutes. Serve immediately.

Quick Tuna Tacos
Servings: 4
Cooking Time: 20 Minutes
Ingredients:
- 2 cups torn romaine lettuce
- 1 lb fresh tuna steak, cubed
- 1 tbsp grated fresh ginger
- 2 garlic cloves, minced
- ½ tsp toasted sesame oil
- 4 tortillas
- ¼ cup mild salsa
- 1 red bell pepper, sliced

Directions:
1. Preheat air fryer to 390°F/200°C. Combine the tuna, ginger, garlic, and sesame oil in a bowl and allow to marinate for 10 minutes. Lay the marinated tuna in the fryer and Grill for 4-7 minutes. Serve right away with tortillas, mild salsa, lettuce, and bell pepper for delicious tacos.

Cilantro Sea Bass
Servings: 2
Cooking Time: 15 Minutes
Ingredients:
- Salt and pepper to taste
- 1 tsp olive oil
- 2 sea bass fillets
- ½ tsp berbere seasoning
- 2 tsp chopped cilantro
- 1 tsp dried thyme
- ½ tsp garlic powder
- 4 lemon quarters

Directions:
1. Preheat air fryer at 375°F/190°C. Rub sea bass fillets with olive oil, thyme, garlic powder, salt and black pepper. Season with berbere seasoning. Place fillets in the greased frying basket and Air Fry for 6-8 minutes. Let rest for 5 minutes on a serving plate. Scatter with cilantro and serve with lemon quarters on the side.

Crab Cakes
Servings: 2
Cooking Time: 10 Minutes
Ingredients:
- 1 teaspoon butter
- ⅓ cup finely diced onion
- ⅓ cup finely diced celery
- ¼ cup mayonnaise
- 1 teaspoon Dijon mustard
- 1 egg
- pinch ground cayenne pepper
- 1 teaspoon salt
- freshly ground black pepper
- 16 ounces lump crabmeat
- ½ cup + 2 tablespoons panko breadcrumbs, divided

Directions:
1. Melt the butter in a skillet over medium heat. Sauté the onion and celery until it starts to soften, but not brown – about 4 minutes. Transfer the cooked vegetables to a large bowl. Add the mayonnaise, Dijon mustard, egg, cayenne pepper, salt and freshly ground black pepper to the bowl. Gently fold in the lump crabmeat and 2 tablespoons of panko breadcrumbs. Stir carefully so you don't break up all the crab pieces.
2. Preheat the air fryer to 400°F/205°C.
3. Place the remaining panko breadcrumbs in a shallow dish. Divide the crab mixture into 4 portions and shape each portion into a round patty. Dredge the crab patties in the breadcrumbs, coating both sides as well as the edges with the crumbs.
4. Air-fry the crab cakes for 5 minutes. Using a flat spatula, gently turn the cakes over and air-fry for another 5 minutes. Serve the crab cakes with tartar sauce or cocktail sauce, or dress it up with the suggestion below.

Crunchy Flounder Gratin
Servings: 4
Cooking Time: 20 Minutes
Ingredients:
- ¼ cup grated Parmesan
- 4 flounder fillets
- 4 tbsp butter, melted
- ¼ cup panko bread crumbs
- ½ tsp paprika
- 1 egg

Tower Air Fryer Cookbook

- Salt and pepper to taste
- ½ tsp dried oregano
- ½ tsp dried basil
- 1 tsp dried thyme
- 1 lemon, quartered
- 1 tbsp chopped parsley

Directions:
1. Preheat air fryer to 375°F/190°C. In a bowl, whisk together egg until smooth. Brush the fillets on both sides with some of the butter. Combine the rest of the butter, bread crumbs, Parmesan cheese, salt, paprika, thyme, oregano, basil, and pepper in a small bowl until crumbly. Dip the fish into the egg and then into the bread crumb mixture and coat completely. Transfer the fish to the frying basket and bake for 5 minutes. Carefully flip the fillets and bake for another 6 minutes until crispy and golden on the outside. Garnish with lemon wedges and parsley. Serve and enjoy.

Herb-crusted Sole

Servings: 4
Cooking Time: 20 Minutes
Ingredients:
- ½ lemon, juiced and zested
- 4 sole fillets
- ½ tsp dried thyme
- ½ tsp dried marjoram
- ½ tsp dried parsley
- Black pepper to taste
- 1 bread slice, crumbled
- 2 tsp olive oil

Directions:
1. Preheat air fryer to 320°F/160°C. In a bowl, combine the lemon zest, thyme, marjoram, parsley, pepper, breadcrumbs, and olive oil and stir. Arrange the sole fillets on a lined baking pan, skin-side down. Pour the lemon juice over the fillets, then press them firmly into the breadcrumb mixture to coat. Air Fry for 8-11 minutes, until the breadcrumbs are crisp and golden brown. Serve warm.

Restaurant-style Breaded Shrimp

Servings: 2
Cooking Time: 35 Minutes
Ingredients:
- ½ lb fresh shrimp, peeled
- 2 eggs, beaten
- ½ cup breadcrumbs
- ½ onion, finely chopped
- ½ tsp ground ginger
- ½ tsp garlic powder
- ½ tsp turmeric
- ½ tsp red chili powder
- Salt and pepper to taste
- ½ tsp amchur powder

Directions:
1. Preheat air fryer to 350°F/175°C. Place the beaten eggs in a bowl and dip in the shrimp. Blend the bread crumbs with all the dry ingredients in another bowl. Add in the shrimp and toss to coat. Place the coated shrimp in the greased frying basket. Air Fry for 12-14 minutes until the breaded crust of the shrimp is golden brown. Toss the basket two or three times during the cooking time. Serve.

Black Cod With Grapes, Fennel, Pecans And Kale

Servings: 2
Cooking Time: 15 Minutes
Ingredients:
- 2 (6- to 8-ounce) fillets of black cod (or sablefish)
- salt and freshly ground black pepper
- olive oil
- 1 cup grapes, halved
- 1 small bulb fennel, sliced ¼-inch thick
- ½ cup pecans
- 3 cups shredded kale
- 2 teaspoons white balsamic vinegar or white wine vinegar
- 2 tablespoons extra virgin olive oil

Directions:
1. Preheat the air fryer to 400°F/205°C.
2. Season the cod fillets with salt and pepper and drizzle, brush or spray a little olive oil on top. Place the fish, presentation side up (skin side down), into the air fryer basket. Air-fry for 10 minutes.
3. When the fish has finished cooking, remove the fillets to a side plate and loosely tent with foil to rest.
4. Toss the grapes, fennel and pecans in a bowl with a drizzle of olive oil and season with salt and pepper. Add the grapes, fennel and pecans to the air fryer basket and air-fry for 5 minutes at 400°F, shaking the basket once during the cooking time.
5. Transfer the grapes, fennel and pecans to a bowl with the kale. Dress the kale with the balsamic vinegar and olive oil, season to taste with salt and pepper and serve along side the cooked fish.

Dijon Shrimp Cakes

Servings: 4
Cooking Time: 30 Minutes
Ingredients:
- 1 cup cooked shrimp, minced
- ¾ cup saltine cracker crumbs
- 1 cup lump crabmeat
- 3 green onions, chopped
- 1 egg, beaten
- ¼ cup mayonnaise
- 2 tbsp Dijon mustard
- 1 tbsp lemon juice

Directions:
1. Preheat the air fryer to 375°F/190°C. Combine the crabmeat, shrimp, green onions, egg, mayonnaise, mustard, ¼ cup of cracker crumbs, and the lemon juice in a bowl and mix gently. Make 4 patties, sprinkle with the rest of the cracker crumbs on both sides, and spray with cooking oil. Line the frying basket with a round parchment paper with holes poked in it. Coat the paper with cooking spray and lay the patties on it. Bake for 10-14 minutes or until the patties are golden brown. Serve warm.

Beef, Pork & Lamb Recipes

Beef Short Ribs

Servings: 4
Cooking Time: 20 Minutes
Ingredients:
- 2 tablespoons soy sauce
- 1 tablespoon sesame oil
- 2 tablespoons brown sugar
- 1 teaspoon ground ginger
- 2 garlic cloves, crushed
- 1 pound beef short ribs

Directions:
1. In a small bowl, mix together the soy sauce, sesame oil, brown sugar, and ginger. Transfer the mixture to a large resealable plastic bag, and place the garlic cloves and short ribs into the bag. Secure and place in the refrigerator for an hour (or overnight).
2. When you're ready to prepare the dish, preheat the air fryer to 330°F/165°C.
3. Liberally spray the air fryer basket with olive oil mist and set the beef short ribs in the basket.
4. Cook for 10 minutes, flip the short ribs, and then cook another 10 minutes.
5. Remove the short ribs from the air fryer basket, loosely cover with aluminum foil, and let them rest. The short ribs will continue to cook after they're removed from the basket. Check the internal temperature after 5 minutes to make sure it reached 145°F/60°C if you prefer a well-done meat. If it didn't reach 145°F/60°C and you would like it to be cooked longer, you can put it back into the air fryer basket at 330°F/165°C for another 3 minutes.
6. Remove from the basket and let it rest, covered with aluminum foil, for 5 minutes. Serve immediately.

Stress-free Beef Patties

Servings: 2
Cooking Time: 30 Minutes
Ingredients:
- ½ lb ground beef
- 1 ½ tbsp ketchup
- 1 ½ tbsp tamari
- ½ tsp jalapeño powder
- ½ tsp mustard powder
- Salt and pepper to taste

Directions:
1. Preheat air fryer to 350°F/175°C. Add the beef, ketchup, tamari, jalapeño, mustard salt, and pepper in a bowl and mix until evenly combined. Shape into 2 patties, then place them on the greased frying basket. Air Fry for 18-20 minutes, turning once. Serve and enjoy!

Honey Pork Links

Servings: 4
Cooking Time: 20 Minutes
Ingredients:
- 12 oz ground mild pork sausage, removed from casings
- 1 tsp rubbed sage
- 2 tbsp honey
- ⅛ tsp cayenne pepper
- ⅛ tsp paprika
- Salt and pepper to taste

Directions:
1. Preheat air fryer to 400°F/205°C. Remove the sausage from the casings. Transfer to a bowl and add the remaining ingredients. Mix well. Make 8 links out of the mixture. Add the links to the frying basket and Air Fry for 8-10 minutes, flipping once. Serve right away.

Beef Fajitas

Servings: 2
Cooking Time: 15 Minutes
Ingredients:
- 8 oz sliced mushrooms
- ½ onion, cut into half-moons
- 1 tbsp olive oil
- Salt and pepper to taste
- 1 strip steak
- ½ tsp smoked paprika
- ½ tsp fajita seasoning
- 2 tbsp corn

Directions:
1. Preheat air fryer to 400°F/205°C. Combine the olive oil, onion, and salt in a bowl. Add the mushrooms and toss to coat. Spread in the frying basket. Sprinkle steak with salt, paprika, fajita seasoning and black pepper. Place steak on top of the mushroom mixture and Air Fry for 9 minutes, flipping steak once. Let rest onto a cutting board for 5 minutes before cutting in half. Divide steak, mushrooms, corn, and onions between 2 plates and serve.

Country-style Pork Ribs[2]

Servings: 4
Cooking Time: 50 Minutes
Ingredients:
- 1 tsp smoked paprika
- 1 tsp ground cumin
- 1 tsp garlic powder
- 1 tsp onion powder
- 1 tbsp honey
- ½ tsp ground mustard
- Salt and pepper to taste
- 2 tbsp olive oil
- 1 tbsp fresh orange juice
- 2 lb country-style pork ribs

Directions:
1. Preheat air fryer to 350°F/175°C. Combine all spices and honey in a bowl. In another bowl, whisk olive oil and orange juice and massage onto pork ribs. Sprinkle with the spice mixture. Place the pork ribs in the frying basket and Air Fry for 40 minutes, flipping every 10 minutes. Serve.

Sweet Potato - crusted Pork Rib Chops

Servings: 2
Cooking Time: 14 Minutes
Ingredients:
- 2 Large egg white(s), well beaten
- 1½ cups (about 6 ounces) Crushed sweet potato chips (certified gluten-free, if a concern)
- 1 teaspoon Ground cinnamon
- 1 teaspoon Ground dried ginger
- 1 teaspoon Table salt (optional)
- 2 10-ounce, 1-inch-thick bone-in pork rib chop(s)

Directions:
1. Preheat the air fryer to 375°F/190°C.
2. Set up and fill two shallow soup plates or small pie plates on your counter: one for the beaten egg white(s); and one for the crushed chips, mixed with the cinnamon, ginger, and salt (if using).
3. Dip a chop in the egg white(s), coating it on both sides as well as the edges. Let the excess egg white slip back into the rest, then set it in the crushed chip mixture. Turn it several times, pressing gently, until evenly coated on both sides and the edges. If necessary, set the chop aside and coat the remaining chop(s).
4. Set the chop(s) in the basket with as much air space between them as possible. Air-fry undisturbed for 12 minutes, or until crunchy and browned and an instant-read meat thermometer inserted into the center of a chop (without touching bone) registers 145°F. If the machine is at 360°F/180°C, you may need to add 2 minutes to the cooking time.
5. Use kitchen tongs to transfer the chop(s) to a wire rack. Cool for 2 or 3 minutes before serving.

Beef & Barley Stuffed Bell Peppers

Servings: 4
Cooking Time: 30 Minutes
Ingredients:
- 1 cup pulled cooked roast beef
- 4 bell peppers, tops removed
- 1 onion, chopped
- ½ cup grated carrot
- 2 tsp olive oil
- 2 tomatoes, chopped
- 1 cup cooked barley
- 1 tsp dried marjoram

Directions:
1. Preheat air fryer to 400°F/205°C. Cut the tops of the bell peppers, then remove the stems. Put the onion, carrots, and olive oil in a baking pan and cook for 2-4 minutes. The veggies should be crispy but soft. Put the veggies in a bowl, toss in the tomatoes, barley, roast beef, and marjoram, and mix to combine. Spoon the veggie mix into the cleaned bell peppers and put them in the frying basket. Bake for 12-16 minutes or until the peppers are tender. Serve warm.

Barbecue-style London Broil

Servings: 5
Cooking Time: 17 Minutes
Ingredients:
- ¾ teaspoon Mild smoked paprika
- ¾ teaspoon Dried oregano
- ¾ teaspoon Table salt
- ¾ teaspoon Ground black pepper
- ¼ teaspoon Garlic powder
- ¼ teaspoon Onion powder
- 1½ pounds Beef London broil (in one piece)
- Olive oil spray

Directions:
1. Preheat the air fryer to 400°F/205°C.
2. Mix the smoked paprika, oregano, salt, pepper, garlic powder, and onion powder in a small bowl until uniform.
3. Pat and rub this mixture across all surfaces of the beef. Lightly coat the beef on all sides with olive oil spray.
4. When the machine is at temperature, lay the London broil flat in the basket and air-fry undisturbed for 8 minutes for the small batch, 10 minutes for the medium batch, or 12 minutes for the large batch for medium-rare, until an instant-read meat thermometer inserted into the center of the meat registers 130°F/55°C (not USDA-approved). Add 1, 2, or 3 minutes, respectively (based on the size of the cut) for medium, until an instant-read meat thermometer registers 135°F/55°C (not USDA-approved). Or add 3, 4, or 5 minutes respectively for medium, until an instant-read meat thermometer registers 145°F/60°C (USDA-approved).
5. Use kitchen tongs to transfer the London broil to a cutting board. Let the meat rest for 10 minutes. It needs a long time for the juices to be reincorporated into the meat's fibers. Carve it against the grain into very thin (less than ¼-inch-thick) slices to serve.

Sage Pork With Potatoes

Servings: 4
Cooking Time: 30 Minutes
Ingredients:
- 2 cups potatoes
- 2 tsp olive oil
- 1 lb pork tenderloin, cubed
- 1 onion, chopped
- 1 red bell pepper, chopped
- 2 garlic cloves, minced
- ½ tsp dried sage
- ½ tsp fennel seeds, crushed
- 2 tbsp chicken broth

Directions:
1. Preheat air fryer to 370°F/185°C. Add the potatoes and olive oil to a bowl and toss to coat. Transfer them to the frying basket and Air Fry for 15 minutes. Remove the bowl. Add the pork, onion, red bell pepper, garlic, sage, and fennel seeds, to the potatoes, add chicken broth and stir gently. Return the bowl to the frying basket and cook for 10 minutes. Be sure to shake the basket at least once. The pork should be cooked through and the potatoes soft and crispy. Serve immediately.

Rack Of Lamb With Pistachio Crust

Servings: 2
Cooking Time: 19 Minutes
Ingredients:
- ½ cup finely chopped pistachios
- 3 tablespoons panko breadcrumbs
- 1 teaspoon chopped fresh rosemary
- 2 teaspoons chopped fresh oregano
- salt and freshly ground black pepper
- 1 tablespoon olive oil
- 1 rack of lamb, bones trimmed of fat and frenched

- 1 tablespoon Dijon mustard

Directions:
1. Preheat the air fryer to 380°F/195°C.
2. Combine the pistachios, breadcrumbs, rosemary, oregano, salt and pepper in a small bowl. Drizzle in the olive oil and stir to combine.
3. Season the rack of lamb with salt and pepper on all sides and transfer it to the air fryer basket with the fat side facing up. Air-fry the lamb for 12 minutes. Remove the lamb from the air fryer and brush the fat side of the lamb rack with the Dijon mustard. Coat the rack with the pistachio mixture, pressing the breadcrumbs onto the lamb with your hands and rolling the bottom of the rack in any of the crumbs that fall off.
4. Return the rack of lamb to the air fryer and air-fry for another 3 to 7 minutes or until an instant read thermometer reads 140°F/60°C for medium. Add or subtract a couple of minutes for lamb that is more or less well cooked. (Your time will vary depending on how big the rack of lamb is.)
5. Let the lamb rest for at least 5 minutes. Then, slice into chops and serve.

Crispy Steak Subs

Servings: 2
Cooking Time: 30 Minutes
Ingredients:
- 1 hoagie bun baguette, halved
- 6 oz flank steak, sliced
- ½ white onion, sliced
- ½ red pepper, sliced
- 2 mozzarella cheese slices

Directions:
1. Preheat air fryer to 320°F/160°C. Place the flank steak slices, onion, and red pepper on one side of the frying basket. Add the hoagie bun halves, crusty side up, to the other half of the air fryer. Bake for 10 minutes. Flip the hoagie buns. Cover both sides with one slice of mozzarella cheese. Gently stir the steak, onions, and peppers. Cook for 6 more minutes until the cheese is melted and the steak is juicy on the inside and crispy on the outside.
2. Remove the cheesy hoagie halves to a serving plate. Cover one side with the steak, and top with the onions and peppers. Close with the other cheesy hoagie half, slice into two pieces, and enjoy!

Italian Sausage & Peppers

Servings: 6
Cooking Time: 25 Minutes
Ingredients:
- 1 6-ounce can tomato paste
- ⅔ cup water
- 1 8-ounce can tomato sauce
- 1 teaspoon dried parsley flakes
- ½ teaspoon garlic powder
- ⅛ teaspoon oregano
- ½ pound mild Italian bulk sausage
- 1 tablespoon extra virgin olive oil
- ½ large onion, cut in 1-inch chunks
- 4 ounces fresh mushrooms, sliced
- 1 large green bell pepper, cut in 1-inch chunks
- 8 ounces spaghetti, cooked
- Parmesan cheese for serving

Directions:
1. In a large saucepan or skillet, stir together the tomato paste, water, tomato sauce, parsley, garlic, and oregano. Heat on stovetop over very low heat while preparing meat and vegetables.
2. Break sausage into small chunks, about ½-inch pieces. Place in air fryer baking pan.
3. Cook at 390°F/200°C for 5 minutes. Stir. Cook 7 minutes longer or until sausage is well done. Remove from pan, drain on paper towels, and add to the sauce mixture.
4. If any sausage grease remains in baking pan, pour it off or use paper towels to soak it up. (Be careful handling that hot pan!)
5. Place olive oil, onions, and mushrooms in pan and stir. Cook for 5 minutes or just until tender. Using a slotted spoon, transfer onions and mushrooms from baking pan into the sauce and sausage mixture.
6. Place bell pepper chunks in air fryer baking pan and cook for 8 minutes or until tender. When done, stir into sauce with sausage and other vegetables.
7. Serve over cooked spaghetti with plenty of Parmesan cheese.

Sweet And Sour Pork

Servings: 2
Cooking Time: 11 Minutes
Ingredients:
- ⅓ cup all-purpose flour
- ⅓ cup cornstarch
- 2 teaspoons Chinese 5-spice powder
- 1 teaspoon salt
- freshly ground black pepper
- 1 egg
- 2 tablespoons milk
- ¾ pound boneless pork, cut into 1-inch cubes
- vegetable or canola oil, in a spray bottle
- 1½ cups large chunks of red and green peppers
- ½ cup ketchup
- 2 tablespoons rice wine vinegar or apple cider vinegar
- 2 tablespoons brown sugar
- ¼ cup orange juice
- 1 tablespoon soy sauce
- 1 clove garlic, minced
- 1 cup cubed pineapple
- chopped scallions

Directions:
1. Set up a dredging station with two bowls. Combine the flour, cornstarch, Chinese 5-spice powder, salt and pepper in one large bowl. Whisk the egg and milk together in a second bowl. Dredge the pork cubes in the flour mixture first, then dip them into the egg and then back into the flour to coat on all sides. Spray the coated pork cubes with vegetable or canola oil.
2. Preheat the air fryer to 400°F/205°C.
3. Toss the pepper chunks with a little oil and air-fry at 400°F/205°C for 5 minutes, shaking the basket halfway through the cooking time.
4. While the peppers are cooking, start making the sauce. Combine the ketchup, rice wine vinegar, brown sugar, orange juice, soy sauce, and garlic in a medium saucepan and bring the mixture to a boil on the stovetop. Reduce the heat and simmer for 5 minutes. When the peppers have finished air-frying, add them to the saucepan along with the pineapple chunks. Simmer the peppers and pineapple in the sauce for an additional 2 minutes. Set aside and keep warm.

5. Add the dredged pork cubes to the air fryer basket and air-fry at 400°F/205°C for 6 minutes, shaking the basket to turn the cubes over for the last minute of the cooking process.
6. When ready to serve, toss the cooked pork with the pineapple, peppers and sauce. Serve over white rice and garnish with chopped scallions.

Chipotle Pork Meatballs

Servings: 4
Cooking Time: 35 Minutes
Ingredients:
- 1 lb ground pork
- 1 egg
- ¼ cup chipotle sauce
- ¼ cup grated celery
- ¼ cup chopped parsley
- ¼ cup chopped cilantro
- ¼ cup flour
- ¼ tsp salt

Directions:
1. Preheat air fryer to 350°F/175°C. In a large bowl, combine the ground pork, egg, chipotle sauce, celery, parsley, cilantro, flour, and salt. Form mixture into 16 meatballs. Place the meatballs in the lightly greased frying basket and Air Fry for 8-10 minutes, flipping once. Serve immediately!

City "chicken"

Servings: 3
Cooking Time: 10 Minutes
Ingredients:
- 1 pound Pork tenderloin, cut into 2-inch cubes
- ½ cup All-purpose flour or tapioca flour
- 1 Large egg(s)
- 1 teaspoon Dried poultry seasoning blend
- 1¼ cups Plain panko bread crumbs (gluten-free, if a concern)
- Vegetable oil spray

Directions:
1. Preheat the air fryer to 350°F/175°C .
2. Thread 3 or 4 pieces of pork on a 4-inch bamboo skewer. You'll need 2 or 3 skewers for a small batch, 3 or 4 for a medium, and up to 6 for a large batch.
3. Set up and fill three shallow soup plates or small pie plates on your counter: one for the flour; one for the egg(s), beaten with the poultry seasoning until foamy; and one for the bread crumbs.
4. Dip and roll one skewer into the flour, coating all sides of the meat. Gently shake off any excess flour, then dip and roll the skewer in the egg mixture. Let any excess egg mixture slip back into the rest, then set the skewer in the bread crumbs and roll it around, pressing gently, until the exterior surfaces of the meat are evenly coated. Generously coat the meat on the skewer with vegetable oil spray. Set aside and continue dredging, dipping, coating, and spraying the remaining skewers.
5. Set the skewers in the basket in one layer and air-fry undisturbed for 10 minutes, or until brown and crunchy.
6. Use kitchen tongs to transfer the skewers to a wire rack. Cool for a minute or two before serving.

Crispy Smoked Pork Chops

Servings: 3
Cooking Time: 8 Minutes
Ingredients:
- ⅔ cup All-purpose flour or tapioca flour
- 1 Large egg white(s)
- 2 tablespoons Water
- 1½ cups Corn flake crumbs (gluten-free, if a concern)
- 3 ½-pound, ½-inch-thick bone-in smoked pork chops

Directions:
1. Preheat the air fryer to 375°F/190°C.
2. Set up and fill three shallow soup plates or small pie plates on your counter: one for the flour; one for the egg white(s), whisked with the water until foamy; and one for the corn flake crumbs.
3. Set a chop in the flour and turn it several times, coating both sides and the edges. Gently shake off any excess flour, then set it in the beaten egg white mixture. Turn to coat both sides as well as the edges. Let any excess egg white slip back into the rest, then set the chop in the corn flake crumbs. Turn it several times, pressing gently to coat the chop evenly on both sides and around the edge. Set the chop aside and continue coating the remaining chop(s) in the same way.
4. Set the chops in the basket with as much air space between them as possible. Air-fry undisturbed for 8 minutes, or until the coating is crunchy and the chops are heated through.
5. Use kitchen tongs to transfer the chops to a wire rack and cool for a couple of minutes before serving.

Fried Spam

Servings: 2
Cooking Time: 12 Minutes
Ingredients:
- ½ cup All-purpose flour or gluten-free all-purpose flour
- 1 Large egg(s)
- 1 tablespoon Wasabi paste
- 1⅓ cups Plain panko bread crumbs (gluten-free, if a concern)
- 4 ½-inch-thick Spam slices
- Vegetable oil spray

Directions:
1. Preheat the air fryer to 400°F/205°C.
2. Set up and fill three shallow soup plates or small pie plates on your counter: one for the flour; one for the egg(s), whisked with the wasabi paste until uniform; and one for the bread crumbs.
3. Dip a slice of Spam in the flour, coating both sides. Slip it into the egg mixture and turn to coat on both sides, even along the edges. Let any excess egg mixture slip back into the rest, then set the slice in the bread crumbs. Turn it several times, pressing gently to make an even coating on both sides. Generously coat both sides of the slice with vegetable oil spray. Set aside so you can dip, coat, and spray the remaining slice(s).
4. Set the slices in the basket in a single layer so that they don't touch (even if they're close together). Air-fry undisturbed for 12 minutes, or until very brown and quite crunchy.
5. Use kitchen tongs to transfer the slices to a wire rack. Cool for a minute or two before serving.

Pork Chops

Servings: 2
Cooking Time: 16 Minutes
Ingredients:
- 2 bone-in, centercut pork chops, 1-inch thick (10 ounces each)
- 2 teaspoons Worcestershire sauce
- salt and pepper
- cooking spray

Directions:
1. Rub the Worcestershire sauce into both sides of pork chops.
2. Season with salt and pepper to taste.
3. Spray air fryer basket with cooking spray and place the chops in basket side by side.
4. Cook at 360°F/180°C for 16 minutes or until well done. Let rest for 5minutes before serving.

Italian Meatballs

Servings: 4
Cooking Time: 12 Minutes
Ingredients:
- 12 ounces lean ground beef
- 4 ounces Italian sausage, casing removed
- ½ cup breadcrumbs
- 1 cup grated Parmesan cheese
- 1 egg
- 2 tablespoons milk
- 2 teaspoons Italian seasoning
- ½ teaspoon onion powder
- ½ teaspoon garlic powder
- Pinch of red pepper flakes

Directions:
1. In a large bowl, place all the ingredients and mix well. Roll out 24 meatballs.
2. Preheat the air fryer to 360°F/180°C.
3. Place the meatballs in the air fryer basket and cook for 12 minutes, tossing every 4 minutes. Using a food thermometer, check to ensure the internal temperature of the meatballs is 165°F.

Ground Beef Calzones

Servings: 6
Cooking Time: 30 Minutes
Ingredients:
- 1 refrigerated pizza dough
- 1 cup shredded mozzarella
- ½ cup chopped onion
- 2 garlic cloves, minced
- ¼ cup chopped mushrooms
- 1 lb ground beef
- 1 tbsp pizza seasoning
- Salt and pepper to taste
- 1 ½ cups marinara sauce
- 1 tsp flour

Directions:
1. Warm 1 tbsp of oil in a skillet over medium heat. Stir-fry onion, garlic and mushrooms for 2-3 minutes or until aromatic. Add beef, pizza seasoning, salt and pepper. Use a large spoon to break up the beef. Cook for 3 minutes or until brown. Stir in marinara sauce and set aside.
2. On a floured work surface, roll out pizza dough and cut into 6 equal-sized rectangles. On each rectangle, add ½ cup of beef and top with 1 tbsp of shredded cheese. Fold one side of the dough over the filling to the opposite side. Press the edges using the back of a fork to seal them. Preheat air fryer to 400°F/205°C. Place the first batch of calzones in the air fryer and spray with cooking oil. Bake for 10 minutes. Let cool slightly and serve warm.

Spicy Hoisin Bbq Pork Chops

Servings: 2
Cooking Time: 12 Minutes
Ingredients:
- 3 tablespoons hoisin sauce
- ¼ cup honey
- 1 tablespoon soy sauce
- 3 tablespoons rice vinegar
- 2 tablespoons brown sugar
- 1½ teaspoons grated fresh ginger
- 1 to 2 teaspoons Sriracha sauce, to taste
- 2 to 3 bone-in center cut pork chops, 1-inch thick (about 1¼ pounds)
- chopped scallions, for garnish

Directions:
1. Combine the hoisin sauce, honey, soy sauce, rice vinegar, brown sugar, ginger, and Sriracha sauce in a small saucepan. Whisk the ingredients together and bring the mixture to a boil over medium-high heat on the stovetop. Reduce the heat and simmer the sauce until it has reduced in volume and thickened slightly – about 10 minutes.
2. Preheat the air fryer to 400°F/205°C.
3. Place the pork chops into the air fryer basket and pour half the hoisin BBQ sauce over the top. Air-fry for 6 minutes. Then, flip the chops over, pour the remaining hoisin BBQ sauce on top and air-fry for 6 more minutes, depending on the thickness of the pork chops. The internal temperature of the pork chops should be 155°F/70°C when tested with an instant read thermometer.
4. Let the pork chops rest for 5 minutes before serving. You can spoon a little of the sauce from the bottom drawer of the air fryer over the top if desired. Sprinkle with chopped scallions and serve.

Meatloaf With Tangy Tomato Glaze

Servings: 6
Cooking Time: 50 Minutes
Ingredients:
- 1 pound ground beef
- ½ pound ground pork
- ½ pound ground veal (or turkey)
- 1 medium onion, diced
- 1 small clove of garlic, minced
- 2 egg yolks, lightly beaten
- ½ cup tomato ketchup
- 1 tablespoon Worcestershire sauce
- ½ cup plain breadcrumbs*
- 2 teaspoons salt
- freshly ground black pepper
- ½ cup chopped fresh parsley, plus more for garnish
- 6 tablespoons ketchup
- 1 tablespoon balsamic vinegar
- 2 tablespoons brown sugar

Directions:

Tower Air Fryer Cookbook

99

1. Combine the meats, onion, garlic, egg yolks, ketchup, Worcestershire sauce, breadcrumbs, salt, pepper and fresh parsley in a large bowl and mix well.
2. Preheat the air fryer to 350°F/175°C and pour a little water into the bottom of the air fryer drawer. (This will help prevent the grease that drips into the bottom drawer from burning and smoking.)
3. Transfer the meatloaf mixture to the air fryer basket, packing it down gently. Run a spatula around the meatloaf to create a space about ½-inch wide between the meat and the side of the air fryer basket.
4. Air-fry at 350°F/175°C for 20 minutes. Carefully invert the meatloaf onto a plate (remember to remove the basket from the air fryer drawer so you don't pour all the grease out) and slide it back into the air fryer basket to turn it over. Re-shape the meatloaf with a spatula if necessary. Air-fry for another 20 minutes at 350°F/175°C.
5. Combine the ketchup, balsamic vinegar and brown sugar in a bowl and spread the mixture over the meatloaf. Air-fry for another 10 minutes, until an instant read thermometer inserted into the center of the meatloaf registers 160°F/70°C.
6. Allow the meatloaf to rest for a few more minutes and then transfer it to a serving platter using a spatula. Slice the meatloaf, sprinkle a little chopped parsley on top if desired, and serve.

Balsamic Beef & Veggie Skewers
Servings: 4
Cooking Time: 25 Minutes
Ingredients:
- 2 tbsp balsamic vinegar
- 2 tsp olive oil
- ½ tsp dried oregano
- Salt and pepper to taste
- ¾ lb round steak, cubed
- 1 red bell pepper, sliced
- 1 yellow bell pepper, sliced
- 1 cup cherry tomatoes

Directions:
1. Preheat air fryer to 390°F/200°C. Put the balsamic vinegar, olive oil, oregano, salt, and black pepper in a bowl and stir. Toss the steak in and allow to marinate for 10 minutes. Poke 8 metal skewers through the beef, bell peppers, and cherry tomatoes, alternating ingredients as you go. Place the skewers in the air fryer and Air Fry for 5-7 minutes, turning once until the beef is golden and cooked through and the veggies are tender. Serve and enjoy!

Extra Crispy Country-style Pork Riblets
Servings: 3
Cooking Time: 30 Minutes
Ingredients:
- ⅓ cup Tapioca flour
- 2½ tablespoons Chile powder
- ¾ teaspoon Table salt (optional)
- 1¼ pounds Boneless country-style pork ribs, cut into 1½-inch chunks
- Vegetable oil spray

Directions:
1. Preheat the air fryer to 375°F/190°C.
2. Mix the tapioca flour, chile powder, and salt (if using) in a large bowl until well combined. Add the country-style rib chunks and toss well to coat thoroughly.
3. When the machine is at temperature, gently shake off any excess tapioca coating from the chunks. Generously coat them on all sides with vegetable oil spray. Arrange the chunks in the basket in one (admittedly fairly tight) layer. The pieces may touch. Air-fry for 30 minutes, rearranging the pieces at the 10- and 20-minute marks to expose any touching bits, until very crisp and well browned.
4. Gently pour the contents of the basket onto a wire rack. Cool for 5 minutes before serving.

Indonesian Pork Satay
Servings: 4
Cooking Time: 30 Minutes
Ingredients:
- 1 lb pork tenderloin, cubed
- ¼ cup minced onion
- 2 garlic cloves, minced
- 1 jalapeño pepper, minced
- 2 tbsp lime juice
- 2 tbsp coconut milk
- ½ tbsp ground coriander
- ½ tsp ground cumin
- 2 tbsp peanut butter
- 2 tsp curry powder

Directions:
1. Combine the pork, onion, garlic, jalapeño, lime juice, coconut milk, peanut butter, ground coriander, cumin, and curry powder in a bowl. Stir well and allow to marinate for 10 minutes.
2. Preheat air fryer to 380°F/195°C. Use a holey spoon and take the pork out of the marinade and set the marinade aside. Poke 8 bamboo skewers through the meat, then place the skewers in the air fryer. Use a cooking brush to rub the marinade on each skewer, then Grill for 10-14 minutes, adding more marinade if necessary. The pork should be golden and cooked through when finished. Serve warm.

Pork Cutlets With Almond-lemon Crust
Servings: 3
Cooking Time: 14 Minutes
Ingredients:
- ¾ cup Almond flour
- ¾ cup Plain dried bread crumbs (gluten-free, if a concern)
- 1½ teaspoons Finely grated lemon zest
- 1¼ teaspoons Table salt
- ¾ teaspoon Garlic powder
- ¾ teaspoon Dried oregano
- 1 Large egg white(s)
- 2 tablespoons Water
- 3 6-ounce center-cut boneless pork loin chops (about ¾ inch thick)
- Olive oil spray

Directions:
1. Preheat the air fryer to 375°F/190°C.
2. Mix the almond flour, bread crumbs, lemon zest, salt, garlic powder, and dried oregano in a large bowl until well combined.
3. Whisk the egg white(s) and water in a shallow soup plate or small pie plate until uniform.

4. Dip a chop in the egg white mixture, turning it to coat all sides, even the ends. Let any excess egg white mixture slip back into the rest, then set it in the almond flour mixture. Turn it several times, pressing gently to coat it evenly. Generously coat the chop with olive oil spray, then set aside to dip and coat the remaining chop(s).
5. Set the chops in the basket with as much air space between them as possible. Air-fry undisturbed for 12 minutes, or until browned and crunchy. You may need to add 2 minutes to the cooking time if the machine is at 360°F/180°C.
6. Use kitchen tongs to transfer the chops to a wire rack. Cool for a few minutes before serving.

Golden Pork Quesadillas

Servings: 2
Cooking Time: 50 Minutes
Ingredients:
- ¼ cup shredded Monterey jack cheese
- 2 tortilla wraps
- 4 oz pork shoulder, sliced
- 1 tsp taco seasoning
- ½ white onion, sliced
- ½ red bell pepper, sliced
- ½ green bell pepper, sliced
- ½ yellow bell pepper, sliced
- 1 tsp chopped cilantro

Directions:
1. Preheat air fryer to 350°F/175°C. Place the pork, onion, bell peppers, and taco seasoning in the greased frying basket. Air Fry for 20 minutes, stirring twice; remove.
2. Sprinkle half the shredded Monterey jack cheese over one of the tortilla wraps, cover with the pork mixture, and scatter with the remaining cheese and cilantro. Top with the second tortilla wrap. Place in the frying basket. Bake for 12 minutes, flipping once halfway through cooking until the tortillas are browned and crisp. Let cool for a few minutes before slicing. Serve and enjoy!

Broccoli & Mushroom Beef

Servings: 4
Cooking Time: 30 Minutes
Ingredients:
- 1 lb sirloin strip steak, cubed
- 1 cup sliced cremini mushrooms
- 2 tbsp potato starch
- ½ cup beef broth
- 1 tsp soy sauce
- 2 ½ cups broccoli florets
- 1 onion, chopped
- 1 tbsp grated fresh ginger
- 1 cup cooked quinoa

Directions:
1. Add potato starch, broth, and soy sauce to a bowl and mix, then add in the beef and coat thoroughly. Marinate for 5 minutes. Preheat air fryer to 400°F/205°C. Set aside the broth and move the beef to a bowl. Add broccoli, onion, mushrooms, and ginger and transfer the bowl to the air fryer. Bake for 12-15 minutes until the beef is golden brown and the veggies soft. Pour the reserved broth over the beef and cook for 2-3 more minutes until the sauce is bubbling. Serve warm over cooked quinoa.

Tarragon Pork Tenderloin

Servings: 4
Cooking Time: 25 Minutes
Ingredients:
- ½ tsp dried tarragon
- 1 lb pork tenderloin, sliced
- Salt and pepper to taste
- 2 tbsp Dijon mustard
- 1 clove garlic, minced
- 1 cup bread crumbs
- 2 tbsp olive oil

Directions:
1. Preheat air fryer to 390°F/200°C. Using a rolling pin, pound the pork slices until they are about ¾ inch thick. Season both sides with salt and pepper. Coat the pork with mustard and season with garlic and tarragon. In a shallow bowl, mix bread crumbs and olive oil. Dredge the pork with the bread crumbs, pressing firmly, so that it adheres. Put the pork in the frying basket and Air Fry until the pork outside is brown and crisp, 12-14 minutes. Serve warm.

Crispy Pork Medallions With Radicchio And Endive Salad

Servings: 4
Cooking Time: 7 Minutes
Ingredients:
- 1 (8-ounce) pork tenderloin
- salt and freshly ground black pepper
- ¼ cup flour
- 2 eggs, lightly beaten
- ¾ cup cracker meal
- 1 teaspoon paprika
- 1 teaspoon dry mustard
- 1 teaspoon garlic powder
- 1 teaspoon dried thyme
- 1 teaspoon salt
- vegetable or canola oil, in spray bottle
- Vinaigrette
- ¼ cup white balsamic vinegar
- 2 tablespoons agave syrup (or honey or maple syrup)
- 1 tablespoon Dijon mustard
- juice of ½ lemon
- 2 tablespoons chopped chervil or flat-leaf parsley
- salt and freshly ground black pepper
- ½ cup extra-virgin olive oil
- Radicchio and Endive Salad
- 1 heart romaine lettuce, torn into large pieces
- ½ head radicchio, coarsely chopped
- 2 heads endive, sliced
- ½ cup cherry tomatoes, halved
- 3 ounces fresh mozzarella, diced
- salt and freshly ground black pepper

Directions:
1. Slice the pork tenderloin into 1-inch slices. Using a meat pounder, pound the pork slices into thin ½-inch medallions. Generously season the pork with salt and freshly ground black pepper on both sides.
2. Set up a dredging station using three shallow dishes. Place the flour in one dish and the beaten eggs in a second dish. Combine the cracker meal, paprika, dry mustard, garlic powder, thyme and salt in a third dish.
3. Preheat the air fryer to 400°F/205°C.

4. Dredge the pork medallions in flour first and then into the beaten egg. Let the excess egg drip off and coat both sides of the medallions with the cracker meal crumb mixture. Spray both sides of the coated medallions with vegetable or canola oil.
5. Air-fry the medallions in two batches at 400°F/205°C for 5 minutes. Once you have air-fried all the medallions, flip them all over and return the first batch of medallions back into the air fryer on top of the second batch. Air-fry at 400°F/205°C for an additional 2 minutes.
6. While the medallions are cooking, make the salad and dressing. Whisk the white balsamic vinegar, agave syrup, Dijon mustard, lemon juice, chervil, salt and pepper together in a small bowl. Whisk in the olive oil slowly until combined and thickened.
7. Combine the romaine lettuce, radicchio, endive, cherry tomatoes, and mozzarella cheese in a large salad bowl. Drizzle the dressing over the vegetables and toss to combine. Season with salt and freshly ground black pepper.
8. Serve the pork medallions warm on or beside the salad.

Lamb Chops In Currant Sauce

Servings: 4
Cooking Time: 30 Minutes
Ingredients:
- ½ cup chicken broth
- 2 tbsp red currant jelly
- 2 tbsp Dijon mustard
- 1 tbsp lemon juice
- ½ tsp dried thyme
- ½ tsp dried mint
- 8 lamb chops
- Salt and pepper to taste

Directions:
1. Preheat the air fryer to 375°F/190°C. Combine the broth, jelly, mustard, lemon juice, mint, and thyme and mix with a whisk until smooth. Sprinkle the chops with salt and pepper and brush with some of the broth mixture.
2. Set 4 chops in the frying basket in a single layer, then add a raised rack and lay the rest of the chops on top. Bake for 15-20 minutes. Then, lay them in a cake pan and add the chicken broth mix. Put in the fryer and Bake for 3-5 more minutes or until the sauce is bubbling and the chops are tender.

Pesto-rubbed Veal Chops

Servings: 2
Cooking Time: 12-15 Minutes
Ingredients:
- ¼ cup Purchased pesto
- 2 10-ounce bone-in veal loin or rib chop(s)
- ½ teaspoon Ground black pepper

Directions:
1. Preheat the air fryer to 400°F/205°C.
2. Rub the pesto onto both sides of the veal chop(s). Sprinkle one side of the chop(s) with the ground black pepper. Set aside at room temperature as the machine comes up to temperature.
3. Set the chop(s) in the basket. If you're cooking more than one chop, leave as much air space between them as possible. Air-fry undisturbed for 12 minutes for medium-rare, or until an instant-read meat thermometer inserted into the center of a chop (without touching bone) registers 135°F/55°C (not USDA-approved). Or air-fry undisturbed for 15 minutes for medium-well, or until an instant-read meat thermometer registers 145°F/60°C (USDA-approved).
4. Use kitchen tongs to transfer the chops to a cutting board or a wire rack. Cool for 5 minutes before serving.

Bacon, Blue Cheese And Pear Stuffed Pork Chops

Servings: 3
Cooking Time: 24 Minutes
Ingredients:
- 4 slices bacon, chopped
- 1 tablespoon butter
- ½ cup finely diced onion
- ⅓ cup chicken stock
- 1½ cups seasoned stuffing cubes
- 1 egg, beaten
- ½ teaspoon dried thyme
- ½ teaspoon salt
- ⅛ teaspoon black pepper
- 1 pear, finely diced
- ⅓ cup crumbled blue cheese
- 3 boneless center-cut pork chops (2-inch thick)
- olive oil
- salt and freshly ground black pepper

Directions:
1. Preheat the air fryer to 400°F/205°C.
2. Place the bacon into the air fryer basket and air-fry for 6 minutes, stirring halfway through the cooking time. Remove the bacon and set it aside on a paper towel. Pour out the grease from the bottom of the air fryer.
3. To make the stuffing, melt the butter in a medium saucepan over medium heat on the stovetop. Add the onion and sauté for a few minutes, until it starts to soften. Add the chicken stock and simmer for 1 minute. Remove the pan from the heat and add the stuffing cubes. Stir until the stock has been absorbed. Add the egg, dried thyme, salt and freshly ground black pepper, and stir until combined. Fold in the diced pear and crumbled blue cheese.
4. Place the pork chops on a cutting board. Using the palm of your hand to hold the chop flat and steady, slice into the side of the pork chop to make a pocket in the center of the chop. Leave about an inch of chop uncut and make sure you don't cut all the way through the pork chop. Brush both sides of the pork chops with olive oil and season with salt and freshly ground black pepper. Stuff each pork chop with a third of the stuffing, packing the stuffing tightly inside the pocket.
5. Preheat the air fryer to 360°F/180°C.
6. Spray or brush the sides of the air fryer basket with oil. Place the pork chops in the air fryer basket with the open stuffed edge of the pork chop facing the outside edges of the basket.
7. Air-fry the pork chops for 18 minutes, turning the pork chops over halfway through the cooking time. When the chops are done, let them rest for 5 minutes and then transfer to a serving platter.

Smokehouse-style Beef Ribs

Servings: 3
Cooking Time: 25 Minutes
Ingredients:
- ¼ teaspoon Mild smoked paprika
- ¼ teaspoon Garlic powder
- ¼ teaspoon Onion powder

- ¼ teaspoon Table salt
- ¼ teaspoon Ground black pepper
- 3 10- to 12-ounce beef back ribs (not beef short ribs)

Directions:
1. Preheat the air fryer to 350°F/175°C.
2. Mix the smoked paprika, garlic powder, onion powder, salt, and pepper in a small bowl until uniform. Massage and pat this mixture onto the ribs.
3. When the machine is at temperature, set the ribs in the basket in one layer, turning them on their sides if necessary, sort of like they're spooning but with at least ¼ inch air space between them. Air-fry for 25 minutes, turning once, until deep brown and sizzling.
4. Use kitchen tongs to transfer the ribs to a wire rack. Cool for 5 minutes before serving.

Berbere Beef Steaks

Servings: 4
Cooking Time: 45 Minutes
Ingredients:
- 1 chipotle pepper in adobo sauce, minced
- 1 lb skirt steak
- 2 tbsp chipotle sauce
- ¼ tsp Berbere seasoning
- Salt and pepper to taste

Directions:
1. Cut the steak into 4 equal pieces, then place them on a plate. Mix together chipotle pepper, adobo sauce, salt, pepper, and Berbere seasoning in a bowl. Spread the mixture on both sides of the steak. Chill for 2 hours.
2. Preheat air fryer to 390°F/200°C. Place the steaks in the frying basket and Bake for 5 minutes on each side for well-done meat. Allow the steaks to rest for 5 more minutes. To serve, slice against the grain.

Authentic Sausage Kartoffel Salad

Servings: 4
Cooking Time: 50 Minutes
Ingredients:
- ½ lb cooked Polish sausage, sliced
- 2 cooked potatoes, cubed
- 1 cup chicken broth
- 2 tbsp olive oil
- 1 onion, chopped
- 2 garlic cloves, minced
- ¼ cup apple cider vinegar
- 3 tbsp light brown sugar
- 2 tbsp cornstarch
- ¼ cup sour cream
- 1 tsp yellow mustard
- 2 tbsp chopped chives

Directions:
1. Preheat the air fryer to 370°F/185°C. Combine the olive oil, onion, garlic, and sausage in a baking pan and put it in the air basket. Bake for 4-7 minutes or until the onions are crispy but tender and the sausages are hot. Add the stock, vinegar, brown sugar, and cornstarch to the mixture in the pan and stir. Bake for 5 more minutes until hot. Stir the sour cream and yellow mustard into the sauce, add the potatoes, and stir to coat. Cook for another 2-3 minutes or until hot. Serve topped with freshly chopped chives.

Tandoori Lamb Samosas

Servings: 2
Cooking Time: 20 Minutes
Ingredients:
- 6 oz ground lamb, sautéed
- ¼ cup spinach, torn
- ½ onion, minced
- 1 tsp tandoori masala
- ½ tsp ginger-garlic paste
- ½ tsp red chili powder
- ½ tsp turmeric powder
- Salt and pepper to taste
- 3 puff dough sheets

Directions:
1. Preheat air fryer to 350°F/175°C. Put the ground lamb, tandoori masala, ginger garlic paste, red chili powder, turmeric powder, salt, and pepper in a bowl and stir to combine. Add in the spinach and onion and stir until the ingredients are evenly blended. Divide the mixture into three equal segments.
2. Lay the pastry dough sheets out on a lightly floured surface. Fill each sheet of dough with one of the three portions of lamb mix, then fold the pastry over into a triangle, sealing the edges with a bit of water. Transfer the samosas to the greased frying basket and Air Fry for 12 minutes, flipping once until the samosas are crispy and flaky. Remove and leave to cool for 5 minutes. Serve.

Chinese-style Lamb Chops

Servings: 4
Cooking Time: 25 Minutes
Ingredients:
- 8 lamb chops, trimmed
- 2 tbsp scallions, sliced
- ¼ tsp Chinese five-spice
- 3 garlic cloves, crushed
- ½ tsp ginger powder
- ¼ cup dark soy sauce
- 2 tsp orange juice
- 3 tbsp honey
- ½ tbsp light brown sugar
- ¼ tsp red pepper flakes

Directions:
1. Season the chops with garlic, ginger, soy sauce, five-spice powder, orange juice, and honey in a bowl. Toss to coat. Cover the bowl with plastic wrap and marinate for 2 hours and up to overnight.
2. Preheat air fryer to 400°F/205°C. Remove the chops from the bowl but reserve the marinade. Place the chops in the greased frying basket and Bake for 5 minutes. Using tongs, flip the chops. Brush the lamb with the reserved marinade, then sprinkle with brown sugar and pepper flakes. Cook for another 4 minutes until brown and caramelized medium-rare. Serve with scallions on top.

French-style Pork Medallions

Servings: 4
Cooking Time: 25 Minutes
Ingredients:
- 1 lb pork medallions
- Salt and pepper to taste
- ½ tsp dried marjoram
- 2 tbsp butter

- 1 tbsp olive oil
- 1 tsp garlic powder
- 1 shallot, diced
- 1 cup chicken stock
- 2 tbsp Dijon mustard
- 2 tbsp grainy mustard
- 1/3 cup heavy cream

Directions:
1. Preheat the air fryer to 350°F/175°C. Pound the pork medallions with a rolling pin to about ¼ inch thickness. Rub them with salt, pepper, garlic, and marjoram. Place into the greased frying basket and Bake for 7 minutes or until almost done. Remove and wipe the basket clean. Combine the butter, olive oil, shallot, and stock in a baking pan, and set it in the frying basket. Bake for 5 minutes or until the shallot is crispy and tender. Add the mustard and heavy cream and cook for 4 more minutes or until the mix starts to thicken. Then add the pork to the sauce and cook for 5 more minutes, or until the sauce simmers. Remove and serve warm.

Pizza Tortilla Rolls

Servings: 4
Cooking Time: 8 Minutes
Ingredients:
- 1 teaspoon butter
- ½ medium onion, slivered
- ½ red or green bell pepper, julienned
- 4 ounces fresh white mushrooms, chopped
- 8 flour tortillas (6- or 7-inch size)
- ½ cup pizza sauce
- 8 thin slices deli ham
- 24 pepperoni slices (about 1½ ounces)
- 1 cup shredded mozzarella cheese (about 4 ounces)
- oil for misting or cooking spray

Directions:
1. Place butter, onions, bell pepper, and mushrooms in air fryer baking pan. Cook at 390°F/200°C for 3minutes. Stir and cook 4 minutes longer until just crisp and tender. Remove pan and set aside.
2. To assemble rolls, spread about 2 teaspoons of pizza sauce on one half of each tortilla. Top with a slice of ham and 3 slices of pepperoni. Divide sautéed vegetables among tortillas and top with cheese.
3. Roll up tortillas, secure with toothpicks if needed, and spray with oil.
4. Place 4 rolls in air fryer basket and cook for 4minutes. Turn and cook 4 minutes, until heated through and lightly browned.
5. Repeat step 4 to cook remaining pizza rolls.

Garlic-buttered Rib Eye Steak

Servings: 2
Cooking Time: 25 Minutes
Ingredients:
- 1 lb rib eye steak
- Salt and pepper to taste
- 1 tbsp butter
- 1 tsp paprika
- 1 tbsp chopped rosemary
- 2 garlic cloves, minced
- 2 tbsp chopped parsley
- 1 tbsp chopped mint

Directions:
1. Preheat air fryer to 400°F/205°C. Sprinkle salt and pepper on both sides of the rib eye. Transfer the rib eye to the greased frying basket, then top with butter, mint, paprika, rosemary, and garlic. Bake for 6 minutes, then flip the steak. Bake for another 6 minutes. For medium-rare, the steak needs to reach an internal temperature of 140°F/60°C. Allow resting for 5 minutes before slicing. Serve sprinkled with parsley and enjoy!

Vietnamese Beef Lettuce Wraps

Servings: 4
Cooking Time: 12 Minutes
Ingredients:
- ⅓ cup low-sodium soy sauce*
- 2 teaspoons fish sauce*
- 2 teaspoons brown sugar
- 1 tablespoon chili paste
- juice of 1 lime
- 2 cloves garlic, minced
- 2 teaspoons fresh ginger, minced
- 1 pound beef sirloin
- Sauce
- ⅓ cup low-sodium soy sauce*
- juice of 2 limes
- 1 tablespoon mirin wine
- 2 teaspoons chili paste
- Serving
- 1 head butter lettuce
- ½ cup julienned carrots
- ½ cup julienned cucumber
- ½ cup sliced radishes, sliced into half moons
- 2 cups cooked rice noodles
- ⅓ cup chopped peanuts

Directions:
1. Combine the soy sauce, fish sauce, brown sugar, chili paste, lime juice, garlic and ginger in a bowl. Slice the beef into thin slices, then cut those slices in half. Add the beef to the marinade and marinate for 1 to 3 hours in the refrigerator. When you are ready to cook, remove the steak from the refrigerator and let it sit at room temperature for 30 minutes.
2. Preheat the air fryer to 400°F/205°C.
3. Transfer the beef and marinade to the air fryer basket. Air-fry at 400°F/205°C for 12 minutes, shaking the basket a few times during the cooking process.
4. While the beef is cooking, prepare a wrap-building station. Combine the soy sauce, lime juice, mirin wine and chili paste in a bowl and transfer to a little pouring vessel. Separate the lettuce leaves from the head of lettuce and put them in a serving bowl. Place the carrots, cucumber, radish, rice noodles and chopped peanuts all in separate serving bowls.
5. When the beef has finished cooking, transfer it to another serving bowl and invite your guests to build their wraps. To build the wraps, place some beef in a lettuce leaf and top with carrots, cucumbers, some rice noodles and chopped peanuts. Drizzle a little sauce over top, fold the lettuce around the ingredients and enjoy!

Tamari-seasoned Pork Strips

Servings: 4
Cooking Time: 40 Minutes
Ingredients:
- 3 tbsp olive oil
- 2 tbsp tamari
- 2 tsp red chili paste
- 2 tsp yellow mustard
- 2 tsp granulated sugar
- 1 lb pork shoulder strips
- 1 cup white rice, cooked
- 6 scallions, chopped
- ½ tsp garlic powder
- 1 tbsp lemon juice
- 1 tsp lemon zest
- ½ tsp salt

Directions:
1. Add 2 tbsp of olive oil, tamari, chili paste, mustard, and sugar to a bowl and whisk until everything is well mixed. Set aside half of the marinade. Toss pork strips in the remaining marinade and put in the fridge for 30 minutes.
2. Preheat air fryer to 350ºF/175°C. Place the pork strips in the frying basket and Air Fry for 16-18 minutes, tossing once. Transfer cooked pork to the bowl along with the remaining marinade and toss to coat. Set aside. In a medium bowl, stir in the cooked rice, garlic, lemon juice, lemon zest, and salt and cover. Spread on a serving plate. Arrange the pork strips over and top with scallions. Serve.

Wasabi Pork Medallions

Servings: 4
Cooking Time: 20 Minutes + Marinate Time
Ingredients:
- 1 lb pork medallions
- 1 cup soy sauce
- 1 tbsp mirin
- ½ cup olive oil
- 3 cloves garlic, crushed
- 1 tsp fresh grated ginger
- 1 tsp wasabi paste
- 1 tbsp brown sugar

Directions:
1. Place all ingredients, except for the pork, in a resealable bag and shake to combine. Add the pork medallions to the bag, shake again, and place in the fridge to marinate for 2 hours. Preheat air fryer to 360°F/180°C. Remove pork medallions from the marinade and place them in the frying basket in rows. Air Fry for 14-16 minutes or until the medallions are cooked through and juicy. Serve.

Grilled Pork & Bell Pepper Salad

Servings: 4
Cooking Time: 25 Minutes
Ingredients:
- 1 cup sautéed button mushrooms, sliced
- 2 lb pork tenderloin, sliced
- 1 tsp olive oil
- 1 tsp dried marjoram
- 6 tomato wedges
- 6 green olives
- 6 cups mixed salad greens
- 1 red bell pepper, sliced
- 1/3 cup vinaigrette dressing

Directions:
1. Preheat air fryer to 400°F/205°C. Combine the pork and olive oil, making sure the pork is well-coated. Season with marjoram. Lay the pork in the air fryer. Grill for 4-6 minutes, turning once until the pork is cooked through.
2. While the pork is cooking, toss the salad greens, red bell pepper, tomatoes, olives, and mushrooms into a bowl. Lay the pork slices on top of the salad, season with vinaigrette, and toss. Serve while the pork is still warm.

Argentinian Steak Asado Salad

Servings: 2
Cooking Time: 35 Minutes
Ingredients:
- 1 jalapeño pepper, sliced thin
- ¼ cup shredded pepper Jack cheese
- 1 avocado, peeled and pitted
- ¼ cup diced tomatoes
- ½ diced shallot
- 2 tsp chopped cilantro
- 2 tsp lime juice
- ½ lb flank steak
- 1 garlic clove, minced
- 1 tsp ground cumin
- Salt and pepper to taste
- ¼ lime
- 3 cups mesclun mix
- ½ cup pico de gallo

Directions:
1. Mash the avocado in a small bowl. Add tomatoes, shallot, cilantro, lime juice, salt, and pepper. Set aside. Season the steak with garlic, salt, pepper, and cumin.
2. Preheat air fryer to 400°F/205°C. Put the steak into the greased frying basket. Bake 8-10 minutes, flipping once until your desired doneness. Remove and let rest. Squeeze the lime over the steak and cut into thin slices. For one serving, plate half of mesclun, 2 tbsp of cheese, and ¼ cup guacamole. Place half of the steak slices on top t, then add ¼ cup pico de gallo and jalapeño if desired.

Homemade Pork Gyoza

Servings: 4
Cooking Time: 50 Minutes
Ingredients:
- 8 wonton wrappers
- 4 oz ground pork, browned
- 1 green apple
- 1 tsp rice vinegar
- 1 tbsp vegetable oil
- ½ tbsp oyster sauce
- 1 tbsp soy sauce
- A pinch of white pepper

Directions:
1. Preheat air fryer to 350°F/175°C. Combine the oyster sauce, soy sauce, rice vinegar, and white pepper in a small bowl. Add in the pork and stir thoroughly. Peel and core the apple, and slice into small cubes. Add the apples to the meat mixture, and combine thoroughly. Divide the filling between the wonton wrappers. Wrap the wontons into triangles and seal with a bit of water. Brush the wrappers with vegetable oil. Place them in the greased frying basket. Bake for 25 minutes until crispy golden brown on the outside and juicy and delicious on the inside. Serve.

Wiener Schnitzel

Servings: 4
Cooking Time: 14 Minutes
Ingredients:
- 4 thin boneless pork loin chops
- 2 tablespoons lemon juice
- ½ cup flour
- 1 teaspoon salt
- ¼ teaspoon marjoram
- 1 cup plain breadcrumbs
- 2 eggs, beaten
- oil for misting or cooking spray

Directions:
1. Rub the lemon juice into all sides of pork chops.
2. Mix together the flour, salt, and marjoram.
3. Place flour mixture on a sheet of wax paper.
4. Place breadcrumbs on another sheet of wax paper.
5. Roll pork chops in flour, dip in beaten eggs, then roll in breadcrumbs. Mist all sides with oil or cooking spray.
6. Spray air fryer basket with nonstick cooking spray and place pork chops in basket.
7. Cook at 390°F/200°C for 7minutes. Turn, mist again, and cook for another 7 minutes, until well done. Serve with lemon wedges.

Pork Chops With Cereal Crust

Servings: 2
Cooking Time: 20 Minutes
Ingredients:
- ¼ cup grated Parmesan
- 1 egg
- 1 tbsp Dijon mustard
- ¼ cup crushed bran cereal
- ¼ tsp black pepper
- ¼ tsp cumin powder
- ¼ tsp nutmeg
- 1 tsp horseradish powder
- 2 pork chops

Directions:
1. Preheat air fryer at 350ºF/175°C. Whisk egg and mustard in a bowl. In another bowl, combine Parmesan cheese, cumin powder, nutmeg, horseradish powder, bran cereal, and black pepper. Dip pork chops in the egg mixture, then dredge them in the cheese mixture. Place pork chops in the frying basket and Air Fry for 12 minutes, tossing once. Let rest onto a cutting board for 5 minutes. Serve.

Orange Glazed Pork Tenderloin

Servings: 3
Cooking Time: 23 Minutes
Ingredients:
- 2 tablespoons brown sugar
- 2 teaspoons cornstarch
- 2 teaspoons Dijon mustard
- ½ cup orange juice
- ½ teaspoon soy sauce*
- 2 teaspoons grated fresh ginger
- ¼ cup white wine
- zest of 1 orange
- 1 pound pork tenderloin
- salt and freshly ground black pepper
- oranges, halved (for garnish)
- fresh parsley or other green herb (for garnish)

Directions:
1. Combine the brown sugar, cornstarch, Dijon mustard, orange juice, soy sauce, ginger, white wine and orange zest in a small saucepan and bring the mixture to a boil on the stovetop. Lower the heat and simmer while you cook the pork tenderloin or until the sauce has thickened.
2. Preheat the air fryer to 370°F/185°C.
3. Season all sides of the pork tenderloin with salt and freshly ground black pepper. Transfer the tenderloin to the air fryer basket, bending the pork into a wide "U" shape if necessary to fit in the basket. Air-fry at 370°F/185°C for 20 to 23 minutes, or until the internal temperature reaches 145°F. Flip the tenderloin over halfway through the cooking process and baste with the sauce.
4. Transfer the tenderloin to a cutting board and let it rest for 5 minutes. Slice the pork at a slight angle and serve immediately with orange halves and fresh herbs to dress it up. Drizzle any remaining glaze over the top.

Sausage-cheese Calzone

Servings: 8
Cooking Time: 8 Minutes
Ingredients:
- Crust
- 2 cups white wheat flour, plus more for kneading and rolling
- 1 package (¼ ounce) RapidRise yeast
- 1 teaspoon salt
- ½ teaspoon dried basil
- 1 cup warm water (115°F to 125°F)
- 2 teaspoons olive oil
- Filling
- ¼ pound Italian sausage
- ½ cup ricotta cheese
- 4 ounces mozzarella cheese, shredded
- ¼ cup grated Parmesan cheese
- oil for misting or cooking spray
- marinara sauce for serving

Directions:
1. Crumble Italian sausage into air fryer baking pan and cook at 390°F/200°C for 5minutes. Stir, breaking apart, and cook for 3 to 4minutes, until well done. Remove and set aside on paper towels to drain.
2. To make dough, combine flour, yeast, salt, and basil. Add warm water and oil and stir until a soft dough forms. Turn out onto lightly floured board and knead for 3 or 4minutes. Let dough rest for 10minutes.
3. To make filling, combine the three cheeses in a medium bowl and mix well. Stir in the cooked sausage.
4. Cut dough into 8 pieces.
5. Working with 4 pieces of the dough, press each into a circle about 5 inches in diameter. Top each dough circle with 2 heaping tablespoons of filling. Fold over to create a half-moon shape and press edges firmly together. Be sure that edges are firmly sealed to prevent leakage. Spray both sides with oil or cooking spray.
6. Place 4 calzones in air fryer basket and cook at 360°F/180°C for 5minutes. Mist with oil and cook for 3 minutes, until crust is done and nicely browned.
7. While the first batch is cooking, press out the remaining dough, fill, and shape into calzones.
8. Spray both sides with oil and cook for 5minutes. If needed, mist with oil and continue cooking for 3 minutes longer. This second batch will cook a little faster than the first because your air fryer is already hot.
9. Serve with marinara sauce on the side for dipping.

Italian Sausage Rolls

Servings: 4
Cooking Time: 20 Minutes
Ingredients:
- 1 red bell pepper, cut into strips
- 4 Italian sausages
- 1 zucchini, cut into strips
- ½ onion, cut into strips
- 1 tsp dried oregano
- ½ tsp garlic powder
- 5 Italian rolls

Directions:
1. Preheat air fryer to 360°F/180°C. Place all sausages in the air fryer. Bake for 10 minutes. While the sausages are cooking, season the bell pepper, zucchini and onion with oregano and garlic powder. When the time is up, flip the sausages, then add the peppers and onions. Cook for another 5 minutes or until the vegetables are soft and the sausages are cooked through. Put the sausage on Italian rolls, then top with peppers and onions. Serve.

Peachy Pork Chops

Servings: 2
Cooking Time: 20 Minutes
Ingredients:
- 2 tbsp peach preserves
- 2 tbsp tomato paste
- 1 tbsp Dijon mustard
- 1 tsp BBQ sauce
- 1 tbsp lime juice
- 1 tbsp olive oil
- 2 cloves garlic, minced
- 2 pork chops

Directions:
1. Whisk all ingredients in a bowl until well mixed and let chill covered in the fridge for 30 minutes. Preheat air fryer to 350ºF/175°C. Place pork chops in the frying basket and Air Fry for 12 minutes or until cooked through and tender. Transfer the chops to a cutting board and let sit for 5 minutes before serving.

Bbq Back Ribs

Servings: 4
Cooking Time: 40 Minutes
Ingredients:
- 2 tbsp light brown sugar
- Salt and pepper to taste
- 2 tsp onion powder
- 1 tsp garlic powder
- 1 tsp mustard powder
- 1 tsp dried marjoram
- ½ tsp smoked paprika
- 1 tsp cayenne pepper
- 1 ½ pounds baby back ribs
- 2 tbsp barbecue sauce

Directions:
1. Preheat the air fryer to 375°F/190°C. Combine the brown sugar, salt, pepper, onion and garlic powder, mustard, paprika, cayenne, and marjoram in a bowl and mix. Pour into a small glass jar. Brush the ribs with barbecue sauce and sprinkle 1 tbsp of the seasoning mix. Rub the seasoning all over the meat. Set the ribs in the greased frying basket. Bake for 25 minutes until nicely browned, flipping them once halfway through cooking. Serve hot!

Lazy Mexican Meat Pizza

Servings: 4
Cooking Time: 35 Minutes
Ingredients:
- 1 ¼ cups canned refried beans
- 2 cups shredded cheddar
- ½ cup chopped cilantro
- 2/3 cup salsa
- 1 red bell pepper, chopped
- 1 sliced jalapeño
- 1 pizza crust
- 16 meatballs, halved

Directions:
1. Preheat the air fryer to 375°F/190°C. Combine the refried beans, salsa, jalapeño, and bell pepper in a bowl and spread on the pizza crust. Top with meatball halves and sprinkle with cheddar cheese. Put the pizza in the greased frying basket and Bake for 7-10 minutes until hot and the cheese is brown. Sprinkle with the fresh cilantro and serve.

Zesty London Broil

Servings: 4
Cooking Time: 28 Minutes
Ingredients:
- ⅔ cup ketchup
- ¼ cup honey
- ¼ cup olive oil
- 2 tablespoons apple cider vinegar
- 2 tablespoons Worcestershire sauce
- 2 tablespoons minced onion
- ½ teaspoon paprika
- 1 teaspoon salt
- 1 teaspoon freshly ground black pepper
- 2 pounds London broil, top round or flank steak (about 1-inch thick)

Directions:
1. Combine the ketchup, honey, olive oil, apple cider vinegar, Worcestershire sauce, minced onion, paprika, salt and pepper in a small bowl and whisk together.
2. Generously pierce both sides of the meat with a fork or meat tenderizer and place it in a shallow dish. Pour the marinade mixture over the steak, making sure all sides of the meat get coated with the marinade. Cover and refrigerate overnight.
3. Preheat the air fryer to 400°F/205°C.
4. Transfer the London broil to the air fryer basket and air-fry for 28 minutes, depending on how rare or well done you like your steak. Flip the steak over halfway through the cooking time.
5. Remove the London broil from the air fryer and let it rest for five minutes on a cutting board. To serve, thinly slice the meat against the grain and transfer to a serving platter.

Glazed Meatloaf

Servings: 4
Cooking Time: 35-55 Minutes
Ingredients:
- ½ cup Seasoned Italian-style panko bread crumbs (gluten-free, if a concern)
- ¼ cup Whole or low-fat milk

- 1 pound Lean ground beef
- 1 pound Bulk mild Italian sausage meat (gluten-free, if a concern)
- 1 Large egg(s), well beaten
- 1 teaspoon Dried thyme
- 1 teaspoon Onion powder
- 1 teaspoon Garlic powder
- Vegetable oil spray
- 1 tablespoon Ketchup (gluten-free, if a concern)
- 1 tablespoon Hoisin sauce (see here; gluten-free, if a concern)
- 2 teaspoons Pickle brine, preferably from a jar of jalapeño rings (gluten-free, if a concern)

Directions:
1. Pour the bread crumbs into a large bowl, add the milk, stir gently, and soak for 10 minutes.
2. Preheat the air fryer to 350°F/175°C.
3. Add the ground beef, Italian sausage meat, egg(s), thyme, onion powder, and garlic powder to the bowl with the bread crumbs. Blend gently until well combined. (Clean, dry hands work best!) Form this mixture into an oval loaf about 2 inches tall (its length will vary depending on the amount of ingredients) but with a flat bottom. Generously coat the top, bottom, and all sides of the loaf with vegetable oil spray.
4. Use a large, nonstick-safe spatula or perhaps silicone baking mitts to transfer the loaf to the basket. Air-fry undisturbed for 30 minutes for a small meatloaf, 40 minutes for a medium one, or 50 minutes for a large, until an instant-read meat thermometer inserted into the center of the loaf registers 165°F.
5. Whisk the ketchup, hoisin, and pickle brine in a small bowl until smooth. Brush this over the top and sides of the meatloaf and continue air-frying undisturbed for 5 minutes, or until the glaze has browned a bit. Use that same spatula or those same baking mitts to transfer the meatloaf to a cutting board. Cool for 10 minutes before slicing.

Carne Asada
Servings: 4
Cooking Time: 15 Minutes
Ingredients:
- 4 cloves garlic, minced
- 3 chipotle peppers in adobo, chopped
- ⅓ cup chopped fresh parsley
- ⅓ cup chopped fresh oregano
- 1 teaspoon ground cumin seed
- juice of 2 limes
- ⅓ cup olive oil
- 1 to 1½ pounds flank steak (depending on your appetites)
- salt
- tortillas and guacamole (optional – for serving)

Directions:
1. Make the marinade: Combine the garlic, chipotle, parsley, oregano, cumin, lime juice and olive oil in a non-reactive bowl. Coat the flank steak with the marinade and let it marinate for 30 minutes to 8 hours. (Don't leave the steak out of refrigeration for longer than 2 hours, however.)
2. Preheat the air fryer to 390°F/200°C.
3. Remove the steak from the marinade and place it in the air fryer basket. Season the steak with salt and air-fry for 15 minutes, turning the steak over halfway through the cooking time and seasoning again with salt. This should cook the steak to medium. Add or subtract two minutes for medium-well or medium-rare.
4. Remember to let the steak rest before slicing the meat against the grain. Serve with warm tortillas, guacamole and a fresh salsa like the Tomato-Corn Salsa below.

Jerk Meatballs
Servings: 6
Cooking Time: 30 Minutes
Ingredients:
- 1 tsp minced habanero
- 1 tsp Jamaican jerk seasoning
- 1 sandwich bread slice, torn
- 2 tbsp whole milk
- 1 lb ground beef
- 1 egg
- 2 tbsp diced onion
- 1 tsp smoked paprika
- 1 tsp black pepper
- 1 tbsp chopped parsley
- ½ lime

Directions:
1. Preheat air fryer at 350ºF/175°C. In a bowl, combine bread pieces with milk. Add in ground beef, egg, onion, smoked paprika, black pepper, habanero, and jerk seasoning, and using your hands, squeeze ingredients together until fully combined. Form mixture into meatballs. Place meatballs in the greased frying basket and Air Fry for 8 minutes, flipping once. Squeeze lime and sprinkle the parsley over.

Lamb Koftas Meatballs
Servings: 3
Cooking Time: 8 Minutes
Ingredients:
- 1 pound ground lamb
- 1 teaspoon ground cumin
- 1 teaspoon ground coriander
- 2 tablespoons chopped fresh mint
- 1 egg, beaten
- ½ teaspoon salt
- freshly ground black pepper

Directions:
1. Combine all ingredients in a bowl and mix together well. Divide the mixture into 10 portions. Roll each portion into a ball and then by cupping the meatball in your hand, shape it into an oval.
2. Preheat the air fryer to 400°F/205°C.
3. Air-fry the koftas for 8 minutes.
4. Serve warm with the cucumber-yogurt dip.

Barbecue Country-style Pork Ribs
Servings: 3
Cooking Time: 30 Minutes
Ingredients:
- 3 8-ounce boneless country-style pork ribs
- 1½ teaspoons Mild smoked paprika
- 1½ teaspoons Light brown sugar
- ¾ teaspoon Onion powder
- ¾ teaspoon Ground black pepper
- ¼ teaspoon Table salt
- Vegetable oil spray

Directions:

1. Preheat the air fryer to 350°F/175°C. Set the ribs in a bowl on the counter as the machine heats.
2. Mix the smoked paprika, brown sugar, onion powder, pepper, and salt in a small bowl until well combined. Rub this mixture over all the surfaces of the country-style ribs. Generously coat the country-style ribs with vegetable oil spray.
3. Set the ribs in the basket with as much air space between them as possible. Air-fry undisturbed for 30 minutes, or until browned and sizzling and an instant-read meat thermometer inserted into one rib registers at least 145°F/60°C.
4. Use kitchen tongs to transfer the country-style ribs to a wire rack. Cool for 5 minutes before serving.

Chile Con Carne Galette

Servings: 4
Cooking Time: 30 Minutes
Ingredients:
- 1 can chili beans in chili sauce
- ½ cup canned fire-roasted diced tomatoes, drained
- ½ cup grated Mexican cheese blend
- 2 tsp olive oil
- ½ lb ground beef
- ½ cup dark beer
- ½ onion, diced
- 1 carrot, peeled and diced
- 1 celery stalk, diced
- ½ tsp ground cumin
- ½ tsp chili powder
- ¼ tsp salt
- 1 cup corn chips
- 3 tbsp beef broth
- 2 tsp corn masa

Directions:
1. Warm the olive oil in a skillet over -high heat for 30 seconds. Add in ground beef, onion, carrot, and celery and cook for 5 minutes until the beef is no longer pink. Drain the fat. Mix 3 tbsp beef broth and 2 tsp corn mass until smooth and then toss it in beans, chili sauce, dark beer, tomatoes, cumin, chili powder, and salt. Cook until thickened. Turn the heat off.
2. Preheat air fryer at 350°F/175°C. Spoon beef mixture into a cake pan, then top with corn chips, followed by cheese blend. Place cake pan in the frying basket and Bake for 6 minutes. Let rest for 10 minutes before serving.

Mongolian Beef

Servings: 4
Cooking Time: 15 Minutes
Ingredients:
- 1½ pounds flank steak, thinly sliced
- on the bias into ¼-inch strips
- Marinade
- 2 tablespoons soy sauce*
- 1 clove garlic, smashed
- big pinch crushed red pepper flakes
- Sauce
- 1 tablespoon vegetable oil
- 2 cloves garlic, minced
- 1 tablespoon finely grated fresh ginger
- 3 dried red chili peppers
- ¾ cup soy sauce*
- ¾ cup chicken stock
- 5 to 6 tablespoons brown sugar (depending on how sweet you want the sauce)
- ½ cup cornstarch, divided
- 1 bunch scallions, sliced into 2-inch pieces

Directions:
1. Marinate the beef in the soy sauce, garlic and red pepper flakes for one hour.
2. In the meantime, make the sauce. Preheat a small saucepan over medium heat on the stovetop. Add the oil, garlic, ginger and dried chili peppers and sauté for just a minute or two. Add the soy sauce, chicken stock and brown sugar and continue to simmer for a few minutes. Dissolve 3 tablespoons of cornstarch in 3 tablespoons of water and stir this into the saucepan. Stir the sauce over medium heat until it thickens. Set this aside.
3. Preheat the air fryer to 400°F/205°C.
4. Remove the beef from the marinade and transfer it to a zipper sealable plastic bag with the remaining cornstarch. Shake it around to completely coat the beef and transfer the coated strips of beef to a baking sheet or plate, shaking off any excess cornstarch. Spray the strips with vegetable oil on all sides and transfer them to the air fryer basket.
5. Air-fry at 400°F/205°C for 15 minutes, shaking the basket to toss and rotate the beef strips throughout the cooking process. Add the scallions for the last 4 minutes of the cooking. Transfer the hot beef strips and scallions to a bowl and toss with the sauce (warmed on the stovetop if necessary), coating all the beef strips with the sauce. Serve warm over white rice.

Tonkatsu

Servings: 3
Cooking Time: 10 Minutes
Ingredients:
- ½ cup All-purpose flour or tapioca flour
- 1 Large egg white(s), well beaten
- ¾ cup Plain panko bread crumbs (gluten-free, if a concern)
- 3 4-ounce center-cut boneless pork loin chops (about ½ inch thick)
- Vegetable oil spray

Directions:
1. Preheat the air fryer to 375°F/190°C.
2. Set up and fill three shallow soup plates or small pie plates on your counter: one for the flour, one for the beaten egg white(s), and one for the bread crumbs.
3. Set a chop in the flour and roll it to coat all sides, even the ends. Gently shake off any excess flour and set it in the egg white(s). Gently roll and turn to coat all sides. Let any excess egg white slip back into the rest, then set the chop in the bread crumbs. Turn it several times, pressing gently to get an even coating on all sides and the ends. Generously coat the breaded chop with vegetable oil spray, then set it aside so you can dredge, coat, and spray the remaining chop(s).
4. Set the chops in the basket with as much air space between them as possible. Air-fry undisturbed for 10 minutes, or until golden brown and crisp.
5. Use kitchen tongs to transfer the chops to a wire rack and cool for a couple of minutes before serving.

Lemon-garlic Strip Steak
Servings: 2
Cooking Time: 15 Minutes
Ingredients:
- 3 cloves garlic, minced
- 1 tbsp lemon juice
- 1 tbsp olive oil
- Salt and pepper to taste
- 1 tbsp chopped parsley
- ½ tsp chopped rosemary
- ½ tsp chopped sage
- 1 strip steak

Directions:
1. In a small bowl, whisk all ingredients. Brush mixture over strip steak and let marinate covered in the fridge for 30 minutes. Preheat air fryer at 400°F/205°C. Place strip steak in the greased frying basket and Bake for 8 minutes until rare, turning once. Let rest onto a cutting board for 5 minutes before serving.

Cal-mex Chimichangas
Servings: 4
Cooking Time: 30 Minutes
Ingredients:
- 1 can diced tomatoes with chiles
- 1 cup shredded cheddar
- ½ cup chopped onions
- 2 garlic cloves, minced
- 1 lb ground beef
- 2 tbsp taco seasoning
- Salt and pepper to taste
- 4 flour tortillas
- ½ cup Pico de Gallo

Directions:
1. Warm the olive oil in a skillet over medium heat and stir-fry the onion and garlic for 3 minutes or until fragrant. Add ground beef, taco seasoning, salt and pepper. Stir and break up the beef with a spoon. Cook for 3-4 minutes or until it is browned. Stir in diced tomatoes with chiles. Scoop ½ cup of beef onto each tortilla. Form chimichangas by folding the sides of the tortilla into the middle, then roll up from the bottom. Use a toothpick to secure the chimichanga.
2. Preheat air fryer to 400°F/205°C. Lightly spray the chimichangas with cooking oil. Place the first batch in the fryer and Bake for 8 minutes. Transfer to a serving dish and top with shredded cheese and pico de gallo.

Basil Cheese & Ham Stromboli
Servings: 6
Cooking Time: 30 Minutes
Ingredients:
- 1 can refrigerated pizza dough
- ½ cup shredded mozzarella
- ½ red bell pepper, sliced
- 2 tsp all-purpose flour
- 6 Havarti cheese slices
- 12 deli ham slices
- ½ tsp dried basil
- 1 tsp garlic powder
- ½ tsp oregano
- Black pepper to taste

Directions:
1. Preheat air fryer to 400°F/205°C. Flour a flat work surface and roll out the pizza dough. Use a knife to cut into 6 equal-sized rectangles. On each rectangle, add 1 slice of Havarti, 1 tbsp of mozzarella, 2 slices of ham, and some red pepper slices. Season with basil, garlic, oregano, and black pepper. Fold one side of the dough over the filling to the opposite side. Press the edges with the back of a fork to seal them. Place one batch of stromboli in the fryer and lightly spray with cooking oil. Air Fry for 10 minutes. Serve and enjoy!

Thyme Steak Finger Strips
Servings: 2
Cooking Time: 25 Minutes
Ingredients:
- ½ lb top sirloin strips
- 1 cup breadcrumbs
- ½ tsp garlic powder
- ½ tsp steak seasoning
- 2 eggs, beaten
- Salt and pepper to taste
- ½ tbsp dried thyme

Directions:
1. Preheat air fryer to 350°F/175°C. Put the breadcrumbs, garlic powder, steak seasoning, thyme, salt, and pepper in a bowl and stir to combine. Add in the sirloin steak strips and toss to coat all sides. Dip into the beaten eggs, then dip again into the dry ingredients. Lay the coated steak pieces on the greased frying basket in an even layer. Air Fry for 16-18 minutes, turning once. Serve and enjoy!

Pepperoni Bagel Pizzas
Servings: 4
Cooking Time: 20 Minutes
Ingredients:
- 2 bagels, halved horizontally
- 2 cups shredded mozzarella
- ¼ cup grated Parmesan
- 1 cup passata
- 1/3 cup sliced pepperoni
- 2 scallions, chopped
- 2 tbsp minced fresh chives
- 1 tsp red chili flakes

Directions:
1. Preheat the air fryer to 375°F/190°C. Put the bagel halves, cut side up, in the frying basket. Bake for 2-3 minutes until golden. Remove and top them with passata, pepperoni, scallions, and cheeses. Put the bagels topping-side up to the frying basket and cook for 8-12 more minutes or until the bagels are hot and the cheese has melted and is bubbling. Top with the chives and chili flakes and serve.

Leftover Roast Beef Risotto
Servings: 4
Cooking Time: 30 Minutes
Ingredients:
- ½ chopped red bell pepper
- ½ chopped cooked roast beef
- 3 tbsp grated Parmesan
- 2 tsp butter, melted
- 1 shallot, finely chopped
- 3 garlic cloves, minced
- ¾ cup short-grain rice
- 1¼ cups beef broth

Directions:
1. Preheat air fryer to 390°F/200°C. Add the melted butter, shallot, garlic, and red bell pepper to a baking pan and stir to combine. Air Fry for 2 minutes, or until the vegetables are crisp-tender. Remove from the air fryer and stir in the rice, broth, and roast beef. Put the cooking pan back into the fryer and Bake for 18-22 minutes, stirring once during cooking until the rice is al dente and the beef is cooked through. Sprinkle with Parmesan and serve.

Balsamic Marinated Rib Eye Steak With Balsamic Fried Cipollini Onions

Servings: 2
Cooking Time: 22-26 Minutes
Ingredients:
- 3 tablespoons balsamic vinegar
- 2 cloves garlic, sliced
- 1 tablespoon Dijon mustard
- 1 teaspoon fresh thyme leaves
- 1 (16-ounce) boneless rib eye steak
- coarsely ground black pepper
- salt
- 1 (8-ounce) bag cipollini onions, peeled
- 1 teaspoon balsamic vinegar

Directions:
1. Combine the 3 tablespoons of balsamic vinegar, garlic, Dijon mustard and thyme in a small bowl. Pour this marinade over the steak. Pierce the steak several times with a paring knife or
2. a needle-style meat tenderizer and season it generously with coarsely ground black pepper. Flip the steak over and pierce the other side in a similar fashion, seasoning again with the coarsely ground black pepper. Marinate the steak for 2 to 24 hours in the refrigerator. When you are ready to cook, remove the steak from the refrigerator and let it sit at room temperature for 30 minutes.
3. Preheat the air fryer to 400°F/205°C.
4. Season the steak with salt and air-fry at 400°F/205°C for 12 minutes (medium-rare), 14 minutes (medium), or 16 minutes (well-done), flipping the steak once half way through the cooking time.
5. While the steak is air-frying, toss the onions with 1 teaspoon of balsamic vinegar and season with salt.
6. Remove the steak from the air fryer and let it rest while you fry the onions. Transfer the onions to the air fryer basket and air-fry for 10 minutes, adding a few more minutes if your onions are very large. Then, slice the steak on the bias and serve with the fried onions on top.

Meat Loaves

Servings: 4
Cooking Time: 19 Minutes
Ingredients:
- Sauce
- ¼ cup white vinegar
- ¼ cup brown sugar
- 2 tablespoons Worcestershire sauce
- ½ cup ketchup
- Meat Loaves
- 1 pound very lean ground beef
- ⅔ cup dry bread (approx. 1 slice torn into small pieces)
- 1 egg
- ⅓ cup minced onion
- 1 teaspoon salt
- 2 tablespoons ketchup

Directions:
1. In a small saucepan, combine all sauce ingredients and bring to a boil. Remove from heat and stir to ensure that brown sugar dissolves completely.
2. In a large bowl, combine the beef, bread, egg, onion, salt, and ketchup. Mix well.
3. Divide meat mixture into 4 portions and shape each into a thick, round patty. Patties will be about 3 to 3½ inches in diameter, and all four should fit easily into the air fryer basket at once.
4. Cook at 360°F/180°C for 18 minutes, until meat is well done. Baste tops of mini loaves with a small amount of sauce, and cook 1 minute.
5. Serve hot with additional sauce on the side.

Flank Steak With Roasted Peppers And Chimichurri

Servings: 4
Cooking Time: 22 Minutes
Ingredients:
- 2 cups flat-leaf parsley leaves
- ¼ cup fresh oregano leaves
- 3 cloves garlic
- ½ cup olive oil
- ¼ cup red wine vinegar
- ½ teaspoon salt
- freshly ground black pepper
- ¼ teaspoon crushed red pepper flakes
- ½ teaspoon ground cumin
- 1 pound flank steak
- 1 red bell pepper, cut into strips
- 1 yellow bell pepper, cut into strips

Directions:
1. Make the chimichurri sauce by chopping the parsley, oregano and garlic in a food processor. Add the olive oil, vinegar and seasonings and process again. Pour half of the sauce into a shallow dish with the flank steak and set the remaining sauce aside. Pierce the flank steak with a needle-style meat tenderizer or a paring knife and marinate the steak for 2 to 24 hours in the refrigerator. When you are ready to cook, remove the steak from the refrigerator and let it sit at room temperature for 30 minutes.
2. Preheat the air fryer to 400°F/205°C.
3. Cut the flank steak in half so that it fits more easily into the air fryer and transfer both pieces to the air fryer basket. Air-fry for 14 minutes, depending on how you like your steak cooked (10 minutes will give you medium for a 1-inch thick flank steak). Flip the steak over halfway through the cooking time.
4. When the flank steak is cooked to your liking, transfer it to a cutting board, loosely tent with foil and let it rest while you cook the peppers.
5. Toss the peppers in a little olive oil, salt and freshly ground black pepper and transfer them to the air fryer basket. Air-fry at 400°F/205°C for 8 minutes, shaking the basket once or twice throughout the cooking process. To serve, slice the flank steak against the grain of the meat and top with the roasted peppers. Drizzle the reserved chimichurri sauce on top, thinning the sauce with another tablespoon of olive oil if desired.

Paprika Fried Beef

Servings: 4
Cooking Time: 30 Minutes
Ingredients:
- Celery salt to taste
- 4 beef cube steaks
- ½ cup milk
- 1 cup flour
- 2 tsp paprika
- 1 egg
- 1 cup bread crumbs
- 2 tbsp olive oil

Directions:
1. Preheat air fryer to 350°F/175°C. Place the cube steaks in a zipper sealed bag or between two sheets of cling wrap. Gently pound the steaks until they are slightly thinner. Set aside. In a bowl, mix together milk, flour, paprika, celery salt, and egg until just combined. In a separate bowl, mix together the crumbs and olive oil. Take the steaks and dip them into the buttermilk batter, shake off some of the excess, and return to a plate for 5 minutes. Next, dip the steaks in the bread crumbs, patting the crumbs into both sides. Air Fry the steaks until the crust is crispy and brown, 12-16 minutes. Serve warm.

Lamb Meatballs With Quick Tomato Sauce

Servings: 4
Cooking Time: 8 Minutes
Ingredients:
- ½ small onion, finely diced
- 1 clove garlic, minced
- 1 pound ground lamb
- 2 tablespoons fresh parsley, finely chopped (plus more for garnish)
- 2 teaspoons fresh oregano, finely chopped
- 2 tablespoons milk
- 1 egg yolk
- salt and freshly ground black pepper
- ½ cup crumbled feta cheese, for garnish
- Tomato Sauce:
- 2 tablespoons butter
- 1 clove garlic, smashed
- pinch crushed red pepper flakes
- ¼ teaspoon ground cinnamon
- 1 (28-ounce) can crushed tomatoes
- salt, to taste

Directions:
1. Combine all ingredients for the meatballs in a large bowl and mix just until everything is combined. Shape the mixture into 1½-inch balls or shape the meat between two spoons to make quenelles (little three-sided footballs).
2. Preheat the air fryer to 400°F/205°C.
3. While the air fryer is Preheating, start the quick tomato sauce. Place the butter, garlic and red pepper flakes in a sauté pan and heat over medium heat on the stovetop. Let the garlic sizzle a little, but before the butter starts to brown, add the cinnamon and tomatoes. Bring to a simmer and simmer for 15 minutes. Season to taste with salt (but not too much as the feta that you will be sprinkling on at the end will be salty).
4. Brush the bottom of the air fryer basket with a little oil and transfer the meatballs to the air fryer basket in one layer, air-frying in batches if necessary.
5. Air-fry at 400°F/205°C for 8 minutes, giving the basket a shake once during the cooking process to turn the meatballs over.
6. To serve, spoon a pool of the tomato sauce onto plates and add the meatballs in a decorative manner. Sprinkle the feta cheese on top and garnish with more fresh parsley. Serve immediately.

Stuffed Cabbage Rolls

Servings: 4
Cooking Time: 50 Minutes
Ingredients:
- ½ cup long-grain brown rice
- 12 green cabbage leaves
- 1 lb ground beef
- 4 garlic cloves, minced
- Salt and pepper to taste
- 1 tsp ground cinnamon
- ½ tsp ground cumin
- 2 tbsp chopped mint
- 1 lemon, juiced and zested
- ½ cup beef broth
- 1 tbsp olive oil
- 2 tbsp parsley, chopped

Directions:
1. Place a large pot of salted water over medium heat and bring to a boil. Add the cabbage leaves and boil them for 3 minutes. Remove from the water and set aside. Combine the ground beef, rice, garlic, salt, pepper, cinnamon, cumin, mint, lemon juice and zest in a bowl.
2. Preheat air fryer to 360°F/180°C. Divide the beef mixture between the cabbage leaves and roll them up. Place the finished rolls into a greased baking dish. Pour the beef broth over the cabbage rolls and then brush the tops with olive oil. Put the casserole dish into the frying basket and Bake for 30 minutes. Top with parsley and enjoy!

Perfect Strip Steaks

Servings: 2
Cooking Time: 17 Minutes
Ingredients:
- 1½ tablespoons Olive oil
- 1½ tablespoons Minced garlic
- 2 teaspoons Ground black pepper
- 1 teaspoon Table salt
- 2 ¾-pound boneless beef strip steak(s)

Directions:
1. Preheat the air fryer to 375°F/190°C (or 380°F/195°C or 390°F/200°C, if one of these is the closest setting).
2. Mix the oil, garlic, pepper, and salt in a small bowl, then smear this mixture over both sides of the steak(s).
3. When the machine is at temperature, put the steak(s) in the basket with as much air space as possible between them for the larger batch. They should not overlap or even touch. That said, even just a ¼-inch between them will work. Air-fry for 12 minutes, turning once, until an instant-read meat thermometer inserted into the thickest part of a steak registers 127°F/50°C for rare (not USDA-approved). Or air-fry for 15 minutes, turning once, until an instant-read meat thermometer registers 145°F/60°C for medium (USDA-approved). If the machine is at 390°F/200°C, the steaks may cook 2 minutes more quickly than the stated timing.
4. Use kitchen tongs to transfer the steak(s) to a wire rack. Cool for 5 minutes before serving.

Friday Night Cheeseburgers

Servings: 4
Cooking Time: 20 Minutes
Ingredients:
- 1 lb ground beef
- 1 tsp Worcestershire sauce
- 1 tbsp allspice
- Salt and pepper to taste
- 4 cheddar cheese slices
- 4 buns

Directions:
1. Preheat air fryer to 360°F/180°C. Combine beef, Worcestershire sauce, allspice, salt and pepper in a large bowl. Divide into 4 equal portions and shape into patties. Place the burgers in the greased frying basket and Air Fry for 8 minutes. Flip and cook for another 3-4 minutes. Top each burger with cheddar cheese and cook for another minute so the cheese melts. Transfer to a bun and serve.

Barbecue-style Beef Cube Steak

Servings: 2
Cooking Time: 14 Minutes
Ingredients:
- 2 4-ounce beef cube steak(s)
- 2 cups (about 8 ounces) Fritos (original flavor) or a generic corn chip equivalent, crushed to crumbs (see here)
- 6 tablespoons Purchased smooth barbecue sauce, any flavor (gluten-free, if a concern)

Directions:
1. Preheat the air fryer to 375°F/190°C.
2. Spread the Fritos crumbs in a shallow soup plate or a small pie plate. Rub the barbecue sauce onto both sides of the steak(s). Dredge the steak(s) in the Fritos crumbs to coat well and thoroughly, turning several times and pressing down to get the little bits to adhere to the meat.
3. When the machine is at temperature, set the steak(s) in the basket. Leave as much air space between them as possible if you're working with more than one piece of beef. Air-fry undisturbed for 12 minutes, or until lightly brown and crunchy. If the machine is at 360°F/180°C, you may need to add 2 minutes to the cooking time.
4. Use kitchen tongs to transfer the steak(s) to a wire rack. Cool for 5 minutes before serving.

Chicken Fried Steak

Servings: 4
Cooking Time: 15 Minutes
Ingredients:
- 2 eggs
- ½ cup buttermilk
- 1½ cups flour
- ¾ teaspoon salt
- ½ teaspoon pepper
- 1 pound beef cube steaks
- salt and pepper
- oil for misting or cooking spray

Directions:
1. Beat together eggs and buttermilk in a shallow dish.
2. In another shallow dish, stir together the flour, ½ teaspoon salt, and ¼ teaspoon pepper.
3. Season cube steaks with remaining salt and pepper to taste. Dip in flour, buttermilk egg wash, and then flour again.
4. Spray both sides of steaks with oil or cooking spray.
5. Cooking in 2 batches, place steaks in air fryer basket in single layer. Cook at 360°F/180°C for 10minutes. Spray tops of steaks with oil and cook 5minutes or until meat is well done.
6. Repeat to cook remaining steaks.

Vegetable Side Dishes Recipes

Sriracha Green Beans
Servings: 4
Cooking Time: 30 Minutes
Ingredients:
- ½ tbsp toasted sesame seeds
- 1 tbsp tamari
- ½ tbsp Sriracha sauce
- 4 tsp canola oil
- 12 oz trimmed green beans
- 1 tbsp cilantro, chopped

Directions:
1. Mix the tamari, sriracha, and 1 tsp of canola oil in a small bowl. In a large bowl, toss green beans with the remaining oil. Preheat air fryer to 375°F/190°C. Place the green beans in the frying basket and Air Fry for 8 minutes, shaking the basket once until the beans are charred and tender. Toss the beans with sauce, cilantro, and sesame seeds. Serve.

Horseradish Potato Mash
Servings: 4
Cooking Time: 50 Minutes
Ingredients:
- 1 lb baby potatoes
- 1 tbsp horseradish sauce
- ½ cup vegetable broth
- ½ tsp sea salt
- 3 tbsp butter
- 2 garlic cloves, minced
- 2 tsp chili powder

Directions:
1. Preheat the air fryer to 400°F/205°C. Combine the potatoes, broth, and salt in a cake pan, then cover with foil and put it in the frying basket. Bake for 20 minutes, stirring once until they are almost tender. Drain and place them on a baking sheet. With the bottom of a glass, smash the potatoes, but don't break them apart. Put a small saucepan on the stove and mix butter, garlic, chili powder, and horseradish sauce. Melt the butter over low heat, then brush over the potatoes. Put as many as will fit in the basket in a single layer, butter-side down. Brush the tops with more of the butter mix, and Bake for 12-17 minutes, turning once until they're crisp. Keep the cooked potatoes warm in the oven at 250°F while air frying the rest of the potatoes.

Pecorino Dill Muffins
Servings: 4
Cooking Time: 25 Minutes
Ingredients:
- ¼ cup grated Pecorino cheese
- 1 cup flour
- 1 tsp dried dill
- ⅛ tsp salt
- ¼ tsp onion powder
- 2 tsp baking powder
- 1 egg
- ¼ cup Greek yogurt

Directions:
1. Preheat air fryer to 350°F/175°C. In a bowl, combine dry the ingredients. Set aside. In another bowl, whisk the wet ingredients. Add the wet ingredients to the dry ingredients and combine until blended.
2. Transfer the batter to 6 silicone muffin cups lightly greased with olive oil. Place muffin cups in the frying basket and Bake for 12 minutes. Serve right away.

Layered Mixed Vegetables
Servings: 4
Cooking Time: 30 Minutes
Ingredients:
- 1 Yukon Gold potato, sliced
- 1 eggplant, sliced
- 1 carrot, thinly sliced
- ¼ cup minced onions
- 3 garlic cloves, minced
- ¾ cup milk
- 2 tbsp cornstarch
- ½ tsp dried thyme

Directions:
1. Preheat air fryer to 380°F/195°C. In layers, add the potato, eggplant, carrot, onion, and garlic to a baking pan. Combine the milk, cornstarch, and thyme in a bowl, then pour this mix over the veggies. Put the pan in the air fryer and Bake for 15 minutes. The casserole should be golden on top with softened veggies. Serve immediately.

Perfect Asparagus
Servings: 3
Cooking Time: 10 Minutes
Ingredients:
- 1 pound Very thin asparagus spears
- 2 tablespoons Olive oil
- 1 teaspoon Coarse sea salt or kosher salt
- ¾ teaspoon Finely grated lemon zest

Directions:
1. Preheat the air fryer to 400°F/205°C.
2. Trim just enough off the bottom of the asparagus spears so they'll fit in the basket. Put the spears on a large plate and drizzle them with some of the olive oil. Turn them over and drizzle more olive oil, working to get all the spears coated.
3. When the machine is at temperature, place the spears in one direction in the basket. They may be touching. Air-fry for 10 minutes, tossing and rearranging the spears twice, until tender.
4. Dump the contents of the basket on a serving platter. Spread out the spears. Sprinkle them with the salt and lemon zest while still warm. Serve at once.

Fried Cauliflower with Parmesan Lemon Dressing

Servings: 2
Cooking Time: 12 Minutes
Ingredients:
- 4 cups cauliflower florets (about half a large head)
- 1 tablespoon olive oil
- salt and freshly ground black pepper
- 1 teaspoon finely chopped lemon zest
- 1 tablespoon fresh lemon juice (about half a lemon)
- ¼ cup grated Parmigiano-Reggiano cheese
- 4 tablespoons extra virgin olive oil
- ¼ teaspoon salt
- lots of freshly ground black pepper
- 1 tablespoon chopped fresh parsley

Directions:
1. Preheat the air fryer to 400°F/205°C.
2. Toss the cauliflower florets with the olive oil, salt and freshly ground black pepper. Air-fry for 12 minutes, shaking the basket a couple of times during the cooking process.
3. While the cauliflower is frying, make the dressing. Combine the lemon zest, lemon juice, Parmigiano-Reggiano cheese and olive oil in a small bowl. Season with salt and lots of freshly ground black pepper. Stir in the parsley.
4. Turn the fried cauliflower out onto a serving platter and drizzle the dressing over the top.

Vegetable Roast

Servings: 6
Cooking Time: 20 Minutes
Ingredients:
- 2 tbsp dill, chopped
- 2 zucchini, cubed
- 1 red bell pepper, diced
- 2 garlic cloves, sliced
- 2 tbsp olive oil
- ½ tsp salt
- ½ tsp red pepper flakes

Directions:
1. Preheat air fryer to 380°F/195°C. Combine the zucchini, bell pepper, red pepper flakes, dill and garlic with olive oil and salt in a bowl. Pour the mixture into the frying basket and Roast for 14-16 minutes, shaking once. Serve warm.

Perfect Broccolini

Servings: 4
Cooking Time: 15 Minutes
Ingredients:
- 1 pound Broccolini
- Olive oil spray
- Coarse sea salt or kosher salt

Directions:
1. Preheat the air fryer to 375°F/190°C.
2. Place the broccolini on a cutting board. Generously coat it with olive oil spray, turning the vegetables and rearranging them before spraying a couple of times more, to make sure everything's well coated, even the flowery bits in their heads.
3. When the machine is at temperature, pile the broccolini in the basket, spreading it into as close to one layer as you can. Air-fry for 5 minutes, tossing once to get any covered or touching parts exposed to the air currents, until the leaves begin to get brown and even crisp. Watch carefully and use this visual cue to know the moment to stop the cooking.
4. Transfer the broccolini to a platter. Spread out the pieces and sprinkle them with salt to taste.

Summer Watermelon And Cucumber Salad

Servings: 4
Cooking Time: 15 Minutes
Ingredients:
- ½ red onion, sliced into half-moons
- 2 tbsp crumbled goat cheese
- 10 chopped basil leaves
- 4 cups watermelon cubes
- ½ cucumber, sliced
- 4 tsp olive oil
- Salt and pepper to taste
- 3 cups arugula
- 1 tsp balsamic vinegar
- 1 tsp honey
- 1 tbsp chopped mint

Directions:
1. Preheat air fryer at 375°F/190°C. Toss watermelon, cucumber, onion, 2 tsp of olive oil, salt, and pepper in a bowl. Place it in the frying basket and Air Fry for 4 minutes, tossing once. In a salad bowl, whisk the arugula, balsamic vinegar, honey, and the remaining olive oil until the arugula is coated. Add in watermelon mixture. Scatter with goat cheese, basil leaves and mint to serve.

Honey-roasted Parsnips

Servings: 3
Cooking Time: 23 Minutes
Ingredients:
- 1½ pounds Medium parsnips, peeled
- Olive oil spray
- 1 tablespoon Honey
- 1½ teaspoons Water
- ¼ teaspoon Table salt

Directions:
1. Preheat the air fryer to 350°F/175°C.
2. If the thick end of a parsnip is more than ½ inch in diameter, cut the parsnip just below where it swells to its large end, then slice the large section in half lengthwise. If the parsnips are larger than the basket (or basket attachment), trim off the thin end so the parsnips will fit. Generously coat the parsnips on all sides with olive oil spray.
3. When the machine is at temperature, set the parsnips in the basket with as much air space between them as possible. Air-fry undisturbed for 20 minutes.
4. Whisk the honey, water, and salt in a small bowl until smooth. Brush this mixture over the parsnips. Air-fry undisturbed for 3 minutes more, or until the glaze is lightly browned.
5. Use kitchen tongs to transfer the parsnips to a wire rack or a serving platter. Cool for a couple of minutes before serving.

Corn On The Cob

Servings: 4
Cooking Time: 12 Minutes
Ingredients:
- 2 large ears fresh corn
- olive oil for misting
- salt (optional)

Directions:

Tower Air Fryer Cookbook

1. Shuck corn, remove silks, and wash.
2. Cut or break each ear in half crosswise.
3. Spray corn with olive oil.
4. Cook at 390°F/200°C for 12 minutes or until browned as much as you like.
5. Serve plain or with coarsely ground salt.

Grits Casserole

Servings: 4
Cooking Time: 30 Minutes
Ingredients:
- 10 fresh asparagus spears, cut into 1-inch pieces
- 2 cups cooked grits, cooled to room temperature
- 1 egg, beaten
- 2 teaspoons Worcestershire sauce
- ½ teaspoon garlic powder
- ¼ teaspoon salt
- 2 slices provolone cheese (about 1½ ounces)
- oil for misting or cooking spray

Directions:
1. Mist asparagus spears with oil and cook at 390°F/200°C for 5minutes, until crisp-tender.
2. In a medium bowl, mix together the grits, egg, Worcestershire, garlic powder, and salt.
3. Spoon half of grits mixture into air fryer baking pan and top with asparagus.
4. Tear cheese slices into pieces and layer evenly on top of asparagus.
5. Top with remaining grits.
6. Bake at 360°F/180°C for 25 minutes. The casserole will rise a little as it cooks. When done, the top will have browned lightly with just a hint of crispiness.

Butternut Medallions With Honey Butter And Sage

Servings: 2
Cooking Time: 15 Minutes
Ingredients:
- 1 butternut squash, peeled
- olive oil, in a spray bottle
- salt and freshly ground black pepper
- 2 tablespoons butter, softened
- 2 tablespoons honey
- pinch ground cinnamon
- pinch ground nutmeg
- chopped fresh sage

Directions:
1. Preheat the air fryer to 370°F/185°C.
2. Cut the neck of the butternut squash into disks about ½-inch thick. (Use the base of the butternut squash for another use.) Brush or spray the disks with oil and season with salt and freshly ground black pepper.
3. Transfer the butternut disks to the air fryer in one layer (or just ever so slightly overlapping). Air-fry at 370°F for 5 minutes.
4. While the butternut squash is cooking, combine the butter, honey, cinnamon and nutmeg in a small bowl. Brush this mixture on the butternut squash, flip the disks over and brush the other side as well. Continue to air-fry at 370°F/185°C for another 5 minutes. Flip the disks once more, brush with more of the honey butter and air-fry for another 5 minutes. The butternut should be browning nicely around the edges.
5. Remove the butternut squash from the air-fryer and repeat with additional batches if necessary. Transfer to a serving platter, sprinkle with the fresh sage and serve.

Honey-mustard Roasted Cabbage

Servings: 4
Cooking Time: 35 Minutes
Ingredients:
- 4 cups chopped green cabbage
- 1/3 cup honey mustard dressing
- 1 shallot, chopped
- 2 garlic cloves, minced
- 2 tbsp olive oil
- 1 tbsp lemon juice
- 1 tbsp cornstarch
- ½ tsp fennel seeds

Directions:
1. Preheat the air fryer to 370°F/185°C. Toss the cabbage, shallot, olive oil and garlic in a cake pan. Bake for 10 minutes or until the cabbage is wilted, then drain the excess liquid. While the cabbage is cooking, combine the salad dressing, lemon juice, cornstarch, and fennel seeds in a bowl. Take cake pan out of the fryer and pour out any excess liquid. Pour the dressing mix over the drained cabbage and mix well. Return the pan to the fryer and Bake for 7-11 minutes more, stirring twice during cooking until the cabbage is tender and the sauce has thickened. Serve warm.

Speedy Baked Caprese With Avocado

Servings:4
Cooking Time: 15 Minutes
Ingredients:
- 4 oz fresh mozzarella
- 8 cherry tomatoes
- 2 tsp olive oil
- 2 halved avocados, pitted
- ¼ tsp salt
- 2 tbsp basil, torn

Directions:
1. Preheat air fryer to 375ºF/190°C. In a bowl, combine tomatoes and olive oil. Set aside. Add avocado halves, cut sides up, in the frying basket, scatter tomatoes around halves, and Bake for 7 minutes. Divide avocado halves between 4 small plates, top each with 2 tomatoes and sprinkle with salt. Cut mozzarella cheese and evenly distribute over tomatoes. Scatter with the basil to serve.

Crunchy Green Beans

Servings: 4
Cooking Time: 15 Minutes
Ingredients:
- 1 tbsp tahini
- 1 tbsp lemon juice
- 1 tsp allspice
- 1 lb green beans, trimmed

Directions:
1. Preheat air fryer to 400°F/205°C. Whisk tahini, lemon juice, 1 tbsp of water, and allspice in a bowl. Put in the green beans and toss to coat. Roast for 5 minutes until golden brown and cooked. Serve immediately.

Best-ever Brussels Sprouts

Servings: 4
Cooking Time: 30 Minutes
Ingredients:
- 1 lb Brussels sprouts, halved lengthwise
- 2 tbsp olive oil
- 3 tsp chili powder
- 1 tbsp lemon juice

Directions:
1. Preheat air fryer to 390°F/200°C. Add the sprouts in a bowl, drizzle with olive oil and 2 tsp of chili powder, and toss to coat. Set them in the frying basket and Air Fry for 12 minutes. Shake at least once. Season with the remaining chili powder and lemon juice, shake once again, and cook for 3-5 minutes until golden and crispy. Serve warm.

Simple Roasted Sweet Potatoes

Servings: 2
Cooking Time: 45 Minutes
Ingredients:
- 2 10- to 12-ounce sweet potato(es)

Directions:
1. Preheat the air fryer to 350°F/175°C.
2. Prick the sweet potato(es) in four or five different places with the tines of a flatware fork (not in a line but all around).
3. When the machine is at temperature, set the sweet potato(es) in the basket with as much air space between them as possible. Air-fry undisturbed for 45 minutes, or until soft when pricked with a fork.
4. Use kitchen tongs to transfer the sweet potato(es) to a wire rack. Cool for 5 minutes before serving.

Roasted Heirloom Carrots With Orange And Thyme

Servings: 2
Cooking Time: 12 Minutes
Ingredients:
- 10 to 12 heirloom or rainbow carrots (about 1 pound), scrubbed but not peeled
- 1 teaspoon olive oil
- salt and freshly ground black pepper
- 1 tablespoon butter
- 1 teaspoon fresh orange zest
- 1 teaspoon chopped fresh thyme

Directions:
1. Preheat the air fryer to 400°F/205°C.
2. Scrub the carrots and halve them lengthwise. Toss them in the olive oil, season with salt and freshly ground black pepper and transfer to the air fryer.
3. Air-fry at 400°F/205°C for 12 minutes, shaking the basket every once in a while to rotate the carrots as they cook.
4. As soon as the carrots have finished cooking, add the butter, orange zest and thyme and toss all the ingredients together in the air fryer basket to melt the butter and coat evenly. Serve warm.

Five-spice Roasted Sweet Potatoes

Servings: 4
Cooking Time: 12 Minutes
Ingredients:
- ½ teaspoon ground cinnamon
- ¼ teaspoon ground cumin
- ¼ teaspoon paprika
- 1 teaspoon chile powder
- ⅛ teaspoon turmeric
- ½ teaspoon salt (optional)
- freshly ground black pepper
- 2 large sweet potatoes, peeled and cut into ¾-inch cubes (about 3 cups)
- 1 tablespoon olive oil

Directions:
1. In a large bowl, mix together cinnamon, cumin, paprika, chile powder, turmeric, salt, and pepper to taste.
2. Add potatoes and stir well.
3. Drizzle the seasoned potatoes with the olive oil and stir until evenly coated.
4. Place seasoned potatoes in the air fryer baking pan or an ovenproof dish that fits inside your air fryer basket.
5. Cook for 6minutes at 390°F/200°C, stop, and stir well.
6. Cook for an additional 6minutes.

Green Peas With Mint

Servings: 4
Cooking Time: 5 Minutes
Ingredients:
- 1 cup shredded lettuce
- 1 10-ounce package frozen green peas, thawed
- 1 tablespoon fresh mint, shredded
- 1 teaspoon melted butter

Directions:
1. Lay the shredded lettuce in the air fryer basket.
2. Toss together the peas, mint, and melted butter and spoon over the lettuce.
3. Cook at 360°F/180°C for 5minutes, until peas are warm and lettuce wilts.

Garlic-parmesan Popcorn

Servings: 2
Cooking Time: 15 Minutes
Ingredients:
- 2 tsp grated Parmesan cheese
- ¼ cup popcorn kernels
- 1 tbsp lemon juice
- 1 tsp garlic powder

Directions:
1. Preheat air fryer to 400°F/205°C. Line the basket with aluminum foil. Put the popcorn kernels in a single layer and Grill for 6-8 minutes until they stop popping. Remove them into a bowl. Drizzle with lemon juice and toss until well coated. Sprinkle with garlic powder and grated Parmesan and toss to coat. Drizzle with more lemon juice. Serve.

Rosemary New Potatoes

Servings: 4
Cooking Time: 6 Minutes
Ingredients:
- 3 large red potatoes (enough to make 3 cups sliced)
- ¼ teaspoon ground rosemary
- ¼ teaspoon ground thyme
- ⅛ teaspoon salt
- ⅛ teaspoon ground black pepper
- 2 teaspoons extra-light olive oil

Directions:
1. Preheat air fryer to 330°F/165°C.
2. Place potatoes in large bowl and sprinkle with rosemary, thyme, salt, and pepper.
3. Stir with a spoon to distribute seasonings evenly.
4. Add oil to potatoes and stir again to coat well.
5. Cook at 330°F/165°C for 4minutes. Stir and break apart any that have stuck together.
6. Cook an additional 2 minutes or until fork-tender.

Chili-oiled Brussels Sprouts

Servings: 4
Cooking Time: 30 Minutes
Ingredients:
- 1 cup Brussels sprouts, quartered
- 1 tsp olive oil
- 1 tsp chili oil
- Salt and pepper to taste

Directions:
1. Preheat air fryer to 350°F/175°C. Coat the Brussels sprouts with olive oil, chili oil, salt, and black pepper in a bowl. Transfer to the frying basket. Bake for 20 minutes, shaking the basket several times throughout cooking until the sprouts are crispy, browned on the outside, and juicy inside. Serve and enjoy!

Hot Okra Wedges

Servings: 2
Cooking Time: 35 Minutes
Ingredients:
- 1 cup okra, sliced
- 1 cup breadcrumbs
- 2 eggs, beaten
- A pinch of black pepper
- 1 tsp crushed red peppers
- 2 tsp hot Tabasco sauce

Directions:
1. Preheat air fryer to 350°F/175°C. Place the eggs and Tabasco sauce in a bowl and stir thoroughly; set aside. In a separate mixing bowl, combine the breadcrumbs, crushed red peppers, and pepper. Dip the okra into the beaten eggs, then coat in the crumb mixture. Lay the okra pieces on the greased frying basket. Air Fry for 14-16 minutes, shaking the basket several times during cooking. When ready, the okra will be crispy and golden brown. Serve.

Smashed Fried Baby Potatoes

Servings: 3
Cooking Time: 18 Minutes
Ingredients:
- 1½ pounds baby red or baby Yukon gold potatoes
- ¼ cup butter, melted
- 1 teaspoon olive oil
- ½ teaspoon paprika
- 1 teaspoon dried parsley
- salt and freshly ground black pepper
- 2 scallions, finely chopped

Directions:
1. Bring a large pot of salted water to a boil. Add the potatoes and boil for 18 minutes or until the potatoes are fork-tender.
2. Drain the potatoes and transfer them to a cutting board to cool slightly. Spray or brush the bottom of a drinking glass with a little oil. Smash or flatten the potatoes by pressing the glass down on each potato slowly. Try not to completely flatten the potato or smash it so hard that it breaks apart.
3. Combine the melted butter, olive oil, paprika, and parsley together.
4. Preheat the air fryer to 400°F/205°C.
5. Spray the bottom of the air fryer basket with oil and transfer one layer of the smashed potatoes into the basket. Brush with some of the butter mixture and season generously with salt and freshly ground black pepper.
6. Air-fry at 400°F/205°C for 10 minutes. Carefully flip the potatoes over and air-fry for an additional 8 minutes until crispy and lightly browned.
7. Keep the potatoes warm in a 170°F/75°C oven or tent with aluminum foil while you cook the second batch. Sprinkle minced scallions over the potatoes and serve warm.

Gorgonzola Stuffed Mushrooms

Servings: 2
Cooking Time: 15 Minutes
Ingredients:
- 12 white button mushroom caps
- 2 tbsp diced white button mushroom stems
- ¼ cup Gorgonzola cheese, crumbled
- 1 tsp olive oil
- 1 green onion, chopped
- 2 tbsp bread crumbs

Directions:
1. Preheat air fryer to 350°F/175°C. Rub around the top of each mushroom cap with olive oil. Mix the mushroom stems, green onion, and Gorgonzola cheese in a bowl.
2. Distribute and press mixture into the cups of mushrooms, then sprinkle bread crumbs on top. Place stuffed mushrooms in the frying basket and Bake for 5-7 minutes. Serve right away.

Roasted Brussels Sprouts

Servings: 4
Cooking Time: 25 Minutes
Ingredients:
- ½ cup balsamic vinegar
- 2 tablespoons honey
- 1 pound Brussels sprouts, halved lengthwise
- 2 slices bacon, chopped
- ½ teaspoon garlic powder
- 1 teaspoon salt
- 1 tablespoon extra-virgin olive oil
- ¼ cup grated Parmesan cheese

Directions:
1. Preheat the air fryer to 370°F/185°C.
2. In a small saucepan, heat the vinegar and honey for 8 to 10 minutes over medium-low heat, or until the balsamic vinegar reduces by half to create a thick balsamic glazing sauce.
3. While the balsamic glaze is reducing, in a large bowl, toss together the Brussels sprouts, bacon, garlic powder, salt, and olive oil. Pour the mixture into the air fryer basket and cook for 10 minutes; check for doneness. Cook another 2 to 5 minutes or until slightly crispy and tender.
4. Pour the balsamic glaze into a serving bowl and add the cooked Brussels sprouts to the dish, stirring to coat. Top with grated Parmesan cheese and serve.

Mom's Potatoes Au Gratin

Servings: 4
Cooking Time: 50 Minutes
Ingredients:
- 4 Yukon Gold potatoes, peeled
- 1 cup shredded cheddar cheese
- 2 tbsp grated Parmesan cheese
- 2 garlic cloves, minced
- 1/3 cup heavy cream
- 1/3 cup whole milk
- ½ tsp dried marjoram

- Salt and pepper to taste

Directions:
1. Preheat the air fryer to 350°F/175°C. Spray a 7-inch round pan thoroughly with cooking oil. Cut the potatoes into ⅛-inch-thick slices and layer the potatoes inside the pan along with cheddar cheese and garlic. Mix the cream, milk, marjoram, salt, and pepper in a bowl, then slowly pour the mix over the potatoes. Sprinkle with Parmesan and put the pan in the fryer. Bake for 25-35 minutes or until the potatoes are tender, the sauce is bubbling, and the top is golden. Serve warm.

Cheesy Texas Toast

Servings: 2
Cooking Time: 4 Minutes
Ingredients:
- 2 1-inch-thick slice(s) Italian bread (each about 4 inches across)
- 4 teaspoons Softened butter
- 2 teaspoons Minced garlic
- ¼ cup (about ¾ ounce) Finely grated Parmesan cheese

Directions:
1. Preheat the air fryer to 400°F/205°C.
2. Spread one side of a slice of bread with 2 teaspoons butter. Sprinkle with 1 teaspoon minced garlic, followed by 2 tablespoons grated cheese. Repeat this process if you're making one or more additional toasts.
3. When the machine is at temperature, put the bread slice(s) cheese side up in the basket (with as much air space between them as possible if you're making more than one). Air-fry undisturbed for 4 minutes, or until browned and crunchy.
4. Use a nonstick-safe spatula to transfer the toasts cheese side up to a wire rack. Cool for 5 minutes before serving.

Balsamic Beet Chips

Servings: 4
Cooking Time: 40 Minutes
Ingredients:
- ½ tsp balsamic vinegar
- 4 beets, peeled and sliced
- 1 garlic clove, minced
- 2 tbsp chopped mint
- Salt and pepper to taste
- 3 tbsp olive oil

Directions:
1. Preheat air fryer to 380°F/195°C. Coat all ingredients in a bowl, except balsamic vinegar. Pour the beet mixture into the frying basket and Roast for 25-30 minutes, stirring once. Serve, drizzled with vinegar and enjoy!

Sage & Thyme Potatoes

Servings: 4
Cooking Time: 30 Minutes
Ingredients:
- 2 red potatoes, peeled and cubed
- ¼ cup olive oil
- 1 tsp dried sage
- ½ tsp dried thyme
- ½ tsp salt
- 2 tbsp grated Parmesan

Directions:
1. Preheat air fryer to 360°F/180°C. Coat the red potatoes with olive oil, sage, thyme and salt in a bowl. Pour the potatoes into the air frying basket and Roast for 10 minutes. Stir the potatoes and sprinkle the Parmesan over the top. Continue roasting for 8 more minutes. Serve hot.

Onions

Servings: 4
Cooking Time: 18 Minutes
Ingredients:
- 2 yellow onions (Vidalia or 1015 recommended)
- salt and pepper
- ¼ teaspoon ground thyme
- ¼ teaspoon smoked paprika
- 2 teaspoons olive oil
- 1 ounce Gruyère cheese, grated

Directions:
1. Peel onions and halve lengthwise (vertically).
2. Sprinkle cut sides of onions with salt, pepper, thyme, and paprika.
3. Place each onion half, cut-surface up, on a large square of aluminum foil. Pull sides of foil up to cup around onion. Drizzle cut surface of onions with oil.
4. Crimp foil at top to seal closed.
5. Place wrapped onions in air fryer basket and cook at 390°F/200°C for 18 minutes. When done, onions should be soft enough to pierce with fork but still slightly firm.
6. Open foil just enough to sprinkle each onion with grated cheese.
7. Cook for 30 seconds to 1 minute to melt cheese.

Crispy, Cheesy Leeks

Servings: 4
Cooking Time: 15 Minutes
Ingredients:
- 2 Medium leek(s), about 9 ounces each
- Olive oil spray
- ¼ cup Seasoned Italian-style dried bread crumbs (gluten-free, if a concern)
- ¼ cup (about ¾ ounce) Finely grated Parmesan cheese
- 2 tablespoons Olive oil

Directions:
1. Preheat the air fryer to 350°F/175°C.
2. Trim off the root end of the leek(s) as well as the dark green top(s), leaving about a 5-inch usable section. Split the leek section(s) in half lengthwise. Set the leek halves cut side up on your work surface. Pull out and remove in one piece the semicircles that make up the inner structure of the leek, about halfway down. Set the removed "inside" next to the outer leek "shells" on your cutting board. Generously coat them all on all sides (particularly the "bottoms") with olive oil spray.
3. Set the leeks and their insides cut side up in the basket with as much air space between them as possible. Air-fry undisturbed for 12 minutes.
4. Meanwhile, mix the bread crumbs, cheese, and olive oil in a small bowl until well combined.
5. After 12 minutes in the air fryer, sprinkle this mixture inside the leek shells and on top of the leek insides. Increase the machine's temperature to 375°F/190°C (or 380°F/195°C or 390°F/200°C, if one of these is the closest setting). Air-fry undisturbed for 3 minutes, or until the topping is lightly browned.
6. Use a nonstick-safe spatula to transfer the leeks to a serving platter. Cool for a few minutes before serving warm.

Salmon Salad With Steamboat Dressing

Servings: 4
Cooking Time: 18 Minutes
Ingredients:
- ¼ teaspoon salt
- 1½ teaspoons dried dill weed
- 1 tablespoon fresh lemon juice
- 8 ounces fresh or frozen salmon fillet (skin on)
- 8 cups shredded romaine, Boston, or other leaf lettuce
- 8 spears cooked asparagus, cut in 1-inch pieces
- 8 cherry tomatoes, halved or quartered

Directions:
1. Mix the salt and dill weed together. Rub the lemon juice over the salmon on both sides and sprinkle the dill and salt all over. Refrigerate for 15 to 20minutes.
2. Make Steamboat Dressing and refrigerate while cooking salmon and preparing salad.
3. Cook salmon in air fryer basket at 330°F/165°C for 18 minutes. Cooking time will vary depending on thickness of fillets. When done, salmon should flake with fork but still be moist and tender.
4. Remove salmon from air fryer and cool slightly. At this point, the skin should slide off easily. Cut salmon into 4 pieces and discard skin.
5. Divide the lettuce among 4 plates. Scatter asparagus spears and tomato pieces evenly over the lettuce, allowing roughly 2 whole spears and 2 whole cherry tomatoes per plate.
6. Top each salad with one portion of the salmon and drizzle with a tablespoon of dressing. Serve with additional dressing to pass at the table.

Yellow Squash

Servings: 4
Cooking Time: 10 Minutes
Ingredients:
- 1 large yellow squash (about 1½ cups)
- 2 eggs
- ¼ cup buttermilk
- 1 cup panko breadcrumbs
- ¼ cup white cornmeal
- ½ teaspoon salt
- oil for misting or cooking spray

Directions:
1. Preheat air fryer to 390°F/200°C.
2. Cut the squash into ¼-inch slices.
3. In a shallow dish, beat together eggs and buttermilk.
4. In sealable plastic bag or container with lid, combine ¼ cup panko crumbs, white cornmeal, and salt. Shake to mix well.
5. Place the remaining ¾ cup panko crumbs in a separate shallow dish.
6. Dump all the squash slices into the egg/buttermilk mixture. Stir to coat.
7. Remove squash from buttermilk mixture with a slotted spoon, letting excess drip off, and transfer to the panko/cornmeal mixture. Close bag or container and shake well to coat.
8. Remove squash from crumb mixture, letting excess fall off. Return squash to egg/buttermilk mixture, stirring gently to coat. If you need more liquid to coat all the squash, add a little more buttermilk.
9. Remove each squash slice from egg wash and dip in a dish of ¾ cup panko crumbs.
10. Mist squash slices with oil or cooking spray and place in air fryer basket. Squash should be in a single layer, but it's okay if the slices crowd together and overlap a little.
11. Cook at 390°F for 5minutes. Shake basket to break up any that have stuck together. Mist again with oil or spray.
12. Cook 5minutes longer and check. If necessary, mist again with oil and cook an additional two minutes, until squash slices are golden brown and crisp.

Zucchini Fries

Servings: 3
Cooking Time: 12 Minutes
Ingredients:
- 1 large Zucchini
- ½ cup All-purpose flour or tapioca flour
- 2 Large egg(s), well beaten
- 1 cup Seasoned Italian-style dried bread crumbs (gluten-free, if a concern)
- Olive oil spray

Directions:
1. Preheat the air fryer to 400°F/205°C.
2. Trim the zucchini into a long rectangular block, taking off the ends and four "sides" to make this shape. Cut the block lengthwise into ½-inch-thick slices. Lay these slices flat and cut in half widthwise. Slice each of these pieces into ½-inch-thick batons.
3. Set up and fill three shallow soup plates or small pie plates on your counter: one for the flour, one for the beaten egg(s), and one for the bread crumbs.
4. Set a zucchini baton in the flour and turn it several times to coat all sides. Gently shake off any excess flour, then dip it in the egg(s), turning it to coat. Let any excess egg slip back into the rest, then set the baton in the bread crumbs and turn it several times, pressing gently to coat all sides, even the ends. Set aside on a cutting board and continue coating the remainder of the batons in the same way.
5. Lightly coat the batons on all sides with olive oil spray. Set them in two flat layers in the basket, the top layer at a 90-degree angle to the bottom one, with a little air space between the batons in each layer. In the end, the whole thing will look like a crosshatch pattern. Air-fry undisturbed for 6 minutes.
6. Use kitchen tongs to gently rearrange the batons so that any covered parts are now uncovered. The batons no longer need to be in a crosshatch pattern. Continue air-frying undisturbed for 6 minutes, or until lightly browned and crisp.
7. Gently pour the contents of the basket onto a wire rack. Spread the batons out and cool for only a minute or two before serving.

Acorn Squash Halves With Maple Butter Glaze

Servings: 2
Cooking Time: 33 Minutes
Ingredients:
- 1 medium (1 to 1¼ pounds) Acorn squash
- Vegetable oil spray
- ¼ teaspoon Table salt
- 1½ tablespoons Butter, melted
- 1½ tablespoons Maple syrup

Directions:

1. Preheat the air fryer to 325°F/160°C (or 330°F/165°C, if that's the closest setting).
2. Cut a squash in half through the stem end. Use a flatware spoon (preferably, a serrated grapefruit spoon) to scrape out and discard the seeds and membranes in each half. Use a paring knife to make a crisscross pattern of cuts about ½ inch apart and ¼ inch deep across the "meat" of the squash. If working with a second squash, repeat this step for that one.
3. Generously coat the cut side of the squash halves with vegetable oil spray. Sprinkle the halves with the salt. Set them in the basket cut side up with at least ¼ inch between them. Air-fry undisturbed for 30 minutes.
4. Increase the machine's temperature to 400°F. Mix the melted butter and syrup in a small bowl until uniform. Brush this mixture over the cut sides of the squash(es), letting it pool in the center. Air-fry undisturbed for 3 minutes, or until the glaze is bubbling.
5. Use a nonstick-safe spatula and kitchen tongs to transfer the squash halves cut side up to a wire rack. Cool for 5 to 10 minutes before serving.

Sweet Roasted Pumpkin Rounds

Servings: 4
Cooking Time: 35 Minutes
Ingredients:
- 1 pumpkin
- 1 tbsp honey
- 1 tbsp melted butter
- ¼ tsp cardamom
- ¼ tsp sea salt

Directions:
1. Preheat the air fryer to 370°F/185°C. Cut the pumpkin in half lengthwise and remove the seeds. Slice each half crosswise into 1-inch-wide half-circles, then cut each half-circle in half again to make quarter rounds. Combine the honey, butter, cardamom, and salt in a bowl and mix well. Toss the pumpkin in the mixture until coated, then put into the frying basket. Bake for 15-20 minutes, shaking once during cooking until the edges start to brown and the squash is tender.

Blistered Shishito Peppers

Servings: 2
Cooking Time: 15 Minutes
Ingredients:
- 20 shishito peppers
- 1 tsp sesame oil
- ½ tsp soy sauce
- ½ tsp grated ginger
- Salt to taste
- 1 tsp sesame seeds

Directions:
1. Preheat air fryer to 375°F/190°C. Coat the peppers with sesame oil and salt in a bowl. Transfer them to the frying basket and Air Fry for 8 minutes or until blistered and softened, shaking the basket to turn the peppers. Drizzle with soy sauce and sprinkle with ginger and sesame seeds to serve.

Broccoli Au Gratin

Servings: 2
Cooking Time: 25 Minutes
Ingredients:
- 2 cups broccoli florets, chopped
- 6 tbsp grated Gruyère cheese
- 1 tbsp grated Pecorino cheese
- ½ tbsp olive oil
- 1 tbsp flour
- 1/3 cup milk
- ½ tsp ground coriander
- Salt and black pepper
- 2 tbsp panko bread crumbs

Directions:
1. Whisk the olive oil, flour, milk, coriander, salt, and pepper in a bowl. Incorporate broccoli, Gruyere cheese, panko bread crumbs, and Pecorino cheese until well combined. Pour in a greased baking dish.
2. Preheat air fryer to 330°F/165°C. Put the baking dish into the frying basket. Bake until the broccoli is crisp-tender and the top is golden, or about 12-15 minutes. Serve warm.

Dilly Sesame Roasted Asparagus

Servings: 6
Cooking Time: 15 Minutes
Ingredients:
- 1 lb asparagus, trimmed
- 1 tbsp butter, melted
- ¼ tsp salt
- 1 clove garlic, minced
- 2 tsp chopped dill
- 3 tbsp sesame seeds

Directions:
1. Preheat air fryer to 370°F/185°C. Combine asparagus and butter in a bowl. Place asparagus mixture in the frying basket and Roast for 9 minutes, tossing once. Transfer it to a serving dish and stir in salt, garlic, sesame seeds and dill until coated. Serve immediately.

Asparagus

Servings: 4
Cooking Time: 9 Minutes
Ingredients:
- 1 bunch asparagus (approx. 1 pound), washed and trimmed
- ⅛ teaspoon dried tarragon, crushed
- salt and pepper
- 1 to 2 teaspoons extra-light olive oil

Directions:
1. Spread asparagus spears on cookie sheet or cutting board.
2. Sprinkle with tarragon, salt, and pepper.
3. Drizzle with 1 teaspoon of oil and roll the spears or mix by hand. If needed, add up to 1 more teaspoon of oil and mix again until all spears are lightly coated.
4. Place spears in air fryer basket. If necessary, bend the longer spears to make them fit. It doesn't matter if they don't lie flat.
5. Cook at 390°F/200°C for 5 minutes. Shake basket or stir spears with a spoon.
6. Cook for an additional 4 minutes or just until crisp-tender.

Mexican-style Frittata

Servings: 4
Cooking Time: 35 Minutes
Ingredients:
- ½ cup shredded Cotija cheese
- ½ cup cooked black beans

- 1 cooked potato, sliced
- 3 eggs, beaten
- Salt and pepper to taste

Directions:
1. Preheat air fryer to 350°F/175°C. Mix the eggs, beans, half of Cotija cheese, salt, and pepper in a bowl. Pour the mixture into a greased baking dish. Top with potato slices. Place the baking dish in the frying basket and Air Fry for 10 minutes. Slide the basket out and sprinkle the remaining Cotija cheese over the dish. Cook for 10 more minutes or until golden and bubbling. Slice into wedges to serve.

Stuffed Onions

Servings: 6
Cooking Time: 27 Minutes
Ingredients:
- 6 Small 3½- to 4-ounce yellow or white onions
- Olive oil spray
- 6 ounces Bulk sweet Italian sausage meat (gluten-free, if a concern)
- 9 Cherry tomatoes, chopped
- 3 tablespoons Seasoned Italian-style dried bread crumbs (gluten-free, if a concern)
- 3 tablespoons (about ½ ounce) Finely grated Parmesan cheese

Directions:
1. Preheat the air fryer to 325°F/160°C (or 330°F/165°C, if that's the closest setting).
2. Cut just enough off the root ends of the onions so they will stand up on a cutting board when this end is turned down. Carefully peel off just the brown, papery skin. Now cut the top quarter off each and place the onion back on the cutting board with this end facing up. Use a flatware spoon (preferably a serrated grapefruit spoon) or a melon baller to scoop out the "insides" (interior layers) of the onion, leaving enough of the bottom and side walls so that the onion does not collapse. Depending on the thickness of the layers in the onion, this may be one or two of those layers—or even three, if they're very thin.
3. Coat the insides and outsides of the onions with olive oil spray. Set the onion "shells" in the basket and air-fry for 15 minutes.
4. Meanwhile, make the filling. Set a medium skillet over medium heat for a couple of minutes, then crumble in the sausage meat. Cook, stirring often, until browned, about 4 minutes. Transfer the contents of the skillet to a medium bowl (leave the fat behind in the skillet or add it to the bowl, depending on your cross-trainer regimen). Stir in the tomatoes, bread crumbs, and cheese until well combined.
5. When the onions are ready, use a nonstick-safe spatula to gently transfer them to a cutting board. Increase the air fryer's temperature to 350°F/175°C.
6. Pack the sausage mixture into the onion shells, gently compacting the filling and mounding it up at the top.
7. When the machine is at temperature, set the onions stuffing side up in the basket with at least ¼ inch between them. Air-fry for 12 minutes, or until lightly browned and sizzling hot.
8. Use a nonstick-safe spatula, and perhaps a flatware fork for balance, to transfer the onions to a cutting board or serving platter. Cool for 5 minutes before serving.

Easy Parmesan Asparagus

Servings: 4
Cooking Time: 15 Minutes
Ingredients:
- 3 tsp grated Parmesan cheese
- 1 lb asparagus, trimmed
- 2 tsp olive oil
- Salt to taste
- 1 clove garlic, minced
- ½ lemon

Directions:
1. Preheat air fryer at 375°F/190°C. Toss the asparagus and olive oil in a bowl, place them in the frying basket, and Air Fry for 8-10 minutes, tossing once. Transfer them into a large serving dish. Sprinkle with salt, garlic, and Parmesan cheese and toss until coated. Serve immediately with a squeeze of lemon. Enjoy!

Honey-mustard Asparagus Puffs

Servings: 4
Cooking Time: 35 Minutes
Ingredients:
- 8 asparagus spears
- ½ sheet puff pastry
- 2 tbsp honey mustard
- 1 egg, lightly beaten

Directions:
1. Preheat the air fryer to 375°F/190°C. Spread the pastry with honey mustard and cut it into 8 strips. Wrap the pastry, honey mustard–side in, around the asparagus. Put a rack in the frying basket and lay the asparagus spears on the rack. Brush all over pastries with beaten egg and Air Fry for 12-17 minutes or until the pastry is golden. Serve.

Parmesan Asparagus

Servings: 2
Cooking Time: 5 Minutes
Ingredients:
- 1 bunch asparagus, stems trimmed
- 1 teaspoon olive oil
- salt and freshly ground black pepper
- ¼ cup coarsely grated Parmesan cheese
- ½ lemon

Directions:
1. Preheat the air fryer to 400°F/205°C.
2. Toss the asparagus with the oil and season with salt and freshly ground black pepper.
3. Transfer the asparagus to the air fryer basket and air-fry at 400°F/205°C for 5 minutes, shaking the basket to turn the asparagus once or twice during the cooking process.
4. When the asparagus is cooked to your liking, sprinkle the asparagus generously with the Parmesan cheese and close the air fryer drawer again. Let the asparagus sit for 1 minute in the turned-off air fryer. Then, remove the asparagus, transfer it to a serving dish and finish with a grind of black pepper and a squeeze of lemon juice.

Sticky Broccoli Florets

Servings: 4
Cooking Time: 20 Minutes
Ingredients:
- 4 cups broccoli florets
- 2 tbsp olive oil
- ½ tsp salt
- ½ cup grapefruit juice
- 1 tbsp raw honey

- 4-6 grapefruit wedges

Directions:
1. Preheat air fryer to 360°F/180°C. Add the broccoli, olive oil, salt, grapefruit juice, and honey to a bowl. Toss the broccoli in the liquid until well coated. Pour the broccoli mixture into the frying basket and Roast for 12 minutes, stirring once. Serve with grapefruit wedges.

Smoky Roasted Veggie Chips

Servings: 4
Cooking Time: 40 Minutes
Ingredients:
- 2 tbsp butter
- 2 tsp smoked paprika
- 1 tsp dried dill
- Salt and pepper to taste
- 2 carrots, cut into rounds
- 1 parsnip, cut into rounds
- 1 tbsp chopped fresh dill

Directions:
1. Preheat the air fryer to 375°F/190°C. Combine the butter, paprika, dried dill, salt, and pepper in a small pan, over low heat until the butter melts. Put the carrots and parsnip in the frying basket, top with the butter mix, and toss. Air Fry for 20-25 minutes or until the veggies are tender and golden around the edges. Toss with fresh dill and serve.

Simple Green Bake

Servings: 4
Cooking Time: 15 Minutes
Ingredients:
- 1 cup asparagus, chopped
- 2 cups broccoli florets
- 1 tbsp olive oil
- 1 tbsp lemon juice
- 1 cup green peas
- 2 tbsp honey mustard
- Salt and pepper to taste

Directions:
1. Preheat air fryer to 330°F/165°C. Add asparagus and broccoli to the frying basket. Drizzle with olive oil and lemon juice and toss. Bake for 6 minutes. Remove the basket and add peas. Steam for another 3 minutes or until the vegetables are hot and tender. Pour the vegetables into a serving dish. Drizzle with honey mustard and season with salt and pepper. Toss and serve warm.

Sesame Carrots And Sugar Snap Peas

Cooking Time: 16 Minutes
Servings: 4
Ingredients:
- 1 pound carrots, peeled sliced on the bias (½-inch slices)
- 1 teaspoon olive oil
- salt and freshly ground black pepper
- ⅓ cup honey
- 1 tablespoon sesame oil
- 1 tablespoon soy sauce
- ½ teaspoon minced fresh ginger
- 4 ounces sugar snap peas (about 1 cup)
- 1½ teaspoons sesame seeds

Directions:
1. Preheat the air fryer to 360°F/180°C.
2. Toss the carrots with the olive oil, season with salt and pepper and air-fry for 10 minutes, shaking the basket once or twice during the cooking process.
3. Combine the honey, sesame oil, soy sauce and minced ginger in a large bowl. Add the sugar snap peas and the air-fried carrots to the honey mixture, toss to coat and return everything to the air fryer basket.
4. Turn up the temperature to 400°F/205°C and air-fry for an additional 6 minutes, shaking the basket once during the cooking process.
5. Transfer the carrots and sugar snap peas to a serving bowl. Pour the sauce from the bottom of the cooker over the vegetables and sprinkle sesame seeds over top. Serve immediately.

Roasted Broccoli And Red Bean Salad

Servings: 3
Cooking Time: 14 Minutes
Ingredients:
- 3 cups (about 1 pound) 1- to 1½-inch fresh broccoli florets (not frozen)
- 1½ tablespoons Olive oil spray
- 1¼ cups Canned red kidney beans, drained and rinsed
- 3 tablespoons Minced yellow or white onion
- 2 tablespoons plus 1 teaspoon Red wine vinegar
- ¾ teaspoon Dried oregano
- ¼ teaspoon Table salt
- ¼ teaspoon Ground black pepper

Directions:
1. Preheat the air fryer to 375°F/190°C.
2. Put the broccoli florets in a big bowl, coat them generously with olive oil spray, then toss to coat all surfaces, even down into the crannies, spraying them a couple of times more.
3. Pour the florets into the basket, spreading them into as close to one layer as you can. Air-fry for 12 minutes, tossing and rearranging the florets twice so that any touching or covered parts are eventually exposed to the air currents, until light browned but still a bit firm. (If the machine is at 360°F/180°C, you may need to add 2 minutes to the cooking time.)
4. Dump the contents of the basket onto a large cutting board. Cool for a minute or two, then chop the florets into small bits. Scrape these into a bowl and add the kidney beans, onion, vinegar, oregano, salt, and pepper. Toss well and serve warm or at room temperature.

Asparagus Wrapped In Pancetta

Servings: 4
Cooking Time: 30 Minutes
Ingredients:
- 20 asparagus trimmed
- Salt and pepper pepper
- 4 pancetta slices
- 1 tbsp fresh sage, chopped

Directions:
1. Sprinkle the asparagus with fresh sage, salt and pepper. Toss to coat. Make 4 bundles of 5 spears by wrapping the center of the bunch with one slice of pancetta.
2. Preheat air fryer to 400°F/205°C. Put the bundles in the greased frying basket and Air Fry for 8-10 minutes or until the pancetta is brown and the asparagus are starting to char on the edges. Serve immediately.

Chicken Eggrolls

Servings: 10
Cooking Time: 17 Minutes
Ingredients:
- 1 tablespoon vegetable oil
- ¼ cup chopped onion
- 1 clove garlic, minced
- 1 cup shredded carrot
- ½ cup thinly sliced celery
- 2 cups cooked chicken
- 2 cups shredded white cabbage
- ½ cup teriyaki sauce
- 20 egg roll wrappers
- 1 egg, whisked
- 1 tablespoon water

Directions:
1. Preheat the air fryer to 390°F/200°C.
2. In a large skillet, heat the oil over medium-high heat. Add in the onion and sauté for 1 minute. Add in the garlic and sauté for 30 seconds. Add in the carrot and celery and cook for 2 minutes. Add in the chicken, cabbage, and teriyaki sauce. Allow the mixture to cook for 1 minute, stirring to combine. Remove from the heat.
3. In a small bowl, whisk together the egg and water for brushing the edges.
4. Lay the eggroll wrappers out at an angle. Place ¼ cup filling in the center. Fold the bottom corner up first and then fold in the corners; roll up to complete eggroll.
5. Place the eggrolls in the air fryer basket, spray with cooking spray, and cook for 8 minutes, turn over, and cook another 2 to 4 minutes.

Lemony Fried Fennel Slices

Servings: 2
Cooking Time: 15 Minutes
Ingredients:
- 1 tbsp minced fennel fronds
- 1 fennel bulb
- 2 tsp olive oil
- ¼ tsp salt
- 2 lemon wedges
- 1 tsp fennel seeds

Directions:
1. Preheat air fryer to 350°F/175°C. Remove the fronds from the fennel bulb and reserve them. Cut the fennel into thin slices. Rub fennel chips with olive oil on both sides and sprinkle with salt and fennel seeds. Place fennel slices in the frying basket and Bake for 8 minutes. Squeeze lemon on top and scatter with chopped fronds. Serve.

Citrusy Brussels Sprouts

Servings: 4
Cooking Time: 15 Minutes
Ingredients:
- 1 lb Brussels sprouts, quartered
- 1 clementine, cut into rings
- 2 garlic cloves, minced
- 1 tbsp olive oil
- 1 tbsp butter, melted
- ½ tsp salt

Directions:
1. Preheat air fryer to 360°F/180°C. Add the quartered Brussels sprouts with the garlic, olive oil, butter and salt in a bowl and toss until well coated. Pour the Brussels sprouts into the air fryer, top with the clementine slices, and Roast for 10 minutes. Remove from the air fryer and set the clementines aside. Toss the Brussels sprouts and serve.

Jerk Rubbed Corn On The Cob

Servings: 4
Cooking Time: 6 Minutes
Ingredients:
- 1 teaspoon ground allspice
- 1 teaspoon dried thyme
- ½ teaspoon ground ginger
- ½ teaspoon ground cinnamon
- ¼ teaspoon ground nutmeg
- ⅛ teaspoon ground cayenne pepper
- 1 teaspoon salt
- 2 tablespoons butter, melted
- 4 ears of corn, husked

Directions:
1. Preheat the air fryer to 380°F/195°C.
2. Combine all the spices in a bowl. Brush the corn with the melted butter and then sprinkle the spices generously on all sides of each ear of corn.
3. Transfer the ears of corn to the air fryer basket. It's ok if they are crisscrossed on top of each other. Air-fry at 380°F/195°C for 6 minutes, rotating the ears as they cook.
4. Brush more butter on at the end and sprinkle with any remaining spice mixture.

Tasty Brussels Sprouts With Guanciale

Servings: 4
Cooking Time: 50 Minutes
Ingredients:
- 3 guanciale slices, halved
- 1 lb Brussels sprouts, halved
- 2 tbsp olive oil
- ¼ tsp salt
- ¼ tsp dried thyme

Directions:
1. Preheat air fryer to 350°F/175°C. Air Fry Lay the guanciale in the air fryer, until crispy, 10 minutes. Remove and drain on a paper towel. Give the guanciale a rough chop and Set aside. Coat Brussels sprouts with olive oil in a large bowl. Add salt and thyme, then toss. Place the sprouts in the frying basket. Air Fry for about 12-15 minutes, shake the basket once until the sprouts are golden and tender. Top with guanciale and serve.

Crispy Brussels Sprouts

Servings: 3
Cooking Time: 12 Minutes
Ingredients:
- 1¼ pounds Medium, 2-inch-in-length Brussels sprouts
- 1½ tablespoons Olive oil
- ¾ teaspoon Table salt

Directions:
1. Preheat the air fryer to 400°F/205°C.
2. Halve each Brussels sprout through the stem end, pulling off and discarding any discolored outer leaves. Put the sprout halves in a large bowl, add the oil and salt, and stir well to coat evenly, until the Brussels sprouts are glistening.

3. When the machine is at temperature, scrape the contents of the bowl into the basket, gently spreading the Brussels sprout halves into as close to one layer as possible. Air-fry for 12 minutes, gently tossing and rearranging the vegetables twice to get all covered or touching parts exposed to the air currents, until crisp and browned at the edges.
4. Gently pour the contents of the basket onto a wire rack. Cool for a minute or two before serving.

Rosemary Potato Salad

Servings: 4
Cooking Time: 30 Minutes
Ingredients:
- 3 tbsp olive oil
- 2 lb red potatoes, halved
- Salt and pepper to taste
- 1 red bell pepper, chopped
- 2 green onions, chopped
- 1/3 cup lemon juice
- 3 tbsp Dijon mustard
- 1 tbsp rosemary, chopped

Directions:
1. Preheat air fryer to 350°F/175°C. Add potatoes to the frying basket and drizzle with 1 tablespoon olive oil. Season with salt and pepper. Roast the potatoes for 25 minutes, shaking twice. Potatoes will be tender and lightly golden.
2. While the potatoes are roasting, add peppers and green onions in a bowl. In a separate bowl, whisk olive oil, lemon juice, and mustard. When the potatoes are done, transfer them to a large bowl. Pour the mustard dressing over and toss to coat. Serve sprinkled with rosemary.

Sage Hasselback Potatoes

Servings: 4
Cooking Time: 45 Minutes
Ingredients:
- 1 lb fingerling potatoes
- 1 tbsp olive oil
- 1 tbsp butter
- 1 tsp dried sage
- Salt and pepper to taste

Directions:
1. Preheat the air fryer to 400°F/205°C. Rinse the potatoes dry, then set them on a work surface and put two chopsticks lengthwise on either side of each so you won't cut all the way through. Make vertical, crosswise cuts in the potato, about 1/8 inch apart. Repeat with the remaining potatoes. Combine the olive oil and butter in a bowl and microwave for 30 seconds or until melted. Stir in the sage, salt, and pepper. Put the potatoes in a large bowl and drizzle with the olive oil mixture. Toss to coat, then put the potatoes in the fryer and Air Fry for 22-27 minutes, rearranging them after 10-12 minutes. Cook until the potatoes are tender. Serve hot and enjoy!

Garlicky Brussels Sprouts

Servings: 4
Cooking Time: 35 Minutes
Ingredients:
- 1 lb Brussels sprouts, halved lengthwise
- 1 tbsp olive oil
- 1 tbsp lemon juice
- ½ tsp sea salt
- ⅛ tsp garlic powder
- 4 garlic cloves, sliced
- 2 tbsp parsley, chopped
- ½ tsp red chili flakes

Directions:
1. Preheat the air fryer to 375°F/190°C. Combine the olive oil, lemon juice, salt, and garlic powder in a bowl and mix well. Add the Brussels sprouts and toss to coat. Put the Brussels sprouts in the frying basket. Air Fry for 15-20 minutes, shaking the basket once until golden and crisp. Sprinkle with garlic slices, parsley, and chili flakes. Toss and cook for 2-4 minutes more until the garlic browns a bit.

Carrots & Parsnips With Tahini Sauce

Servings: 4
Cooking Time: 20 Minutes
Ingredients:
- 2 parsnips, cut into half-moons
- 2 tsp olive oil
- ½ tsp salt
- 1 carrot, cut into sticks
- 1 tbsp tahini
- 1 tbsp lemon juice
- 1 clove garlic, minced
- 1 tbsp chopped parsley

Directions:
1. Preheat air fryer to 375°F/190°C. Coat the parsnips and carrots with some olive oil and salt. Place them in the frying basket and Air Fry for 10 minutes, tossing once. In a bowl, whisk tahini, lemon juice, 1 tsp of water, and garlic. Pour the sauce over the cooked veggies. Scatter with parsley and serve.

Provence French Fries

Servings: 4
Cooking Time: 25 Minutes
Ingredients:
- 2 russet potatoes
- 1 tbsp olive oil
- 1 tbsp herbs de Provence

Directions:
1. Preheat air fryer to 400°F/205°C. Slice the potatoes lengthwise into ½-inch thick strips. In a bowl, whisk the olive oil and herbs de Provence. Toss in the potatoes to coat. Arrange them in a single and Air Fry for 18-20 minutes, shaking once, until crispy. Serve warm.

Cheese & Bacon Pasta Bake

Servings: 4
Cooking Time: 35 Minutes
Ingredients:
- ½ cup shredded sharp cheddar cheese
- ½ cup shredded mozzarella cheese
- 4 oz cooked bacon, crumbled
- 3 tbsp butter, divided
- 1 tbsp flour
- 1 tsp black pepper
- 2 oz crushed feta cheese
- ¼ cup heavy cream
- ½ lb cooked rotini
- ¼ cup bread crumbs

Directions:
1. Melt 2 tbsp of butter in a skillet over medium heat. Stir in flour until the sauce thickens. Stir in all cheeses, black

pepper and heavy cream and cook for 2 minutes until creamy. Toss in rotini and bacon until well coated. Spoon rotini mixture into a greased cake pan.

2. Preheat air fryer at 370°F/185°C. Microwave the remaining butter in 10-seconds intervals until melted. Then stir in breadcrumbs. Scatter over pasta mixture. Place cake pan in the frying basket and Bake for 15 minutes. Let sit for 10 minutes before serving.

Onion Rings

Servings: 4
Cooking Time: 12 Minutes
Ingredients:
- 1 large onion (preferably Vidalia or 1015)
- ½ cup flour, plus 2 tablespoons
- ½ teaspoon salt
- ½ cup beer, plus 2 tablespoons
- 1 cup crushed panko breadcrumbs
- oil for misting or cooking spray

Directions:
1. Peel onion, slice, and separate into rings.
2. In a large bowl, mix together the flour and salt. Add beer and stir until it stops foaming and makes a thick batter.
3. Place onion rings in batter and stir to coat.
4. Place breadcrumbs in a sealable plastic bag or container with lid.
5. Working with a few at a time, remove onion rings from batter, shaking off excess, and drop into breadcrumbs. Shake to coat, then lay out onion rings on cookie sheet or wax paper.
6. When finished, spray onion rings with oil or cooking spray and pile into air fryer basket.
7. Cook at 390°F/200°C for 5minutes. Shake basket and mist with oil. Cook 5minutes and mist again. Cook an additional 2 minutes, until golden brown and crispy.

Roasted Eggplant Halves With Herbed Ricotta

Servings: 3
Cooking Time: 20 Minutes
Ingredients:
- 3 5- to 6-ounce small eggplants, stemmed
- Olive oil spray
- ¼ teaspoon Table salt
- ¼ teaspoon Ground black pepper
- ½ cup Regular or low-fat ricotta
- 1½ tablespoons Minced fresh basil leaves
- 1¼ teaspoons Minced fresh oregano leaves
- Honey

Directions:
1. Preheat the air fryer to 325°F/160°C (or 330°F/165°C, if that's the closest setting).
2. Cut the eggplants in half lengthwise. Set them cut side up on your work surface. Using the tip of a paring knife, make a series of slits about three-quarters down into the flesh of each eggplant half; work at a 45-degree angle to the (former) stem across the vegetable and make the slits about ½ inch apart. Make a second set of equidistant slits at a 90-degree angle to the first slits, thus creating a crosshatch pattern in the vegetable.
3. Generously coat the cut sides of the eggplants with olive oil spray. Sprinkle the salt and pepper over the cut surfaces.
4. Set the eggplant halves cut side up in the basket with as much air space between them as possible. Air-fry undisturbed for 20 minutes, or until soft and golden.
5. Use kitchen tongs to gently transfer the eggplant halves to serving plates or a platter. Cool for 5 minutes.
6. Whisk the ricotta, basil, and oregano in a small bowl until well combined. Top the eggplant halves with this mixture. Drizzle the halves with honey to taste before serving warm.

Buttery Radish Wedges

Servings: 2
Cooking Time: 20 Minutes
Ingredients:
- 2 tbsp butter, melted
- 2 cloves garlic, minced
- ¼ tsp salt
- 20 radishes, quartered
- 2 tbsp feta cheese crumbles
- 1 tbsp chopped parsley

Directions:
1. Preheat air fryer to 370°F/185°C. Mix the butter, garlic, and salt in a bowl. Stir in radishes. Place the radish wedges in the frying basket and Roast for 10 minutes, shaking once. Transfer to a large serving dish and stir in feta cheese. Scatter with parsley and serve.

Mushrooms, Sautéed

Servings: 4
Cooking Time: 4 Minutes
Ingredients:
- 8 ounces sliced white mushrooms, rinsed and well drained
- ¼ teaspoon garlic powder
- 1 tablespoon Worcestershire sauce

Directions:
1. Place mushrooms in a large bowl and sprinkle with garlic powder and Worcestershire. Stir well to distribute seasonings evenly.
2. Place in air fryer basket and cook at 390°F for 4 minutes, until tender.

Grilled Lime Scallions

Servings: 6
Cooking Time: 15 Minutes
Ingredients:
- 2 bunches of scallions
- 1 tbsp olive oil
- 2 tsp lime juice
- Salt and pepper to taste
- ¼ tsp Italian seasoning
- 2 tsp lime zest

Directions:
1. Preheat air fryer to 370°F/185°C. Trim the scallions and cut them in half lengthwise. Place them in a bowl and add olive oil and lime juice. Toss to coat. Place the mix in the frying basket and Air Fry for 7 minutes, tossing once. Transfer to a serving dish and stir in salt, pepper, Italian seasoning and lime zest. Serve immediately.

Fingerling Potatoes

Servings: 4
Cooking Time: 15 Minutes
Ingredients:
- 1 pound fingerling potatoes
- 1 tablespoon light olive oil
- ½ teaspoon dried parsley
- ½ teaspoon lemon juice
- coarsely ground sea salt

Directions:
1. Cut potatoes in half lengthwise.
2. In a large bowl, combine potatoes, oil, parsley, and lemon juice. Stir well to coat potatoes.
3. Place potatoes in air fryer basket and cook at 360°F/180°C for 15 minutes or until lightly browned and tender inside.
4. Sprinkle with sea salt before serving.

Basic Corn On The Cob

Servings: 4
Cooking Time: 15 Minutes
Ingredients:
- 3 ears of corn, shucked and halved
- 2 tbsp butter, melted
- Salt and pepper to taste
- 1 tsp minced garlic
- 1 tsp paprika

Directions:
1. Preheat air fryer at 400ºF/205°C. Toss all ingredients in a bowl. Place corn in the frying basket and Bake for 7 minutes, turning once. Serve immediately.

Buttery Stuffed Tomatoes

Servings: 6
Cooking Time: 15 Minutes
Ingredients:
- 3 8-ounce round tomatoes
- ½ cup plus 1 tablespoon Plain panko bread crumbs (gluten-free, if a concern)
- 3 tablespoons (about ½ ounce) Finely grated Parmesan cheese
- 3 tablespoons Butter, melted and cooled
- 4 teaspoons Stemmed and chopped fresh parsley leaves
- 1 teaspoon Minced garlic
- ¼ teaspoon Table salt
- Up to ¼ teaspoon Red pepper flakes
- Olive oil spray

Directions:
1. Preheat the air fryer to 375°F/190°C.
2. Cut the tomatoes in half through their "equators" (that is, not through the stem ends). One at a time, gently squeeze the tomato halves over a trash can, using a clean finger to gently force out the seeds and most of the juice inside, working carefully so that the tomato doesn't lose its round shape or get crushed.
3. Stir the bread crumbs, cheese, butter, parsley, garlic, salt, and red pepper flakes in a bowl until the bread crumbs are moistened and the parsley is uniform throughout the mixture. Pile this mixture into the spaces left in the tomato halves. Press gently to compact the filling. Coat the tops of the tomatoes with olive oil spray.
4. Place the tomatoes cut side up in the basket. They may touch each other. Air-fry for 15 minutes, or until the filling is lightly browned and crunchy.
5. Use nonstick-safe spatula and kitchen tongs for balance to gently transfer the stuffed tomatoes to a platter or a cutting board. Cool for a couple of minutes before serving.

Farmers' Market Veggie Medley

Servings: 4
Cooking Time: 45 Minutes
Ingredients:
- 3 tsp grated Parmesan cheese
- ½ lb carrots, sliced
- ½ lb asparagus, sliced
- ½ lb zucchini, sliced
- 3 tbsp olive oil
- Salt and pepper to taste
- ½ tsp garlic powder
- 1 tbsp thyme, chopped

Directions:
1. Preheat air fryer to 390°F/200°C. Coat the carrots with some olive oil in a bowl. Air fry the carrots for 5 minutes. Meanwhile, mix the asparagus and zucchini together and drizzle with the remaining olive oil. Season with salt, pepper, and garlic powder.
2. When the time is over, slide the basket out and spread the zucchini-squash mixture on top of the carrots. Bake for 10-15 more minutes, stirring the vegetables several times during cooking. Sprinkle with Parmesan cheese and thyme. Serve and enjoy!

Crispy Cauliflower Puffs

Servings: 12
Cooking Time: 9 Minutes
Ingredients:
- 1½ cups Riced cauliflower
- 1 cup (about 4 ounces) Shredded Monterey Jack cheese
- ¾ cup Seasoned Italian-style panko bread crumbs (gluten-free, if a concern)
- 2 tablespoons plus 1 teaspoon All-purpose flour or potato starch
- 2 tablespoons plus 1 teaspoon Vegetable oil
- 1 plus 1 large yolk Large egg(s)
- ¾ teaspoon Table salt
- Vegetable oil spray

Directions:
1. Preheat the air fryer to 375°F/190°C.
2. Stir the riced cauliflower, cheese, bread crumbs, flour or potato starch, oil, egg(s) and egg yolk (if necessary), and salt in a large bowl to make a thick batter.
3. Using 2 tablespoons of the batter, form a compact ball between your clean, dry palms. Set it aside and continue forming more balls: 7 more for a small batch, 11 more for a medium batch, or 15 more for a large batch.
4. Generously coat the balls on all sides with vegetable oil spray. Set them in the basket with as much air space between them as possible. Air-fry undisturbed for 7 minutes, or until golden brown and crisp. If the machine is at 360°F/180°C, you may need to add 2 minutes to the cooking time.
5. Gently pour the contents of the basket onto a wire rack. Cool the puffs for 5 minutes before serving.

Balsamic Stuffed Mushrooms

Servings: 4
Cooking Time: 30 Minutes
Ingredients:
- ¼ cup chopped roasted red peppers
- 12 portobello mushroom caps
- 2 tsp grated Parmesan cheese
- 10 oz spinach, chopped
- 3 scallions, chopped
- ¼ cup chickpea flour
- 1 tsp garlic powder
- 1 tbsp balsamic vinegar
- ½ lemon

Directions:
1. Preheat air fryer to 360°F/180°C. In a bowl, squeeze any excess water from the spinach; discard the water. Stir in scallions, red pepper, chickpea flour, Parmesan cheese, garlic, and balsamic vinegar until well combined. Fill each mushroom cap with spinach mixture until covering the tops, pressing down slightly. Bake for 12 minutes until crispy. Drizzle with lemon juice before serving.

Moroccan-spiced Carrots

Servings: 4
Cooking Time: 30 Minutes
Ingredients:
- 1¼ pounds Baby carrots
- 2 tablespoons Butter, melted and cooled
- 1 teaspoon Mild smoked paprika
- 1 teaspoon Ground cumin
- ¾ teaspoon Ground coriander
- ¾ teaspoon Ground dried ginger
- ¼ teaspoon Ground cinnamon
- ½ teaspoon Table salt
- ¼ teaspoon Ground black pepper

Directions:
1. Preheat the air fryer to 400°F/205°C.
2. Toss the carrots, melted butter, smoked paprika, cumin, coriander, ginger, cinnamon, salt, and pepper in a large bowl until the carrots are evenly and thoroughly coated.
3. When the machine is at temperature, scrape the carrots into the basket, spreading them into as close to one layer as you can. Air-fry for 30 minutes, tossing and rearranging the carrots every 8 minutes (that is, three times), until crisp-tender and lightly browned in spots.
4. Pour the contents of the basket into a serving bowl or platter. Cool for a couple of minutes, then serve warm or at room temperature.

Rosemary Roasted Potatoes With Lemon

Cooking Time: 12 Minutes
Servings: 4
Ingredients:
- 1 pound small red-skinned potatoes, halved or cut into bite-sized chunks
- 1 tablespoon olive oil
- 1 teaspoon finely chopped fresh rosemary
- ¼ teaspoon salt
- freshly ground black pepper
- 1 tablespoon lemon zest

Directions:
1. Preheat the air fryer to 400°F/205°C.
2. Toss the potatoes with the olive oil, rosemary, salt and freshly ground black pepper.
3. Air-fry for 12 minutes (depending on the size of the chunks), tossing the potatoes a few times throughout the cooking process.
4. As soon as the potatoes are tender to a knifepoint, toss them with the lemon zest and more salt if desired.

Smoked Avocado Wedges

Servings: 4
Cooking Time: 15 Minutes
Ingredients:
- ½ tsp smoked paprika
- 2 tsp olive oil
- ½ lime, juiced
- 8 peeled avocado wedges
- 1 tsp chipotle powder
- ¼ tsp salt

Directions:
1. Preheat air fryer to 400°F/205°C. Drizzle the avocado wedges with olive oil and lime juice. In a bowl, combine chipotle powder, smoked paprika, and salt. Sprinkle over the avocado wedges. Place them in the frying basket and Air Fry for 7 minutes. Serve immediately.

Tower Air Fryer Cookbook

Desserts And Sweets

Cherry Cheesecake Rolls

Servings: 6
Cooking Time: 30 Minutes
Ingredients:
- 1 can crescent rolls
- 4 oz cream cheese
- 1 tbsp cherry preserves
- 1/3 cup sliced fresh cherries

Directions:
1. Roll out the dough into a large rectangle on a flat work surface. Cut the dough into 12 rectangles by cutting 3 cuts across and 2 cuts down. In a microwave-safe bowl, soften cream cheese for 15 seconds. Stir together with cherry preserves. Mound 2 tsp of the cherries-cheese mix on each piece of dough. Carefully spread the mixture but not on the edges. Top with 2 tsp of cherries each. Roll each triangle to make a cylinder.
2. Preheat air fryer to 350°F/175°C. Place the first batch of the rolls in the greased air fryer. Spray the rolls with cooking oil and Bake for 8 minutes. Let cool in the air fryer for 2-3 minutes before removing. Serve.

S' mores Pockets

Servings: 6
Cooking Time: 5 Minutes
Ingredients:
- 12 sheets phyllo dough, thawed
- 1½ cups butter, melted
- ¾ cup graham cracker crumbs
- 1 (7-ounce) Giant Hershey's® milk chocolate bar
- 12 marshmallows, cut in half

Directions:
1. Place one sheet of the phyllo on a large cutting board. Keep the rest of the phyllo sheets covered with a slightly damp, clean kitchen towel. Brush the phyllo sheet generously with some melted butter. Place a second phyllo sheet on top of the first and brush it with more butter. Repeat with one more phyllo sheet until you have a stack of 3 phyllo sheets with butter brushed between the layers. Cover the phyllo sheets with one quarter of the graham cracker crumbs leaving a 1-inch border on one of the short ends of the rectangle. Cut the phyllo sheets lengthwise into 3 strips.
2. Take 2 of the strips and crisscross them to form a cross with the empty borders at the top and to the left. Place 2 of the chocolate rectangles in the center of the cross. Place 4 of the marshmallow halves on top of the chocolate. Now fold the pocket together by folding the bottom phyllo strip up over the chocolate and marshmallows. Then fold the right side over, then the top strip down and finally the left side over. Brush all the edges generously with melted butter to seal shut. Repeat with the next three sheets of phyllo, until all the sheets have been used. You will be able to make 2 pockets with every second batch because you will have an extra graham cracker crumb strip from the previous set of sheets.
3. Preheat the air fryer to 350°F/175°C.
4. Transfer 3 pockets at a time to the air fryer basket. Air-fry at 350°F/175°C for 4 to 5 minutes, until the phyllo dough is light brown in color. Flip the pockets over halfway through the cooking process. Repeat with the remaining 3 pockets.
5. Serve warm.

Home-style Pumpkin Pie Pudding

Servings: 4
Cooking Time: 30 Minutes
Ingredients:
- 1 cup canned pumpkin purée
- ¼ cup sugar
- 3 tbsp all-purpose flour
- 1 tbsp butter, melted
- 1 egg
- 1 orange, zested
- 2 tbsp milk
- 1 tsp vanilla extract
- 4 vanilla wafers, crumbled

Directions:
1. Preheat air fryer to 350°F/175°C. Beat the pumpkin puree, sugar, flour, butter, egg, orange zest, milk, and vanilla until well-mixed. Spritz a baking pan with the cooking spray, then pour the pumpkin mix in. Place it in the air fryer and Bake for 11-17 minutes or until golden brown. Take the pudding out of the fryer and let it chill. Serve with vanilla wager crumbs.

Lemon Iced Donut Balls

Servings: 6
Cooking Time: 25 Minutes
Ingredients:
- 1 can jumbo biscuit dough
- 2 tsp lemon juice
- ½ cup icing sugar, sifted

Directions:
1. Preheat air fryer to 360°F/180°C. Divide the biscuit dough into 16 equal portions. Roll the dough into balls of 1½ inches thickness. Place the donut holes in the greased frying basket and Air Fry for 8 minutes, flipping once. Mix the icing sugar and lemon juice until smooth. Spread the icing over the top of the donuts. Leave to set a bit. Serve.

Mixed Berry Pie

Servings: 4
Cooking Time: 25 Minutes
Ingredients:
- 2/3 cup blackberries, cut into thirds
- ¼ cup sugar
- 2 tbsp cornstarch
- ¼ tsp vanilla extract
- ¼ tsp peppermint extract
- ½ tsp lemon zest
- 1 cup sliced strawberries
- 1 cup raspberries
- 1 refrigerated piecrust

Tower Air Fryer Cookbook

- 1 large egg

Directions:
1. Mix the sugar, cornstarch, vanilla, peppermint extract, and lemon zest in a bowl. Toss in all berries gently until combined. Pour into a greased dish. On a clean workspace, lay out the dough and cut into a 7-inch diameter round. Cover the baking dish with the round and crimp the edges. With a knife, cut 4 slits in the top to vent.
2. Beat 1 egg and 1 tbsp of water to make an egg wash. Brush the egg wash over the crust. Preheat air fryer to 350°F/175°C. Put the baking dish into the frying basket. Bake for 15 minutes or until the crust is golden and the berries are bubbling through the vents. Remove from the air fryer and let cool for 15 minutes. Serve warm.

Nutty Banana Bread

Servings: 6
Cooking Time: 30 Minutes
Ingredients:
- 2 bananas
- 2 tbsp ground flaxseed
- ¼ cup milk
- 1 tbsp apple cider vinegar
- 1 tbsp vanilla extract
- ½ tsp ground cinnamon
- 2 tbsp honey
- ½ cup oat flour
- ½ tsp baking soda
- 3 tbsp butter

Directions:
1. Preheat air fryer to 320°F/160°C. Using a fork, mash the bananas until chunky. Mix in flaxseed, milk, apple vinegar, vanilla extract, cinnamon, and honey. Finally, toss in oat flour and baking soda until smooth but still chunky. Divide the batter between 6 cupcake molds. Top with one and a half teaspoons of butter each and swirl it a little. Bake for 18 minutes until golden brown and puffy. Let cool completely before serving.

Carrot-oat Cake Muffins

Servings: 4
Cooking Time: 20 Minutes
Ingredients:
- 3 tbsp butter, softened
- ¼ cup brown sugar
- 1 tbsp maple syrup
- 1 egg white
- ½ tsp vanilla extract
- 1/3 cup finely grated carrots
- ½ cup oatmeal
- 1/3 cup flour
- ½ tsp baking soda
- ¼ cup raisins

Directions:
1. Preheat air fryer to 350°F/175°C. Mix the butter, brown sugar, and maple syrup until smooth, then toss in the egg white, vanilla, and carrots. Whisk well and add the oatmeal, flour, baking soda, and raisins. Divide the mixture between muffin cups. Bake in the fryer for 8-10 minutes.

Strawberry Donuts

Servings: 4
Cooking Time: 55 Minutes
Ingredients:
- ¾ cup Greek yogurt
- 2 tbsp maple syrup
- 1 tbsp vanilla extract
- 2 tsp active dry yeast
- 1 ½ cups all-purpose flour
- 3 tbsp milk
- ½ cup strawberry jam

Directions:
1. Preheat air fryer to 350°F/175°C. Whisk the Greek yogurt, maple syrup, vanilla extract, and yeast until well combined. Then toss in flour until you get a sticky dough. Let rest covered for 10 minutes. Flour a parchment paper on a flat surface, lay the dough, sprinkle with some flour, and flatten to ½-inch thick with a rolling pin.
2. Using a 3-inch cookie cutter, cut the donuts. Repeat the process until no dough is left. Place the donuts in the basket and let rise for 15-20 minutes. Spread some milk on top of each donut and Air Fry for 4 minutes. Turn the donuts, spread more milk, and Air Fry for 4 more minutes until golden brown. Let cool for 15 minutes. Using a knife, cut the donuts 3/4 lengthwise, brush 1 tbsp of strawberry jam on each and close them. Serve.

Coconut Rice Cake

Servings: 8
Cooking Time: 30 Minutes
Ingredients:
- 1 cup all-natural coconut water
- 1 cup unsweetened coconut milk
- 1 teaspoon almond extract
- ¼ teaspoon salt
- 4 tablespoons honey
- cooking spray
- ¾ cup raw jasmine rice
- 2 cups sliced or cubed fruit

Directions:
1. In a medium bowl, mix together the coconut water, coconut milk, almond extract, salt, and honey.
2. Spray air fryer baking pan with cooking spray and add the rice.
3. Pour liquid mixture over rice.
4. Cook at 360°F/180°C for 15minutes. Stir and cook for 15 minutes longer or until rice grains are tender.
5. Allow cake to cool slightly. Run a dull knife around edge of cake, inside the pan. Turn the cake out onto a platter and garnish with fruit.

Fried Cannoli Wontons

Servings: 10
Cooking Time: 8 Minutes
Ingredients:
- 8 ounces Neufchâtel cream cheese
- ¼ cup powdered sugar
- 1 teaspoon vanilla extract
- ¼ teaspoon salt
- ¼ cup mini chocolate chips
- 2 tablespoons chopped pecans (optional)
- 20 wonton wrappers
- ¼ cup filtered water

Directions:
1. Preheat the air fryer to 370°F/185°C.
2. In a large bowl, use a hand mixer to combine the cream cheese with the powdered sugar, vanilla, and salt. Fold in the chocolate chips and pecans. Set aside.

3. Lay the wonton wrappers out on a flat, smooth surface and place a bowl with the filtered water next to them.
4. Use a teaspoon to evenly divide the cream cheese mixture among the 20 wonton wrappers, placing the batter in the center of the wontons.
5. Wet the tip of your index finger, and gently moisten the outer edges of the wrapper. Then fold each wrapper until it creates a secure pocket.
6. Liberally spray the air fryer basket with olive oil mist.
7. Place the wontons into the basket, and cook for 5 to 8 minutes. When the outer edges begin to brown, remove the wontons from the air fryer basket. Repeat cooking with remaining wontons.
8. Serve warm.

Cheesecake Wontons

Servings: 16
Cooking Time: 6 Minutes
Ingredients:
- ¼ cup Regular or low-fat cream cheese (not fat-free)
- 2 tablespoons Granulated white sugar
- 1½ tablespoons Egg yolk
- ¼ teaspoon Vanilla extract
- ⅛ teaspoon Table salt
- 1½ tablespoons All-purpose flour
- 16 Wonton wrappers (vegetarian, if a concern)
- Vegetable oil spray

Directions:
1. Preheat the air fryer to 400°F/205°C.
2. Using a flatware fork, mash the cream cheese, sugar, egg yolk, and vanilla in a small bowl until smooth. Add the salt and flour and continue mashing until evenly combined.
3. Set a wonton wrapper on a clean, dry work surface so that one corner faces you (so that it looks like a diamond on your work surface). Set 1 teaspoon of the cream cheese mixture in the middle of the wrapper but just above a horizontal line that would divide the wrapper in half. Dip your clean finger in water and run it along the edges of the wrapper. Fold the corner closest to you up and over the filling, lining it up with the corner farthest from you, thereby making a stuffed triangle. Press gently to seal. Wet the two triangle tips nearest you, then fold them up and together over the filling. Gently press together to seal and fuse. Set aside and continue making more stuffed wontons, 11 more for the small batch, 15 more for the medium batch, or 23 more for the large one.
4. Lightly coat the stuffed wrappers on all sides with vegetable oil spray. Set them with the fused corners up in the basket with as much air space between them as possible. Air-fry undisturbed for 6 minutes, or until golden brown and crisp.
5. Gently dump the contents of the basket onto a wire rack. Cool for at least 5 minutes before serving.

Mini Carrot Cakes

Servings: 6
Cooking Time: 25 Minutes
Ingredients:
- 1 cup grated carrots
- ¼ cup raw honey
- ¼ cup olive oil
- ½ tsp vanilla extract
- ½ tsp lemon zest
- 1 egg
- ¼ cup applesauce
- 1 1/3 cups flour
- ¾ tsp baking powder
- ½ tsp baking soda
- ½ tsp ground cinnamon
- ¼ tsp ground nutmeg
- ⅛ tsp ground ginger
- ⅛ tsp salt
- ¼ cup chopped hazelnuts
- 2 tbsp chopped sultanas

Directions:
1. Preheat air fryer to 380°F/195°C. Combine the carrots, honey, olive oil, vanilla extract, lemon zest, egg, and applesauce in a bowl. Sift the flour, baking powder, baking soda, cinnamon, nutmeg, ginger, and salt in a separate bowl. Add the wet ingredients to the dry ingredients, mixing until just combined. Fold in the hazelnuts and sultanas. Fill greased muffin cups three-quarters full with the batter, and place them in the frying basket. Bake for 10-12 minutes until a toothpick inserted in the center of a cupcake comes out clean. Serve and enjoy!

Black And Blue Clafoutis

Servings: 2
Cooking Time: 15 minutes
Ingredients:
- 6-inch pie pan
- 3 large eggs
- ½ cup sugar
- 1 teaspoon vanilla extract
- 2 tablespoons butter, melted 1 cup milk
- ½ cup all-purpose flour*
- 1 cup blackberries
- 1 cup blueberries
- 2 tablespoons confectioners' sugar

Directions:
1. Preheat the air fryer to 320°F/160°C.
2. Combine the eggs and sugar in a bowl and whisk vigorously until smooth, lighter in color and well combined. Add the vanilla extract, butter and milk and whisk together well. Add the flour and whisk just until no lumps or streaks of white remain.
3. Scatter half the blueberries and blackberries in a greased (6-inch) pie pan or cake pan. Pour half of the batter (about 1¼ cups) on top of the berries and transfer the tart pan to the air fryer basket. You can use an aluminum foil sling to help with this by taking a long piece of aluminum foil, folding it in half lengthwise twice until it is roughly 26-inches by 3-inches. Place this under the pie dish and hold the ends of the foil to move the pie dish in and out of the air fryer basket. Tuck the ends of the foil beside the pie dish while it cooks in the air fryer.
4. Air-fry at 320°F/160°C for 15 minutes or until the clafoutis has puffed up and is still a little jiggly in the center. Remove the clafoutis from the air fryer, invert it onto a plate and let it cool while you bake the second batch. Serve the clafoutis warm, dusted with confectioners' sugar on top.

Fudgy Brownie Cake

Servings: 6
Cooking Time: 25-35 Minutes
Ingredients:
- 6½ tablespoons All-purpose flour
- ¼ cup plus 1 teaspoon Unsweetened cocoa powder

- ½ teaspoon Baking powder
- ¼ teaspoon Table salt
- 6½ tablespoons Butter, at room temperature
- 9½ tablespoons Granulated white sugar
- 1 egg plus 1 large egg white Large egg(s)
- ¾ teaspoon Vanilla extract
- Baking spray (see here)

Directions:
1. Preheat the air fryer to 325°F/160°C (or 330°F/165°C, if that's the closest setting).
2. Mix the flour, cocoa powder, baking powder, and salt in a small bowl until well combined.
3. Using an electric hand mixer at medium speed, beat the butter and sugar in a medium bowl until creamy and smooth, about 3 minutes, occasionally scraping down the inside of the bowl.
4. Beat in the egg(s) and the white or yolk (as necessary), as well as the vanilla, until smooth. Turn off the beaters and add the flour mixture. Beat at low speed until thick and smooth.
5. Use the baking spray to generously coat the inside of a 6-inch round cake pan for a small batch, a 7-inch round cake pan for a medium batch, or an 8-inch round cake pan for a large batch. Scrape and spread the batter into the pan, smoothing the batter out to an even layer.
6. Set the pan in the basket and air-fry for 25 minutes for a 6-inch layer, 30 minutes for a 7-inch layer, or 35 minutes for an 8-inch layer, or until the cake is set but soft to the touch. Start checking it at the 20-minute mark to know where you are.
7. Use hot pads or silicone baking mitts to transfer the cake pan to a wire rack. Cool for at least 1 hour or up to 4 hours. Using a nonstick-safe knife, slice the cake into wedges right in the pan and lift them out one by one.

Cherry Hand Pies

Servings: 8
Cooking Time: 8 Minutes
Ingredients:
- 4 cups frozen or canned pitted tart cherries (if using canned, drain and pat dry)
- 2 teaspoons lemon juice
- ½ cup sugar
- ¼ cup cornstarch
- 1 teaspoon vanilla extract
- 1 Basic Pie Dough (see the preceding recipe) or store-bought pie dough

Directions:
1. In a medium saucepan, place the cherries and lemon juice and cook over medium heat for 10 minutes, or until the cherries begin to break down.
2. In a small bowl, stir together the sugar and cornstarch. Pour the sugar mixture into the cherries, stirring constantly. Cook the cherry mixture over low heat for 2 to 3 minutes, or until thickened. Remove from the heat and stir in the vanilla extract. Allow the cherry mixture to cool to room temperature, about 30 minutes.
3. Meanwhile, bring the pie dough to room temperature. Divide the dough into 8 equal pieces. Roll out the dough to ¼-inch thickness in circles. Place ¼ cup filling in the center of each rolled dough. Fold the dough to create a half-circle. Using a fork, press around the edges to seal the hand pies. Pierce the top of the pie with a fork for steam release while cooking. Continue until 8 hand pies are formed.
4. Preheat the air fryer to 350°F/175°C.
5. Place a single layer of hand pies in the air fryer basket and spray with cooking spray. Cook for 8 to 10 minutes or until golden brown and cooked through.

Pumpkin Brownies

Servings: 4
Cooking Time: 30 Minutes
Ingredients:
- ¼ cup canned pumpkin
- ½ cup maple syrup
- 2 eggs, beaten
- 1 tbsp vanilla extract
- ¼ cup tapioca flour
- ¼ cup flour
- ½ tsp baking powder

Directions:
1. Preheat air fryer to 320°F/160°C. Mix the pumpkin, maple syrup, eggs, and vanilla extract in a bowl. Toss in tapioca flour, flour, and baking powder until smooth. Pour the batter into a small round cake pan and Bake for 20 minutes until a toothpick comes out clean. Let cool completely before slicing into 4 brownies. Serve and enjoy!

Honey-roasted Mixed Nuts

Servings: 8
Cooking Time: 15 Minutes
Ingredients:
- ½ cup raw, shelled pistachios
- ½ cup raw almonds
- 1 cup raw walnuts
- 2 tablespoons filtered water
- 2 tablespoons honey
- 1 tablespoon vegetable oil
- 2 tablespoons sugar
- ½ teaspoon salt

Directions:
1. Preheat the air fryer to 300°F/150°C.
2. Lightly spray an air-fryer-safe pan with olive oil; then place the pistachios, almonds, and walnuts inside the pan and place the pan inside the air fryer basket.
3. Cook for 15 minutes, shaking the basket every 5 minutes to rotate the nuts.
4. While the nuts are roasting, boil the water in a small pan and stir in the honey and oil. Continue to stir while cooking until the water begins to evaporate and a thick sauce is formed. Note: The sauce should stick to the back of a wooden spoon when mixed. Turn off the heat.
5. Remove the nuts from the air fryer (cooking should have just completed) and spoon the nuts into the stovetop pan. Use a spatula to coat the nuts with the honey syrup.
6. Line a baking sheet with parchment paper and spoon the nuts onto the sheet. Lightly sprinkle the sugar and salt over the nuts and let cool in the refrigerator for at least 2 hours.
7. When the honey and sugar have hardened, store the nuts in an airtight container in the refrigerator.

Chocolate Macaroons

Servings: 16
Cooking Time: 8 Minutes
Ingredients:
- 2 Large egg white(s), at room temperature
- ⅛ teaspoon Table salt
- ½ cup Granulated white sugar

- 1½ cups Unsweetened shredded coconut
- 3 tablespoons Unsweetened cocoa powder

Directions:
1. Preheat the air fryer to 375°F/190°C.
2. Using an electric mixer at high speed, beat the egg white(s) and salt in a medium or large bowl until stiff peaks can be formed when the turned-off beaters are dipped into the mixture.
3. Still working with the mixer at high speed, beat in the sugar in a slow stream until the meringue is shiny and thick.
4. Scrape down and remove the beaters. Fold in the coconut and cocoa with a rubber spatula until well combined, working carefully to deflate the meringue as little as possible.
5. Scoop up 2 tablespoons of the mixture. Wet your clean hands and roll that little bit of coconut bliss into a ball. Set it aside and continue making more balls: 7 more for a small batch, 15 more for a medium batch, or 23 more for a large one.
6. Line the bottom of the machine's basket or the basket attachment with parchment paper. Set the balls on the parchment with as much air space between them as possible. Air-fry undisturbed for 8 minutes, or until dry, set, and lightly browned.
7. Use a nonstick-safe spatula to transfer the macaroons to a wire rack. Cool for at least 10 minutes before serving. Or cool to room temperature, about 30 minutes, then store in a sealed container at room temperature for up to 3 days.

Giant Buttery Oatmeal Cookie

Servings: 4
Cooking Time: 16 Minutes
Ingredients:
- 1 cup Rolled oats (not quick-cooking or steel-cut oats)
- ½ cup All-purpose flour
- ½ teaspoon Baking soda
- ½ teaspoon Ground cinnamon
- ½ teaspoon Table salt
- 3½ tablespoons Butter, at room temperature
- ⅓ cup Packed dark brown sugar
- 1½ tablespoons Granulated white sugar
- 3 tablespoons (or 1 medium egg, well beaten) Pasteurized egg substitute, such as Egg Beaters
- ¾ teaspoon Vanilla extract
- ⅓ cup Chopped pecans
- Baking spray

Directions:
1. Preheat the air fryer to 350°F/175°C.
2. Stir the oats, flour, baking soda, cinnamon, and salt in a bowl until well combined.
3. Using an electric hand mixer at medium speed, beat the butter, brown sugar, and granulated white sugar until creamy and thick, about 3 minutes, scraping down the inside of the bowl occasionally. Beat in the egg substitute or egg (as applicable) and vanilla until uniform.
4. Scrape down and remove the beaters. Fold in the flour mixture and pecans with a rubber spatula just until all the flour is moistened and the nuts are even throughout the dough.
5. For a small air fryer, coat the inside of a 6-inch round cake pan with baking spray. For a medium air fryer, coat the inside of a 7-inch round cake pan with baking spray. And for a large air fryer, coat the inside of an 8-inch round cake pan with baking spray. Scrape and gently press the dough into the prepared pan, spreading it into an even layer to the perimeter.
6. Set the pan in the basket and air-fry undisturbed for 16 minutes, or until puffed and browned.
7. Transfer the pan to a wire rack and cool for 10 minutes. Loosen the cookie from the perimeter with a spatula, then invert the pan onto a cutting board and let the cookie come free. Remove the pan and reinvert the cookie onto the wire rack. Cool for 5 minutes more before slicing into wedges to serve.

Famous Chocolate Lava Cake

Servings: 4
Cooking Time: 15 Minutes
Ingredients:
- ¼ cup flour
- 1 tbsp cocoa powder
- ⅛ tsp salt
- ½ tsp baking powder
- 1 tsp vanilla extract
- ¼ cup raw honey
- 1 egg, beaten
- 2 tbsp olive oil
- 2 tbsp icing sugar, to dust

Directions:
1. Preheat air fryer to 380°F/195°C. Sift the flour, cocoa powder, salt, vanilla, and baking powder in a bowl. Add in honey, egg, and olive oil and stir to combine. Divide the batter evenly among greased ramekins. Put the filled ramekins inside the air fryer and Bake for 10 minutes. Remove the lava cakes from the fryer and slide a knife around the outside edge of each cake. Turn each ramekin upside down on a saucer and serve dusted with icing sugar.

Vanilla-strawberry Muffins

Servings: 4
Cooking Time: 25 Minutes
Ingredients:
- ¼ cup diced strawberries
- 2 tbsp powdered sugar
- 1 cup flour
- ½ tsp baking soda
- 1/3 cup granulated sugar
- ¼ tsp salt
- 1 tsp vanilla extract
- 1 egg
- 1 tbsp butter, melted
- ½ cup diced strawberries
- 2 tbsp chopped walnuts
- 6 tbsp butter, softened
- 1 ½ cups powdered sugar
- 1/8 tsp peppermint extract

Directions:
1. Preheat air fryer at 375°F/190°C. Combine flour, baking soda, granulated sugar, and salt in a bowl. In another bowl, combine the vanilla, egg, walnuts and melted butter. Pour wet ingredients into dry ingredients and toss to combine. Fold in half of the strawberries and spoon mixture into 8 greased silicone cupcake liners.
2. Place cupcakes in the frying basket and Bake for 6-8 minutes. Let cool onto a cooling rack for 10 minutes. Blend the remaining strawberries in a food processor until smooth. Slowly add powdered sugar to softened butter while beating in a bowl. Stir in peppermint extract and puréed strawberries until blended. Spread over cooled cupcakes. Serve sprinkled with powdered sugar

Party S'mores

Servings: 6
Cooking Time: 15 Minutes
Ingredients:
- 2 dark chocolate bars, cut into 12 pieces
- 12 buttermilk biscuits
- 12 marshmallows

Directions:
1. Preheat air fryer to 350°F/175°C. Place 6 biscuits in the air fryer. Top each square with a piece of dark chocolate. Bake for 2 minutes. Add a marshmallow to each piece of chocolate. Cook for another minute. Remove and top with another piece of biscuit. Serve warm.

Chocolate Bars

Servings: 4
Cooking Time: 30 Minutes
Ingredients:
- 2 tbsp chocolate toffee chips
- ¼ cup chopped pecans
- 2 tbsp raisins
- 1 tbsp dried blueberries
- 2 tbsp maple syrup
- ¼ cup light brown sugar
- 1/3 cup peanut butter
- 2 tbsp chocolate chips
- 2 tbsp butter, melted
- ½ tsp vanilla extract
- Salt to taste

Directions:
1. Preheat air fryer at 350ºF/175°C. In a bowl, combine the pecans, maple syrup, sugar, peanut butter, toffee chips, raisins, dried blueberries, chocolate chips, butter, vanilla extract, and salt. Press mixture into a lightly greased cake pan and cover it with aluminum foil. Place cake pan in the frying basket and Bake for 15 minutes. Remove the foil and cook for 5 more minutes. Let cool completely for 15 minutes. Turn over on a place and cut into 6 bars. Enjoy!

Molten Chocolate Almond Cakes

Servings: 3
Cooking Time: 13 Minutes
Ingredients:
- butter and flour for the ramekins
- 4 ounces bittersweet chocolate, chopped
- ½ cup (1 stick) unsalted butter
- 2 eggs
- 2 egg yolks
- ¼ cup sugar
- ½ teaspoon pure vanilla extract, or almond extract
- 1 tablespoon all-purpose flour
- 3 tablespoons ground almonds
- 8 to 12 semisweet chocolate discs (or 4 chunks of chocolate)
- cocoa powder or powdered sugar, for dusting
- toasted almonds, coarsely chopped

Directions:
1. Butter and flour three (6-ounce) ramekins. (Butter the ramekins and then coat the butter with flour by shaking it around in the ramekin and dumping out any excess.)
2. Melt the chocolate and butter together, either in the microwave or in a double boiler. In a separate bowl, beat the eggs, egg yolks and sugar together until light and smooth. Add the vanilla extract. Whisk the chocolate mixture into the egg mixture. Stir in the flour and ground almonds.
3. Preheat the air fryer to 330°F/165°C.
4. Transfer the batter carefully to the buttered ramekins, filling halfway. Place two or three chocolate discs in the center of the batter and then fill the ramekins to ½-inch below the top with the remaining batter. Place the ramekins into the air fryer basket and air-fry at 330°F for 13 minutes. The sides of the cake should be set, but the centers should be slightly soft. Remove the ramekins from the air fryer and let the cakes sit for 5 minutes. (If you'd like the cake a little less molten, air-fry for 14 minutes and let the cakes sit for 4 minutes.)
5. Run a butter knife around the edge of the ramekins and invert the cakes onto a plate. Lift the ramekin off the plate slowly and carefully so that the cake doesn't break. Dust with cocoa powder or powdered sugar and serve with a scoop of ice cream and some coarsely chopped toasted almonds.

Carrot Cake With Cream Cheese Icing

Servings: 6
Cooking Time: 55 Minutes
Ingredients:
- 1¼ cups all-purpose flour
- 1 teaspoon baking powder
- ½ teaspoon baking soda
- 1 teaspoon ground cinnamon
- ¼ teaspoon ground nutmeg
- ¼ teaspoon salt
- 2 cups grated carrot (about 3 to 4 medium carrots or 2 large)
- ¾ cup granulated sugar
- ¼ cup brown sugar
- 2 eggs
- ¾ cup canola or vegetable oil
- For the icing:
- 8 ounces cream cheese, softened at room , Temperature: 8 tablespoons butter (4 ounces or 1 stick), softened at room , Temperature: 1 cup powdered sugar
- 1 teaspoon pure vanilla extract

Directions:
1. Grease a 7-inch cake pan.
2. Combine the flour, baking powder, baking soda, cinnamon, nutmeg and salt in a bowl. Add the grated carrots and toss well. In a separate bowl, beat the sugars and eggs together until light and frothy. Drizzle in the oil, beating constantly. Fold the egg mixture into the dry ingredients until everything is just combined and you no longer see any traces of flour. Pour the batter into the cake pan and wrap the pan completely in greased aluminum foil.
3. Preheat the air fryer to 350°F/175°C.
4. Lower the cake pan into the air fryer basket using a sling made of aluminum foil (fold a piece of aluminum foil into a strip about 2-inches wide by 24-inches long). Fold the ends of the aluminum foil into the air fryer, letting them rest on top of the cake. Air-fry for 40 minutes. Remove the aluminum foil cover and air-fry for an additional 15 minutes or until a skewer inserted into the center of the cake comes out clean and the top is nicely browned.
5. While the cake is cooking, beat the cream cheese, butter, powdered sugar and vanilla extract together using a hand

mixer, stand mixer or food processor (or a lot of elbow grease!).
6. Remove the cake pan from the air fryer and let the cake cool in the cake pan for 10 minutes or so. Then remove the cake from the pan and let it continue to cool completely. Frost the cake with the cream cheese icing and serve.

Apple-carrot Cupcakes
Servings: 6
Cooking Time: 25 Minutes
Ingredients:
- 1 cup grated carrot
- 1/3 cup chopped apple
- ¼ cup raisins
- 2 tbsp maple syrup
- 1/3 cup milk
- 1 cup oat flour
- 1 tsp ground cinnamon
- ½ tsp ground ginger
- 1 tsp baking powder
- ½ tsp baking soda
- 1/3 cup chopped walnuts

Directions:
1. Preheat air fryer to 350°F/175°C. Combine carrot, apple, raisins, maple syrup, and milk in a bowl. Stir in oat flour, cinnamon, ginger, baking powder, and baking soda until combined. Divide the batter between 6 cupcake molds. Top with chopped walnuts each and press down a little. Bake for 15 minutes until golden brown and a toothpick comes out clean. Let cool completely before serving.

Nutty Cookies
Servings: 6
Cooking Time: 25 Minutes
Ingredients:
- ¼ cup pistachios
- ¼ cup evaporated cane sugar
- ¼ cup raw almonds
- ½ cup almond flour
- 1 tsp pure vanilla extract
- 1 egg white

Directions:
1. Preheat air fryer to 375°F/190°C. Add ¼ cup of pistachios and almonds into a food processor. Pulse until they resemble crumbles. Roughly chop the rest of the pistachios with a sharp knife. Combine all ingredients in a large bowl until completely incorporated. Form 6 equally-sized balls and transfer to the parchment-lined frying basket. Allow for 1 inch between each portion. Bake for 7 minutes. Cool on a wire rack for 5 minutes. Serve and enjoy.

Fried Snickers Bars
Servings: 8
Cooking Time: 4 Minutes
Ingredients:
- 1/3 cup All-purpose flour
- 1 Large egg white(s), beaten until foamy
- 1½ cups (6 ounces) Vanilla wafer cookie crumbs
- 8 Fun-size (0.6-ounce/17-gram) Snickers bars, frozen
- Vegetable oil spray

Directions:
1. Preheat the air fryer to 400°F/205°C.
2. Set up and fill three shallow soup plates or small pie plates on your counter: one for the flour, one for the beaten egg white(s), and one for the cookie crumbs.
3. Unwrap the frozen candy bars. Dip one in the flour, turning it to coat on all sides. Gently shake off any excess, then set it in the beaten egg white(s). Turn it to coat all sides, even the ends, then let any excess egg white slip back into the rest. Set the candy bar in the cookie crumbs. Turn to coat on all sides, even the ends. Dip the candy bar back in the egg white(s) a second time, then into the cookie crumbs a second time, making sure you have an even coating all around. Coat the covered candy bar all over with vegetable oil spray. Set aside so you can dip and coat the remaining candy bars.
4. Set the coated candy bars in the basket with as much air space between them as possible. Air-fry undisturbed for 4 minutes, or until golden brown.
5. Remove the basket from the machine and let the candy bars cool in the basket for 10 minutes. Use a nonstick-safe spatula to transfer them to a wire rack and cool for 5 minutes more before chowing down.

Cinnamon Pear Cheesecake
Servings: 6
Cooking Time: 60 Minutes + Cooling Time
Ingredients:
- 16 oz cream cheese, softened
- 1 cup crumbled graham crackers
- 4 peeled pears, sliced
- 1 tsp vanilla extract
- 1 tbsp brown sugar
- 1 tsp ground cinnamon
- 1 egg
- 1 cup condensed milk
- 2 tbsp white sugar
- 1 ½ tsp butter, melted

Directions:
1. Preheat air fryer to 350°F/175°C. Place the crumbled graham cracker, white sugar, and butter in a large bowl and stir to combine. Spoon the mixture into a greased pan and press around the edges to flatten it against the dish. Place the pan into the frying basket and Bake for 5 minutes. Remove and let it cool for 30 minutes to harden.
2. Place the cream cheese, vanilla extract, brown sugar, cinnamon, condensed milk and egg in a large bowl and whip until the ingredients are thoroughly mixed. Arrange the pear slices on the cooled crust and spoon the wet mixture over. Level the top with a spatula. Place the pan in the frying basket. Bake for 40 minutes. Allow to cool completely. Serve and enjoy!

Baked Apple Crisp
Servings: 4
Cooking Time: 23 Minutes
Ingredients:
- 2 large Granny Smith apples, peeled, cored, and chopped
- ¼ cup granulated sugar
- ¼ cup plus 2 teaspoons flour, divided
- 2 teaspoons milk
- ¼ teaspoon cinnamon
- ¼ cup oats
- ¼ cup brown sugar
- 2 tablespoons unsalted butter
- ⅛ teaspoon baking powder

- ⅛ teaspoon salt

Directions:
1. Preheat the air fryer to 350°F/175°C.
2. In a medium bowl, mix the apples, the granulated sugar, 2 teaspoons of the flour, the milk, and the cinnamon.
3. Spray 4 oven-safe ramekins with cooking spray. Divide the filling among the four ramekins.
4. In a small bowl, mix the oats, the brown sugar, the remaining ¼ cup of flour, the butter, the baking powder, and the salt. Use your fingers or a pastry blender to crumble the butter into pea-size pieces. Divide the topping over the top of the apple filling. Cover the apple crisps with foil.
5. Place the covered apple crisps in the air fryer basket and cook for 20 minutes. Uncover and continue cooking for 3 minutes or until the surface is golden and crunchy.

Cinnamon Canned Biscuit Donuts

Servings: 4
Cooking Time: 25 Minutes
Ingredients:
- 1 can jumbo biscuits
- 1 cup cinnamon sugar

Directions:
1. Preheat air fryer to 360°F/180°C. Divide biscuit dough into 8 biscuits and place on a flat work surface. Cut a small circle in the center of the biscuit with a small cookie cutter. Place a batch of 4 donuts in the air fryer. Spray with oil and Bake for 8 minutes, flipping once. Drizzle the cinnamon sugar over the donuts and serve.

Air-fried Beignets

Servings: 24
Cooking Time: 5 Minutes
Ingredients:
- ¾ cup lukewarm water (about 90°F)
- ¼ cup sugar
- 1 generous teaspoon active dry yeast (½ envelope)
- 3½ to 4 cups all-purpose flour
- ½ teaspoon salt
- 2 tablespoons unsalted butter, room temperature and cut into small pieces
- 1 egg, lightly beaten
- ½ cup evaporated milk
- ¼ cup melted butter
- 1 cup confectioners' sugar
- chocolate sauce or raspberry sauce, to dip

Directions:
1. Combine the lukewarm water, a pinch of the sugar and the yeast in a bowl and let it proof for 5 minutes. It should froth a little. If it doesn't froth, your yeast is not active and you should start again with new yeast.
2. Combine 3½ cups of the flour, salt, 2 tablespoons of butter and the remaining sugar in a large bowl, or in the bowl of a stand mixer. Add the egg, evaporated milk and yeast mixture to the bowl and mix with a wooden spoon (or the paddle attachment of the stand mixer) until the dough comes together in a sticky ball. Add a little more flour if necessary to get the dough to form. Transfer the dough to an oiled bowl, cover with plastic wrap or a clean kitchen towel and let it rise in a warm place for at least 2 hours or until it has doubled in size. Longer is better for flavor development and you can even let the dough rest in the refrigerator overnight (just remember to bring it to room temperature before proceeding with the recipe).
3. Roll the dough out to ½-inch thickness. Cut the dough into rectangular or diamond-shaped pieces. You can make the beignets any size you like, but this recipe will give you 24 (2-inch x 3-inch) rectangles.
4. Preheat the air fryer to 350°F/175°C.
5. Brush the beignets on both sides with some of the melted butter and air-fry in batches at 350°F /175°C for 5 minutes, turning them over halfway through if desired. (They will brown on all sides without being flipped, but flipping them will brown them more evenly.)
6. As soon as the beignets are finished, transfer them to a plate or baking sheet and dust with the confectioners' sugar. Serve warm with a chocolate or raspberry sauce.

Baked Stuffed Pears

Servings: 4
Cooking Time: 15 Minutes + Cooling Time
Ingredients:
- 4 cored pears, halved
- ½ cup chopped cashews
- ½ cup dried cranberries
- ¼ cup agave nectar
- ½ stick butter, softened
- ½ tsp ground cinnamon
- ½ cup apple juice

Directions:
1. Preheat the air fryer to 350°F/175°C. Combine the cashews, cranberries, agave nectar, butter, and cinnamon and mix well. Stuff this mixture into the pears, heaping it up on top. Set the pears in a baking pan and pour the apple juice into the bottom of the pan. Put the pan in the fryer and Bake for 10-12 minutes or until the pears are tender. Let cool before serving.

Apple & Blueberry Crumble

Servings: 4
Cooking Time: 20 Minutes
Ingredients:
- 5 apples, peeled and diced
- ½ lemon, zested and juiced
- ½ cup blueberries
- 1 cup brown sugar
- 1 tsp cinnamon
- ½ cup butter
- ½ cup flour

Directions:
1. Preheat air fryer to 340°F/170°C. Place the apple chunks, blueberries, lemon juice and zest, half of the butter, half of the brown sugar, and cinnamon in a greased baking dish. Combine thoroughly until all is well mixed. Combine the flour with the remaining butter and brown sugar in a separate bowl. Stir until it forms a crumbly consistency. Spread the mixture over the fruit. Bake in the air fryer for 10-15 minutes until golden and bubbling. Serve and enjoy!

Giant Buttery Chocolate Chip Cookie

Servings: 4
Cooking Time: 16 Minutes
Ingredients:
- ⅔ cup plus 1 tablespoon All-purpose flour
- ¼ teaspoon Baking soda
- ¼ teaspoon Table salt
- Baking spray (see the headnote)

- 4 tablespoons (¼ cup/½ stick) plus 1 teaspoon Butter, at room temperature
- ¼ cup plus 1 teaspoon Packed dark brown sugar
- 3 tablespoons plus 1 teaspoon Granulated white sugar
- 2½ tablespoons Pasteurized egg substitute, such as Egg Beaters
- ½ teaspoon Vanilla extract
- ¾ cup plus 1 tablespoon Semisweet or bittersweet chocolate chips

Directions:
1. Preheat the air fryer to 350°F /175°C.
2. Whisk the flour, baking soda, and salt in a bowl until well combined.
3. For a small air fryer, coat the inside of a 6-inch round cake pan with baking spray. For a medium air fryer, coat the inside of a 7-inch round cake pan with baking spray. And for a large air fryer, coat the inside of an 8-inch round cake pan with baking spray.
4. Using a hand electric mixer at medium speed, beat the butter, brown sugar, and granulated white sugar in a bowl until smooth and thick, about 3 minutes, scraping down the inside of the bowl several times.
5. Beat in the pasteurized egg substitute or egg (as applicable) and vanilla until uniform. Scrape down and remove the beaters. Fold in the flour mixture and chocolate chips with a rubber spatula, just until combined. Scrape and gently press this dough into the prepared pan, getting it even across the pan to the perimeter.
6. Set the pan in the basket and air-fry undisturbed for 16 minutes, or until the cookie is puffed, browned, and feels set to the touch.
7. Transfer the pan to a wire rack and cool for 10 minutes. Loosen the cookie from the perimeter with a spatula, then invert the pan onto a cutting board and let the cookie come free. Remove the pan and reinvert the cookie onto the wire rack. Cool for 5 minutes more before slicing into wedges to serve.

Holiday Peppermint Cake

Servings: 4
Cooking Time: 20 Minutes
Ingredients:
- 1 ½ cups flour
- 3 eggs
- 1/3 cup molasses
- ½ cup olive oil
- ½ cup almond milk
- ½ tsp vanilla extract
- ½ tsp peppermint extract
- 1 tsp baking powder
- ½ tsp salt

Directions:
1. Preheat air fryer to 380°F/195°C. Whisk the eggs and molasses in a bowl until smooth. Slowly mix in the olive oil, almond milk, and vanilla and peppermint extracts until combined. Sift the flour, baking powder, and salt in another bowl. Gradually incorporate the dry ingredients into the wet ingredients until combined. Pour the batter into a greased baking pan and place in the fryer. Bake for 12-15 minutes until a toothpick inserted in the center comes out clean. Serve and enjoy!

Fluffy Orange Cake

Servings: 6
Cooking Time: 30 Minutes
Ingredients:
- 1/3 cup cornmeal
- 1 ¼ cups flour
- ¾ cup white sugar
- 1 tsp baking soda
- ¼ cup safflower oil
- 1 ¼ cups orange juice
- 1 tsp orange zest
- ¼ cup powdered sugar

Directions:
1. Preheat air fryer to 340°F/170°C. Mix cornmeal, flour, sugar, baking soda, safflower oil, 1 cup of orange juice, and orange zest in a medium bowl. Mix until combined.
2. Pour the batter into a greased baking pan and set into the air fryer. Bake until a toothpick in the center of the cake comes out clean. Remove the cake and place it on a cooling rack. Use the toothpick to make 20 holes in the cake. Meanwhile, combine the rest of the juice with the powdered sugar in a small bowl. Drizzle the glaze over the hot cake and allow it to absorb. Leave to cool completely, then cut into pieces. Serve and enjoy!

Custard

Servings: 4
Cooking Time: 45 Minutes
Ingredients:
- 2 cups whole milk
- 2 eggs
- ¼ cup sugar
- ⅛ teaspoon salt
- ¼ teaspoon vanilla
- cooking spray
- ⅛ teaspoon nutmeg

Directions:
1. In a blender, process milk, egg, sugar, salt, and vanilla until smooth.
2. Spray a 6 x 6-inch baking pan with nonstick spray and pour the custard into it.
3. Cook at 300°F/150°C for 45 minutes. Custard is done when the center sets.
4. Sprinkle top with the nutmeg.
5. Allow custard to cool slightly.
6. Serve it warm, at room temperature, or chilled.

Rich Blueberry Biscuit Shortcakes

Servings: 4
Cooking Time: 35 Minutes
Ingredients:
- 1 lb blueberries, halved
- ¼ cup granulated sugar
- 1 tsp orange zest
- 1 cup heavy cream
- 1 tbsp orange juice
- 2 tbsp powdered sugar
- ¼ tsp cinnamon
- ¼ tsp nutmeg
- 2 cups flour
- 1 egg yolk
- 1 tbsp baking powder
- ½ tsp baking soda
- ½ tsp cornstarch

- ½ tsp salt
- ½ tsp vanilla extract
- ½ tsp honey
- 4 tbsp cold butter, cubed
- 1 ¼ cups buttermilk

Directions:
1. Combine blueberries, granulated sugar, and orange zest in a bowl. Let chill the topping covered in the fridge until ready to use. Beat heavy cream, orange juice, egg yolk, vanilla extract and powdered sugar in a metal bowl until peaks form. Let chill the whipped cream covered in the fridge until ready to use.
2. Preheat air fryer at 350°F/175°C. Combine flour, cinnamon, nutmeg, baking powder, baking soda, cornstarch, honey, butter cubes, and buttermilk in a bowl until a sticky dough forms. Flour your hands and form dough into 8 balls. Place them on a lightly greased pizza pan. Place pizza pan in the frying basket and Air Fry for 8 minutes. Transfer biscuits to serving plates and cut them in half. Spread blueberry mixture to each biscuit bottom and place tops of biscuits. Garnish with whipped cream and serve.

British Bread Pudding

Servings: 4
Cooking Time: 30 Minutes
Ingredients:
- 4 bread slices
- 1 cup milk
- ¼ cup sugar
- 2 eggs, beaten
- 1 tbsp vanilla extract
- ½ tsp ground cinnamon

Directions:
1. Preheat air fryer to 320°F/160°C. Slice bread into bite-size pieces. Set aside in a small cake pan. Mix the milk, sugar, eggs, vanilla extract, and cinnamon in a bowl until well combined. Pour over the bread and toss to coat. Bake for 20 minutes until crispy and all liquid is absorbed. Slice into 4 pieces. Serve and enjoy!

Apple Dumplings

Servings: 4
Cooking Time: 25 Minutes
Ingredients:
- 1 Basic Pie Dough (see the following recipe)
- 4 medium Granny Smith or Pink Lady apples, peeled and cored
- 4 tablespoons sugar
- 4 teaspoons cinnamon
- ½ teaspoon ground nutmeg
- 4 tablespoons unsalted butter, melted
- 4 scoops ice cream, for serving

Directions:
1. Preheat the air fryer to 330°F/165°C.
2. Bring the pie crust recipe to room temperature.
3. Place the pie crust on a floured surface. Divide the dough into 4 equal pieces. Roll out each piece to ¼-inch-thick rounds. Place an apple onto each dough round. Sprinkle 1 tablespoon of sugar in the core part of each apple; sprinkle 1 teaspoon cinnamon and ⅛ teaspoon nutmeg over each. Place 1 tablespoon of butter into the center of each. Fold up the sides and fully cover the cored apples.
4. Place the dumplings into the air fryer basket and spray with cooking spray. Cook for 25 minutes. Check after 14 minutes cooking; if they're getting too brown, reduce the heat to 320°F/160°C and complete the cooking.
5. Serve hot apple dumplings with a scoop of ice cream.

One-bowl Chocolate Buttermilk Cake

Servings: 6
Cooking Time: 16-20 Minutes
Ingredients:
- ¾ cup All-purpose flour
- ½ cup Granulated white sugar
- 3 tablespoons Unsweetened cocoa powder
- ½ teaspoon Baking soda
- ¼ teaspoon Table salt
- ½ cup Buttermilk
- 2 tablespoons Vegetable oil
- ¾ teaspoon Vanilla extract
- Baking spray (see here)

Directions:
1. Preheat the air fryer to 325°F/160°C (or 330°F/165°C, if that's the closest setting).
2. Stir the flour, sugar, cocoa powder, baking soda, and salt in a large bowl until well combined. Add the buttermilk, oil, and vanilla. Stir just until a thick, grainy batter forms.
3. Use the baking spray to generously coat the inside of a 6-inch round cake pan for a small batch, a 7-inch round cake pan for a medium batch, or an 8-inch round cake pan for a large batch. Scrape and spread the chocolate batter into this pan, smoothing the batter out to an even layer.
4. Set the pan in the basket and air-fry undisturbed for 16 minutes for a 6-inch layer, 18 minutes for a 7-inch layer, or 20 minutes for an 8-inch layer, or until a toothpick or cake tester inserted into the center of the cake comes out clean. Start checking it at the 14-minute mark to know where you are.
5. Use hot pads or silicone baking mitts to transfer the cake pan to a wire rack. Cool for 5 minutes. To unmold, set a cutting board over the baking pan and invert both the board and the pan. Lift the still-warm pan off the cake layer. Set the wire rack on top of the cake layer and invert all of it with the cutting board so that the cake layer is now right side up on the wire rack. Remove the cutting board and continue cooling the cake for at least 10 minutes or to room temperature, about 30 minutes, before slicing into wedges.

Fall Pumpkin Cake

Servings: 6
Cooking Time: 50 Minutes
Ingredients:
- 1/3 cup pecan pieces
- 5 gingersnap cookies
- 1/3 cup light brown sugar
- 6 tbsp butter, melted
- 3 eggs
- ½ tsp vanilla extract
- 1 cup pumpkin purée
- 2 tbsp sour cream
- ½ cup flour
- ¼ cup tapioca flour
- ½ tsp cornstarch
- ½ cup granulated sugar
- ½ tsp baking soda
- 1 tsp baking powder
- 1 tsp pumpkin pie spice

- 6 oz mascarpone cheese
- 1 1/3 cups powdered sugar
- 1 tsp cinnamon
- 2 tbsp butter, softened
- 1 tbsp milk
- 1 tbsp flaked almonds

Directions:
1. Blitz the pecans, gingersnap cookies, brown sugar, and 3 tbsp of melted butter in a food processor until combined. Press mixture into the bottom of a lightly greased cake pan. Preheat air fryer at 350°F. In a bowl, whisk the eggs, remaining melted butter, ½ tsp of vanilla extract, pumpkin purée, and sour cream. In another bowl, combine the flour, tapioca flour, cornstarch, granulated sugar, baking soda, baking powder, and pumpkin pie spice. Add wet ingredients to dry ingredients and combine. Do not overmix. Pour the batter into a cake pan and cover it with aluminum foil. Place cake pan in the frying basket and Bake for 30 minutes. Remove the foil and cook for another 5 minutes. Let cool onto a cooling rack for 10 minutes. Then, turn cake onto a large serving platter. In a small bowl, whisk the mascarpone cheese, powdered sugar, remaining vanilla extract, cinnamon, softened butter, and milk. Spread over cooled cake and cut into slices. Serve sprinkled with almonds and enjoy!

Annie's Chocolate Chunk Hazelnut Cookies

Servings: 24
Cooking Time: 12 Minutes
Ingredients:
- 1 cup butter, softened
- 1 cup brown sugar
- ½ cup granulated sugar
- 2 eggs, lightly beaten
- 1½ teaspoons vanilla extract
- 1½ cups all-purpose flour
- ½ cup rolled oats
- 1 teaspoon baking soda
- ½ teaspoon salt
- 2 cups chocolate chunks
- ½ cup toasted chopped hazelnuts

Directions:
1. Cream the butter and sugars together until light and fluffy using a stand mixer or electric hand mixer. Add the eggs and vanilla, and beat until well combined.
2. Combine the flour, rolled oats, baking soda and salt in a second bowl. Gradually add the dry ingredients to the wet ingredients with a wooden spoon or spatula. Stir in the chocolate chunks and hazelnuts until distributed throughout the dough.
3. Shape the cookies into small balls about the size of golf balls and place them on a baking sheet. Freeze the cookie balls for at least 30 minutes, or package them in as airtight a package as you can and keep them in your freezer.
4. When you're ready for a delicious snack or dessert, Preheat the air fryer to 350°F/175°C. Cut a piece of parchment paper to fit the number of cookies you are baking. Place the parchment down in the air fryer basket and place the frozen cookie ball or balls on top (remember to leave room for them to expand).
5. Air-fry the cookies at 350°F/175°C for 12 minutes, or until they are done to your liking. Let them cool for a few minutes before enjoying your freshly baked cookie.

Apple Crisp

Servings: 4
Cooking Time: 16 Minutes
Ingredients:
- Filling
- 3 Granny Smith apples, thinly sliced (about 4 cups)
- ¼ teaspoon ground cinnamon
- ⅛ teaspoon salt
- 1½ teaspoons lemon juice
- 2 tablespoons honey
- 1 tablespoon brown sugar
- cooking spray
- Crumb Topping
- 2 tablespoons oats
- 2 tablespoons oat bran
- 2 tablespoons cooked quinoa
- 2 tablespoons chopped walnuts
- 2 tablespoons brown sugar
- 2 teaspoons coconut oil

Directions:
1. Combine all filling ingredients and stir well so that apples are evenly coated.
2. Spray air fryer baking pan with nonstick cooking spray and spoon in the apple mixture.
3. Cook at 360°F/180°C for 5minutes. Stir well, scooping up from the bottom to mix apples and sauce.
4. At this point, the apples should be crisp-tender. Continue cooking in 3-minute intervals until apples are as soft as you like.
5. While apples are cooking, combine all topping ingredients in a small bowl. Stir until coconut oil mixes in well and distributes evenly. If your coconut oil is cold, it may be easier to mix in by hand.
6. When apples are cooked to your liking, sprinkle crumb mixture on top. Cook at 360°F for 8 minutes or until crumb topping is golden brown and crispy.

Caramel Blondies With Macadamia Nuts

Servings: 4
Cooking Time: 35 Minutes + Cooling Time
Ingredients:
- 1/3 cup ground macadamia
- ½ cup unsalted butter
- 1 cup white sugar
- 1 tsp vanilla extract
- 2 eggs
- ½ cup all-purpose flour
- ½ cup caramel chips
- ¼ tsp baking powder
- A pinch of salt

Directions:
1. Preheat air fryer to 340°F/170°C. Whisk the eggs in a bowl. Add the melted butter and vanilla extract and whip thoroughly until slightly fluffy. Combine the flour, sugar, ground macadamia, caramel chips, salt, and baking powder in another bowl. Slowly pour the dry ingredients into the wet ingredients, stirring until thoroughly blended and until there are no lumps in the batter. Spoon the batter into a greased cake pan. Place the pan in the air fryer. Bake for 20 minutes until a knife comes out dry and clean. Let cool for a few minutes before cutting and serving.

Cinnamon Sugar Banana Rolls

Servings: 6
Cooking Time: 8 Minutes
Ingredients:
- ¼ cup Granulated white sugar
- 2 teaspoons Ground cinnamon
- 2 tablespoons Peach or apricot jam or orange marmalade
- 6 Spring roll wrappers, thawed if necessary
- 2 Ripe banana(s), peeled and cut into 3-inch-long sections
- 1 Large egg, well beaten
- Vegetable oil spray

Directions:
1. Preheat the air fryer to 400°F/205°C.
2. Stir the sugar and cinnamon in a small bowl until well combined. Stir the jam or marmalade with a fork to loosen it up.
3. Set a spring roll wrapper on a clean, dry work surface. Roll a banana section in the sugar mixture until evenly and well coated. Set the coated banana along one edge of the wrapper. Top it with about 1 teaspoon of the jam or marmalade. Fold the sides of the wrapper perpendicular to the banana up and over the banana, partially covering it. Brush beaten egg over the side of the wrapper farthest from the banana. Starting with the banana, roll the wrapper closed, ending at the part with the beaten egg. Press gently to seal. Set the roll aside seam side down and continue filling and rolling the remaining wrappers in the same way.
4. Lightly coat the wrappers with vegetable oil spray. Set them seam side down in the basket with as much air space between them as possible. Air-fry undisturbed for 8 minutes, or until crisp and golden brown.
5. Use kitchen tongs to gently transfer the rolls to a wire rack. Cool for at least 5 minutes or up to 30 minutes before serving.

White Chocolate Cranberry Blondies

Servings: 6
Cooking Time: 18 Minutes
Ingredients:
- ⅓ cup butter
- ½ cup sugar
- 1 teaspoon vanilla extract
- 1 large egg
- 1 cup all-purpose flour
- ½ teaspoon baking powder
- ⅛ teaspoon salt
- ¼ cup dried cranberries
- ¼ cup white chocolate chips

Directions:
1. Preheat the air fryer to 320°F/160°C.
2. In a large bowl, cream the butter with the sugar and vanilla extract. Whisk in the egg and set aside.
3. In a separate bowl, mix the flour with the baking powder and salt. Then gently mix the dry ingredients into the wet. Fold in the cranberries and chocolate chips.
4. Liberally spray an oven-safe 7-inch springform pan with olive oil and pour the batter into the pan.
5. Cook for 17 minutes or until a toothpick inserted in the center comes out clean.

6. Remove and let cool 5 minutes before serving.

Honeyed Tortilla Fritters

Servings: 8
Cooking Time: 10 Minutes
Ingredients:
- 2 tbsp granulated sugar
- ½ tsp ground cinnamon
- 1 tsp vanilla powder
- Salt to taste
- 8 flour tortillas, quartered
- 2 tbsp butter, melted
- 4 tsp honey
- 1 tbsp almond flakes

Directions:
1. Preheat air fryer at 400°F/205°C. Combine the sugar, cinnamon, vanilla powder, and salt in a bowl. Set aside. Brush tortilla quarters with melted butter and sprinkle with sugar mixture. Place tortilla quarters in the frying basket and Air Fry for 4 minutes, turning once. Let cool on a large plate for 5 minutes until hardened. Drizzle with honey and scatter with almond flakes to serve.

Berry Streusel Cake

Servings: 6
Cooking Time: 60 Minutes
Ingredients:
- 2 tbsp demerara sugar
- 2 tbsp sunflower oil
- ¼ cup almond flour
- 1 cup pastry flour
- ½ cup brown sugar
- 1 tsp baking powder
- 1 tbsp lemon zest
- ¼ tsp salt
- ¾ cup milk
- 2 tbsp olive oil
- 1 tsp vanilla
- 1 cup blueberries
- ½ cup powdered sugar
- 1 tbsp lemon juice
- ⅛ tsp salt

Directions:
1. Mix the demerara sugar, sunflower oil, and almond flour in a bowl and put it in the refrigerator. Whisk the pastry flour, brown sugar, baking powder, lemon zest, and salt in another bowl. Add the milk, olive oil, and vanilla and stir with a rubber spatula until combined. Add the blueberries and stir slowly. Coat the inside of a baking pan with oil and pour the batter into the pan.
2. Preheat air fryer to 310°F/155°C. Remove the almond mix from the fridge and spread it over the cake batter. Put the cake in the air fryer and Bake for 45 minutes or until a knife inserted in the center comes out clean and the top is golden. Combine the powdered sugar, lemon juice and salt in a bowl. Once the cake has cooled, slice it into 4 pieces and drizzle each with icing. Serve.

Peanut Butter S'mores

Servings: 10
Cooking Time: 1 Minute
Ingredients:
- 10 Graham crackers (full, double-square cookies as they come out of the package)
- 5 tablespoons Natural-style creamy or crunchy peanut butter
- ½ cup Milk chocolate chips
- 10 Standard-size marshmallows (not minis and not jumbo campfire ones)

Directions:
1. Preheat the air fryer to 350°F /175°C.
2. Break the graham crackers in half widthwise at the marked place, so the rectangle is now in two squares. Set half of the squares flat side up on your work surface. Spread each with about 1½ teaspoons peanut butter, then set 10 to 12 chocolate chips point side up into the peanut butter on each, pressing gently so the chips stick.
3. Flatten a marshmallow between your clean, dry hands and set it atop the chips. Do the same with the remaining marshmallows on the other coated graham crackers. Do not set the other half of the graham crackers on top of these coated graham crackers.
4. When the machine is at temperature, set the treats graham cracker side down in a single layer in the basket. They may touch, but even a fraction of an inch between them will provide better air flow. Air-fry undisturbed for 45 seconds.
5. Use a nonstick-safe spatula to transfer the topped graham crackers to a wire rack. Set the other graham cracker squares flat side down over the marshmallows. Cool for a couple of minutes before serving.

Oatmeal Blackberry Crisp

Servings: 6
Cooking Time: 20 Minutes
Ingredients:
- 1 cup rolled oats
- ½ cup flour
- ¼ cup olive oil
- ¼ tsp salt
- 1 tsp cinnamon
- 1/3 cup honey
- 4 cups blackberries

Directions:
1. Preheat air fryer to 350°F/175°C. Combine rolled oats, flour, olive oil, salt, cinnamon, and honey in a large bowl. Mix well. Spread blackberries on the bottom of a greased cooking pan. Cover them with the oat mixture. Place pan in air fryer and Bake for 15 minutes. Cool for a few minutes. Serve and enjoy.

Strawberry Donut Bites

Servings: 6
Cooking Time: 25 Minutes
Ingredients:
- 2/3 cup flour
- A pinch of salt
- ½ tsp baking powder
- 1 tsp vanilla extract
- 2 tbsp light brown sugar
- 1 tbsp honey
- ½ cup diced strawberries
- 1 tbsp butter, melted
- 2 tbsp powdered sugar
- 2 tsp sour cream
- ¼ cup crushed pretzels

Directions:
1. Preheat air fryer at 325°F/160°C. In a bowl, sift flour, baking powder, and salt. Add in vanilla, brown sugar, honey, 2 tbsp of water, butter, and strawberries and whisk until combined. Form dough into balls. Place the balls on a lightly greased pizza pan, place them in the frying basket, and Air Fry for 10-12 minutes. Let cool onto a cooling rack for 5 minutes. Mix the powdered sugar and sour cream in a small bowl, 1 tsp of sour cream at a time until you reach your desired consistency. Gently pour over the donut bites. Scatter with crushed pretzels and serve.

Cheese Blintzes

Servings: 6
Cooking Time: 10 Minutes
Ingredients:
- 1½ 7½-ounce package(s) farmer cheese
- 3 tablespoons Regular or low-fat cream cheese (not fat-free)
- 3 tablespoons Granulated white sugar
- ¼ teaspoon Vanilla extract
- 6 Egg roll wrappers
- 3 tablespoons Butter, melted and cooled

Directions:
1. Preheat the air fryer to 375°F/190°C.
2. Use a flatware fork to mash the farmer cheese, cream cheese, sugar, and vanilla in a small bowl until smooth.
3. Set one egg roll wrapper on a clean, dry work surface. Place ¼ cup of the filling at the edge closest to you, leaving a ½-inch gap before the edge of the wrapper. Dip your clean finger in water and wet the edges of the wrapper. Fold the perpendicular sides over the filling, then roll the wrapper closed with the filling inside. Set it aside seam side down and continue filling the remainder of the wrappers.
4. Brush the wrappers on all sides with the melted butter. Be generous. Set them seam side down in the basket with as much space between them as possible. Air-fry undisturbed for 10 minutes, or until lightly browned.
5. Use a nonstick-safe spatula to transfer the blintzes to a wire rack. Cool for at least 5 minutes or up to 20 minutes before serving.

Cheese & Honey Stuffed Figs

Servings: 4
Cooking Time: 15 Minutes
Ingredients:
- 8 figs, stem off
- 2 oz cottage cheese
- ¼ tsp ground cinnamon
- ¼ tsp orange zest
- ¼ tsp vanilla extract
- 2 tbsp honey
- 1 tbsp olive oil

Directions:
1. Preheat air fryer to 360°F/180°C. Cut an "X" in the top of each fig 1/3 way through, leaving intact the base. Mix together the cottage cheese, cinnamon, orange zest, vanilla extract and 1 tbsp of honey in a bowl. Spoon the cheese mixture into the cavity of each fig. Put the figs in a single layer in the frying basket. Drizzle the olive oil over the top of the figs and Roast for 10 minutes. Drizzle with the remaining honey. Serve and enjoy!

Maple Cinnamon Cheesecake

Servings: 4
Cooking Time: 12 Minutes
Ingredients:
- 6 sheets of cinnamon graham crackers
- 2 tablespoons butter
- 8 ounces Neufchâtel cream cheese
- 3 tablespoons pure maple syrup
- 1 large egg
- ½ teaspoon ground cinnamon
- ¼ teaspoon salt

Directions:
1. Preheat the air fryer to 350°F/175°C.
2. Place the graham crackers in a food processor and process until crushed into a flour. Mix with the butter and press into a mini air-fryer-safe pan lined at the bottom with parchment paper. Place in the air fryer and cook for 4 minutes.
3. In a large bowl, place the cream cheese and maple syrup. Use a hand mixer or stand mixer and beat together until smooth. Add in the egg, cinnamon, and salt and mix on medium speed until combined.
4. Remove the graham cracker crust from the air fryer and pour the batter into the pan.
5. Place the pan back in the air fryer, adjusting the temperature to 315°F/155°C. Cook for 18 minutes. Carefully remove when cooking completes. The top should be lightly browned and firm.
6. Keep the cheesecake in the pan and place in the refrigerator for 3 or more hours to firm up before serving.

Spiced Fruit Skewers

Servings: 4
Cooking Time: 15 Minutes
Ingredients:
- 2 peeled peaches, thickly sliced
- 3 plums, halved and pitted
- 3 peeled kiwi, quartered
- 1 tbsp honey
- ½ tsp ground cinnamon
- ¼ tsp ground allspice
- ¼ tsp cayenne pepper

Directions:
1. Preheat air fryer to 400°F/205°C. Combine the honey, cinnamon, allspice, and cayenne and set aside. Alternate fruits on 8 bamboo skewers, then brush the fruit with the honey mix. Lay the skewers in the air fryer and Air Fry for 3-5 minutes. Allow to chill for 5 minutes before serving.

Coconut Cream Roll-ups

Servings: 4
Cooking Time: 20 Minutes
Ingredients:
- ½ cup cream cheese, softened
- 1 cup fresh raspberries
- ¼ cup brown sugar
- ¼ cup coconut cream
- 1 egg
- 1 tsp corn starch
- 6 spring roll wrappers

Directions:
1. Preheat air fryer to 350°F/175°C. Add the cream cheese, brown sugar, coconut cream, cornstarch, and egg to a bowl and whisk until all ingredients are completely mixed and fluffy, thick and stiff. Spoon even amounts of the creamy filling into each spring roll wrapper, then top each dollop of filling with several raspberries. Roll up the wraps around the creamy raspberry filling, and seal the seams with a few dabs of water.
2. Place each roll on the foil-lined frying basket, seams facing down. Bake for 10 minutes, flipping them once until golden brown and perfect on the outside, while the raspberries and cream filling will have cooked together in a glorious fusion. Remove with tongs and serve hot or cold. Serve and enjoy!

Mango-chocolate Custard

Servings: 4
Cooking Time: 40 Minutes
Ingredients:
- 4 egg yolks
- 2 tbsp granulated sugar
- 1/8 tsp almond extract
- 1 ½ cups half-and-half
- 3/4 cup chocolate chips
- 1 mango, pureed
- 1 mango, chopped
- 1 tsp fresh mint, chopped

Directions:
1. Beat the egg yolks, sugar, and almond extract in a bowl. Set aside. Place half-and-half in a saucepan over low heat and bring it to a low simmer. Whisk a spoonful of heated half-and-half into egg mixture, then slowly whisk egg mixture into saucepan. Stir in chocolate chips and mango purée for 10 minutes until chocolate melts. Divide between 4 ramekins.
2. Preheat air fryer at 350°F/175°C. Place ramekins in the frying basket and Bake for 6-8 minutes. Let cool onto a cooling rack for 15 minutes, then let chill covered in the fridge for at least 2 hours or up to 2 days. Serve with chopped mangoes and mint on top.

Grilled Pineapple Dessert

Servings: 4
Cooking Time: 12 Minutes
Ingredients:
- oil for misting or cooking spray
- 4 ½-inch-thick slices fresh pineapple, core removed
- 1 tablespoon honey
- ¼ teaspoon brandy
- 2 tablespoons slivered almonds, toasted
- vanilla frozen yogurt or coconut sorbet

Directions:
1. Spray both sides of pineapple slices with oil or cooking spray. Place on grill plate or directly into air fryer basket.
2. Cook at 390°F/200°C for 6minutes. Turn slices over and cook for an additional 6minutes.
3. Mix together the honey and brandy.
4. Remove cooked pineapple slices from air fryer, sprinkle with toasted almonds, and drizzle with honey mixture.
5. Serve with a scoop of frozen yogurt or sorbet on the side.

Fruit Turnovers

Servings: 6
Cooking Time: 25 Minutes
Ingredients:
- 1 sheet puff pastry dough
- 6 tsp peach preserves
- 3 kiwi, sliced
- 1 large egg, beaten

- 1 tbsp icing sugar

Directions:
1. Prepare puff pastry by cutting it into 6 rectangles. Roll out the pastry with a rolling pin into 5-inch squares. On your workspace, position one square so that it looks like a diamond with points to the top and bottom. Spoon 1 tsp of the preserves on the bottom half and spread it, leaving a ½-inch border from the edge. Place half of one kiwi on top of the preserves. Brush the clean edges with the egg, then fold the top corner over the filling to make a triangle. Crimp with a fork to seal the pastry. Brush the top of the pastry with egg. Preheat air fryer to 350°F/175°C. Put the pastries in the greased frying basket. Air Fry for 10 minutes, flipping once until golden and puffy. Remove from the fryer, let cool and dush with icing sugar. Serve.

Coconut Crusted Bananas With Pineapple Sauce

Servings: 4
Cooking Time: 5 Minutes
Ingredients:
- Pineapple Sauce
- 1½ cups puréed fresh pineapple
- 2 tablespoons sugar
- juice of 1 lemon
- ¼ teaspoon ground cinnamon
- 3 firm bananas
- ¼ cup sweetened condensed milk
- 1¼ cups shredded coconut
- ⅓ cup crushed graham crackers (crumbs)*
- vegetable or canola oil, in a spray bottle
- vanilla frozen yogurt or ice cream

Directions:
1. Make the pineapple sauce by combining the pineapple, sugar, lemon juice and cinnamon in a saucepan. Simmer the mixture on the stovetop for 20 minutes, and then set it aside.
2. Slice the bananas diagonally into ½-inch thick slices and place them in a bowl. Pour the sweetened condensed milk into the bowl and toss the bananas gently to coat. Combine the coconut and graham cracker crumbs together in a shallow dish. Remove the banana slices from the condensed milk and let any excess milk drip off. Dip the banana slices in the coconut and crumb mixture to coat both sides. Spray the coated slices with oil.
3. Preheat the air fryer to 400°F/205°C.
4. Grease the bottom of the air fryer basket with a little oil. Air-fry the bananas in batches at 400°F/205°C for 5 minutes, turning them over halfway through the cooking time. Air-fry until the bananas are golden brown on both sides.
5. Serve warm over vanilla frozen yogurt with some of the pineapple sauce spooned over top.

Brownies After Dark

Servings: 4
Cooking Time: 13 Minutes
Ingredients:
- 1 egg
- ½ cup granulated sugar
- ¼ teaspoon salt
- ½ teaspoon vanilla
- ¼ cup butter, melted
- ¼ cup flour, plus 2 tablespoons
- ¼ cup cocoa
- cooking spray
- Optional

- vanilla ice cream
- caramel sauce
- whipped cream

Directions:
1. Beat together egg, sugar, salt, and vanilla until light.
2. Add melted butter and mix well.
3. Stir in flour and cocoa.
4. Spray 6 x 6-inch baking pan lightly with cooking spray.
5. Spread batter in pan and cook at 330°F/165°C for 13 minutes. Cool and cut into 4 large squares or 16 small brownie bites.

Puff Pastry Apples

Servings: 4
Cooking Time: 10 Minutes
Ingredients:
- 3 Rome or Gala apples, peeled
- 2 tablespoons sugar
- 1 teaspoon all-purpose flour
- 1 teaspoon ground cinnamon
- ⅛ teaspoon ground ginger
- pinch ground nutmeg
- 1 sheet puff pastry
- 1 tablespoon butter, cut into 4 pieces
- 1 egg, beaten
- vegetable oil
- vanilla ice cream (optional)
- caramel sauce (optional)

Directions:
1. Remove the core from the apple by cutting the four sides off the apple around the core. Slice the pieces of apple into thin half-moons, about ¼-inch thick. Combine the sugar, flour, cinnamon, ginger, and nutmeg in a large bowl. Add the apples to the bowl and gently toss until the apples are evenly coated with the spice mixture. Set aside.
2. Cut the puff pastry sheet into a 12-inch by 12-inch square. Then quarter the sheet into four 6-inch squares. Save any remaining pastry for decorating the apples at the end.
3. Divide the spiced apples between the four puff pastry squares, stacking the apples in the center of each square and placing them flat on top of each other in a circle. Top the apples with a piece of the butter.
4. Brush the four edges of the pastry with the egg wash. Bring the four corners of the pastry together, wrapping them around the apple slices and pinching them together at the top in the style of a "beggars purse" appetizer. Fold the ends of the pastry corners down onto the apple making them look like leaves. Brush the entire apple with the egg wash.
5. Using the leftover dough, make leaves to decorate the apples. Cut out 8 leaf shapes, about 1½-inches long, "drawing" the leaf veins on the pastry leaves with a paring knife. Place 2 leaves on the top of each apple, tucking the ends of the leaves under the pastry in the center of the apples. Brush the top of the leaves with additional egg wash. Sprinkle the entire apple with some granulated sugar.
6. Preheat the air fryer to 350°F/175°C.
7. Spray or brush the inside of the air fryer basket with oil. Place the apples in the basket and air-fry for 6 minutes. Carefully turn the apples over – it's easiest to remove one apple, then flip the others over and finally return the last apple to the air fryer. Air-fry for an additional 4 minutes.
8. Serve the puff pastry apples warm with vanilla ice cream and drizzle with some caramel sauce.

Baked Caramelized Peaches

Servings: 6
Cooking Time: 25 Minutes
Ingredients:
- 3 pitted peaches, halved
- 2 tbsp brown sugar
- 1 cup heavy cream
- 1 tsp vanilla extract
- ¼ tsp ground cinnamon
- 1 cup fresh blueberries

Directions:
1. Preheat air fryer to 380°F/195°C. Lay the peaches in the frying basket with the cut side up, then top them with brown sugar. Bake for 7-11 minutes, allowing the peaches to brown around the edges. In a mixing bowl, whisk heavy cream, vanilla, and cinnamon until stiff peaks form. Fold the peaches into a plate. Spoon the cream mixture into the peach cups, top with blueberries, and serve.

Roasted Pears

Servings: 4
Cooking Time: 10 Minutes
Ingredients:
- 2 Ripe pears, preferably Anjou, stemmed, peeled, halved lengthwise, and cored
- 2 tablespoons Butter, melted
- 2 teaspoons Granulated white sugar
- Grated nutmeg
- ¼ cup Honey
- ½ cup (about 1½ ounces) Shaved Parmesan cheese

Directions:
1. Preheat the air fryer to 400°F/205°C.
2. Brush each pear half with about 1½ teaspoons of the melted butter, then sprinkle their cut sides with ½ teaspoon sugar. Grate a pinch of nutmeg over each pear.
3. When the machine is at temperature, set the pear halves cut side up in the basket with as much air space between them as possible. Air-fry undisturbed for 10 minutes, or until hot and softened.
4. Use a nonstick-safe spatula, and perhaps a flatware tablespoon for balance, to transfer the pear halves to a serving platter or plates. Cool for a minute or two, then drizzle each pear half with 1 tablespoon of the honey. Lay about 2 tablespoons of shaved Parmesan over each half just before serving.

Banana-almond Delights

Servings: 4
Cooking Time: 30 Minutes
Ingredients:
- 1 ripe banana, mashed
- 1 tbsp almond liqueur
- ½ tsp ground cinnamon
- 2 tbsp coconut sugar
- 1 cup almond flour
- ¼ tsp baking soda
- 8 raw almonds

Directions:
1. Preheat air fryer to 300°F/150°C. Add the banana to a bowl and stir in almond liqueur, cinnamon, and coconut sugar until well combined. Toss in almond flour and baking soda until smooth. Make 8 balls out of the mixture. Place the balls onto the parchment-lined frying basket, flatten each into ½-inch thick, and press 1 almond into the center. Bake for 12 minutes, turn and Bake for 6 more minutes. Let cool slightly before serving.

Lemon Pound Cake Bites

Servings: 6
Cooking Time: 20 Minutes
Ingredients:
- 1 pound cake, cubed
- 1/3 cup cinnamon sugar
- ½ stick butter, melted
- 1 cup vanilla yogurt
- 3 tbsp brown sugar
- 1 tsp lemon zest

Directions:
1. Preheat the air fryer to 350°F/175°C. Drizzle the cake cubes with melted butter, then put them in the cinnamon sugar and toss until coated. Put them in a single layer in the frying basket and Air Fry for 4 minutes or until golden. Remove and place on a serving plate. Combine the yogurt, brown sugar, and lemon zest in a bowl. Serve with the cake bites.

Chocolate Rum Brownies

Servings: 6
Cooking Time: 30 Minutes + Cooling Time
Ingredients:
- ½ cup butter, melted
- 1 cup white sugar
- 1 tsp dark rum
- 2 eggs
- ½ cup flour
- 1/3 cup cocoa powder
- ¼ tsp baking powder
- Pinch of salt

Directions:
1. Preheat air fryer to 350°F/175°C. Whisk the melted butter, eggs, and dark rum in a mixing bowl until slightly fluffy and all ingredients are thoroughly combined. Place the flour, sugar, cocoa, salt, and baking powder in a separate bowl and stir to combine. Gradually pour the dry ingredients into the wet ingredients, stirring continuously until thoroughly blended and there are no lumps in the batter. Spoon the batter into a greased cake pan. Put the pan in the frying basket and Bake for 20 minutes until a toothpick comes out dry and clean. Let cool for several minutes. Cut and serve. Enjoy!

Ricotta Stuffed Apples

Servings: 4
Cooking Time: 25 Minutes
Ingredients:
- ½ cup cheddar cheese
- ¼ cup raisins
- 2 apples
- ½ tsp ground cinnamon

Directions:
1. Preheat air fryer to 350°F/175°C. Combine cheddar cheese and raisins in a bowl and set aside. Chop apples lengthwise and discard the core and stem. Sprinkle each half with cinnamon and stuff each half with 1/4 of the cheddar mixture. Bake for 7 minutes, turn, and Bake for 13 minutes more until the apples are soft. Serve immediately.

RECIPE INDEX

A

Acorn Squash Halves With Maple Butter Glaze	120
Air-fried Beignets	136
Almond-crusted Fish	80
Almond-pumpkin Porridge	47
Annie's Chocolate Chunk Hazelnut Cookies	139
Apple & Blueberry Crumble	136
Apple Crisp	139
Apple Dumplings	138
Apple-carrot Cupcakes	135
Argentinian Steak Asado Salad	105
Aromatic Mushroom Omelet	45
Artichoke Samosas	24
Artichoke-spinach Dip	29
Asian Meatball Tacos	77
Asparagus Wrapped In Pancetta	123
Asparagus	121
Authentic Sausage Kartoffel Salad	103
Avocado Egg Rolls	24
Avocado Fries With Quick Salsa Fresca	12
Avocado Fries, Vegan	21
Avocado Toast With Lemony Shrimp	27
Avocado Toasts With Poached Eggs	35

B

Bacon & Blue Cheese Tartlets	28
Bacon Candy	25
Bacon Puff Pastry Pinwheels	42
Bacon, Blue Cheese And Pear Stuffed Pork Chops	102
Bagel Chips	23
Baked Apple Crisp	135
Baked Caramelized Peaches	144
Baked Stuffed Pears	136
Balsamic Beef & Veggie Skewers	100
Balsamic Beet Chips	119
Balsamic Grape Dip	23
Balsamic Marinated Rib Eye Steak With Balsamic Fried Cipollini Onions	111
Balsamic Stuffed Mushrooms	128
Banana Bread	34
Banana-almond Delights	144
Banana-blackberry Muffins	46
Banana-strawberry Cakecups	31
Barbecue Country-style Pork Ribs	108
Barbecue-style Beef Cube Steak	113
Barbecue-style London Broil	96
Basic Chicken Breasts(2)	66
Basic Corn On The Cob	127
Basil Cheese & Ham Stromboli	110
Bbq Back Ribs	107
Bbq Fried Oysters	89
Beef & Barley Stuffed Bell Peppers	96
Beef Fajitas	95
Beef Short Ribs	95
Beer-battered Onion Rings	23
Beet Chips	21
Bengali Samosa With Mango Chutney	61
Berbere Beef Steaks	103
Berbere Eggplant Dip	59
Berry Streusel Cake	140
Best-ever Brussels Sprouts	117
Black And Blue Clafoutis	131
Black Cod With Grapes, Fennel, Pecans And Kale	94
Black-olive Jalapeño Poppers	26
Blistered Shishito Peppers	121
Blooming Onion	19
Blueberry Muffins	40
Boss Chicken Cobb Salad	67
Breaded Avocado Tacos	62
Breaded Mozzarella Sticks	28
Breaded Parmesan Perch	81
Breakfast Chimichangas	41
Breakfast Pot Pies	40
Breakfast Sausage Bites	42
British Bread Pudding	138
Broccoli & Mushroom Beef	101
Broccoli Au Gratin	121
Brown Sugar Grapefruit	47
Brownies After Dark	143
Buffalo Cauliflower	26
Buffalo French Fries	14
Buttered Swordfish Steaks	86
Buttered Turkey Breasts	70
Butternut Medallions With Honey Butter And Sage	116
Buttery Lobster Tails	87
Buttery Radish Wedges	126
Buttery Spiced Pecans	25
Buttery Stuffed Tomatoes	127

C

Cajun Breakfast Potatoes	43
Cajun Chicken Livers	74
Cajun Flounder Fillets	90
Cajun-seasoned Shrimp	83
Californian Tilapia	83
Cal-mex Chimichangas	110
Cal-mex Turkey Patties	78
Canadian-inspired Waffle Poutine	16
Caprese-style Sandwiches	59
Caramel Blondies With Macadamia Nuts	139
Carne Asada	108
Carrot Cake With Cream Cheese Icing	134
Carrot Muffins	35
Carrot Orange Muffins	43
Carrot-oat Cake Muffins	130
Carrots & Parsnips With Tahini Sauce	125
Catalan Sardines With Romesco Sauce	84
Catfish Nuggets	90
Cauliflower-crust Pizza	25
Cheddar & Sausage Tater Tots	40
Cheddar Bean Taquitos	48
Cheddar Cheese Biscuits	40

Tower Air Fryer Cookbook

Cheddar Stuffed Jalapeños	15
Cheddar Stuffed Portobellos With Salsa	62
Cheddar-ham-corn Muffins	38
Cheese & Bacon Pasta Bake	125
Cheese & Crab Stuffed Mushrooms	92
Cheese & Honey Stuffed Figs	141
Cheese Blintzes	141
Cheesecake Wontons	131
Cheesy Chicken-avocado Paninis	73
Cheesy Enchilada Stuffed Baked Potatoes	64
Cheesy Green Dip	25
Cheesy Green Pitas	16
Cheesy Green Wonton Triangles	18
Cheesy Spinach Dip(2)	23
Cheesy Texas Toast	119
Cherry Beignets	31
Cherry Cheesecake Rolls	129
Cherry Hand Pies	132
Chicano Rice Bowls	51
Chicken & Fruit Biryani	78
Chicken & Rice Sautée	66
Chicken Adobo	74
Chicken Breast Burgers	79
Chicken Burgers With Blue Cheese Sauce	70
Chicken Chimichangas	71
Chicken Cordon Bleu	65
Chicken Cutlets With Broccoli Rabe And Roasted Peppers	76
Chicken Eggrolls	124
Chicken Fried Steak	113
Chicken Hand Pies	69
Chicken Nachos	29
Chicken Nuggets	76
Chicken Parmigiana	77
Chicken Pasta Pie	72
Chicken Souvlaki Gyros	65
Chicken Tenders With Basil-strawberry Glaze	75
Chicken Wellington	75
Chicken Wings Al Ajillo	79
Chile Con Carne Galette	109
Chili Tofu & Quinoa Bowls	61
Chili-oiled Brussels Sprouts	118
Chinese Fish Noodle Bowls	88
Chinese-style Lamb Chops	103
Chipotle Chicken Drumsticks	78
Chipotle Pork Meatballs	98
Chive Potato Pierogi	52
Chocolate Bars	134
Chocolate Macaroons	132
Chocolate Rum Brownies	144
Chorizo Sausage & Cheese Balls	37
Christmas Chicken & Roasted Grape Salad	65
Cilantro Sea Bass	93
Cinnamon Apple Crisps	24
Cinnamon Canned Biscuit Donuts	136
Cinnamon Pear Cheesecake	135
Cinnamon Pumpkin Donuts	38
Cinnamon Sugar Banana Rolls	140
Cinnamon Sugar Donut Holes	34
Cinnamon Sweet Potato Fries	12
Cinnamon-coconut Doughnuts	44
Citrusy Brussels Sprouts	124
City "chicken"	98
Classic Cinnamon Rolls	41
Classic Potato Chips	23
Coconut Cream Roll-ups	142
Coconut Crusted Bananas With Pineapple Sauce	143
Coconut Rice Cake	130
Coconut Shrimp	85
Coconut-shrimp Po' Boys	80
Coffee Cake	39
Colorful French Toast Sticks	39
Colorful Vegetable Medley	55
Corn Dog Bites	27
Corn Dog Muffins	17
Corn On The Cob	115
Country Chicken Hoagies	66
Country-style Pork Ribs(2)	95
Crab Cakes On A Budget	84
Crab Cakes	93
Crab Rangoon Dip With Wonton Chips	28
Crabmeat-stuffed Flounder	90
Cream Cheese Deviled Eggs	36
Creamy Broccoli & Mushroom Casserole	48
Crispy Apple Fries With Caramel Sauce	62
Crispy Bacon	32
Crispy Brussels Sprouts	124
Crispy Cauliflower Puffs	127
Crispy Chicken Bites With Gorgonzola Sauce	15
Crispy Cordon Bleu	79
Crispy Pork Medallions With Radicchio And Endive Salad	101
Crispy Samosa Rolls	35
Crispy Smoked Pork Chops	98
Crispy Spiced Chickpeas	29
Crispy Steak Subs	97
Crispy, Cheesy Leeks	119
Crunchy And Buttery Cod With Ritz® Cracker Crust	91
Crunchy Clam Strips	89
Crunchy Flounder Gratin	93
Crunchy Green Beans	116
Crunchy Pickle Chips	20
Crunchy Rice Paper Samosas	48
Curried Pickle Chips	14
Curried Potato, Cauliflower And Pea Turnovers	60
Custard	137

D

Dijon Shrimp Cakes	94
Dilly Red Snapper	87
Dilly Sesame Roasted Asparagus	121

E

Easy Asian-style Tuna	84
Easy Cheese & Spinach Lasagna	60
Easy Corn Dog Cupcakes	41
Easy Parmesan Asparagus	122
Easy Turkey Meatballs	69
Easy Vanilla Muffins	34
Easy Zucchini Lasagna Roll-ups	50
Easy-peasy Shrimp	92
Effortless Mac `n´ Cheese	59
Egg Muffins	33
Egg Rolls	62
Eggless Mung Bean Tart	35
English Muffin Sandwiches	37
English Scones	35
Extra Crispy Country-style Pork Riblets	100

F

Falafel 63
Fall Pumpkin Cake 138
Family Chicken Fingers 79
Family Fish Nuggets With Tartar Sauce 83
Famous Chocolate Lava Cake 133
Fantasy Sweet Chili Chicken Strips 74
Farfalle With White Sauce 58
Farmer's Fried Chicken 70
Farmers' Market Veggie Medley 127
Favorite Blueberry Muffins 46
Fennel Tofu Bites 62
Fiery Bacon-wrapped Dates 23
Filled Mushrooms With Crab & Cheese 81
Fingerling Potatoes 127
Fish Sticks With Tartar Sauce 83
Fish Tacos With Jalapeño-lime Sauce 81
Fish Tortillas With Coleslaw 92
Five Spice Fries 16
Five Spice Red Snapper With Green Onions And Orange Salsa 83
Five-spice Roasted Sweet Potatoes 117
Flank Steak With Roasted Peppers And Chimichurri 111
Fluffy Orange Cake 137
French Toast And Turkey Sausage Roll-ups 32
French-style Pork Medallions 103
Friday Night Cheeseburgers 113
Fried Brie With Cherry Tomatoes 19
Fried Cannoli Wontons 130
Fried Cauliflowerwith Parmesan Lemon Dressing 115
Fried Cheese Ravioli With Marinara Sauce 29
Fried Gyoza 22
Fried Pb&j 46
Fried Peaches 13
Fried Shrimp 89
Fried Snickers Bars 135
Fried Spam 98
Fried String Beans With Greek Sauce 21
Fruit Turnovers 142
Fudgy Brownie Cake 131

G

Garlic And Dill Salmon 91
Garlic Bread Knots 42
Garlic Breadsticks 29
Garlic Chicken 68
Garlic Wings 14
Garlic-buttered Rib Eye Steak 104
Garlic-herb Pita Chips 19
Garlicky Brussel Sprouts With Saffron Aioli 56
Garlicky Brussels Sprouts 125
Garlicky Roasted Mushrooms 52
Garlicky Sea Bass With Root Veggies 80
Garlic-parmesan Popcorn 117
General Tso's Cauliflower 54
Giant Buttery Chocolate Chip Cookie 136
Giant Buttery Oatmeal Cookie 133
Gingery Turkey Meatballs 72
Glazed Chicken Thighs 68
Glazed Meatloaf 107
Gluten-free Nutty Chicken Fingers 70
Golden Pork Quesadillas 101
Gorgeous Jalapeño Poppers 53
Gorgonzola Stuffed Mushrooms 118

Granola Three Ways 22
Greek Chicken Wings 73
Greek Gyros With Chicken & Rice 76
Green Bean & Baby Potato Mix 52
Green Bean Sautée 49
Green Onion Pancakes 32
Green Peas With Mint 117
Grilled Cheese Sandwich 52
Grilled Ham & Muenster Cheese On Raisin Bread 13
Grilled Lime Scallions 126
Grilled Pineapple Dessert 142
Grilled Pork & Bell Pepper Salad 105
Grits Casserole 116
Ground Beef Calzones 99
Gruyère Asparagus & Chicken Quiche 72
Guajillo Chile Chicken Meatballs 66

H

Ham & Cheese Sandwiches 45
Harissa Chicken Wings 77
Hashbrown Potatoes Lyonnaise 37
Hearty Salad 56
Herb-crusted Sole 94
Herbed Cheese Brittle 26
Herb-marinated Chicken 77
Hole In One 42
Holiday Peppermint Cake 137
Holiday Shrimp Scampi 89
Holliday Lobster Salad 87
Homemade Pork Gyoza 105
Home-style Cinnamon Rolls 56
Home-style Pumpkin Pie Pudding 129
Honey Donuts 44
Honey Lemon Thyme Glazed Cornish Hen 74
Honey Oatmeal 46
Honey Pear Chips 57
Honey Pork Links 95
Honey Tater Tots With Bacon 12
Honeyed Tortilla Fritters 140
Honey-mustard Asparagus Puffs 122
Honey-mustard Chicken Wings 21
Honey-mustard Roasted Cabbage 116
Honey-roasted Mixed Nuts 132
Honey-roasted Parsnips 115
Horseradish Potato Mash 114
Horseradish-crusted Salmon Fillets 91
Hot Calamari Rings 80
Hot Okra Wedges 118
Huevos Rancheros 41
Hush Puffins 45

I

Indonesian Pork Satay 100
Intense Buffalo Chicken Wings 67
Italian Meatballs 99
Italian Roasted Chicken Thighs 69
Italian Sausage & Peppers 97
Italian Sausage Rolls 107
Italian Stuffed Bell Peppers 55
Italian-style Fried Cauliflower 49

J

Japanese-inspired Glazed Chicken 75

Japanese-style Turkey Meatballs ... 67
Jerk Chicken Drumsticks ... 71
Jerk Meatballs ... 108
Jerk Rubbed Corn On The Cob ... 124

K
Kale & Rice Chicken Rolls ... 77
Katsu Chicken Thighs ... 66
King Prawns Al Ajillo ... 81
Korean-style Chicken Bulgogi ... 68

L
Lamb Chops In Currant Sauce ... 102
Lamb Koftas Meatballs ... 108
Lamb Meatballs With Quick Tomato Sauce ... 112
Layered Mixed Vegetables ... 114
Lazy Mexican Meat Pizza ... 107
Leftover Roast Beef Risotto ... 110
Lemon Iced Donut Balls ... 129
Lemon Pound Cake Bites ... 144
Lemon-garlic Strip Steak ... 110
Lemon-roasted Salmon Fillets ... 86
Lemony Fried Fennel Slices ... 124
Lentil Burritos With Cilantro Chutney ... 58
Light Frittata ... 33
Lime Flaming Halibut ... 85

M
Mahi-mahi "burrito" Fillets ... 91
Mango-chocolate Custard ... 142
Maple Cinnamon Cheesecake ... 142
Maple-peach And Apple Oatmeal ... 32
Mascarpone Iced Cinnamon Rolls ... 36
Meat Loaves ... 111
Meatloaf With Tangy Tomato Glaze ... 99
Mexican Turkey Meatloaves ... 73
Mexican-inspired Chicken Breasts ... 76
Mexican-style Frittata ... 121
Mini Carrot Cakes ... 131
Mixed Berry Pie ... 129
Mojito Fish Tacos ... 90
Mojo Sea Bass ... 85
Molten Chocolate Almond Cakes ... 134
Mom's Potatoes Au Gratin ... 118
Mom's Tuna Melt Toastie ... 82
Mom's Chicken Wings ... 78
Mongolian Beef ... 109
Morning Apple Biscuits ... 36
Morning Burrito ... 36
Morning Chicken Frittata Cups ... 43
Morning Loaded Potato Skins ... 33
Moroccan-spiced Carrots ... 128
Mozzarella Sticks ... 21
Mushroom & Cavolo Nero Egg Muffins ... 37
Mushroom And Fried Onion Quesadilla ... 50
Mushroom Bolognese Casserole ... 51
Mushroom, Zucchini And Black Bean Burgers ... 63
Mushrooms, Sautéed ... 126
Mustardy Chicken Bites ... 78

N
Nicoise Deviled Eggs ... 13
No-guilty Spring Rolls ... 14

Not-so-english Muffins ... 45
Nutty Banana Bread ... 130
Nutty Cookies ... 135
Nutty Whole Wheat Muffins ... 31

O
Oat Muffins With Blueberries ... 42
Oatmeal Blackberry Crisp ... 141
One-bowl Chocolate Buttermilk Cake ... 138
Onion Ring Nachos ... 26
Onion Rings ... 126
Onions ... 119
Orange Cran-bran Muffins ... 33
Orange Glazed Pork Tenderloin ... 106
Orange-glazed Carrots ... 19

P
Paprika Fried Beef ... 112
Paprika Onion Blossom ... 22
Parmesan Asparagus ... 122
Parmesan Chicken Meatloaf ... 71
Parmesan Garlic Naan ... 31
Parmesan Pizza Nuggets ... 27
Party S'mores ... 134
Peachy Pork Chops ... 107
Peanut Butter S'mores ... 141
Peanut Butter-barbeque Chicken ... 68
Pecorino Dill Muffins ... 114
Pepperoni Bagel Pizzas ... 110
Peppery Tilapia Roulade ... 88
Perfect Asparagus ... 114
Perfect Broccolini ... 115
Perfect Strip Steaks ... 112
Pesto Pepperoni Pizza Bread ... 48
Pesto-rubbed Veal Chops ... 102
Pigs In A Blanket ... 44
Pizza Bagel Bites ... 17
Pizza Dough ... 39
Pizza Portobello Mushrooms ... 54
Pizza Tortilla Rolls ... 104
Plantain Chips ... 27
Poblano Bake ... 73
Popcorn Chicken Bites ... 24
Pork Chops With Cereal Crust ... 106
Pork Chops ... 99
Pork Cutlets With Almond-lemon Crust ... 100
Poutine ... 17
Powerful Jackfruit Fritters ... 57
Provence French Fries ... 125
Puff Pastry Apples ... 143
Pulled Turkey Quesadillas ... 74
Pumpkin Brownies ... 132
Pumpkin Empanadas ... 36
Punjabi-inspired Chicken ... 69

Q
Quiche Cups ... 47
Quick Tuna Tacos ... 93

R
Rack Of Lamb With Pistachio Crust ... 96
Rainbow Quinoa Patties ... 53
Restaurant-style Breaded Shrimp ... 94

Restaurant-style Chicken Thighs	78
Rice & Bean Burritos	54
Rich Blueberry Biscuit Shortcakes	137
Rich Clam Spread	12
Rich Salmon Burgers With Broccoli Slaw	92
Rich Turkey Burgers	72
Ricotta Stuffed Apples	144
Ricotta Veggie Potpie	53
Rigatoni With Roasted Onions, Fennel, Spinach And Lemon Pepper Ricotta	49
Roasted Broccoli And Red Bean Salad	123
Roasted Brussels Sprouts	118
Roasted Eggplant Halves With Herbed Ricotta	126
Roasted Heirloom Carrots With Orange And Thyme	117
Roasted Jalapeño Salsa Verde	15
Roasted Pears	144
Roasted Vegetable Pita Pizza	56
Roasted Vegetable Thai Green Curry	50
Roasted Vegetable, Brown Rice And Black Bean Burrito	61
Rosemary New Potatoes	117
Rosemary Potato Salad	125
Rosemary Roasted Potatoes With Lemon	128

S

S'mores Pockets	129
Sage & Paprika Turkey Cutlets	79
Sage & Thyme Potatoes	119
Sage Hasselback Potatoes	125
Sage Pork With Potatoes	96
Salmon Salad With Steamboat Dressing	120
Sardinas Fritas	84
Saucy Shrimp	82
Sausage & Cauliflower Balls	25
Sausage And Cheese Rolls	28
Sausage-cheese Calzone	106
Sea Scallops	87
Seafood Egg Rolls	30
Seared Scallops In Beurre Blanc	87
Seasoned Herbed Sourdough Croutons	43
Sesame Carrots And Sugar Snap Peas	123
Shakshuka Cups	38
Shrimp & Grits	88
Shrimp "scampi"	88
Shrimp Al Pesto	84
Shrimp Egg Rolls	15
Shrimp Patties	82
Shrimp Teriyaki	84
Shrimp-jalapeño Poppers In Prosciutto	86
Sicilian-style Vegetarian Pizza	61
Simple Buttermilk Fried Chicken	71
Simple Green Bake	123
Simple Roasted Sweet Potatoes	117
Smashed Fried Baby Potatoes	118
Smoked Avocado Wedges	128
Smoked Paprika Sweet Potato Fries	60
Smoked Salmon Puffs	18
Smoked Whitefish Spread	17
Smokehouse-style Beef Ribs	102
Smoky Roasted Veggie Chips	123
Smooth Walnut-banana Loaf	46
Soft Pretzels	37
Southeast Asian-style Tuna Steaks	92
Southern Sweet Cornbread	39
Southern-fried Chicken Livers	75
Southern-style Chicken Legs	73
Southwest Cornbread	37
Spaghetti Squash And Kale Fritters With Pomodoro Sauce	49
Speedy Baked Caprese With Avocado	116
Spiced Fruit Skewers	142
Spiced Parsnip Chips	16
Spiced Vegetable Galette	53
Spicy Bean Patties	58
Spicy Hoisin Bbq Pork Chops	99
Spicy Honey Mustard Chicken	66
Spicy Vegetable And Tofu Shake Fry	52
Spinach & Turkey Meatballs	67
Spinach And Cheese Calzone	57
Spinach-bacon Rollups	35
Sriracha Green Beans	114
Sticky Broccoli Florets	122
Strawberry Donut Bites	141
Strawberry Donuts	130
Strawberry Streusel Muffins	44
Stress-free Beef Patties	95
String Bean Fries	13
Stuffed Baby Bella Caps	16
Stuffed Cabbage Rolls	112
Stuffed Onions	122
Stuffed Portobellos	51
Stuffed Shrimp Wrapped In Bacon	86
Stuffed Shrimp	81
Summer Sea Scallops	92
Summer Watermelon And Cucumber Salad	115
Sunday Chicken Skewers	68
Sweet And Salty Snack Mix	14
Sweet And Sour Pork	97
Sweet Corn Bread	59
Sweet Potato & Mushroom Hash	33
Sweet Potato Chips	13
Sweet Potato–crusted Pork Rib Chops	96
Sweet Potato–wrapped Shrimp	85
Sweet Roasted Pumpkin Rounds	121
Sweet-and-sour Chicken	69

T

Tacos	55
Tamari-seasoned Pork Strips	105
Tandoori Lamb Samosas	103
Taquito Quesadillas	18
Tarragon Pork Tenderloin	101
Tasty Brussels Sprouts With Guanciale	124
Teriyaki Chicken Legs	65
Tex-mex Potatoes With Avocado Dressing	57
The Best Oysters Rockefeller	93
The Best Shrimp Risotto	86
Thyme Steak Finger Strips	110
Tilapia Al Pesto	89
Tofu & Spinach Lasagna	55
Tonkatsu	109
Tropical Salsa	48
Tuscan Salmon	91

V

Vanilla-strawberry Muffins	133
Vegan Buddha Bowls(2)	58
Vegetable Couscous	59
Vegetable Roast	115

Vegetable Spring Rolls	18
Vegetarian Fritters With Green Dip	20
Vegetarian Paella	57
Vegetarian Quinoa Cups	32
Vegetarian Shepherd's Pie	63
Veggie & Feta Scramble Bowls	39
Veggie Cheese Bites	15
Veggie Samosas	56
Veggie-stuffed Bell Peppers	51
Vietnamese Beef Lettuce Wraps	104
Viking Toast	47

W

Wake-up Veggie & Ham Bake	41
Warm Spinach Dip With Pita Chips	20
Wasabi Pork Medallions	105
Western Frittata	45
White Chocolate Cranberry Blondies	140
Whole-grain Cornbread	43
Wiener Schnitzel	106
Wild Blueberry Lemon Chia Bread	33

Y

Yellow Squash	120

Z

Zesty London Broil	107
Zucchini & Bell Pepper Stir-fry	55
Zucchini Fries	120
Zucchini Tacos	62
Zucchini Tamale Pie	51

Printed in Great Britain
by Amazon